"This fascinating book is part autobiography, part history, part memoir, part cultural guide, and part poetry.... It works beautifully as both the life story of an individual Crow woman and as the history of her tribe throughout and before her long life.... The stories themselves are interesting [and] the preservation of oral performance lends an intimate and important cultural feel to the work."

—J. B. EDWARDS
Choice

"Hogan's stories read like an epic poem."

—CAL CUMIN
Billings Gazette

"The vignettes are golden, unpolished nuggets. A few biographies of Native women have been released recently, but this is the only one that allows the speaker's words to resonate so that the reader may 'hear' them.... It is an ideal entry into understanding Apsáalooke reservation life. The sensitive presentation of Hogan's words and memories, coupled with the authors' introductory statements, provide insights into the development of the Crow reservation through descriptions of changing lifestyles, struggles of family relations, religious and political commitments, and the resilience of Native beliefs and practices. The Woman Who Loved Mankind is a must-read for anyone interested in Native, feminist, or humanistic studies."

—TIMOTHY P. MCCLEARY
Montana: The Magazine of Western History

"This contribution is unique.... The text as a whole records the voice of a Crow elder and positions this voice in the historical and cultural context in which Hogan's life took place. Any concerns that readers might find Hogan's storytelling style foreign at first is minor in view of what the text as a whole achieves.... The book's greatest contribution is its masterful discussion of kinship and the role of traditional sacred ceremonies during the early reservation period.... It is essential reading for new and seasoned students and scholars of American Indian cultures."

—KELLY M. BRANAM
Great Plains Quarterly

The Woman Who Loved Mankind

The Woman Who Loved Mankind

The Life of a Twentieth-Century Crow Elder

Lillian Bullshows Hogan

As told to Barbara Loeb & Mardell Hogan Plainfeather

University of Nebraska Press
Lincoln

© 2012 by the Board of Regents of the University of Nebraska
All rights reserved
The University of Nebraska Press is part of a land-grant institution with campuses and programs on the past, present, and future homelands of the Pawnee, Ponca, Otoe-Missouria, Omaha, Dakota, Lakota, Kaw, Cheyenne, and Arapaho Peoples, as well as those of the relocated Ho-Chunk, Sac and Fox, and Iowa Peoples.

First Nebraska paperback printing: 2025

This work is funded in part by a grant from Humanities Montana, an affiliate of the National Endowment for the Humanities. The findings and conclusions of the work do not necessarily represent the views of Humanities Montana or the National Endowment for the Humanities.

For customers in the EU with safety/GPSR concerns, contact:
gpsr@mare-nostrum.co.uk
Mare Nostrum Group BV
Mauritskade 21D
1091 GC Amsterdam
The Netherlands

Library of Congress
Cataloging-in-Publication Data

Hogan, Lillian Bullshows, 1905–2003.
The woman who loved mankind: the life of a twentieth-century Crow elder Lillian Bullshows Hogan as told to Barbara Loeb and Mardell Hogan Plainfeather. p. cm.
Includes bibliographical references and index.
ISBN 978-0-8032-1613-6 (cloth: alk. paper)
ISBN 978-1-4962-4337-9 (paperback)
ISBN 978-1-4962-4382-9 (epub)
ISBN 978-0-8032-4330-9 (pdf)
1. Hogan, Lillian Bullshows, 1905–2003.
2. Crow women—Biography. 3. Crow Indians—History. 4. Crow Indians—Social life and customs. I. Loeb, Barbara. II. Plainfeather, Mardell Hogan. III. Title.
e99.c92h64   2012
978.6004'975272—dc23   [B]   2011050259

Set in Sabon by Kim Essman.
Designed by Mikah Tacha.

To our families and to storytellers everywhere

Contents

List of Illustrations viii
Acknowledgments ix
Introduction by Barbara Loeb xi
Thoughts about My Mother by Mardell Hogan Plainfeather xxxi
Genealogies xxxvii
1 Chapter One: My Birth and Infancy
13 Chapter Two: My Mother
25 Chapter Three: My Father
47 Chapter Four: My Parents Meet and Marry
57 Chapter Five: My First Memories
73 Chapter Six: Boarding School
93 Chapter Seven: Memories of Youth
147 Chapter Eight: My Mother Teaches Me to Be a Good Woman
175 Chapter Nine: Tobacco Iipche (Sacred Pipe Society) and the Medicine Dance (Tobacco Society)
197 Chapter Ten: We Were Always Hard Up
205 Chapter Eleven: The Last Years in School
213 Chapter Twelve: My First Marriage Was to Alex
225 Chapter Thirteen: We're Adopted into the Tobacco Society
229 Chapter Fourteen: I Married Robbie Yellowtail
241 Chapter Fifteen: Paul
263 Chapter Sixteen: George
307 Chapter Seventeen: The Kids Are Growing Up
333 Chapter Eighteen: Sacred Experiences
341 Chapter Nineteen: Traditional Healing
357 Chapter Twenty: I Gave Indian Names
363 Chapter Twenty-One: I'm an Old-Timer
379 Chapter Twenty-Two: Education
387 Chapter Twenty-Three: Life as an Elder
Bibliography 405
Index 409

Illustrations
following p. 170

1. The Bullshows and Baumgartner families, circa 1910
2. Little Horse's half sister, Clara White Hip, and husband
3. Lillian, approximately fifteen years old, circa 1920
4. Finds Them and Kills Them (Ohchiish) in front of his home, 1928
5. Bone scraper
6. Lillian and her first husband, Alex Plainfeather, 1921
7. Lillian holding her first child, Samuel Plainfeather, 1922
8. Lillian's second husband, Robert Yellowtail, with Chief Plenty Coups, circa 1929
9. Lillian with her third husband, Paul Singer, and daughters, 1934
10. Detail of elk-tooth dress
11. Lillian's fourth husband, George Hogan Sr.
12. Lillian's sons, Adam Singer and Samuel Plainfeather, circa 1943
13. Lillian's parents, Bull Shows and Little Horse, with Lillian's daughter Mary and her grandson Russell, 1946
14. George and Lillian Hogan with their daughter Mardell, 1951
15. Lillian with Lady Bird Johnson, Betty Babcock, Stewart Udall, 1964
16. Mardell, Mary, and Nellie, 1964
17. Lillian and her daughter Mardell, 1979
18. Floral sketches by Lillian, 1981
19. Lillian's great-grandson Calvin Walks Over Ice, circa 1991
20. Lillian seated with her daughters and many of her grandchildren, 1976
21. Lillian seated in elk-tooth dress, with her daughters, 1976
22. Nellie and Lillian, 1980
23. Lillian in elder years

Map
Crow Country and the areas in Lillian's stories   xliv

Genealogies
1. Family Tree   xxxvii
2. First Marriage   xxxviii
3. Second Marriage   xxxix
4. Third Marriage   xl
5. Fourth Marriage   xli

Acknowledgments

We have been blessed with the memories, knowledge, and skills of many and the encouragement of strangers who heard of our undertaking and cheered us forward.

In the 1990s, when we began to write, the Crow Culture Committee gave us approval and encouraging words. When we struggled to find a better way to bring Lillian's stories to life, Wendy Wickwire and Julie Cruikshank advised us.

Raphaelle Real Bird, Crow Studies instructor at Little Big Horn College, reviewed the spelling of every Apsáalooke word. She was amazing. Timothy Bernardis, director of the Little Big Horn College Library, Crow Agency, solved many research problems. He was always available to help. Linguist Timothy McCleary, Little Big Horn College, gave us spelling advice and cultural information.

Lillian's daughters, Lorena Mae Walks Over Ice, Nellie Sings In the Mountains, and Mary Hogan Wallace, searched their memories and family photographs. They answered countless questions.

Many people read parts or all of the manuscript: Rodney Frey, University of Idaho; Lance Hogan, youth director, St. Dennis Parish; Felice Lucero, San Felipe Pueblo, New Mexico; Becky Matthews, Columbus State University; Timothy McCleary, Little Big Horn College, Crow Agency; and novelist Alison Clement, anthropologist Joan Gross, writer Wendy Madar, and editor Cheryl McLean, all of Corvallis, Oregon.

We also received help from Crow chief Dr. Joseph Medicine Crow; Bill Holm, professor emeritus, University of Washington; Kevin Kooistra-Manning, Western Heritage Center, Billings, Montana; Emma Hansen and Mary Robinson, Buffalo Bill Historical Center, Cody, Wyoming; C. Adrian Heidenreich, professor emeritas, Montana State University Billings; Father Charlie, Crow Agency; Father Randolph, Pryor, Montana; Richard Titt, Cumberland Country Historical Society, Carlisle, Pennsylvania; Bill Blake, photographer, Cody, Wyoming; Bob Richard, the son of the late Jack Richard, another Cody photographer; Mary Braun, Oregon State University Press; Loretta Reilly, Oregon State University Valley Library; Barbara Eben, *Big Horn County News*; and the reference librarians at Parmly Billings Library.

LaRae Bear Claw, Terry Bullis, Marsha Fulton, Joyce Good Luck, Nellie Marydell Little Light, Clara Mae Nomee, Cerise Plainfeather, Dan Plainfeather, Ruby Plain Feather, Selmer Red Star, Marvin Stewart, and Tyrone Ten Bear all found information for us. Vicky Bergstrom, Wendi Gale, and Donna McMaster, all of Corvallis or neighboring towns, supplied copious scrap paper. The computer consultants at Oregon State University solved technical problems, of which there were many.

The Research Council, Oregon State University, funded some of Mardell's travels and gave us the means to thank and honor Lillian in the traditional way, with food and gifts. The Center for the Humanities, Oregon State University, gave Barbara a fellowship and a year's access to a beautiful, peaceful office. Humanities Montana, an affiliate of the National Endowment for the Humanities, funded the index.

We thank all of you for making this a better book.

We also wish to thank Elisabeth Chretien, associate acquisitions editor at the University of Nebraska Press, who understood our vision and encouraged us to preserve this format. We thank Joeth Zucco, senior project editor; Chris Dodge, copy editor; Mikah Tacha, designer; and Kim Essman, typesetter, for their diligent work.

Mardell thanks her husband, Dan Plainfeather, for his patience when she traveled to Big Sky, Montana, or Corvallis to work on this project. Barbara thanks her daughter, Alexa Loeb, who spent much of her youth turning down her music so her mother could concentrate.

Most of all, we wish to express our eternal appreciation to Lillian for telling these stories. They mean so much to us and to the family.

Introduction

Barbara Loeb

"She's a kind little girl" she says.
"She's kind to me—therefore,
I'm going to give her a necklace,
this green necklace."

Says "I have some [green beads] in my stomach" she says "and
   I keep them there.
They're my medicine" she says,
"but you get her a string of green beads,
a-a-nd let her wear that,[1]
she grow to be a big,
good woman" she said.
"I want her to have that green beads for necklace."

–*Lillian Hogan*, from "Green Beads from a Real Old Lady"

    An elderly Native American woman said these words around 1910, giving a small child the privilege to wear green-bead necklaces. The gift was not a simple piece of jewelry, but a special medicine imbued with spiritual power.[2] It was also a prayer that this tender five-year-old would grow to adulthood, enjoy a long life, and prove industrious, skillful, and responsible to the ways of her people (be a good woman).

    The little girl's name was Bachée Issítcheesh (Likes Men, or Loves Mankind). Her English name was Lillian Bullshows, her married name was Hogan, and she belonged to the Apsáalooke (Crow) tribe, one of the most influential on the northern Great Plains. This book is her life story as told to her daughter, Mardell Hogan Plainfeather, and to me, a long-time family friend. It recounts how she was raised, who she became, and what the community was like around her. Sometimes it reaches back to the youths of her mother, Little Horse (Horse, for short), and her father, Bull Shows. Occasionally it goes further, to the customs of elders like the woman with the green-bead necklace. Together her stories cover almost the entire span of Crow Reservation life.

I first met Lillian at her family camp on a hot August day in 1979, when I was a young PhD student studying the tribe's beadwork. I was attending my second Crow Fair, near Crow Agency, Montana, and was looking for Mardell, an interpreter and historian at the Custer Battlefield (now the Little Bighorn Battlefield National Monument). Mardell was not in camp, but her sisters, Mary and Nellie, invited me to wait with them. Two hours later we were still talking. "You feel like a sister," one of them said, and gestured to an empty teepee. "You'd better stay here." That kindness touched my heart and initiated a family friendship that I treasure.

At the time, Lillian was busy in the background. An industrious woman wearing a green-bead necklace and tending to the tasks of camp, she was already about seventy-four years old and the matriarch of several generations. She also knew considerable Crow history, which she relayed generously during my doctoral studies.

Our friendship continued long after the degree. We shared adventures and developed many personal memories, none momentous but the stuff of friendship, richly affecting this book. While recording her memoirs, she was addressing two people she knew well, so she spoke with warmth and intimacy. In turn, my affection spurred me to devote many years to our project.

The stories have been a joy and an education for me, and I hope that you too will enjoy and learn from them. If you are a Crow reader, you can step into history one of your elders lived. If you are a scholar of Plains culture, you will gain access to additional perspectives. And if this is your first exposure to Crow culture, you will be welcomed into a different world, where a woman might keep a medicine power in her stomach.

I wanted this compelling storyteller to speak directly to you from the page, so I have worked to preserve both her words and her expressive speech. My writing technique is related to ethno-poetics, and my version adheres to the rhythms of her voice, changing lines each time she pauses. Readers, however, do not need to pause at each line but can move through the stories at a natural speed. (More information on our format follows, near the end of this introduction.)

Lillian

Lillian Hogan was a member of the Big Lodge Clan, which was her mother's, and a child of the Ties the Bundle Clan, which was her father's. In English, her tribe calls itself Crow because this is the label Europeans gave them when they misunderstood their name. Apsáalooke (pronounced ăb sǎă lō gěh) is the name they use in their own language, meaning Children of the Long Beak Bird, but they also simply call themselves Our Side.[3]

Lillian was born in 1905 or as early as 1902, and she died in 2003, so she lived at least ninety-eight years, possibly one hundred one.[4] With the exception of a short stay in Arizona, she spent all her life on her reservation, near Billings, Montana. She worked hard, developed many skills, and adhered to traditional cultural values. Thus, she fulfilled the wishes of the old lady with the green-bead necklace by becoming a big, good woman: long-lived, hardworking, knowledgeable, and responsible to the Crow way of life.

In many ways, Lillian was a modern woman. She drove a car, maintained a bank account, and read the newspaper. She shopped in supermarkets and department stores, watched television, and picked up her mail at the post office. She fervently urged her children to become well-educated. But she was also a traditional woman, born on the cusp between past ways and modern life and raised by people who remembered the buffalo days and had lived nomadically when young. Carefully schooled in the knowledge Crow women once needed to help their families live in comfort and dignity, she was a good beadworker and she knew how to braintan an animal hide, make a saddle from part of a tree, or find and prepare a whole range of traditional foods.[5] She grew up near Plenty Coups, the last traditional chief of the Crows, she translated for William Wildschut, an important early collector, and she had affectionate memories of Finds Them and Kills Them, the last of the old-time Crow berdaches, men who dressed and lived as women. She witnessed ceremonies that no longer exist and remembered when old people told her to jump toward the moon so she would grow. For everyday wear, she dressed much the way her mother had, with braided hair, a home-made, long-sleeved cotton dress, and a wide, decorative belt. She wore high-top moccasins, which she protected from inclement weather with rubber overshoes, and when she was in public she always carried a wool blanket or fringed shawl, worn across her shoulders, around her hips, or draped over her arm, depending on the season and what she was doing. Only a few older women use the fashion today.

From the start, Lillian had to find her way between Apsáalooke and Euro-American customs. So did her parents and her children, as you will see, but neither could have told this story. Like the rest of her generation, Lillian never lived the nomadic life her grandparents had known and her parents had at least tasted. She learned to read, write, and speak English, so she was more prepared to confront the non-tribal society pressing in. Yet, unlike the generations born after her, she heard mainly Apsáalooke in her first years, so English was still her second language, and she spoke it differently. Unlike today's children, she did not come home each night on a school bus. Instead she was shut into a government boarding school, where she was punished for speaking Apsáalooke. After the boarding schools closed, she traveled to school on horseback.

Lillian was raised in a time when missionaries called Native religious practices ungodly. Torn between Crow customs and her Christian beliefs, she resolved the conflicts by attending traditional rituals without actively participating. This too sets her apart from later generations who live more comfortably with both religions.

She was a strong and determined woman who paid close attention to the teachings of her mother and her elders and remembered the details. She married four times, bearing nine children, and two of her husbands were educated and politically influential men. Robert Yellowtail functioned as the tribe's lawyer and became the first Crow superintendent, forever removing reservation management from white hands.[6] George Hogan, in the years before there was a formal tribal council, often served as secretary for tribal meetings. These men went to Washington DC armed with educations and wearing suits instead of the ermine-fringed shirts of the old chiefs. In later years, Lillian hosted the First Lady, Lady Bird Johnson, at her home. In old age, she was one of the last living members of the Tobacco Iipche, or Sacred Pipe Society, a rare organization even in her childhood. She endured so long that for several years she was the oldest living member of her tribe, yet she remained intellectually acute to almost the end of her life.

In this book her greatest power may be her ability to tell a story. As a child Lillian listened carefully to her parents' memories and to the old storytellers. Some of those storytellers would have been born in the 1830s, 1840s, or earlier, at a time when Europeans in her homeland were few in number and old customs were secure.

[As a child] I like to hear stories—I just sit there and listen and listen.
I tell my mother—I say, "I like them telling stories.
Make some fry bread and make some Indian dessert [berry pudding],
so after they tell the story,
after they finish," I say, "We'll eat the dessert."
And these people a-a-all like it—that's where I got stories.
I sure like them to tell a story.[7]

Lillian too became a mesmerizing speaker, framing her knowledge in the old way, with vivid dialogue, expressive hand gestures, helpful repetition, and careful structuring that places the story within the larger context of community. She had a true gift, supported by sharp memory and considerable artistry. In this account, she creates a history that educates, entertains, and allows us to *feel* her experiences.

Apsáalooke Aliichiiwaaó (History of the Apsáalooke People)

Lillian's long-ago ancestors were semi-sedentary and lived in villages with the Hidatsa, whom the Crow still consider kin. Their home was in present North Dakota, but they made periodic buffalo-hunting forays onto the dry plains to the west, and then, possibly as long ago as the fifteenth or sixteenth century, they began leaving the villages permanently and became full-time Plains people and nomadic buffalo hunters. The changes may have happened over centuries, but descendants still recall two stories. In one, a group left when two factions fought about the division of food, specifically a buffalo paunch.[8] In another, a prominent leader named No Vitals, or No Intestines, received a vision and left with his people to search for the sacred tobacco, the foundation of today's Tobacco Society.[9]

Eventually they claimed a large and beautiful region, stretching across much of southern Montana and northern Wyoming and blessed with handsome, snow-capped mountains and bountiful resources. That land is so beloved by Apsáalooke descendants that tribal historian Joseph

Medicine Crow wrote, "We Crows believe our country is the best place on Earth."[10]

Early visitors praised this land too. In 1862, geologist F. V. Hayden described the territory as "perhaps the best game country in the world."[11] Writing in the 1840s or early 1850s, Edwin Thompson Denig, a prominent, educated fur trader, had reported that "the Crows seldom suffer for want of meat."[12] By then, according to Denig, they were so prosperous that they owned more horses than any other tribe east of the Rocky Mountains. It was common, he said, for a single family to own a hundred, each valued at sixty to one hundred dollars.[13]

The tribe lived in two main divisions, the River Crow in the open plains from the Yellowstone River to the Missouri, and the Mountain Crow and the Kicked In the Bellies in the mountain ranges of southern Montana and northern Wyoming. In summer they reunited, undoubtedly with considerable enjoyment and celebration. Their language was Siouan in root. Their population, never large, was estimated at 3,500–4,000 for the late eighteenth century and much of the nineteenth.[14] Enemies, notably the Lakota, Cheyenne, and Blackfeet, pressed in constantly, but the tribe also had friends, especially the Plateau groups west of the Rocky Mountains.[15]

Like all Plains nomads, the Crow started on foot, carrying belongings on their backs or strapped to dogs, but dogs were small and unpredictable at best, so possessions and traveling distances were limited. Then, in the late seventeenth century, Spanish horses came north through Native trade routes, and Plains life transformed. Like others in the region, the Apsáalooke became master riders, traveling farther and faster, and carrying more belongings, more food, and larger "lodges"—skin teepees.

In general, the Crow lived much as other Plains tribes. They moved frequently in search of roots, berries, buffalo, elk, and other game. They made clothing of soft, brain-tanned animal skins, and lived in portable, cone-shaped teepees. To cleanse body and spirit, they used small, domed sweat lodges where they prayed and created intense steam by ritually pouring water on hot rocks. Like the tribes around them, they fasted in isolated places, seeking visions for medicine powers, and they practiced the sacred Sun Dance, with its rigorous fasting and prayer. They participated in intertribal warfare, and their warriors gained prestige by leading successful war parties or "counting coup" through military feats.

Each Plains tribe had distinctive customs, though, and the one most central to the Crow was the sacred Tobacco Society. Birthed from the vision of No Vitals, the society developed through ceremonial adoption of new members, and the ritual planting and harvesting of tobacco that was not used for smoking. The plant became linked with Crow prosperity, identity, and continuation as a people.[16]

The Crow clan system was distinctive too, based on a matrilineal structure in which each person joined his or her mother's clan but built complex, carefully prescribed relationships with members of his or her father's clan. The system bound the tribe together, providing networks of supportive relatives. As Tom Yellowtail said in his own life story, the clan system reinforces "the cooperation of each person, working toward the common welfare of the tribe."[17]

By the early nineteenth century, the Crow were gaining attention for their dignified bearing and gorgeous, costly dress. Prominent men wore beaded buckskin shirts fringed with snowy ermine. Women wore handsome red or blue wool dresses ornamented with elk teeth that represented the wealth and success of the family.[18] Some women carried soft, animal-skin robes exquisitely decorated with slender, parallel bands of beading. Even moving from camp to camp could be a festive occasion, for they often donned their best, creating a fine sight as they paraded the plains on horseback.[19] As a long-time scholar of Crow art, I have often imagined them talking, joking, and flirting as they trailed across the prairie in colorful splendor.

This nomadic way of life ended because of Europeans. Contact began at a trickle, perhaps through rare meetings with eighteenth-century visitors, and they entered the written record in 1805 in the journal of fur trader François Larocque.[20] Though the Crow did not meet him in person, William Clark, of the Lewis and Clark expedition, passed through their territory the same year.

In 1806, Lewis and Clark returned home, bringing maps and information. Explorers, fur trappers, and traders hurried to retrace their steps, and by 1807 Spanish fur trader Manuel Lisa had established a trading post at the mouth of the Bighorn River. The post did not last long because of Blackfoot attacks, but it marked the beginning of European settlement in Crow territory. By the 1840s, miners were rushing westward, indifferent to indigenous societies, and in 1865 the Civil War ended and a land-hungry nation turned its eyes to the West.[21]

Some tribes fought with guns and arrows to protect their way of life and suffered brutal retaliation. The Crow decided to coexist, negotiate, and do their best to outmaneuver their new opponents. In 1825, they had signed a treaty of friendship, which they never broke, and there is no record of Crow attacking settlers or the military.[22]

Nonetheless, the century ended harshly for the Apsáalooke, as for all Plains tribes, and nomadic life became impossible. The thirty-nine million Crow acres that the 1851 Treaty of Fort Laramie acknowledged shrank to eight million acres in the 1868 Treaty of Fort Laramie, and Washington continued to carve away more.[23] Game declined, and in the early 1880s white hunters purposefully slaughtered the great buffalo herds, shattering the indigenous economy and leaving the landscape reeking of rot. The Crow were confined within ever smaller reservation boundaries and couldn't leave to search for food or other resources.

Vigorous assimilation policies came next. The first Crow agency had been established at Fort Parker, near Livingston, Montana, in 1869, and white, government-appointed agents took control. With the support of churches, schools, and government policy, they attempted to uproot Crow culture, undermine indigenous governance, and turn the Crow into homesteaders and farmers.[24] In 1884, Congress established the Courts of Indian Offenses system, and with further support from Indian agents, prosecuted customs at the heart of Crow life. Congress also passed an act in 1882 and another in 1887 (the Dawes Act) that divided tribal land into individual Indian homesteads called allotments and put more pressure on Indian people to become homesteaders and farmers. The proponents of the bills hoped to open "surplus" acreage to white settlers, one of several such efforts. Boarding schools were built, and children forced to attend, and this removed them from the influences of their parents and grandparents while teachers did their best to reform them into Christians with European habits.

The damage from those years affected the Crow and many other tribes for a long time. Five decades after the buffalo slaughter, Chief Plenty Coups said to his biographer, Frank Linderman, "When the buffalo went away the hearts of my people fell to the ground. . . . After this nothing happened. There was little singing anywhere."[25] Around the same time, Pretty Shield was about seventy-five years old and trying to cope with this new life, and she told Linderman, "I am trying to live a life that I do not understand."[26]

Lillian's parents were born about twenty years after Plenty Coups and Pretty Shield.[27] They too saw nomadic life, but they began the shift from airy skin lodges to log cabins when they were only teenagers. They ate beef and government rations instead of buffalo. They reached maturity under restrictive government laws, without the Sun Dance and other important customs, and were surrounded by English-speaking Christians, farmers, ranchers, and a money-based economy. Confined to reservations, the young men of their generation became the first that couldn't count coup. Sometimes they could not even leave the reservation without written passes from white authorities.[28]

There were also good times, as evident in these stories, but these were hard years. By 1910, disease and malnutrition had reduced the Crow population by 50 percent.[29] Reservation lands were a fraction of their original size. Boarding schools were still in place, and white authorities continued to devalue Crow customs. In that year, Lillian was five years old and just beginning to establish memories.

The Stories

Lillian's stories are deeply marked by the physical and social dislocation of the late nineteenth and early twentieth centuries. Her father and his hungry family had to leave their beloved mountains when he was a boy and move to Reno Creek, Montana, then to Pryor, Montana, abandoning their nomadic life forever. As a teenager, her mother lost a brother when a white man killed him, and in those years of declining population, she buried eight children. Only Lillian and her brother Caleb lived to adulthood. Lillian experienced the forced cultural assimilation of boarding school. She and her brother both had their names changed by white authorities without their parents' permission. She spent much of her life conflicted over Christian and Apsáalooke religious beliefs. The family was wracked by the alcohol that had gained a footing as the old life fell apart, and they struggled with the poverty that resulted. Later her young husband Paul died because of alcohol.

During Lillian's youth and young adulthood, a battle was clearly underway, as agents, the U.S. government, and various tribal factions struggled over land, the distribution of tribal funds, the politics of running the reservation, religious freedom, boarding schools, and other issues. Lillian was closely connected to some of the most prominent figures in those struggles. Her family was close to Chief Plenty Coups and visited him frequently, and she was no doubt sent to his little store as a girl to pick up occasional groceries. She married Robert Yellowtail in the 1920s, while he was prominently involved in Crow politics, and she managed his ranch when he went to Washington DC. After 1934, when John Collier was appointed commissioner of Indian affairs and reversed long-standing policies of oppression, the Crow could once again practice their traditions openly, and Lillian supported her brother Caleb in his efforts to bring back the Sun Dance, an important step toward cultural rebuilding.[30]

Yet Lillian only occasionally spoke of politics or specific historical events, so this is not a history in the academic sense. Nor is it a record of Crow mythology, although she knew many myths. It contains her personal memories of her own life and the lives of those around her, as far back as the 1870s, sometimes earlier, providing a warm, accessible, truly remarkable window into Crow Reservation experience. She gives us a precious record, not of distant, anonymous events, but of individual struggles, sorrows, laughter, celebrations—everyday issues of real people.

We open Lillian's book with her birth because that is how she began her account when she told it. We close with her thoughts about old age, her pride in her accomplishments, and her worries for future generations. In between, of course, is her lifetime of experiences.

The overriding subject is living an Apsáalooke life, for in spite of the best efforts of the early agents, schools, and churches, many Crow are bilingual and conduct much social conversation and tribal business in Apsáalooke.[31] Their clan system thrives and continues to bind them together. They use English names, but they still emphasize Indian names too. They continue to take new members into their Tobacco Society. Although few women tan hides the old way, they still wear spectacular elk-tooth dresses and bead so prodigiously that celebrations are a cornucopia of color.[32] They are generous gift givers, often in formal, distinctly Crow formats. In Apsáalooke terms, as observed by Voget, "there is no better way to show respect for another and to maintain kinship loyalties than by periodic gifts."³³ They find many reasons to "take in," or adopt, additional family members, gaining new children, siblings, or parents while keeping those they have.³⁴ From their perspective good relatives represent a kind of prosperity, and they maximize that wealth. They also find many reasons to celebrate, sing, drum, dance, play hand games, bet on horse races, and generally enjoy being Crow.

In 1892, agent Moses Wyman had reported in frustration, "These Indians are friendly . . . but I have never seen a tribe more attached to their traditions and older customs."³⁵ Even then, the cultural dice may have been cast, for the tribe lost a great deal but still managed to preserve an impressive amount. A century later, Apsáalooke customs were fundamental to Lillian's life. They also dominated the way her book unfolded.

Making This Book

Eight Apsáalooke have previously told their life stories for book-length publications, a large number for a small Native tribe. As already mentioned, Pretty Shield and Plenty Coups recounted their experiences to Frank Linderman in the early 1930s. Others include Two Leggings, an ambitious warrior from the same generation; Tom Yellowtail, an important Sun Dance leader of Lillian's generation; and Agnes Deernose, born just a few years after Lillian.³⁶ Tribal historian Joseph Medicine Crow, who was born in 1913 and descends from the noted Chief Medicine Crow, told his story in a form accessible to young adults.³⁷ Helen Pease Wolf, born in 1906 into a mixed-blood family of ranchers and businessmen, also contributed a story.³⁸ Alma Hogan Snell, who was Pretty Shield's granddaughter, Lillian's stepdaughter, and Mardell's half sister, was born in the generation following Lillian's. She published her life story just a few years ago.³⁹ Now Lillian Hogan's story joins this list, bringing the total to nine.

These are not the only publications on or by the Crow. The tribe has intrigued outsiders since the nineteenth century, and ethnographers, historians, anthropologists, art historians, and early visitors have written extensively about them. The Apsáalooke themselves have actively published too.⁴⁰ These more academic publications are important, and a number are cited in this book. Yet it is the biographies that hold a special place in Crow literature, for through them the Apsáalooke exert rare influence on their written narrative. Native people share many customs, so outsiders sometimes assume they think alike, yet there is a common joke in Indian country that goes something like this: "Ask twenty Indian people for their opinions, and you will get twenty-two opinions." That becomes clear in these books, for all of the speakers share a set of Apsáalooke values, but each is a strong individual with unique views of the world. If you think that Native thought is homogeneous or one-dimensional, read these books. They preserve the details of Crow customs and by sheer numbers succeed in creating an unusually textured record of who they have been and are.

We began our own project in 1993, when Lillian was eighty-eight years old. We sat at my dining table in Big Sky, Montana, with a small, portable tape player between us, surrounded by the sounds one might expect around three women conversing at home: children's voices, telephones, the noises of cooking. The process was slightly untidy, so our tapes are unpolished, but the results are warm, honest, and informative in a way that may not have been possible in a more self-conscious setting.

Our approach centered on collaborative scholarship, with each of us playing critical but different roles. Lillian recorded eighteen hours of stories, speaking mostly in English, sometimes in Apsáalooke, and she decided most of the topics. Mardell and I asked clarifying questions or requested favorite stories, but we did not have a specific agenda or list of questions, so Lillian directed the flow of the narrative. That influenced the very nature of the information we gained, sometimes leading us to knowledge we might not have received through more academic questioning.

Mardell was co-interviewer for the first eight tapes and later translated everything told in Apsáalooke. She contributed research and many endnotes, augmenting the Crow knowledge in this book. We have identified those endnotes with her initials, MP. When time permitted, she reviewed my writing, alerting me to the mistakes that inevitably arise in cross-cultural projects. She is the first Crow to edit an Apsáalooke life story.

My main job was to turn oral stories into a cogent book. I participated in all interviews, transcribed the tapes to disk, designed and implemented our editing methodologies, and did research to clarify confusing sections. I also introduced some stories and added basic endnotes, which are noted with my initials, BL. My introductions and endnotes are, for the most, designed to guide those who are new to Apsáalooke culture.

Sadly, Lillian's health began to decline soon after taping. By the time we translated and transcribed the recordings, she was no longer strong enough to answer questions or decide how she wanted her book to be treated. This plunged me into the writing process without her guidance, but two intentions helped me stay on track: remaining mindful that the stories belonged to Lillian, not to me, and striving to create a beautiful and readable book without distorting her words or reforming them to European standards of writing. Too often we academics distort Native knowledge, even with the best intentions, taking oral information and altering it through Western customs of scholarship. We gather the information, analyze it, rearrange it to suit our inquiry, and edit it to European tastes. That is our training. But like a growing number of academics, I had become increasingly uncomfortable with this cultural overlay. I wanted to protect Lillian's right to speak for herself.[41]

At first, I thought I could attain these goals simply by changing her words minimally. Such optimism came from ignorance, and I immediately ran into trouble. My first problem was the unbending silence of print—I was trying to force active, three-dimensional speech into static, linear paragraphs, and every time I tried, Lillian's beautiful stories fell flat. In the 1920s, Nez Perce scholar Archie Phinney stated the problem well after he put his mother's animal stories into writing. "A sad thing in recording these animal stories is the loss of spirit. . . . [W]hen I read my story mechanically I find only the cold corpse."[42]

My second problem was structure. As Rodney Frey noted in *Stories That Make the World*, "the speech patterns found in literacy-based cultures are significantly grounded in literacy structures and forms and are not equivalent per se to the speech patterns found in oral-based cultures."[43] He confirmed that difference when he learned to speak Apsáalooke.

And then there was language. To the ear, Lillian sounded exactly right. Not so on paper. English was her second language, and her unconventional grammar did not read well. The Apsáalooke language represents gender and tense differently, so Lillian, like many elders, applied "he" and "she" loosely and frequently interchanged past and present tenses. She often used short phrases that seemed choppy in writing, and she randomly dropped subject pronouns such as "they" and "we" from the beginnings of sentences. She left out words or arranged them in seemingly odd ways. And like many who come to English as a second language, she sometimes confused words that sound alike (such as "done" and "don't") or missed the distinction between words such as "them" and "those." Like many old-fashioned storytellers, she tended to repeat herself, a device that helped her listeners remember but felt redundant on paper. She interjected "says" or "say" a lot, often inserting the word at the beginning of every phrase, sometimes two or three times in a single sentence. Indian storytellers do this to tell listeners they are quoting someone else, but that too became intrusive on paper.

In short, in transcription Lillian's beautiful stories lost their grace and became muddled. Accounts that had been clear and compelling to the ear became fragmented, repetitive, and ungrammatical in paragraphs. I was left with two choices, edit heavily or change my approach.

That is when I altered the form of this book, abandoning paragraphs for a verse-like structure that follows the rhythms of Lillian's voice. With earphones in place and foot to the pedal of a cassette transcribing machine, I listened repeatedly to each story, breaking the text to a new line each time Lillian paused. This technique is inspired by ethnopoetics and Dennis Tedlock's concepts of oral history as performance, as well as by the pioneering work of anthropologists such as Dell Hymes and by the authenticity of writing by Wendy Wickwire and Julie Cruikshank.[44]

The approach was time-consuming and unfamiliar, but it transformed the project. The rigidity of the page softened, and Lillian's powerful stories regained their eloquence. Awkward idiosyncrasies stopped being awkward. Odd word orders began to make sense. Choppy sentences began to fit. So did the repetitions. Missing pronouns no longer mattered because they usually fell at pauses. The "says" began to provide emphasis, especially at the beginning of a new line, and, mysteriously but happily, the grammar problems faded into the background. I almost always clarified gender when Lillian transposed "he" and "she" because it was too confusing, but I preserved many of her speech patterns and much of the cyclical, repetitive structure so characteristic of traditional Native histories.[45]

Once the text began to read more smoothly, I felt it could take a few bumps, so I preserved most of her tenses as she spoke them, even when she mixed past and present. This trait also flavors the speech of many elders, but I suspect that readers will be able to decipher the tenses once accustomed to this manner of speaking. In short, ethnopoetics allowed me to stay far closer to the original text than would have been possible with standard editing.

To reclaim still more emotion, I included nonverbal cues such as laughter or weeping. These are framed in parentheses. As noted in an earlier footnote, I used hyphenated letters where Lillian drew out words. Sometimes I preserved those attenuations because they seemed to add meaning. For example, I believe that "tra-a-vel" is more than just the act of changing location; it seems to imply the passing of time and distance. In other cases, drawn out words add emphasis or punctuate pauses, as when she started a new sentence with "a-a-nd" and then paused before continuing with the next piece of the story.

Out of respect for Lillian's ownership, neither Mardell nor I added significantly to the body of the text. Instead we relegated commentary to endnotes and introductory clarifications so we would not interrupt the narrative. Sometimes I inserted words or phrases if essential for clarity. Those are usually in brackets so readers can identify them. I studied unclear sections repeatedly, taking care with any word change, in hopes of protecting subtle meanings. Lillian was not there to title her stories, but I wanted to keep her voice, so I used a phrase from within each story. I also used italics for translations from Apsáalooke to English because these sections do not represent her exact words or speech patterns. The translations are also more formal, and I want readers to know why. Sometimes, I used commas unconventionally, leaving them out of a line to preserve flow or adding them at the end of a line to emphasize pauses, even if not grammatically required.

If I have done my job as carefully and artfully as intended, this book may read as though natural and untouched. Yet my hand print affects every page. Sometimes Lillian framed her stories clearly. Sometimes she was just talking about life, and I had to find the story and decide its beginning and end. I rearranged sections for flow and nudged phrases into coherence and grace. I had to determine what word or two would bring Lillian's meaning into focus, and sometimes, in consultation with Mardell, I had to decide exactly what the meaning was. I also eliminated confused dialogue and private or potentially harmful information about other people. For better or worse, I removed my voice and Mardell's, which allowed for smoother stories but occasionally forced me to add bracketed words of transition. When I titled individual stories, I often had to choose between multiple themes, unavoidably affecting what you as readers will take away from those sections. I also decided how best to order the stories into a picture of Lillian's life, inevitably influencing the way her narrative unfolds. In short, I accepted many little compromises to make this book readable.

Nonetheless, I have done my best to preserve Lillian's words accurately and honestly and to honor both her authority and her wonderfully expressive voice. I hope I have stayed sufficiently out of the way so that you can feel her presence as you read. As I said earlier, perhaps on occasion, she will seem to speak directly to you from the page.

Notes

1. Lillian often elongated words, and I have tried to preserve that expressiveness, as here with a-a-nd. In some cases there may be meaning embedded in the drawn-out sounds.
2. Medicine powers provide spiritual assistance that often originates in visions or dreams. They strengthen the owner by bringing health, material success, special knowledge, or other benefits. See Frey, *World of the Crow*; Curtis, *The North American Indian*; Voget, *Shoshoni-Crow Sun Dance*.
3. "Apsáalooke" has become the standardized spelling, based on the Crow Language Alphabet and Pronunciation Guide. The guide was developed through the Crow Bilingual Materials Development Center as part of a federally funded program to produce bilingual materials for schools. See Tushka, *A Dictionary of Everyday Crow*; Two Leggins, *Apsáalooke Writing Tribal Histories*, 3; McCleary, *The Stars We Know*, xxi–xxii; and Apsáaloke Writing Tribal Histories Project, Little Big Horn College Library, http://lib.lbhc.edu/history/0.01.php.
4. Lillian did not know exactly when she was born. Her family thinks she may have been born in 1902 or 1903, but she always gave the year as 1905, so that is the year we have used.
5. Brain-tanning is a traditional Native American technique that uses animal brains and liver in the softening process. Lillian described the steps in "I Learned How to Make Buckskin," chapter 8.
6. Robert Yellowtail was one of the most influential Crow in the twentieth century. His political involvement is described in Bradley, *Handsome People*; Hoxie, *Parading*, and Poten, "Robert Yellowtail." In 1976 he published personal memories in "A Brief Review." The essay does not cover political activities but provides insight into early reservation life.
7. On another tape, Lillian said they told stories when there was snow on the mountains. She'd ask for stories and her father would tell one of the storytellers that they wanted him over at the house. "And he come in the evening . . . would tie his horse, and I'd sit there, and he comes in and we'd give him supper, and he says,

'All right, fix me a ni-i-ce, soft cushion to sit on, and I'll tell her some stories'."
8. The quarrel started between two women, but according to Denig (*Five Indian Tribes*, 137) evolved into a serious confrontation between two competing chiefs and escalated into violence. Swanton (*Indian Tribes of North America*, 390) lists "Kihnatsa" as one Hidatsa name for the Crow, meaning "they who refused the paunch."
9. According to oral tradition, No Vitals traveled extensively in search of the right place. For details, see Medicine Crow, *From the Heart of the Crow Country*, 16–24.
10. Medicine Crow, *Counting Coup*, 18.
11. Hayden, "On the Ethnology and Philosophy," 392.
12. Denig, *Five Indian Tribes*, 160. Denig lived in the upper Missouri River area from 1833–56 and recorded valuable early information on several tribes. He died in 1858. For more on Denig and his writings, see Ewers, "Editor's Introduction" in Denig, *Five Indian Tribes*, xiii–xxxvii.
13. Denig, *Five Indian Tribes*, 144–47.
14. These population estimates are from Lewis and Clark and Mooney. See Swanton, *Indian Tribes of North America*, 391.
15. The Crow and Nez Perce grew so close that the two tribes often dressed similarly. Thomas Leforge, the "White Crow" who joined the tribe in 1868, recalled in his memoirs that it required "an actual personal acquaintance always to distinguish between members of these differing Indian stocks, so closely united in interest and in purpose had they become" (Leforge in Marquis, *Memoirs*, 97–98). For details on the relationship between Crow and Nez Perce beading styles, see Loeb, "Classic Intermontane Beadwork."
16. In "Cultivating Themselves," Nabokov explores the Tobacco Society as a source of regeneration. McCleary ("Akbaatashee," 35) connects the society with "growth within the tribe, protection from enemies, and an abundance of the things which they need to survive."
17. Yellowtail in Fitzgerald, *Yellowtail*, 21.
18. According to Denig, the tribe valued a man's outfit at two to four horses and an elk-tooth dress at that cost or more (Denig, *Five Indian Tribes*, 155, 158). Swiss artist Rudolph Friederich Kurz sketched Crow women in elk-tooth dresses in the early 1850s, the first known documentation of the garments, but the fashion likely dates to precontact, using buckskin instead of wool trade cloth.
19. Pretty Shield described the fun of moving camp in her biography (Linderman, *Pretty-Shield*, 21–22). Several nineteenth-century visitors referenced the beauty of Crow on the move, including a detailed description by Denig, *Five Indian Tribes*, 158. Noted photographer Edward Curtis (*The North American Indian*, 31) reported new brides particularly festive, bedecking themselves and their horses each time they moved camp.
20. Larocque, *Journal*, 1–82.
21. For detailed analysis of relationships during early contact, see Bradley, *Handsome People*.
22. Plenty Coups, the last traditional chief, attributed this decision to a dream he had in his youth and described the vision quest that led to the dream, as well as its interpretation by Yellow Bear (Linderman, *Plenty-Coups*, 57–75). Helen Pease

Wolf (*Reaching Both Ways*, 14) attributed friendly relations to her great-grandfather, Fellows David Pease, later known as Major Pease.
23. Today's reservation is approximately 2.2 million acres, roughly 8 percent of the original territory. To trace the reduction through treaties and acts, see Medicine Crow and Press, *A Handbook*.
24. Bradley (*Handsome People*, 124) argues that turning every Crow into a homesteader was the primary goal of all agents.
25. Linderman attributed the words to both Pretty Shield (*Pretty-Shield*, 248) and Plenty Coups (*Plenty-Coups*, 311).
26. Linderman, *Pretty-Shield*, 24.
27. According to official records, Lillian's father was born in 1871 and her mother in 1872 (file 3508, Big Horn County Office of the Clerk and Recorder), but these probably represent family guesses. Lillian's own estimates in these stories are inconsistent.
28. Robert Yellowtail recalled being required to obtain passes, complete with time limits, just to visit relatives in the next district. He described the process as "[o]ne of the highlights of autocratic rule on the Crow Reservation." See Yellowtail, "A Brief Review."
29. The census of 1910 reported 1,799 Crow.
30. When John Collier developed the Indian Reorganization Act ending many culturally oppressive laws, the tribe initially misinterpreted it and voted against it (see Bradley, *The Handsome People*, chapter 10), but the act allowed them to openly practice customs without fear of persecution. In 1941 they held the first Crow-organized Sun Dance in over sixty years.
31. An increasing number of young Crow are growing up without speaking their language, but Crow teachers are actively working to correct that. See Brien, "Fading Fluency," in the online version of the Apsáalooke Writing Tribal Histories Project, Little Big Horn College (http://lib.lbhc.edu/history/5.11.php).
32. In the twentieth century, Crow art, especially beadwork, became a powerful tool for resisting forced assimilation. For a detailed discussion of beading and the protecting cultural identity, see Loeb, "Crow Beadwork."
33. Voget, *Shoshoni-Crow Sun Dance*, 33.
34. As Leforge discovered in his many years with the Crow, "The number of genuine-offspring children in any family was not easily discoverable" (Marquis, *Memoirs*, 165). We confronted similar challenges in writing this book and could not always discern how relatives connected.
35. Bradley, *After the Buffalo Days*, 179.
36. Nabokov, *Two Leggings*; Fitzgerald, *Yellowtail*; and Voget, *They Call Me Agnes*.
37. Medicine Crow, *Counting Coup*.
38. Wolf, *Reaching Both Ways*. This small book provides basic history of the influential Pease family, descendants of Europeans, Crows, Hidatsa, and Gros Ventre. The author's great-grandfather, Major Pease, was the Crow agent in the 1870s.
39. Snell, *Grandmother's Grandchild*.
40. Influential leaders Robert Yellowtail and Max Big Man were writing by the first half of the twentieth century. Joseph Medicine Crow began publishing in 1939 and was still writing at the time this book was approaching press. Several Crow contributed to a study of French-Canadian/Cree photographer Richard Thros-

sel (Albright, *Crow Indian Photographer*). Tribal members curated "Parading Through History: The Apsaalooke Nation," for the Western Heritage Center. Several faculty at Little Big Horn College, Crow Agency, have written educational materials for students.

41. For a useful, nuanced discussion of problems embedded in both speaking and not speaking for others, see Alcoff, "The Problem of Speaking for Others," 97–119.
42. Archie Phinney wrote these words in 1927 in a letter to Franz Boaz. The letter is housed in the American Philosophical Society Library in Philadelphia. See Ramsey, "From Mythic to Fictive," 26.
43. Frey, *The World of the Crow Indians*, 142.
44. Frey was the first to apply ethnopoetics to Crow oral literature. His book was published after this project began, so it did not directly influence our methodology, but became an inspiration later. See Frey, *Stories That Make the World*.
45. Frey (*The World of the Crow Indians*, 25) attributes pronoun confusion to the egalitarian nature of Crow society. Noting that men and women are "equally eligible for social recognition and spiritual attainment," he says that equality is "embedded in the Apsaalooke language. In the construction of a sentence containing third-person pronouns, ('he,' 'she,' or 'it'), the Apsaalooke do not distinguish the sex of the subject."

Thoughts about My Mother

Mardell Hogan Plainfeather

Mom shared many stories with me. One was how she got her first Crow name, a story she tells in her own way in this book. My comments are in relation to the title Barbara and I chose. I always thought it was odd that a white man known as "the boss farmer" had named her, so I once asked Mother. She said her father admired white people because they were "inventors of many things." Apparently the boss farmer was a good man whom everyone respected. He had named other children in the Pryor community. Grandpa admired his agricultural knowledge, so he too asked the boss to name his baby daughter. When Mom talked about her name, she said her family had a problem interpreting it from the beginning. They chose to say it as "Loves Man" or "Loves the Man," but they decided to reinterpret it as "Likes Men" in hopes of softening the flirtatious implications.

When my mother was a few years older, she realized the connotations her name suggested, and she did not like it. Grandpa later asked a clan sister, Ella Cashen, to give her another. Both my grandfather and Ella were from the Ties the Bundle Clan, which made Ella Mom's clan mother. Ella's Crow name was Ties the Bundle Woman, so when she was asked to rename Mom, she gave away her own name. I remember Ella Cashen well. As a child, I saw that she and Mom were close, and she always gave Ella gifts, as a token of her respect.

Mom preferred "Ties the Bundle Woman," but people still called her Likes Men. She just couldn't seem to persuade people to call her by her new name. But Mom was a good sport and often laughed about it, like the time we had a birthday party for her and one of her dearest friends, Florence Real Bird, gave her a present with the card addressed "To Likes Men, From Don't Like Men." They teased each other and laughed heartily together.

When Barbara and I talked about the name years later, she offered a theory that my sister Mary and I like. Perhaps, Barbara suggested, when the boss farmer named her, he really meant "Loves Mankind" or "Loves All of Humanity." A Crow name is often given to a child derived from one's own virtues, background, or deeds, or maybe even a dream. Did the boss farmer live among the Crow long enough to know this? At the time, Crow Country was isolated, but he had come and patiently worked with Indian people, something not many white men cared to do. Was it his contribution to humankind? Did he enjoy friendships with all, no matter what color their skin? Mom didn't know much about him, except that Grandpa considered him "a good, kind man." I have wondered about this man who gave my mother her name because, like most Crow people, I consider the names of my children and my grandchildren to be so important that I give much thought and consideration to who will name them. I ask one of the child's clan fathers or clan mothers, a respected veteran or friend.

I am the one who thought of calling this book *The Woman Who Loved Mankind*. Barbara's theory of the interpretation of Mom's name is only a theory, but I think Mom would have liked it, too.

During her lifetime, I heard Mom's "teasing cousins" joking that her name Likes Men was a good name for her due to her four marriages. (A teasing cousin is anyone, male or female, who has a father in the same clan as one's own father.) Mom married her first husband at a very young age and soon divorced. She remarried again, but her husband was in politics and was always gone, sometimes rumors getting back to her of other women, so she divorced him too. Next she married a man from the Black Lodge District, a marriage arranged by her new husband's father. Years later, he died, leaving her with small children to bring up alone. She met my own father, a Crow with blue eyes and fair skin inherited from his half-French mother, while he was visiting people at the old Crow hospital with the Baptist minister, the Rev. Chester Bentley. Mom was an inpatient at the time, and Father was a deacon of the Burgess Memorial Baptist Church in Crow Agency and was a widower himself.

My grandfather, ever an admirer of white people, thought he was a white man and sought out his friendship. When he found out that the man was a Crow and was alone, he began to wish his daughter would marry him. Mother didn't want to because he was much older than she was, but eventually they did marry and had twin daughters and later me. I was their last child. My mother was over forty and my father was about sixty-three or sixty-four when I was born.

Mother took the teasing about her marriages well, but as I began to think about her life, I realized some other things about Crow women of her age. Men had always provided for and protected women, and females married mainly for this reason, especially during the pre-reservation period. Male skills as warriors and hunters determined status in the tribe, but those roles were forever changed after the reservation period began. For a long time, the men protected their roles as providers as well as they could, but times changed, and so did male and female situations.

My mother was in between those periods when she relied on a husband, but she survived long enough to know that a lone woman could also be a good provider, which she was after my father passed on. She became the provider for us, and for all of her life she was always cooking and baking. If it wasn't for her family, it was the pies and buns for which she was known—things she made for the Church of God fund-raisers that benefited needy people in Africa. This is how I will always remember her. She was always worried about providing, always chiding us for being lazy, always on the go, going shopping for this or that, making us go to church whether we wanted to or not, and sewing dresses for other traditionally dressed women free of charge. For whatever reason the boss farmer long ago had named her, she really did live up to the name, for she loved her fellow humans.

Mother promised Father she would not practice Crow ways such as Sun Dancing or attend Tobacco Society gatherings anymore. Father had spent most of his youth at the Carlisle Indian School in Pennsylvania, where the staff emphasized Christianity and criticized Indian religious beliefs as well as Native hairstyles and clothing. Life was kind of contradictory because her brother, Caleb Bullshows, was a Sun Dancer, and we, Father included, always went to the Sun Dances and camped, helping out our uncle with many things. We may not have been participants, but we absorbed much, especially the sacredness of this worship and the faith that Uncle Caleb had. Not long after Father died, Mom gave me to George and Evelyn Old Elk for adoption into the sacred Tobacco Society, and they became my beloved Tobacco Society parents. Mom gave my sister, Mary Elizabeth, to Ted and Martha Bear Cloud for adoption into the society too. She told me she would not participate in the ceremonies herself, as she had promised my father, but she was excited for us to become members. I am ever so grateful to her for this. She was always singing the songs of the society and often spoke of the times when she attended a meeting or the times they planted the sacred tobacco in the area around her hometown, Pryor. Years later she took me and a non-Crow scholar to some of these tobacco-planting places, and while we were there she suddenly lamented in Crow fashion the now-deceased people who had attended these plantings with her so many years ago. Breaking Crow tradition, she cried out their Crow names, not their Christian ones, and somehow it made the lament sound especially forlorn and from the depths of her heart.

Mom, like so many of her generation, accepted the ways of the white people, but she never let go of the traditions she was raised with. Even when she was in the hospital dying, she was doing the hand gestures we use in the dance of the Tobacco Society. Perhaps before her body surrendered to death, her spirit was already in the Other Side Camp, attending a Tobacco Society dance. I'll bet she was happy to be there.

Now, in the years after her death, I try to analyze my mother occasionally, including the contradictions in her life. She worshipped God in the white people's church, but she secretly preferred the Tobacco Society way. She was a good mother, but sometimes she would allow her temper to rage, and now I often wonder if her father's and brother's alcoholism had affected her in some way. In this book she speaks of her father with loving memories and describes him as a successful farmer, but she also talks of his gambling at horse races and card playing.

Some of my relatives may not appreciate Mom speaking of Uncle Caleb's or Grandpa's drinking. It surprised and shocked me at first. My parents were beyond normal childbearing years when I was born and their parents were gone, except for Mother's father. He was the only grandparent I ever knew, and I loved him. We visited him in Pryor often, and he eventually came to live with us in Crow Agency. By that time, he was elderly and never drank, to my knowledge. He enjoyed walking with me and my sister/cousin, Iva, to Butch Clifford's candy store and spoiled us with treats almost daily. He loved to drink soda pop because it made him belch, and Iva and I would roar with laughter. This is how *I* remember him. When he died, it broke my heart, and I still miss my grandpa. I never knew him as someone who drank, but it was a tragic reality for my mother. She was the one who had lived through the sorrow of her brother and her father drinking. She was the one who saw her father be a successful farmer, only to see him gamble their profits away or drink it up and finally give up farming altogether. I only hope that my relatives will understand that alcoholism was a reality then, and it is still a reality now.

How glad I am for my father's gentle Christian ways, and most of all for my mother's love, discipline, prayers, and willingness to let us go back to Crow traditions. My parents both instilled in me the values that I have today—to get an education, to work hard, and to have faith in our Creator. It was my mother who encouraged me to seek him in my own way and also *allowed* me to join in the dancing, or powwow as it is called nowadays, when Crow people celebrate any event.

When I was young, our history was never taught in the schools. We were always the bad guys in movies, and we were taught to be ashamed of being Indian. The Bureau of Indian Affairs encouraged us to leave our homelands to work in big cities. It was a confusing time for many Natives but my father's and mother's pride in being Crow anchored me. I became an interpretive specialist in the National Park Service where I spoke about Crow and Native history. I could not have done it without my mother's encouragement. She even gave me her right to speak in public, a right given to her by Big Ox, a Crow elder, in her young adulthood. My parents' values eventually saved me from living without spirituality, culture, education, or goals. My parents left me much.

When Mom told her stories in the Crow language, she was masterful. She not only used many hand gestures, she used facial expressions and sounds to accompany them, and sometimes even her feet to stomp. I sometimes wondered if she learned this style of storytelling from her favorite storyteller, an old man by the name of Cuts the Bear's Ears, a Crow elder who was invited often to my grandparents' home at the request of my mother.

I thought Mom told her stories masterfully in English too, but English was her second language. Although most Crow people of my generation began grade school with a very limited knowledge of the English language, we managed to learn it quickly and well because our parents' generation had to speak English too, in the boarding schools, eventually in church, in business dealings with land lessees and Bureau of Indian Affairs employees, at the hospital, and in stores. The difference was that we were already exposed to the language. Mom's parents knew only a few words, if any at all.

In our home, Crow was spoken about 99.9 percent of the time so when Mom spoke English it seemed like she had a good command of the language. When I read our first transcriptions of our interviews with her, I was somewhat shocked to read what appeared to be poor grammar. Still, I wanted to keep that grammar because it was part of the way she expressed herself in what was, to Mom, a foreign language.

Later Barbara proposed "ethnopoetics" to help preserve her speech patterns, but I was uncomfortable at first with the style she wanted to offer readers. However, after much thought and reading it over a couple of times, it seemed appropriate. This speed *was* Mom's own, and it was the right thing to do: not to change it or her grammar. Her stories are not from a scholar, they are hers and, to use her own words, she was just a "plain Crow Indian woman."

I would record some of Mom's stories now and then because I wanted to save them for her grandchildren, but I never thought to do anything else with the tapes. I am grateful to my sister and friend, Barbara, for offering to do this book. Early reservation life, as experienced by our mothers, fathers, and grandparents, will never be known unless those of us who cherish them save their stories. The stories are important because they help us remember what others have gone through and because those who came before us made us what we are today. We are Apsáalooke, and I don't want any of my descendants to forget the many chapters of our history, whether the experiences are of the tribe as a whole or personal vignettes like my mother's.

Thank you, Barbara, for all of your work. With all of your talents and interests, you could have been doing something else, but you chose to preserve something very special to me and, I hope, to all the Apsáalooke. I will never forget the weeks we spent at your beautiful, peaceful home near the Spanish Peaks, mountains the Apsáalooke loved so well. You, Mom, and I shared her stories, sometimes with laughter, sometimes with tears, but always with the intense interest of two daughters sitting side by side with their mother. Aho!

Your stories will live, Mom. I love you and thank you for sharing them with me and Barbara.

Genealogies

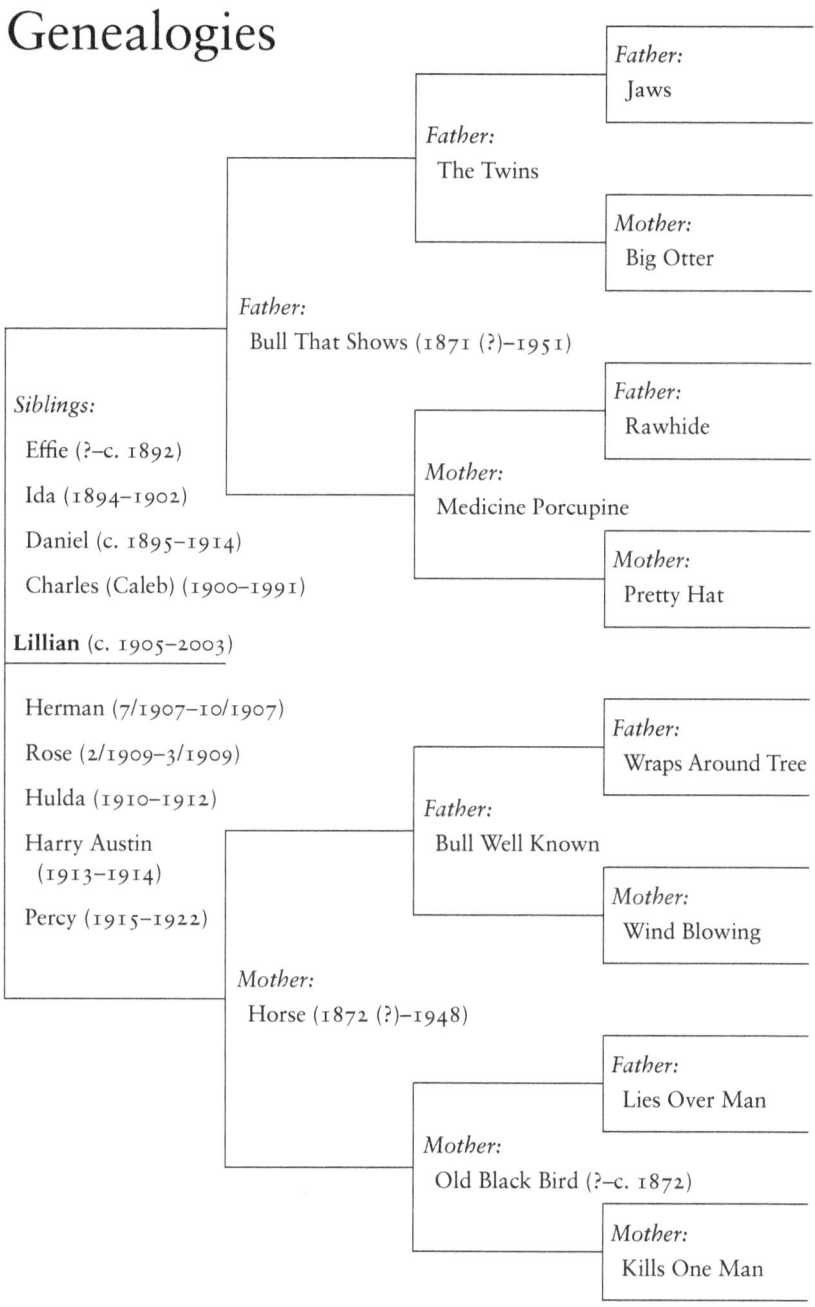

Source: Titles and Records, Bureau of Indian Affairs, Crow Indian Agency.

First Marriage

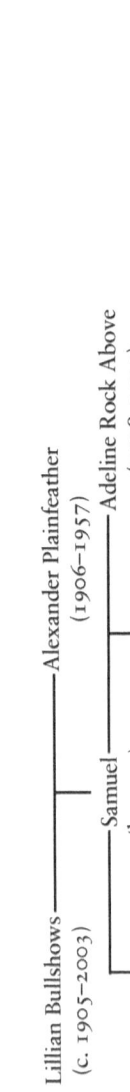

```
Lillian Bullshows ────────── Alexander Plainfeather
(c. 1905–2003)                  (1906–1957)
         │
      Samuel ────────── Adeline Rock Above
      (b. 1922)              (1928–2005)
         │
   Jason Shane
   (b. 1943)
         │
   ┌─────┬─────┬─────┬─────┬─────┬─────┬─────┬─────┐
Russell Gregory Cerise Mary Millie Billie Rebecca Teatta Sara
(b. 1945)(c. 1947–c. 1948)(b. 1949)(b. 1951)(b. 1953)(b. 1955)(b. 1957)(b. 1962)(b. 1966)
```

Second Marriage

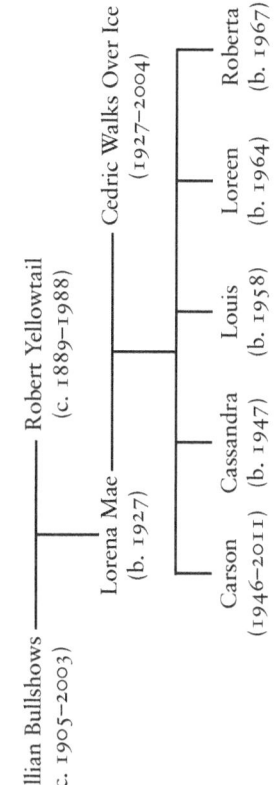

Third Marriage

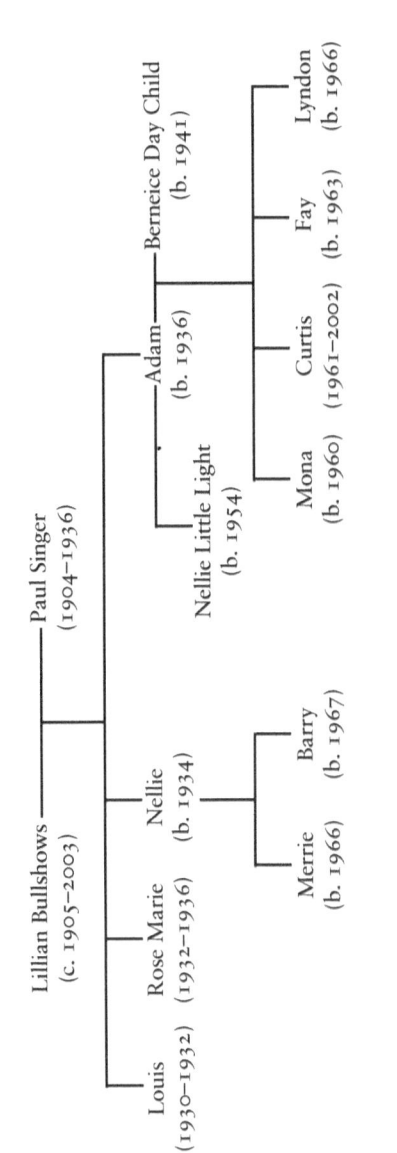

Fourth Marriage

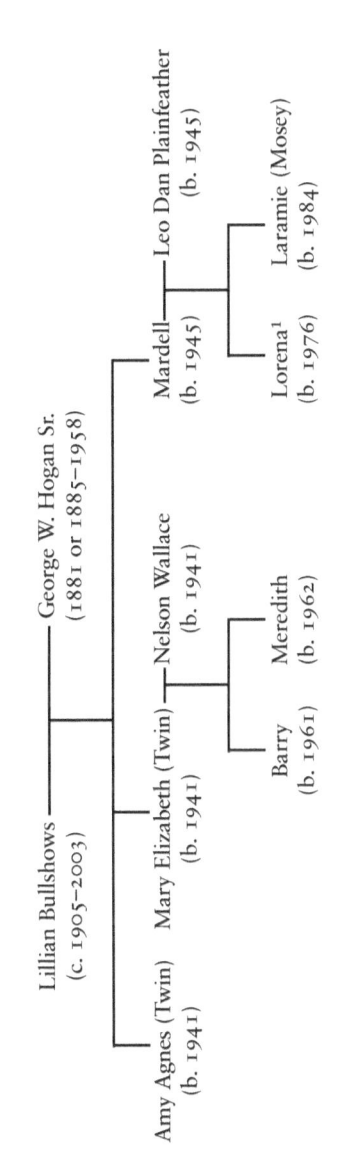

Lillian Bullshows (c. 1905–2003) — George W. Hogan Sr. (1881 or 1885–1958)

- Amy Agnes (Twin) (b. 1941)
- Mary Elizabeth (Twin) (b. 1941) — Nelson Wallace (b. 1941)
  - Barry (b. 1961)
  - Meredith (b. 1962)
- Mardell (b. 1945) — Leo Dan Plainfeather (b. 1945)
  - Lorena[1] (b. 1976)
  - Laramie (Mosey) (b. 1984)

1. Mardell's daughter, adopted by Leo.

The Woman Who Loved Mankind

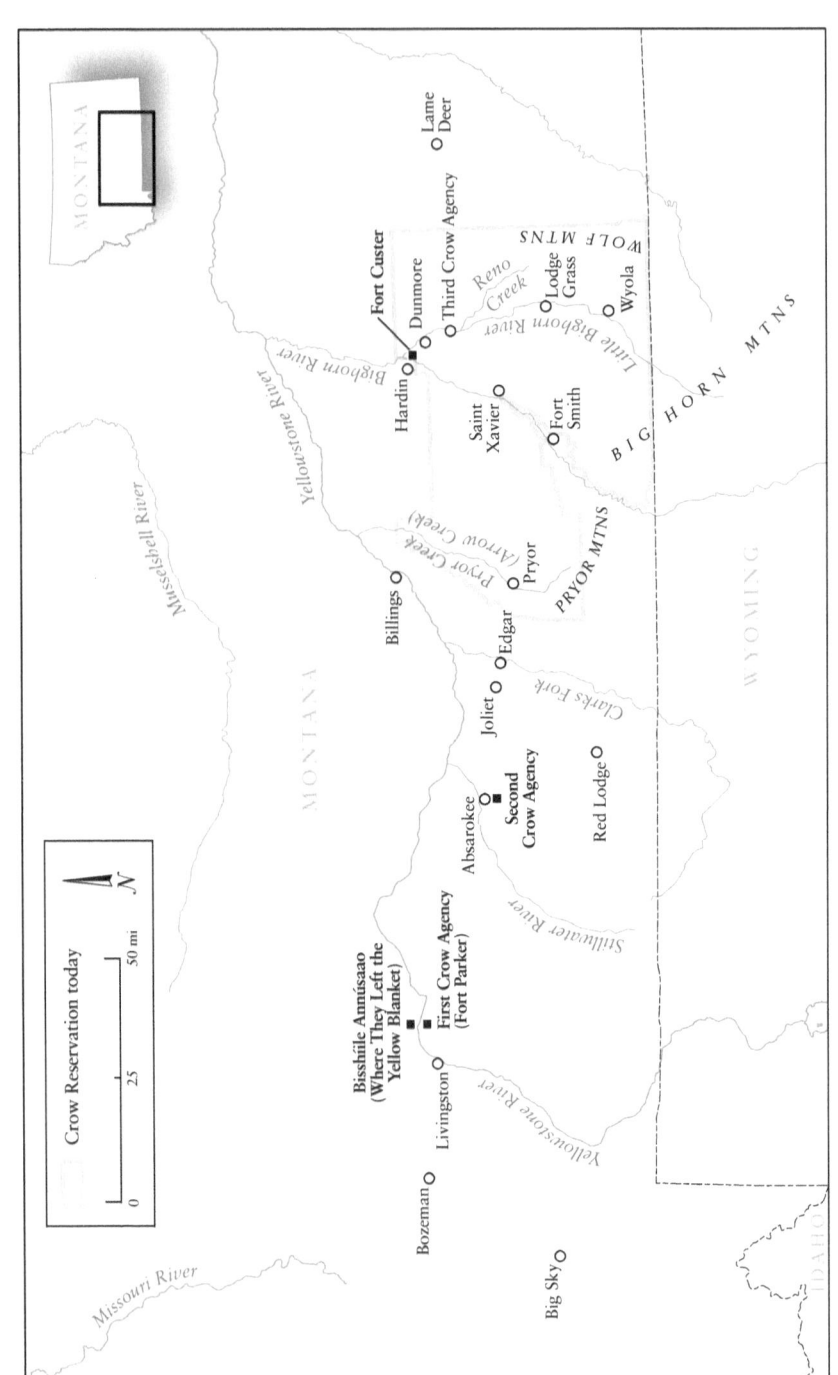

Crow Country and the areas in Lillian's stories.

CHAPTER ONE

My Birth and Infancy

When I Was Born

My mother told me that
when she was pregnant she thought,
"I wish this is a girl."
That's because she lost my sister.
Ida.
I had a older sister, Ida.
A-a-nd
she died with convulsions.
A-a-nd after that my mother felt bad and
when she was carrying me she tells me,
says "now" she says "I wish I have a girl."[1]

And I had two brothers—they were older.
Daniel and Caleb.
Had two brothers.
A-a-nd my sister,
she's between Daniel and Caleb—older than Caleb.
So her name is Ida—I never knew her.
I never knew I had a sister,
till afterwards because they allotted [and I inherited her land].[2]

I had an uncle is well-educated—Henry Russell.
When my mother
has a child he
hurries over to get my father and say,
"We better get over to the Office [Bureau of Indian Affairs] and have this
    child allotted.
Piece of land."[3]

That's why [I know] I have a sister that died.
The older one, Ida.
And then after me I had one little sister and one brother.
And my little sister is Rose.
And my little brother is Harry Austin.
And those I knew, just the two, but I didn't know Ida.

Caleb died last—
last year.
He's about, let's see now,
I think he's
two-o or three years older than I am.
But he died.
Got to live to be an old man.
We kept him in a nursing home for about five years.
Hardin.[4]
Brought him to Billings and he died last year.
A-a-nd
I have just the two brothers [that lived past childhood].[5]

But the other, a brother and a little sister, died when they were little babies.
With a bad cold I guess—my mother doesn't know enough [medical terms].
She don't speak English or
she doesn't know much—of course she just goes by the Indian way.
When they get sick they
call the Indian doctor.
And they do—
they do, they doctor.
Put herbs.
Boil herbs or burn incense.
Hot coal and put that stuff on there and they warm it up and touch.
They get over it, they get cured—like me.[6]

But when I
was a baby,
guess my mother
think a lot of me, she said she want to raise me to be a big—
to be a good woman.

"'Cause I lost one girl and I want this girl."
So when I was born she was really happy.
A-a-nd my father is too.
They both joy and they really happy when I was born.

And I was born in a tent.
It's summer time.
In August.
And I guess she don't remember
exactly the hour or the time but
anyway I was born and when I was a girl she was really glad.
Says "Now I can have a girl,
and I hope to raise her to be a big—
to be a good woman and help me."
That's what my mother says.
Says "Now I have a girl."

1. English was Lillian's second language. Like many Native elders she often transposed past and present tenses. As noted in the introduction, we have preserved those speech patterns. (BL)
2. Lillian learned about her deceased sister, Ida (1894–1902), because she inherited the land Ida had been "allotted" as an infant. The allotment system was established by Congress under the Dawes Act of 1887. For details on issues of land distribution, see introduction and "George Went with My Father to Make a Will" in chapter 16. (BL)
3. Henry Russell learned to read and write in an early agency school, probably in the 1870s. Few Crow could write or speak English then, so educated young Crow like Henry offered essential help with paperwork. For the story of Henry entering school, see "Henry and My Father Go to School," in chapter 3. (BL)
4. Hardin is a town of about three thousand people just north of the reservation. (BL)
5. Only Caleb and Lillian lived to old age, but Little Horse bore many children. Nine siblings are identified in Lillian's allotment folder: Effie, ?–c.1892; Ida, 1894–1902; Daniel, c.1895–1914; Charles (Caleb), 1900–91; Herman, July 1907–October 1907; Rose, February 1909–March 1909; Hulda, 1910–12; Harry Austin, 1913–14; and Percy, 1915–22 (Effie Bull Shows allotment file, Titles and Records, Bureau of Indian Affairs, Crow Agency). Percy is the brother who died of polio, as described in "My Little Brother Had That Infantile Paralysis," chapter 7. (MP, BL)
6. Lillian became ill around 1911 at age six. An Indian doctor cured her after others failed. See "If She Pulls Through, You Can Adopt Her," chapter 9, for Lillian's story and information on Tobacco Society adoption pledges. (BL)

My Maiden Name

My maiden name is
Lillian Bullshows.
Bull
Shows—that's my father's name. [1]
And I think "Lillian," I think the priest named me.
Gave me that name when I was born.

And they have that "Effie" too.
But my father didn't like it—said "I don't like this two names" he says.
Effie came from the Office.[2]
And they have that Lillian in the Office too,
and I don't know how ever it work in they gave me that name—Effie.
  (chuckles)
So I don't know it myself. (laughs)[3]

1. Indian people did not have a tradition of surnames, so white authorities assigned them. Sometimes they assigned seemingly random English ones. Sometimes they used the father's Native name. Lillian's last name, Bullshows, is the English translation of her father's Indian name. (BL)
2. In the late nineteenth and early twentieth centuries, authorities freely replaced Crow names with English ones that they could pronounce, and sometimes they even renamed children who already had English first names. This is what happened to Lillian and her brother, who ended up with two first names. Indian boarding schools and the Bureau of Indian Affairs ("the Office") were especially notorious for changing names. The Office changed Caleb's English name to Charles and Lillian's to Effie, assigning her the same name and allotment number as her deceased older sister, whom she never knew. Government files still list them as Charles and Effie, and many government employees used those names. The family did not. (BL)
3. For more on white authorities assigning English names, see "Henry and My Father Go to School" and "They Took Henry's Indian Name," chapter 3. (BL)

My Indian Name

The Crow use English names with outsiders now, but they still value their Apsáalooke (or "Indian") names. Families usually ask respected relatives to name their children and thank them with generous presents. Name givers, in return, think carefully about the names they bestow. Some pass on their own Indian names. Others draw upon their personal talents and accomplishments, in a sense conveying those abilities to the person they name. Some take ideas from dreams or visions.[1]

As this story recounts, Lillian's parents invited a white man to name their baby. He may have meant to call her "Loves Mankind" or "Loves Humanity," but the family interpreted his choice as fondness for males, a label Lillian never liked. Years later she became sick, and the family asked a clan mother, Ties the Bundle Woman, to rename her. They did this because Crow believe that names can cause illness if they do not suit the owner. They change them to regain health. Ties the Bundle Woman announced Lillian's new name (she "stood to the public") at a Sun Dance so many listeners would be present to hear the new name and the story behind it. Lillian received her first Indian name as an infant, around 1905, and changed it in the 1940s or possibly the early 1950s.
(A reminder to readers: we have italicized translations from Apsáalooke to English. The translations are more formal and do not represent Lillian's exact words.) (BL)

When you're about ten days old,
that's when they name you.
And my father said "I want
no-o relatives to name her."
And "We've been wanting a girl—we lost a girl,
and we want her.
So-o-o,
I don't car-re for any relative to name her."[2]

So he went to the boss farmer, a white man.[3]
We call him *Red Face—a white man*, Vanderhoos.[4]

Said he come to him and says,
"Now mister" he says,
"I got a girl, a baby daughter.
I want you to name her, give her an Indian name."
He's a boss farmer.
And
people come a-a-nd
ask him to name the child—and he does.
Like *Many Different Flowers was one name he gave.
Yellow Flower was another.*[5]
*He gave Indian names.
That's who my father went to.*[6]

*So this man named people.
He stood there thinking, then named me "I Love Man."*
One of my aunts says,
"That's no good, the love part.
Let's just say "Likes Men."
That's why they call me *Likes Men.
When I grew up I didn't like the name.
I got a lot of teasing, especially from my girlfriends.
I didn't like it.*

*I got sick anyway.
I was anemic.
And doctors couldn't build up my blood.
I'd get nervous spells and cry.
Ties the Bundle Woman* [Ella Cashen] *was summoned by my father,
and my name was changed.*[7]

*There was a Sun Dance and there were lots of people.
They gave her lots of gifts*, bla-ankets and quilts and money and she wants a sack of flour.
A fifty-pound sack of flour she said, so this was done [plus] sugar, meat, and stuff like that.
*There was a Sun Dance—lots of people.
Her voice was loud—she could talk real loud.*

She stood to the public *a-a-nd*
said when she was young,
her Indian name was different,
but the Apsáalooke people always
called her Ties the Bundle Woman and it became her name.
"I am old woman now" she said.
"This is my daughter and I give her the name Ties the Bundle Woman on
    this day.[8]
She will carry it—all of you people will know this now."

And that's how I got the name.
Xúhkaalaxchibia [Ties the Bundle Woman].[9]
I've had these girls then.
I may be about forty years old then.
She gave me that name.
My father asked Ties the Bundle Woman for her name.
Gave her lots of gifts and
I carried the name ever since.[10]

My father always
believe in this changing names.
Whenever a child became ill, "change names" they'd say.
I was sick for a long time.
The doctors said I was anemic *and*
put me in the hospital a lot of times.
They couldn't heal me—they said a goiter *was growing too,*
and they said it caused my nervousness.
When my name was changed I became whole and well.
That old lady must have prayed for me.

When my father was a chi-ild he gets si-ick all the time.
He was a twin a-a-nd his sister died,
and they wanted to save him so much that when he gets sick they get
    sca-ared—the parents.
They call the Indian doctors and when the doctor-r,
Indian doctor, work on him,
then the parents say "You give him a name."
And they always give him a name.

They say he had several names—*my father.*
Then toward the end that was his last name [Bull That Shows].
And that's his last name [the last name given].[11]
[One name was] Iáxuhkakaate,
"There's a Red Fox"—Iáxuhkakaate—they're animals.[12]
Iisé Duuptash [Split Face or Double Face[13]]
And another,
Chiilápassiash [Bull That Shows].[14]

Yeah he-e sure believed in those changing names.
When anyone was sick,
he would say "Change the name."
Wanted it done, really believed in it.
I guess it's true 'cause some of us changed names.[15]

1. See Curtis, *The North American Indian*, 25–26; Lowie, *The Crow Indians*, 42–44; and Voget, *They Call Me Agnes*, 41, 65, for information on Crow naming customs. See also Medicine Crow's story on receiving a new name when he was honored upon returning from World War II (Medicine Crow, *Counting Coup*, 122–23). (BL)
2. The Bullshows family had many relatives by blood, clan, and adoption, so it is unclear why he asked an outsider to name his daughter. Mother always said that he was fascinated by white people and called them "inventors" of things, such as cars and farm machinery. Perhaps this is why he wanted a white man to name his precious little daughter. Apparently other Crow families asked the same man to name their children, an honor for him. (MP)
3. Boss farmers were government employees hired by the Indian Bureau (precursor to the Bureau of Indian Affairs) and stationed in every Indian community to teach farming. This had been part of the Treaty of 1868, which Sits In the Middle of the Land and others signed. The government took a long while but lived up to the commitment to teach us to farm. Mom always said that the boss farmer controlled almost every aspect of their lives. (MP)
4. The tape is unclear. "Vanderhoos" is a phonetic approximation. (BL)
5. Like Mom, these others lived in Pryor, a small town at the western end of the present reservation. (MP)
6. The Indian people who lived around that area probably respected him. He must have been a good man to be asked to name their children. But she said he named a child Yellow Flower, and another one that she remembers was Different Kinds of Flowers, so he always named them something to do with plants. She doesn't know why he named her Likes Men. She was just a baby. She says she never has liked that name, and she was glad when it was changed. (MP)
7. Crow believe that sickness can come from a name that ill-suits its owner, so they change names to improve health. It is an old custom. For example, Pretty Shield,

born the mid-1850s, described it to Linderman (*Pretty-Shield*, 19–20). Parents might also "throw away" a sick child to a relative who would provide a new name, new clothes, and a blessing. "This is like a rebirth" (Voget, *They Call Me Agnes*, 42). (BL)

8. Mom's father was a Ties the Bundle Clan member. Ella Cashen used the term "daughter" because she was a member of the Ties the Bundle Clan too, and therefore my mother's clan mother. The Apsáalooke clan system was devised by Old Man Coyote who saw the people living in chaos, without order. He named the clans "driftwood lodges" because he wanted the clans to be individual yet to cling together when necessary. It works this way: you are born into your mother's clan because we are matrilineal. All members of your clan become your sisters and brothers. I would say that these clan brothers and sisters are your confidants. You do not join your father's clan, but you become a "child" of that clan, and its members become your clan mothers and fathers because they are brothers and sisters to your father. They assist you in times of trouble and rejoice with you in times of joy. I would say that all members of your father's clan are your advisors and counselors, and they watch over your behavior. They scold you, if needed, and praise and brag about you in public when you do something of merit, such as graduating from high school or college or returning from the military. The children of your father's clan members belong to the clans of their own mothers, but they too are children of the father's clan and are your "teasing cousins." They have license to ridicule you or joke about you if you do or say something silly or out of the ordinary. Once teased about some strange behavior or act, it is more than likely that the behavior will not be repeated. All of these clan relationships were designed to bring order among the Apsáalooke and control social behavior. Today a clan mother or father is sometimes referred to as "uncle" or "aunt," but these are English terms. The Crow have no term for aunt or uncle, only for mother and father. The clan system is still strong today. (MP)

9. Ella Cashen had two names, Loud Speaker and Ties the Bundle Woman, Ties the Bundle being the name of her clan. She offered "Ties the Bundle" but kept her other name, Loud Speaker. (MP)

10. A few years after Mom told us this story, Christine Rides Horse Decrane asked for "Ties the Bundle Woman" for her own daughter, Melanie. Christine was my mother's grandniece (her granddaughter according to Crow tradition), so Melanie was Mom's great-grandniece (great-granddaughter). My sister Mary and her husband Nelson drove her to the family's home in Pryor, where she gave "Ties the Bundle Woman" away and received fine gifts. That left her without an Indian name, so she had a dinner shortly after, invited her clan mother Alice Mae White Clay LaForge, gave her gifts, and received the name "Owns the Best Camp Site." Alice Mae's husband, Frank, descends from Thomas Leforge, the "White Crow" Indian, but the family spells the name LaForge now. (MP)

11. Bull Shows was his final name and Bullshows eventually became the family's last name. (MP)

12. In English Lillian is translating her father's former name as There's a Red Fox. In Apsáaloke she is saying Little Fox. (MP)

13. This is not the Split Face in old stories. (MP)

14. Chiilápassiash was the name the agent wrote out, and they interpreted it as Bull Shows, Bull That Shows. (MP)
15. I changed my daughter Lorena's Indian name once, and I've changed my son Mosey's name once too, because they were a little sickly and Mosey (Laramie) was asthmatic. I also took them in a Sun Dance to be prayed for because they repeatedly had sore throats and earaches, even though I took all precautions. After I changed the names, they got better. I have a niece, Mary Plain Feather, my brother Samuel's daughter, whose name was changed. Even her Christian name was changed from Renita to Mary, and then her Indian name was changed. My cousin Johnny Bullshows's English name was changed from Randell to Johnny, and his Indian name was changed too, because he was a sickly child. After their names were changed, they got better. I believe in this tradition. (MP)

Red Star and Mary Ann Took Me

Grandparents, childless couples, and other relatives sometimes requested children if they were lonely and wanted company, or they might take in a child if parents divorced, passed away, or developed problems, so Mary Ann Bear Tail is following an old custom when she asks for Lillian in this account. As Agnes Deernose says in her own life story, "Crow like to share children. They don't think of adoption as giving a child up."[1] Some children might stay with their new parents but see their biological parents frequently, even daily. Some might go back and forth. Others would stay with their biological parents but form special bonds with their adoptive ones, as Lillian does in this account. (BL)

Mary Ann was related to my
father.[2]
Wa-ay back *they are related.*
A-a-nd Mary Ann says "I don't have no
child"—*she didn't have a child yet.*
"A-a-nd I want you to give me that little girl."
"*Beewiik,*" *heek.* ["I will keep her," she said.]
A-a-nd my father said "Yes you can have her."

My mother didn't agree with that.
A-a-nd they say when they took me over where they camp,

[when] Red Star
and Mary Ann took me,
they say I was about
nine months old and I was still nursing.

I was nursing—my mom's breasts were so full and hurting,
she tied herself so she wouldn't hurt.
"I'd better go after my baby" and she said e-e-e-arly in the morning, five
   o'clock in the morning,
she went outside, saddle up the horse and came after me.
And when she got to the tent she tied the horse.
Way off so nobody'd see.
Way off she tied the horse—she walked tiptoed.
To the tent.
And she *pulled the door down*—she peeped through and here was Mary
   Ann and Red Star.[3]
Mary Ann was holding me,
and Red Star had a spoon,
feeding me with a little milk.
And
I turned my eyes to the door and saw her eyes peeping in at the door and
I cried and let go of everything.
They were alarmed and said "What is it?"
There was my mother standing there.
She took me back home. (chuckles)
But when I got older they always—
Mary Ann always comes after me, I stay with her.
Back and forth.

Then they had Wallace.[4]
One time when I was young, Mary Ann gave us
some money to buy some bread.
We fought over who'd sit in the saddle.
Wallace finally sat in it and I sat behind him.
I kept telling him to go fast but he wouldn't do it.
I took his reins and I whipped the horse.
The horse galloped, then it ran fast.

Wallace turned around and hit me.
When he hit me he was wearing a hat.
I pulled his hat back and
the strings holding his hat went tight around his neck.
Nearly cut into his skin around the neck.
When he showed what I did,
everyone got mad at both of us. (laughs)

And *later on* Mary Ann married Oliver,
Oliver-r-r Lion Shows.
And
when she married Oliver Lion Shows,
I said "I don't want a stepfather.
Stepfathers are me-ean a-a-nd,
a-a-nd I don't want a stepfather.
I won't call him father [like Red Star]—I don't like a stepfather."

When I got married he says,
"I want to be good to my daughter.
Mary Ann's daughter.
I want to be good to her because I married Mary Ann and she's supposed to be my stepdaughter.
But now after she said those words about me," he said,
"I'm going to be nice to her and I'm going to even give up my pretty white horse to her
husband [Alex]"—*he gave a horse to my husband.*
A white horse, a great horse.
When we first got married he gave him a horse.[5]

1. See Voget, *They Call Me Agnes*, 69. For Deernose's detailed discussion of adopting children, see Voget, *They Call Me Agnes*, 66–69. (BL)
2. This was Mary Ann Bear Tail, a relative of Lillian's biological father, Bull Shows. Red Star was Mary Ann's husband. (BL)
3. The entrance to a tent was usually covered by a blanket. Apparently my grandmother saw the tent lit up and pulled the blanket down so she could peer over the top. (MP)
4. Mary Ann's son, Wallace Red Star, would be Mom's "brother." (MP)
5. This horse was a gift to her first husband, Alex Plainfeather. By Crow tradition, the bride's family always gave horses to a son-in-law or brother-in-law. (MP)

CHAPTER TWO

My Mother

My Mother and Her Mother

This story is about Lillian's mother, Little Horse, known as Horse, and her grandmother, a Shoshone captive. Lillian's grandmother was probably captured in the 1840s or 1850s, and Little Horse was born in 1872 or perhaps a little earlier.[1]

Lillian gives her mother's name because we asked her, but she carefully avoids those of her mother's parents. The Crow traditionally hesitate to name the deceased aloud, saying, "They are at peace now. They are on the other side. Don't call them back." Later Mardell located Lillian's land allotment file at the Bureau of Indian Affairs offices in Crow Agency, so we know Horse's Shoshone mother was Old Black Bird. Horse's father is listed as Bull Well Known in the same files, but Lillian later referred to him as Aakkeetaash (On the Other Bank, or Bank for short), so he probably changed his name, perhaps giving it to someone else or changing it to achieve better health. (BL)

My mother's name was Horse.
Iichíilish.
They call her Horse.
Her Indian name is Horse.[2]
Long time ago when she was young,
they gave her that name,
so she didn't tell me who [named her].

I don't know [where she was born]—she don't know herself.
Maybe she was born down in Wyoming.
Maybe in Montana, she don't know.

Her parents never told her—when she was e-eight months old,
she's still nursing,
when her mother died.
So she don't know—her grandma raised her.
They don't tell her anything [of her birthplace] so she don't know.³

But she knows that her mother's a Shoshone.
Her father went and married this Shoshone because I think she's a prisoner.
They used to fight—the Shoshones and the Crows fight.
And I think when she was a little girl they took her in to Crow.⁴
And after she growed up she married
the man that's my grandfather—they married.⁵
And nice couple.
Lived good until
she gave birth to my mother.

Her grandparents raised her.
The grandmother's [clan] is Big Lodge,
and they told her "You're a Ashshitchíte [Big Lodge]."
So now we all go on Big Lodge.⁶
My mother never claimed
that she's a Shoshone,
but she has relatives now
among the Shoshones.
There's Gloria [Isis].
They're still living.
Sometimes they go to Crow.
At Crow Fair they go and see us.

1. Horse's birth year is listed as 1872 in county records, but the family is unlikely to have known her birth date so this is probably an estimate (File 3508, Big Horn County Office of the Clerk and Recorder, Hardin, Montana). (BL)
2. The Bureau of Indian Affairs recorded her name as Horse. Her complete name was Little Horse, Iichíilikaatesh. (MP)
3. Horse was raised by her paternal grandmother. She might not have known where her daughter-in-law gave birth. (MP)
4. The Crow probably took her in a raid against the Shoshone, possibly for revenge, and gave her to a family to raise. Perhaps this family had lost a child during a Shoshone raid against them. She grew up, married a Crow, and became Mother's

maternal grandmother. When old tribal hostilities subsided in the reservation period, her relatives found her and wanted her to go home with them. She refused, saying her family was Crow now, but the family always kept in touch. We still know our Shoshone relatives, the Wagon, Phillips, and Isis families. (MP)

5. According to Denig (*Five Indian Tribes*, 148), Crow and the Gros Ventre almost always absorbed captured women and children into their tribes, in contrast to more violent treatment from the other tribes he knew. (BL)
6. The tribe's clan system is matrilineal, so children join their mothers' clans, but Horse's Shoshone mother did not have a Crow clan, so the father's side took Horse into the Big Lodge Clan. Her matrilineal descendants have been Big Lodge ever since. (BL)

She's Raised by Two Old Grandmas

My fa-ather and mother <u>ne-ever</u> been to school.
Ne-ever-r.
They say my father learns speaking English by working with some cowboys, cow outfit.
He took his hor-r-se and saddle and some clothing.
He just took off and stayed with some cowboys—that's where he learned to speak a little English.[1]

But my mother ne-e-ever did.
She's—
o-o-oh she's
a little girl and her grandmother raised her because
when she was eight months old her mother died,
and then they had to go around a-a-nd
get a woman that's nursing a baby—they take her a-a-nd
have her feed her and pay her.[2]

But anyway she's raised by
two old grandmas.
My great-grandmother on my mother's side,
she's Wind Blowing.
That's my [great-] grandmother on my mother's side—Wind Blowing.
Her name is Wind Blowing.
Huché Awaashéelash—that's
Wind Blowing.

A-a-nd she's a Crow Indian.
But my mother is a
half
Shoshone and Crow.
Her father's a Crow, her mother's a Shoshone.

A-a-nd the father
married another woman,
and from that other woman my mother has one sister—Clara White Hip.[3]
I don't know Clara's mother, though.
I seen her.
And Clara, that's Clara
White Hip,
and my mother were sisters,
and they look alike, they're dea-a-ad look-alikes [see fig. 2].

1. See "My Father Works With the Cowboys," chapter 3.
2. Payments took the form of generous gifts. On another tape, Lillian said that her father gave a horse to the woman who nursed his baby daughter, a valuable payment. (BL)
3. Clara White Hip was Little Horse's half sister. Her Indian name was Baáitchiilappeesh, meaning Kills Pretty Ones. No one today would know how this name came about. Perhaps the giver killed two handsome men in combat, as the Crow word *itche* means something that is good or nice-looking, or perhaps he killed something pretty, such as birds, perhaps hawks, or elk. Later Clara's granddaughter Clara Nomee became the Crow Tribal chairwoman, holding office from 1990 to 2000. (MP)

My Mother's a Hard Worker

You know,
she's a—
she-e-e <u>is</u>
a hard worker.
She has, o-oh I'd say a aunt of mine in Saint X
would save l-o-ots of pieces for her.[1]
Coats.
Jackets—a lot of stuff.

A-a-nd some quilt pieces for her too—says
her, she don't do anything like that—she's lazy.
Says "I'm too lazy to cut up, make quilts.
I'll save it for my sister-in-law"—that's my mother.

And they bring a whole couple boxes of clothes.
Give it to my mother and I know she'd be out there, hold a scissor.
Couple scissors and a
sharp knife.
She cut through them se-e-ams.
Tear them up and,
and sometimes she wash them and if they're clean she just hang them up.
In the clothesline with the clothespin.
A-a-nd the air and the dampness would smooth out the wrinkles.
And pretty soon she,
when they're smooth and nice, she'd cut them up.
Make nice quilts.
She'd just sit there.
Thread a needle and start sewing—she'd be humming.
Humming a hymn.
She used to just sing—she don't speak English,
but she just hum this "Jesus Loves Me" [song].
(sings) "Jesus loves me, this I know."
She used to just sit there, stitch that quilt,
humming this hymn.
And we used to say "She can speak English." (chuckles)

1. "Saint X" is short for Saint Xavier, a small town near the center of the reservation. The woman is unidentified. First Lillian called her an aunt, later a sister-in-law. Since Crow acknowledge relatives by blood, marriage, clan membership, and adoption, she may have been both. (BL)

I'm Just Like Her

In this brief but revealing story, Lillian begins with her mother's looks, then tells us that Little Horse was industrious, skilled, and respected by her relatives. ("I got relatives who talk to me.") Little Horse would have been esteemed for these characteristics, and Lillian emulated her proudly. (BL)

Yeah I'm-m-m just like my mother.
I got hands just like her.
I got big knuckles.
Br-o-o-own, she looks brown.
I have face
just like the image my mother.
She says "I'm not pretty, I'm not good looking."
But she says,
"I work.
Earn my own living.
I got relatives that
talk to me.
I pick berries, I tan hides.
I sew up their clothes—I cook" she says.
"I make my own living—I learn it
the hard way but
sometimes they say I'm a good cook and all that."
Says "I can do it!" she says.

My Mother Mourns

This account speaks directly to the attitude of some white settlers, but it also describes traditional Apsáalooke mourning. When Crow lost loved ones, they sometimes went alone to the top of a hill for two or three days to grieve, pray, and abstain from food and water. In their depleted state, some, like Lillian's mother, were blessed with advice from a helper or spirit person. If the deceased had been killed in battle or murdered, the bereaved might also seek revenge. That too is part of this story. These events must have happened in the 1880s, as Horse was married by 1890. (BL)

One time,
o-oh my mother may be around
twenty-y-y—
twenty-two—I think she's about twenty-two years old.

She don't know it herself but she tells me
that she must be around twenty-two [perhaps younger].

They were up at this Clarks Fork [Clarks Fork Yellowstone River].[1]
Let's see now.
Here's the Joliet.
Here's Edgar.
And there's the river [between].[2]
Going, you can see Clarks Fork
River that goes through Edgar, this side of Edgar.[3]
In that area.

They camped—she tells me they camp,
there in the timber,
where she stayed with her
grandma and her aunts—and
there's a who-o-le bunch.
People.
They're all camping.
They go out hunting—they could bring elk a-a-nd
women all dry and they all camp and they stayed there.[4]

And that's the fir-r-st year
that white people can come and
buy a land there
and start to settle.
Different people, families, settling.
They build their houses,
start cutting logs and build their houses.
And that day she said
she remember
the old lady.
And her
brother.[5]
She stayed with her brother and aunt that's in Clarks Fork.

And they were having a dance there,
and they said they were in the daytime—this is about noon she said.
At the dance hall, the round teepee, big teepee.[6]
Start
drumming (claps hands rhythmically), singing songs.

And this old lady kept saying,
"Them white people over there in the timber,
they're cutting too much timber."
Said "You better stop them."
Kept saying.
"They're building houses too."
A-a-nd she kept after the men.
That's my mother's brother.
It was her mother-in-law that kept after them.
The old lady.
She kept just fussing over them—
"Them white people is going to cut lots of timber."[7]
So my mother says she must be around twenty-two years old when she
    stayed there.
At Clarks Fork with the relatives.
And there's a dance going on.
And this old lady,
the mother-in-law,
want somebody to go out and stop these white men cutting timber.

So this man that's my uncle,
my mother's brother,
says "All right then—before I go to the dance I'll go and check up on them."
So he took off—went over to them white men, white people,
cutting wood.
And they say he's the be-e-est-natured person that's
among them Indians—they say he was su-u-re nice.
Well he was ready to go to the dance,
but he took off and went to that—
to the men where they were cutting the timber.
He went over there—want to ask they better stop
cutting wood.

And one, one fellow just ran over and took his gun and aim at him and
   (claps hands)
kill him right there.

A-a-nd that's when my mother
mourn—she cried.
Cut all her hair off.[8]
She said she sure take it hard.
And she go up on the hill,
on top of the hill—stayed there,
cry and cry a-a-ll day.
And she said she must be about twenty-two years old then.

And when the Indians heard
that this man was killed,
they quit the dance and flock over there (claps hands) and the white people
   all took off.
No more nobody.
Tried to round them up and they's all gone.

She was only twenty-two years old then.
That's what she told me.
She went out there,
mourning and stayed on top of the hill crying.
And she felt so bad about what happened.
A-a-nd one afternoon,
she said she
fix up her pillow and laid a log there and
she laid there and
slept.
She was so-o-o tired—the sun was hot
and the wind was co-o-ld and
she had been up there two days.
And she said she
dozed off.
Slept—and she heard singing.

She got up quick.
A-a-nd
in her dream somebody said,
"Now,
get over.
Go home.
Wash your face.
Brush up.
Don't feel too bad because [of]
that accident, what happened.
Your brother was killed and they all feel bad.
And there might be
more trouble boding
before long,"
he says—"You just
get over that, your mourning.
Go home."
And they start singing.
And she heard the song.

And then she woke up—look around and there was nobody.
A-a-nd this voice says "Go home."
So she got up and shook up her
bed there, blankets and stuff.
She went home.
"You're going to get revenge.
In couple days,
some of them white people,
they're going to fight among themselves—there's going to be
two white men is going to get killed,
and they're fighting among themselves,
and you get a
good
revenge,
because you lost your brother."
He said "Now don't mourn anymore—go home."
So she got up and went home—that's my mother.

And in two days some white people were fighting among themselves.
Two men got killed.
And she said "That's true,
what I heard up when I was up there mourning."
Says "It's true—I must paint my face,
a-a-nd sing a song and dance."
She did—she took some black coal.
Dab it around her cheeks.⁹
All the people around there heard it.
"Although I cut my hair off,
short,
I get my revenge from these white people.
They kill my brother, now they fight among themselves—that's
two, they kill two and that's revenge.
For what I've been crying."
She says "I've got a
revenge so that's all right.
They better not fight any more."

That's what happened to my mother.
She lost her brother.
And that's up here at Clarks Fork,
this side of Edgar.¹⁰

1. This is the Clarks Fork of the Yellowstone River, which flows into the Yellowstone from south-central Montana, the heart of Crow territory. It is approximately fifteen miles west of the present reservation. (BL)
2. Joliet and Edgar, Montana, are small towns near the Clarks Fork. The first Joliet post office was established in 1893 and the first Edgar post office in 1909. The story surely predates Edgar and may predate Joliet, as well, but Lillian used the present towns to locate the story. (BL)
3. "Going" can refer to the act of traveling or being in the process of traveling. You can see the Clarks Fork if traveling near Edgar. (BL)
4. When Lillian says they were bringing elk and drying the meat, she is indicating that this was a good camping spot. That is why they could stay for a while. (BL)
5. This may be Horse's older half brother, Bull Don't Show, Old Black Bird's son from her prior marriage. Or, according to Roger Turns Plenty, this could have been Shows Little, a blood relative and a brother in Crow terms, though not a biological brother. Shows Little married Roger's grandmother, Itchiikattaa Baaláp-peesh (Kills Good or Kills With Mercy). Later she remarried and had Blanche

Turns Back, mentioned in "My Little Brother Had That Infantile Paralysis," chapter 7. (BL, MP)

6. Today each district has a roomy building used as a community hall. When Crow lived nomadically, they danced outside or used large teepees. (BL)

7. My grandmother, Little Horse, was not yet married. Perhaps this older woman later became my grandmother's mother-in-law. Or perhaps Mom meant to say "his" (the brother's) mother-in-law. The older woman would not have spoken to her son-in-law directly but could have continued to complain and mention the white men until he did something about the situation. (MP)

8. Mourners cut off their hair and sometimes slashed themselves or cut off the tip of a finger, signifying loss so great that they harmed themselves. Some Crows (both male and female) still cut their hair when they lose a close relative, but to my knowledge the last slashing happened when my Aunt Mary Takes the Gun lost her daughter, Susie, in the 1950s. I was a small child, but I remember my father talking about his sister's ordeal. Today there are so many activities among the people that the deceased's family commonly has an announcement made at the burial encouraging others to continue participating in tribal events. The family alone goes into mourning and avoids tribal activities. (MP)

9. Crow people paint their faces black to signify victory. We still do this. When my nephew Carson Walks Over Ice recovered from his wounds in Vietnam, our family paraded him and his friend, Eddie Little Light, another Vietnam veteran, around the Crow Fair camp. A camp crier followed them singing warrior victory songs, and our entire family and the Little Light family smudged our cheeks black, signifying that we were victorious because our warriors had returned from an enemy's country alive. (MP)

10. Crow men once pursued visions by fasting and physically harming themselves, in hopes of a spirit helper offering guidance, protection, and, most importantly, success as a warrior. In contrast, women fasted during personal distress, usually grief, seeking emotional support and, on occasion, revenge. Sometimes they too gained visions and assistance from animal guides. When Lillian's mother fasted and received her vision, she was following that tradition. For related examples, see Curtis, *The North American Indian*, 36; Nabokov, "Vision Quests of Crow Women." (BL)

CHAPTER THREE

My Father

They Saved Lots of Children

This story is from Lillian's father, Bull Shows, who was born about 1871 or a few years earlier.[1] The events happened sometime before his birth, but the tale was passed from generation to generation. His family belonged to the Mountain Crow division of the tribe, and the story takes place in their western range, in a valley near the present town of Livingston, Montana. The tribe had already lost vast sections of traditional land but were still traveling across southern Montana. (BL)

One time my father said they lived
with a who-o-le camp.
Lots of camps.
They camp by Livingston, in that valley.
[They call that place] Bisshíile Annúsaao.
That's "Where They Left the Yellow Blanket."
I don't know who named it but they say
that valley,
the name of that valley, is Bisshíile Annúsaao.
Bishée Shíile Annúsaao.[2]
That's "Where They Left the Yellow Blanket."
That's the name of that valley.

And they said they,
they didn't move
because it's good camping ground there—and all of a sudden there's an
  epidemic.
A-a-nd children die.
Little tots.
Children and on up to about twelve years old.

They die.
He said there's one die, they'll be crying.
In another camp they said "There's another one die."
A-a-nd they said they camp just the other side of Livingston.

A-a-nd one man said they had a girl, they had a girl too,
and this girl was sick down with a sore throat,
and she pretty ne-ear
couldn't hardly breath.
So-o he looked at her and
kept thinking.
And he tell his wife, he says "You watch her real close.
Watch her while I go look for this herb."
A-a-nd he took off.
Went up on the hill or somewhere out in the hill or the woods,
and he got some of that—he looked
re-eal hard—he went down the coulee, up the hill and all that, and he found some of that plant.
He took it a-a-nd "Now my child will live!" he said.

So he bring it back to the camp a-a-nd showed this to his wife.
"How is she?"—and she said "She's pretty bad.
We might loose her."
And [he] say "Hurry up! Hurry up, clean this and boil it now—hurry up!"
And the woman said they just clean this root a-a-nd
shake the dirt off and start to boiling it.
Boiled it and the water turned yellow.
A-a-nd then he said "Now cool it
off and make her take some, hurry up!—if she takes some, if she swallow some down,
that's going to take all that stuff out."
And
said "she'll live.
But if she won't swallow she'll die."

And they said the woman
got her up,
and the little girl was just <u>dying</u> then.

And they got her up
a-a-nd made this
medicine—they boil this herb.
A-a-nd they made her take it.
They open her mouth and take it.
Took some down.
Swallow it—they could hear it and said, that man said,
"*Aho*! [Thank you!]
She swallowed some and she's going to live."
And "Give her some more!"—and they gave her some more.
Little drops, little bit at a time a-a-nd pretty soon
she start to
coughing.
Said she want to cough.
And they got her up and set her up and they said "Cough.
And cough and catch your breath and cough" and then—
then she
threw up, vomit.
And they say she vomits pus.
And blood.
Stuff all come out.
And said she open her eyes, look around, and this man says "Now she's
 going to live!"
All that stuff
stick down from the wi-n-nd pipe and stuff a-a-ll her breathing.
And they all die—swelling.

A-a-nd
this man went out and he said "I'll tell the people that this herb is helping
 our child."
So he did—that's why they saved
what they did—and some that wasn't sick,
they make them take it and they said they saved lots of children.

And that's when they camp up by Livingston.
They say they
take them out on this side of the river, up on the hill, the rim.

Said they buried l-o-ots of
children up there.
Epidemic.
This story was from a different time [before my father was born].
My father heard it told and told us.

1. Bull Shows's birth year, 1871, comes from the Big Horn County Office of the Clerk and Recorder, Hardin, Montana (File 3508), but, as noted in the introduction, it is probably the family's best guess. Lillian estimated her father's ages during several stories, but the dates and his ages are inconsistent. (BL)
2. "Bishíile Annúsaao" is sort of a contraction for "Where They Left the Yellow Blanket": *Bishée* [blanket] *shíile* [yellow] *annúsaa*o [where they leave it]. (MP)

Henry and My Father Go to School

In this story, two curious little boys, Bull Shows and his relative Henry Russell, investigate the new agency school. If they were on the Stillwater River, as Lillian says, then this was the second agency, established in 1875 near present Absarokee, and Henry probably entered school between about 1875 and 1880.¹ The first agency (Fort Parker) had opened in 1869 and the first teacher arrived in 1870, but that agency was on Mission Creek, close to the future site of Livingston and the valley Where They Left the Yellow Blanket. At the first agency, classes were held within the fort. There is no record that it had a separate schoolhouse as here.²

In the story, Bull Shows flees after employees cut Henry's hair and take away his Indian name, two serious affronts to Apsáalooke custom. Henry enters the school willingly, but his treatment foreshadows the bitter experiences of later Indian children who went because they had to, putting up with attacks on their culture and suffering corporal punishment if they spoke their languages. (See "They Put Me in the Boarding School," chapter 6.) Given such troubling treatment, Henry's intellectual curiosity and Lillian's respect for his learning attest to Crow interest in education. (BL)

My father's family live up here by Joliet,
and up in the valley—sometimes they move clear up to the Red Lodge.
And then sometimes over to Livingston.³

Move around there and then come back.
And move camp, up in the valley and all them places.

My father said he used to go hunting.
A-a-nd this time they're down there at Stillwater,
the other side of Columbus.
The one they call the fir-r-st agency [second agency],
on this side Absarokee.[4]
That's where the o-old agency, first agency, established a school,
Indian school,
and then-n the Office [the Bureau of Indian Affairs].
And then-n a-a-ll stretching around on that big area, people
live, Crow Indians.

And he said, if I remember right he says,
"I was-s
six or five years old" he said.
A-a-nd Henry, Henry Russell,
he call him a brother.
This Henry Russell is a brother to Old Dwarf.
And there's my father,
and in that relation,
aunts or-r uncles or I don't know,
but they were relatives and they all camped together and,
a-a-nd have their ways together.[5]

And that afternoon,
Henry Russell
said the father, the old man, fix him bow and arrow.
Fix one for Henry and fix one for my dad.
And Henry said "All right now, let's go down the river,
go hunting and maybe we kill a deer."
They start to pulling this rope [bowstring].
Said "This is pretty strong."
Said "I can aim at a deer and I can kill it.
You try it too"—and my father was about six years old.

He said he tried it.
"Ye-a-ah it's pretty strong!"

And they start out going—instead of going down the river they turned to the schoolhouse.
Where the-e-y start government school right there.
At the agency.
And said "Let's go.
I heard that they're taking children, putting them in school,
and make them talk English,
a-a-nd pretty soon they talk English."
Henry Russell said that to my father.

He says "All right, let's go!"
They come along—instead of going hunting, they turn around and went to the school.
A-a-nd
here they got to the building,
and somebody, a white man he said,
they opened the door—the employees.
They open the door—"Here comes some boys!" they said.
"Come on in!"
They went in the house,
and they put chairs out and they said
they set there
and look on.

And they [the employees] said "Who'll be the first one?"
And Henry—he's older,
older than my father—
Henry set down,
and these employees took a scissor and
clip his hair off.
And as soon as they get through,
they [going to] clip my father's hair off too.[6]
Before they finish [the employees said] "Henry.
We give you the name of Henry."

"And soon as we
cut his [my father's] hair,
we'll give him a name."
And they said my father just sit there waiting for Henry.
And they cut Henry's hair,
and before they got through,
Henry got scared.
He said "They're going to keep me here." (raps on table for emphasis)
"They won't let me go home.
They're going to keep me here,
and I'll be going to school.
See how they clip my hair?
Now before they catch you,
you fly.
Fly out the door.
Get home!"

"And take my bow and arrow—take that home too.
Because I can't use it anymore.
Hurry up and go outside and run for home.
If you don't, they're going to catch you and cut your hair too,
and they make you go to school.
<u>Get home</u>!"
He got after him.[7]

Said they talk Crow,
so these white people don't know what they're saying.
And he took his bow and arrow.
Grabbed them and ran out the door,
and he takes off to the camp—got home.
(raps on table) and that very day,
that's when Henry Russell,
when they kept him in school, make him go to school.
After that, after he's passed
fifteen or sixteen,
they sent him to school up east [to] Indian school—Carlisle.
Way up in [Pennsylvania].[8]

He went to school up there—he never came back for
eight or six years.
How these parents feel bad about that day (raps the table)
when they clip his hair and took him in to school.

But he had really good education,
and he lived to be a Christian man.
All he does is
read the Bible,
read the Bible.
He prays.
He's a Baptist.

And that's what my father told me.
And him [Henry Russell].

1. The 1875 founding date for the second agency is from Hoxie, *Parading*, 108. (BL)
2. The information on the school is from archaeologist Scott Carpenter, who is investigating the Fort Parker site. (Carpenter, e-mail to Loeb, August 2010). The date of the first teacher's arrival is from Algier, *The Crow and the Eagle*, 291. (BL)
3. Joliet is the small town west of the reservation, near where Lillian's uncle was killed by white settlers. (See "My Mother Mourns," chapter 2.) Livingston is about sixty miles west of Joliet, on Interstate 90. Red Lodge is at the base of the Beartooth Mountains, about twenty miles further southwest from Joliet. All of these places were once Crow territory. (BL)
4. Lillian is probably talking about the second agency. The short-lived first agency was near present Livingston. It was built in 1869 on Hide Scraper Creek, now known as Mission Creek. Indian agencies had government offices and other services. They were originally run by government-appointed agents who lived on site and were often infamous for mismanagement and unwelcome efforts to enforce cultural assimilation. Robert Yellowtail described the agent as a "supreme commander" who could make decisions "based on whim," without appeal (Yellowtail, "A Brief Review"). Today's Crow Agency is southeast of Billings. A tribal council now runs the reservation. For more details on the tribe's early agencies, see Leforge in Marquis, *Memoirs*, 32–33, 106–11, and Hoxie, *The Crow*, 82–85. (BL)
5. Bull Shows, Old Dwarf, and Henry Russell were brothers in the Crow way because their parents were related. Even today the family knows them as brothers. Sometimes Crow relationships are difficult to distinguish, especially between blood relatives, because families were close and children were raised together. (MP)
6. Whites disapproved of men with long hair, so authorities frequently forced Native men to cut theirs. Crow men treasured their long hair, a living part of their body,

and some considered the growth of hair sacred. Henry Russell entered school voluntarily but did not volunteer for a haircut. He was probably ashamed that someone had taken his hair without a fight, since hair or scalps were trophies of enemies killed in battle. (MP)

According to Leforge, a white man who joined the Crow in 1868, the school was less popular than the church, partly because teachers urged children to cut their hair for sanitary reasons. "The Indian custom was to cut off the hair only as a sign of mourning, and one who had this disfigurement was known as a 'ghost person'" (Marquis, *Memoirs*, 40). (BL)

7. Since Henry Russell was an elder brother by Crow reckoning, he could tell Bull Shows what to do, and my grandfather looked up to him as his main advisor. My mother always said her father wanted to go to school and learn. I guess he was anxious to go until he saw his brother Henry's hair being lopped off. (MP)

8. Lt. Richard Pratt founded Carlisle in 1879, and several Crow children, including Henry Russell and George Hogan, Lillian's last husband, went there for additional education. Pratt became involved with Indian education in 1875 at Fort Marion, Florida, when overseeing Plains prisoners of war. To continue their education, he took some of them to Hampton, Virginia, in 1878, to the normal school for black students. He founded Carlisle a year later. (For details, see Adams, *Education for Extinction*, 36–51.) Pratt understood that Native people needed English and knowledge of Western culture to survive, but he favored eradicating the Indian within and recommended separating Native children from parental influences. "Pratt liked Indians, but he had little use for Indian cultures" (Adams, *Education for Extinction*, 51). His ideas would influence Indian boarding school education for decades, profoundly affecting the experiences of children like Lillian in the early twentieth century. See "They Put Me in the Boarding School," chapter 6. (BL)

They Took Henry's Indian Name

Henry and Old Dwarf, *they're brothers.*
Henry Russell.
[He got the name "Henry Russell"] *when he went to school.*
They removed his Indian name at school and gave him Russell.
Just like Mardell's dad.
Her dad.
His name is
George Long Time Ago Bear.
A-a-nd the school, the government, says "Your name is too long."
Says "We'll take that Long Time Ago Bear.
Don't carry that name any more—we'll give you Hogan."

And then there's Albert Lincoln.
His name is Albert Thunder Iron,
and they said they'd take that Thunder Iron.
Says "Take it off.
Take Lincoln."
So they call him Albert Lincoln.[1]
And Isaac McAllister, I don't know his Indian name—
says "Your name is too long.
We don't want you to carry that Indian name."

That's when they were going to boarding school.
They go to boarding school up here at Crow Agency.

> 1. Sometimes they gave names of people from history, such as Adams and Lincoln. My dad was named George Washington Hogan. (MP)

Henry Russell Cheated Death Twice

So Henry say he's got good education.
[He went to school] way back here at Absarokee.
That's that first agency [second agency] that's established, up here
the other side of Columbus.
That used to be the agency—all people, all the Crows, flock over there to
    stay.
That's the first agency [second agency].
And after that he went to Carlisle.
School w-a-ay back east.
He's got good education.
Just like Mardell's dad George.

But Henry, he's much older than George.
He went to Carlisle,
and one time he told me, he says,
"One winter there's several boys up on roof, top of the house,
trying to-o-o work the chimney, clean the chimney"—and he said "The
    snow was deep."

"And the sno-o-w slide" and he says "I was in that snow.
Slide down this big building and snow all over.
And before I landed on the lawn" he says,
"I thought sure I was gonna die.
This time I'm gonna die."
But he sure landed on the lawn and the snow—it didn't hurt him,
but he slide down that roof.
And them employee-e-s a-a-nd kids a-a-ll flock over there,
as he come out of the snow. (laughs)
Unhurt, unharmed.

He said that time he came [through] alive.
"And another time" he said "we were at camp up here at Fort Custer."
That's out of Hardin.
There's Custer
army base [Fort Custer] right there.
A-a-nd he said "One of the grandpas said,
'You go down,
where the horses are.
Herd them down to the water,
to the river,
and water them,
and come back.'"

He said "I was just about
ten years old" he said.
"I got on the horse,
saddle up the horse.
I took the horses, herd the horses down the river
and water them and bring them back and put them in the field.
And after that,
after I was climbing on the harness,
the whole harness
slip and
got under the horse"—and he said "my whole leg stuck
in the stirrups and this horse was dragging me a-a-ll day.
Followed the horses and he dragged me."

And he says "My who-o-o-ole back was sticked with cactus."
He said "I cried but after awhile I couldn't cry any more."
Says "Nobody come around, I'll be dead by before sundown."
And this horse was dragging him around.

And pretty soon a man got on top of the hill—says he look at the horses, says "What's this?
That one horse is dragging something.
I'd better go down there and see" (claps hands)—this man ran fast down there and caught the horse.
And the horse was eating but
soon as he moves he's dragging that saddle.
And Henry's leg was stick in there, caught on the saddle—
couldn't get out.
Drag him all day pretty near.

He said "That's the second time of death there" but he said he didn't die.
"And the one I fell off the roof" he said "I didn't die."
(chuckles)
Henry was telling.
Henry said "I cheated death twice."

The First Watermelon, A Story from My Father

[When I was a little girl,] that time,
they have stores.
I come to know,
go to the store and buy.
But when this [happened they'd] come to know Billings then [Billings was just established].
Ammaalapáshkuua [Where They (Anglos) Cut the Wood].[1]

Steamboat come up the river.
They must brin-n-g some,

o-oh flo-our or—a lot of stuff.
In the steamship.
They come up the river and then they unload it there in Billings.
And then-n Billings has l-o-ots of woodpile—
they said it's a big forest there.
L-o-ots of wood, timber.
So they cut it up and
fill it up at the ship and then the steamboat turn around and then go
back east with a load of wood.
Say that's where they always get wood.[2]

Fort Custer [is another place they unload]—they've big barracks.[3]
I've seen the picture.
I had it, in my house up on the wall—I don't know who took it.
I should kept it and I don't know what become of it.

But anyway they say that this man he's an interpreter.
"Honey" was his name—he married a woman on our side.[4]
And this interpreter says, he told these Indians, he says,
"The ship,
the ship is coming in today, sometime today,
and it'll stop a-a-nd unload—some on the other side of the river
and some on this side of the river"—there's the big fort,
army, soldiers living up there.

A-a-nd he says "Now,
you wait and the ship is coming in today that's going to bring some
    watermelon."
He said "This is the first time you'll see anything like that.
It comes from wa-a-a-y down where the sunrise comes.
Where the sun appears is where it comes from."
Says "They're sending a load.
And when the ship stops we're going to unload all the supplies and we'll
    bring them-m
stuff—so you can eat some.

That'll be the first time you eat watermelon."

But anyway they
unload all the stuff.
And they haul it up—it's a big hill.
And they unload the stuff there a-a-nd took it in.
A-a-nd he said "I'll distribute all these to the families.
You have one, you have one, of these big watermelon."
He gave them—they look at it.
"What's this?
We don't know."

"You cut it, take a butcher knife and cut it and,
and you'll see the inside—the inside is red and sweet."
Said "You taste some."
And that's the first time they ever taste.
They cut it with the butcher knife.
Chop it off and then
they taste some and say,
"It tastes like water." (laughs)
Some they ate a little bit of it and some didn't want it.
And some womens, they said "We don't know
how to eat it"—they said "I think we'll cook it."
Says cooked the watermelon, it got all mushy. (laughs)[5]

My father [told me].
He seen it—my uncle even joined the army up there—Pushes Himself.[6]

1. The Apsáalooke call Billings "Where They Cut the Wood" because there was a sawmill there. (MP)
2. The humorous events described here happened when Bull Shows was still a boy. Lillian says the story took place in Billings, but the watermelons came by steamship, so it may have happened in 1877–82, in the little town of Coulson, which Billings later replaced. Coulson was built on the edge of the Yellowstone River and was often supplied by steamship. Like later Billings, it too had a sawmill. In 1882 the Northern Pacific Railway finished its line and established Billings just two miles to the northeast. Both Coulson and steamship service disappeared. (BL)

3. Fort Custer, approximately fifty miles from Billings, was established in 1877, one year after the Battle of the Little Bighorn, supposedly to make military presence known. Even before the reservation was moved to its present location, some Crows lived near the fort so they could work as scouts and livestock tenders. My father's father used to break horses for the army and died there from injuries from a horse. (MP)
4. "On our side" means a Crow. When speaking of an outsider of unknown tribal affiliation, they say from "other lodges." (MP)
5. Snell (*Grandmother's Grandchild*, 157) briefly referenced the same story. She heard it from Hank Bull Chief. (BL)
6. Pushes Himself (Ichiipáachileesh) was an army scout. That he is linked to this story suggests that he joined the army around the same time, perhaps during the same trip, so this would have happened in the late nineteenth century. Her father called him Biiké, which means "elder brother," the Apsáalooke term for maternal uncles, so Pushes Himself was her father's mother's brother. (MP)

At Reno Creek the Crows Were Dispersed

The following story seems to focus on food, but it is Bull Shows's personal memory of a pivotal moment in Crow history, the year they left their nomadic lifestyle forever. The buffalo and other game had been so decimated that they could no longer survive as hunters, and white settlers were demanding lands the tribe could no longer protect. As hunger loomed, they decided to focus on the Big Horn valley, their most promising agricultural lands. Under the guidance of prominent chiefs and agent Henry Armstrong, they left their western territory and converged at Reno Creek, near the present Crow Agency. From there they disbursed to the six districts where they live today.

By the Gregorian calendar, these events happened between 1882 and 1884, but Bull Shows opens with his grandmothers to place his story within Crow life. He is telling us that this happened when these old ladies were fragile but still alive. Then he focuses, not on the politics of this sad time, but his youthful memories of what his hungry family ate. Lillian ends by telling us where the tribe lived before these changes. At the time of the move, Bull Shows and his Mountain Crow relatives had been camped in the western region, not too far from Where They Left the Yellow Blanket. She is explaining how her relatives settled in the Pryor District, where she would be born. (BL)

My father had two grandmothers lived to be into a hundred years old.
A-a-nd my dad says he was about e-eight years old when [he first
 remembered] them two old ladies.
His mother's there—
the mother of my father
is there—and the grandma and then the gre-a-at-grandma is there.
Says "I saw two, two-o o-o-ld grandmas.
They lived to be over a hundred and they don't know the odd
number the hundred—over hundred."

But he says "Every time they'd sit down a-a-nd want to get up a-a-nd,
put their hands down, skin would break."
Say "O-o-o-h my.
Get me some s-a-alve or gre-e-ase to grease this tear."
Their skin would break.[1]
They said there's the <u>gre-a-at</u>-grandma—and then the <u>next</u> grandma,
the second grandma,
she's worse offer than the old one.
He said sometimes she's just,
"Eekaawaa"—"hold onto me"—they would say.[2]
Ever time they would strain to get up,
their skin would break.
"These were my grandmothers and I knew them well" he said.

That time [the time of this story]
they moved a-a-ll the people—all Crows *went to Reno Creek.*[3]
They were put there, [near today's] *agency,*
and they have to wait there until *they sent them away.*[4]
My father *said his age was nine by then.*
Nine years old [perhaps older].
"We had no food.
Winter was coming.
If we had no food the
agency gave us some" he said.
"On weekends if they sent for us" he said.

"[They] issue things like flour, bacon,
sugar, coffee"—what else?⁵
"Rice they would give us and we would take it and eat but
it wasn't good food."
Maybe they didn't know how to cook it. (chuckles)

"Whenever meat ran out my father rode behind me and went with me.
We'd hunt in the Wolfs [Wolf Mountains]" he said.
"Look for deer but we wouldn't find any.
There were lots of pheasants" he said.
"We would kill lots of pheasants and bring them.
Their breast muscles are big,
these pheasants—and they remove the feathers.
And remove the breasts, fillet them."
That's his mother would fillet them.
Hang them up.
He said "They would be pretty big fillets, like
large pieces of dried meat."
When they dry they would pile them up.
When the agency give them food,
give them bacon,
they cut up these dried fillets of pheasant and
cook with the bacon.
"We ate them."
He was nine years old at the time he knew all this.⁶

Then at Reno Creek the Crows were dispersed [to their present districts].
A-a-ll these people from Pryor [their present home]—
the superintendent [the Indian agent] or the government
tell to herd a-a-ll these [to Reno Creek]—they used to live up at Livingston.
On the valley.
[They were] the Mountain Crows, they call them the Mountain Crows.
They camped down around
Livingston, Red Lodge,
and Billings, in that area—that's a-a-ll the who-ole territory.
A-a-nd
the Black Lodge people [the River Crow] lived w-a-ay up on the Musselshell.
The Missouri River.⁶

They a-a-ll wandered around, camp, moved one place to another way up there at Musselshell.

That's the Black Lodge Indians.[7]

[Before Reno Creek] the Crow moved from place to another.[8]

1. When Crow want to indicate someone of great age, they may describe them as so old their skin cracks, breaks, or tears. The phrase appears regularly in Crow literature. See Pretty Shield in Linderman, *Pretty-Shield*, 45, 221; and unnamed informant in Frey, *The World of the Crow Indians*, 92. (BL)
2. *Eekaawaa* is a small sound of alarm or concern and has no real meaning. (MP)
3. Reno Creek is in the foothills of the Wolf Mountains, about five miles from the present Crow Agency, and is named after Maj. Marcus Reno, famous in the Battle of the Little Bighorn. The Crow call it Ash Creek when speaking Apsáalooke. My mother said there were a lot of ash trees growing in the area. The Wolf Mountains lie southeast of Crow Agency, and the tribe went there to hunt and to fast for spiritual quests. They also gathered white clay from a pond there, using it to paint their horses and cure diarrhea. (MP)
4. For a detailed description of these events, see Hoxie, *Parading*, 11–30. (BL)
5. Agent Armstrong issued food within two weeks of reaching the Big Horn valley (Hoxie, *Parading*, 128). Food was also distributed on the Stillwater, but Bull Shows says the family was hunting in the Wolf Mountains, which are near Reno Creek, so this food must have been issued in the months after they moved. Their inability to find deer attests to scarcity of game on the reservation. (BL)
6. Plenty Coups knew his people needed to farm to survive, but he only partially agreed to Armstrong's plan. He bypassed the Big Horn Valley for his birthplace, Arrow Creek, now known as Pryor Creek (Hoxie, *Parading*, 24–25. (BL)
7. The Crow once included two major divisions. The Mountain Crow lived to the south, near the Big Horn Mountains. The River Crow lived on the Musselshell and Judith Rivers and elsewhere north of the Yellowstone. They expected their own reservation near the Musselshell but were forced to move to Livingston, a Mountain Crow region. I think they always yearned for their north country. When the Crow disbursed from Reno (or Ash) Creek, the band leaders had already decided where they would live. The Kicked In the Bellies, a third, smaller division, chose Rotten Grass Creek and the eastern Bighorns, where they had always lived, near present Wyola, Montana. The River Crows eventually settled in what we now know as the Dunmore area or Black Lodge District. Plenty Coups, a Mountain Crow, had always loved the Arrow Creek (Pryor) area and had seen himself living there in his visions, so he and his followers went there. Other Mountain Crows, under Chief Pretty Eagle, settled in the Big Horn valley area between what is now St. Xavier and Fort Smith. Medicine Crow and his bunch stayed in the Greasy Grass area, known today as Lodge Grass. The Crow Agency area is commonly known as the Reno District today but is also known as Center Lodge or Fallen Bell District. The six districts were now formed. (MP)
8. The Crow had already lost thirty million acres of land in the treaty of 1868 (Medicine Crow and Press, *A Handbook*, 15), and more losses followed the move to the Big Horn valley. By 1891, the western territory, including the Stillwater,

was opened to white settlement. The reservation continued to shrink for several more decades and now encompasses approximately 2.2 million acres. (BL)

My Father Works with the Cowboys

This adventure dates to the 1880s before Bullshows married. (BL)

My father has no education,
but he lived to be a
good man—
youth—he said he must be about
twenty-nine years or twenty-eight or,
he said, "around there.
Past twenty anyway" he said.
"I lived to be-e-e a young man—I'm not afraid, I want to do something."
And he said "I want to go and be a cowboy."

So he took off.
He took couple horses.
He told his parents that he's going to work for the cowboys.
And they said, they told him "Be careful.
They give out whiskey to make you drunk and they fight you.
Them white people are mean!
And they might get you drunk and they might kill you."[1]

Try to tell him to keep away from the white people but
he said "There's good cowboys over there—I want to be a cowboy.
I'll go"—and there's where he learn English.
Worked with the cowboys.
He lived,
we don't know [how long]—he said "I might spend a year or two years.
Camp and move camp to another herd, big head of cattle,
I'll be working with the cowboys."
And he says "There's where I learned to cuss" he says. (laughs)
He learned that way.

And he quit after he
didn't like it then—after he work for about a year.
They moved camp another and
he said he didn't go and buy clothes he says.
I'll tell you: this kind of a dirty story but he said,
"From not changing my clothes" he says,
"I wear the same clothes and after that I start to itching
my body" he says.
"I take off my clothes and saw this nits in my—" (laughs)
He said he didn't like it and that's when he quit.
Quit the cowboy outfit.

He'd break horses and,
and watch horses and herd cattle a-a-nd work.
About a year and a half.
He stayed there, w-worked for the outfit, moved from place to another—he
    never seen an Indian.
He lived with the cowboys—a-a-ll that time he learned the English.
He said "Uh-huh, uh-huh,"
when the white men talk to him, he says.
That's how he learned the English, little bit English anyway.

A-a-nd after he found out there a lot of nits in his— (laughs),
he had to quit. (laughs)
Said he quit then
a-a-nd went home to sweat baths and
cleaned up and
don't wear these white clothes.[2]
Bought new ones and start
living different way.

He said "I stayed single
for about four years until I married that old lady" he said—my mother.
    (chuckles)

> 1. Bull Shows's parents had reason to fear both violence and alcohol. For examples of the bitter side of Crow-white relationships and of alcohol, see "My Mother

Mourns," chapter 2; "They Don't Have Much Money," chapter 10, and "Caleb Starts to Drinking," chapter 7. Similarly, Medicine Crow (*Counting Coup*, 70) said he and his great-grandmother both feared white people in his childhood. (BL)

2. Sweat baths are prayer-filled, ritualized, intensely hot steam baths that cleanse and heal both body and spirit, and many tribes have long used them when seeking ritual purification. They are conducted in small, dome-shaped structures of bent saplings covered with thick layers of hides or blankets that retain the intense heat when water is poured over hot rocks inside. For information on ritual uses of sweat baths by the Crow, see Curtis, *North American Indian*; Frey, *World of the Crow Indians*; Lowie, *The Crow Indians*; and Voget, *Shoshoni-Crow Sun Dance*. (BL)

CHAPTER FOUR

My Parents Meet and Marry

My Parents Meet

> *Based on the dates when their children were born, this probably happened around 1890.* (BL)

My father said he never talked to my mother or never seen her,
but there's a train comes from,
from somewhere up by Joliet.
The train was coming slow.
And my mother and her girlfriend was in that train.
He start to coming.
Run-n.
And the train slow up because it was coming close to the station.
And he come in and hang onto the rails (claps hands)—he jump in.

They ride free!
That time they let the Indians ride through in this area
from Joliet and then this area where the train goes,
and Indians can get in there free.
They don't charge them.
So he got in there.

He seen my mother there with a girlfriend.
That's
Ella's mother.[1]

Said they were going to Billings.
They're young—
young girls, young women.
That's when he met my mother.
He said he just set by her and
he says he talked to her.
And pretty soon before the train stops he said,
"We're going to get married." (laughs)

And that's why she can't get away from my father [and] my father
never get away from my mother—they
got off.[2]
Let that other woman go—my father say,
"You go and take off
because you're going to be crazy [flirt].[3]
Go off and don't take her" he says.
"I'm going to marry her now."
So he took her home
and married her.
A-a-nd that's how she
married my father.[4]

   1. Horse was with another Pryor person, the mother of Ella Bell (later Ella Plainbull). Mom refers to her as Baawaxpáleetcheesh (Holds Nothing Is Sacred). (MP)
   2. I believe my mother is saying that they rarely left each other's side after their initial meeting. (MP)
   3. "Crazy" probably refers to running around and flirting. Bull Shows most likely feared that he might lose my grandmother to someone else if he didn't marry her right away. (MP)
   4. Later in the tape Lillian said people used to say her father was a good looking young man, and women were interested in him, but he didn't want to get married until he met Horse. She also said her father thought he might have been about twenty-five when he married and his wife about three years younger, but they did not know for sure because they did not speak much English. If this is true, he was born around 1865, not 1871. (BL)

Medicine Dream for Horses: A Story from My Parents' Early Marriage

When Lillian's parents were newly married and Lillian was not yet born, her uncle, Old Dwarf, dreamed a sacred medicine song that promised many horses. Here he gives the song to the young couple as a dream-blessing. This is a gift of the power within the dream.[1] (BL)

[The Indian way] they have medicine.
Like one time,
my father and mother were living way up on a ranch.
About ten miles from Billings.
They don't know—they always say about ten.
Here's the rough country and they're way down there.[2]
Their parents,
my father's parents,
have a piece of land up there above that Billings road.
And they build a big log house.
And they have a big barn—they said they have a big corral and they have lots of horses.
And
they live up there.
And they only had my brother.
Daniel.
That's the only child they had.

So they live up there and take care of the horses,
and when they need something in the way of food,
my father would saddle up and
go to Billings.
And
my mother would be making bags, beaded bags.
And moccasins, men's moccasins.
And women's moccasin.
And she'd put pretty, nice [bead] work on them.
And my father takes them
to Billings and—
what do we call that—Decker's Curio Store.

My father would take them down to Billings—I don't know—

I'm not there.
And even Caleb's not born.
So we don't know but we were told.
There's my brother [Daniel] and there's a sister that died before that.
So it's my father and mother,
a-a-nd
my brother living there—just the three of them.
And they said they had horses to take care of.

And my uncle [Old Dwarf]
lives way up to Pryor.
He lives close to Pryor Mountain [the Pryor Mountains].
He has a house there and his wife—
together—but he said,
"Last night I dreamt,
a-a-nd
I was given a song [for horses],"
he said.
"But I got plenty of horses.
I think I'll saddle up
and go way down
to Bull Shows."
Says "[He] and his wife are way up.
They live far but" he said "I'll just go alone and I won't be back for maybe ten days or so."
And his wife said "That's all right—go on."

So he saddle up one morning and take his slicker and some clothes tied to the saddle.
And he kept go-o-ing.
This is about, o-oh say about,
maybe sixty-five miles,
from the Pryor Mountain—w-a-ay up to
this place towards Billings, way out in the rugged hill. (chuckles)
And this uncle, my uncle, start to
go and visit them.
Because that night,
he heard a song.

He said "I heard a song—this song that sang" he said.
"The words to that is
'*You'll be given three horses.*'"
That's

> *My song is like water*
> *My song is like water*
> *(chant)*
> *They gave you three [horses]*
> *(chant)*³

That's my uncle heard that song that night in a dream.

So the next morning,
he saddle up and went to my father.
Come along and sometimes gallop or pace and he got to the house.
And my father's "Oh here comes my brother.
Fix a good meal for him."
So my mother [fix]—
I don't know, coffee and I don't know what else.

They fed him when he came.
And he said "Yes I haven't seen you folks and I got lonesome for you folks.
But specially,
I heard a song.
And the words to that is something
true—it's going to be true and I brought you that song."
He says "You-u hang on to that song,
and
don't give it away.
Keep that song and always sing it once in awhile."
And he said "The words to that is

> My song is just like
> the water.
> Never run out.
> And you're going to

be given three horses.

And that's the words to this song.
So you keep this song,
a-a-nd I'll hope you get them horses."[4]

So he stayed around a few days and went back to his own house to his wife.
And then just things go on like that.
And then one afternoon my father says there was a wagon coming.
Somebody coming up the road.
And here it was a wagon
and a man with lots of horses.
Horses—he led about,
said he had about,
twenty-five horses.
And he was driving a team.
And he come in—to the gate.
And open the gate—my father
walked up to the gate and opened the gate for him.

So this man drove in,
and he got off—he says "Can I stay here?
And my horses, turn all the horses in the pasture?"—and my father says yes.
Like I told you, he understands English.
Says "Yes, yes, good, good."
So this man come in and turn all of his horses in and
come to the house and unhitch his horses, turn them loose.
Says, my father says, "Just turn your horses loose.
They been traveling."
[This man] says "I've been traveling
for eight days.
Eight or more days."
And he's going to Livingston.
Or somewhere up in that country.
He said "I'm going over there—I going to buy land, I'm going to live up there.
I got lots of horses."
So he come in and turn the horses.

So they fed him.
They gave him coffee—I don't know what else they gave him.
But he ate and he
fix up a tent—he has tent, said "I'll just put my tent up."
And he did, he put up his tent—he stayed there that night.
And my father [said] "You stay,
maybe three days, maybe two days,
and let your horses rest.
Feed.
And then you [claps hands], later on you can go."

Says "Thank you"—I guess he thank him.
And they start to talking,
and my father understand English, so they start to make friends.
Said "We sure made friends" he said.
And the third day
he said "Well,
time that I go."

My uncle [had] told him,
"When you find a horse,
a buckskin horse,
look like a zebra,"
says "there'll be marks around the
front legs, foot."
He said,
"That's your good luck horse" he says.
"After you find that horse,
you're going to have lots of horses."

And the morning when this man gather up, round up his horse and got to
getting his wagon ready and going, my father
look around these horses.
And he seen a horse that
my uncle told him in this dream—
that "if you ever find a horse, a buckskin horse that's pretty,

prance, that's the horse that you're going to
own—and after that,
you'll have lots of horses."

So he saw this buckskin in that bunch of horses,
and he talked to the man.
He said,
"I want to buy that buckskin."
Says "Then I'm going to
own him,
and I'm going to take care of him,
a-a-nd
I'll buy the horse.
The buckskin.
The horse that my uncle dreamt."
[His uncle] said "If you ever own that horse, after that hold on to that horse and
you'll have more horses.
By that—they'll be given to you."

So this man
said "All right.
I won't sell it to you."
He said "I'll give you the horse,
I got lots of horses there.
You pick two more horses and the buckskin."

See what that song bring in the dream?
"You'll be given three horses."
That's the song he dreamt.
So,
he says "I'll give you the buckskin—don't buy it" he says.
"You helped me out, you pastured my horses and all that—now I'll give you that buckskin.
And two extra—just go and pick two more horses.
Three horses."

And what that song, it say.
"You'll be given three horses."
That's the words to that song and that dream come true.
So this horse, my father own the horse then.
And this man gave him—he would not sell it to him—says "I just give it to you."

That's a tru-ue,
tru-ue thing that
ever happened to my father and uncle.
They tell us that story.
And we know it—we know it's true.
After that we said be good to horses and we do.
We all like horses.
We used to have a bunch of horses.
And pretty ones too.
So that dream come true.

   1. The definition of "dream-blessing" is from Timothy McCleary (e-mail to Barbara Loeb, August 2010).
   2. They were living between Billings and Pryor, near present Blue Creek Road. The area was in some rough hills, and people still call it "the rough country" a century later. (MP)
   3. I have heard the song. There's more, but my mother had a memory lapse here. This may be related to the horse medicine discussed in another story. There was a medicine bundle that was in Grandma's trunk and was later retrieved by my sister Nellie. (MP)
   4. Voget noted (*Shoshoni-Crow Sun Dance*, 38), "Retired warriors known to possess powerful spirit guardians constituted an elite that shaped the careers of young men by offering counsel and the protective influence of a mystical Medicine power, *maxpe*, for a fee." Old Dwarf's gift is not a military medicine, because young men stopped counting coup in the reservation period, but he seems to be performing a modernized version of the same role, providing the younger man with a mystical power intended to bring him success and prosperity. Old Dwarf is not asking for a fee, but Bull Shows will likely reciprocate with a generous gift sometime in the future. Such medicines usually came from visions or dreams, bringing knowledge, skills, or protection. (BL)

CHAPTER FIVE

My First Memories

This chapter begins around 1909 or 1910, when Lillian is four or five. (BL)

I Come to Know

Anyway I was born,
a-a-nd well, in between that I don't know much then. (chuckles)
I just a chi-i-ld, live around.
But I come to know
when I was about fi-i-ve years old.[1]
That's when I get to know
my grandfather and my grandma and we had a big ho-ouse.
A log ho-ouse, oh just all in a big room.
And my grandpa and grandma
used to sleep on that side and Dad and Mother over there and [gesturing to walls]
my brother Caleb w-a-ay over in that corner and they make my bed over here.

I was growing and then my mother al-l-ways
particular.
Says,
"I want to cover her up."[2]

In the night she gets up and cover me up and
that's when I-I-I just have come to know.

Sometimes I see [remember] my grandmother.
And let's see now—
my grandfather died first.
They always take him to Billings to the doctor.
But I know [remember] just one time [with my grandfather]
and that was about—o-oh I may be five years old.
There's three, four buggies, people too and us too.[3]
Taking my grandpa to the doctor I guess.

Anyway we're going to Billings.
So on the way we stopped for dinner,
and my mother fixed the fire and my dad and other people around the fire—
   it was noon day,
and they cook and we ate.[4]
And that's when I remember about my grandpa the fir-r-st time.
He took a piece of cracker—them hardtacks?
He put lard on it.
Put pla-ain lard on it.
And he sprinkled sugar on it
and gave it to me and I ate it,
and I thought that was something grea-a-at—that's the first time I ever knew
   about my grandfather.[5]

His name would be like On the Other Side.[6]
Aakkeetaash.
He's a tal-l-l thin man.
Well, tall.
And he sure looks like my father.
And that's the first time I ever knew a different man from my father.
But then I know that he's my grandpa.

And my mother tells me about her mother.
She said she was only eight months old when her mother died.
She had her half sister, Clara.
Clara White Hip.

She told me that's her sister.
That's her half sister and they look alike.
I never knew about her sister until I was o-oh—
maybe around eight years old or ten, around there.
Then I come to know she had a sister and she looked like her.
So that's when I know
that I had some relatives.

But I know my brother [Caleb] is there and my older brother [Daniel].
And my older brother was su-u-re nice.
And he's good man, young man,
and he goes out trapping in wintertime.

1. "I come to know" is a way of saying this was when she began to remember experiences. (MP)
2. When she was growing older, her mother kept her covered. This went back to teepee living. Modesty was important even in close quarters, and Grandmother probably didn't want Mom to be exposed during sleep, especially to her brother. It was not right to have a male relative see you indecent in any way. (MP)
3. The people in the buggies were relatives. Even today, hospital staff are often surprised that so many family members stay with sick kinfolk. Illness was and is a matter of concern to the whole family, not just the afflicted ones. (MP)
4. Mom pointed this place out to me in September 1997, on our way to the Plenty Coups Day of Honor festivities on Labor Day. Almost ninety years later, she still remembered the exact location. (MP)
5. She is saying that this is her first memory of him. (MP)
6. Her grandfather's name, Aakkeetaash, means "on the other side of a river, bank, or valley," as opposed to being on the side of an enemy. This distinction is important because a Crow term for ourselves is "On Our Side." He was referred to simply as Bank. When a young man, he went on a raid against the Sioux and returned home with a fine horse. He was in the famous battle against the Lakota at Pryor (or Arrow) Creek in the 1860s. We think he was also a warrior with Wraps Up His Tail during the famous rebellion of 1887. (MP)

Snakes and Frogs

Our house is still standing.
Log house.
Still standing there.
There's where I was raised.

Didn't have no water—my father dig a good
spring—a good water there.
A big one there a-a-nd a big [one] over a little further on.
Grea-a-at big,
where we can go and get water.
Haul water.

My grandmother was still living then.
My father's mother.
And they said they called
Caleb.
He's a little boy then.
They call him and he said "That old grandmother of mine
never-r
drink out of the sa-a-me bucket, same water, or let others drink."

She used to have a big,
good pail of water.
Has a cover on there.
She don't let nobody drink out of that—she has her o-own cup, her own
    water.

And she just about ran out of water so she called my brother.
Called him Little Calf—his Indian name is Little Calf.
Says "Little Calf come over and haul some water for me."
"No, no! Grandmother, no, no!" he says.
"Why?"
Says "I'm afraid
to go down the spring and haul water."
"Why?" the grandmother says—"Why?"
"Because there's snakes and the frogs there."
Says "I don't want to go haul water for you—I'm afraid of frogs, afraid of
    snakes." (laughs)
He says "*Binnéesee sáakbisak íaxassaawisshik*"—that's what he said, snakes
    and frogs. (laughs)[1]

So the grandma got mad.
I remember that when I—I may be about
five years old then. (laughs)

   1. The literal translation is "by the water there are frogs, there are snakes." (MP)

When My Grandmother Died

But my grandmother is ne-eat!
She is cle-e-ean and ne-eat.
She has the pail,
a big pail—says "Go get me some water."
We lived close to the spring,
and we'd go.
If we don't go she gets after us.
We go and cle-e-ear nice water.
We take a pailful and take it in.
She put the lid on and says "Don't touch that water."
She take care of her bed, take care of her water, take care of her dishes.
She don't let nobody use them.
A-a-nd any kids come around the bed—
"Go play over there! Don't come near!"[1]
She sure is
neat.

[Her name was] *Her Medicine is Sacred*.[2]
And I remember well that when she died,
she smelled good, whatever was rubbed on her.
Dress her up a-a-nd put her on the bed.
[They had a] brand new quilt, then a blanket, and put her over it and wrap
   her up and
took her up to them hills
and put her in a big cliff.
The rocks were this way [they had crevices] *and they put her in.*
Let her down.[3]

And that's all I remember of that, when my grandma died.

I don't remember my grandpa,
when he died—I guess he was sick the time I told you,
we all take him to the doctor and he took a big
[cracker and put lard and sugar on it].

1. They say she wouldn't let anybody sit on her bed. (MP)
2. According to Lillian's allotment file at the Bureau of Indian Affairs offices, Bull Shows's mother was Medicine Porcupine and his father was The Twins, but in these stories, she refers to this paternal grandmother as Her Medicine Is Sacred. The grandmother probably changed her name, for one of a variety of traditional reasons, but it is also possible that this is a different woman. A number of women could function as grandmothers and be legitimately referred to as such within the Crow system of relationships. (MP, BL)
3. My mother showed me the spot where she remembered they buried her grandmother. It's in Pryor, but I will tell no one ever exactly where. There were cliffs and crevices, and she said they slowly and carefully dropped her into one of the crevices and covered it up. (MP)

They Tell Us to Talk to the Moon

Every afternoon before the
sun goes down in the evening, the moon would be way up shining,
and they make us jump.
Take us outside—"Come on!"
Just a little ways from the house,
and they make us jump.
They said "All right" they say, "Jump"—we'd jump and,
"Tomorrow I'll be
getting
older."
And then we'd jump again and they say "The next day I'll be a lady."
And then the third they say "Jump again.
Say 'I'll be a woman and I'm going to be growing <u>old</u>, older.'"
So they make us talk to the moon—make us jump.
And said "That's all now, run along."

[We do that] once in awhile.

And sometimes they'd be doing something.
They don't do it then—they don't care. (chuckles)
But that's their way.
They said the o-old people, way back in the o-old people,
they make them
jump, talk to the moon like that,
and they say they grow.
Yeh they make us jump—"Say this" they'd say.
"Tomorrow I'll grow.
The next day I'll be
older.
Next day I'll be a
big girl"—go on like that. (chuckles)[1]

So I guess there's some truth to it—I don't know.
Me, I'm an Indian and
sometimes since I read about this Christian
in the Bible, all that—I believe more in that and I
don't care to
believe the Indian way anymore.

   1. Several authors have published references to jumping toward the moon. See McCleary, *The Stars We Know*, 104–5; Medicine Crow, "The Effects of European Culture," 84, 88; and Deernose in Voget, *They Call Me Agnes*, 111. (BL)

Lullabies

This is how you put the baby to sleep.
The mother would wrap it up.
Wrap the baby up,
and says

> O-o-o-o-o-o-o-o-*uh*,
> O-o-o-o-o-o-o-o-*uh*.
> O-o-o-o-o-o-o-o-*uh*,
> O-o-o-o-o-o-o-o-*uh*.[1]

Pretty soon the baby (claps hands) falls asleep.[2]

And they sing some of this—

> Shoonnawoolápshisshiilak
> ammuukáatam kóokoon.
> Awóolapkissheesh
> isáshkaate baaxáhchii.
> Káatak.
> Eelashbachiisáakaataa wahee.
> Koo awóolapchisshe wahee.

That's

> *I found this little child*
> *down the creek.*
> *And I found this dear little child*
> *all wrapped up in the blanket.*
> *And that blanket seems to be too small for it.*
> *But anyway we wrapped the baby up.*
> *And I found the little child so de-ear, so de-ear.*

That's the start of that song.

And

> *I found the baby in a*
> *little low place where it was laying.*
> *And the little blanket was sma-a-ll.*
> *A-a-nd I found the little baby. (chuckles)*

That's the words to that song.

When you sang this, the [next] words to this one it says,

> *The baby was there a-a-nd talking to me a-a-nd*
> *when I start to leaving, leave the baby, take off—*

this is just a song,
this is just a song[3]

> *I start to leaving the baby,*
> *it start to telling me stories, don't want me to go, and it kept*
> *telling [stories], the little child, the baby,*
> *and cried.*

And I told my mama, I says,
"Mom" I said "don't sing that one.
It makes me re-eal sad when they have to
go and leave it and [the baby] start to talking so they won't leave."
And I says "Don't sing that one now—sing another one.
Don't sing that one—makes me re-eal sad." (chuckles)
But I remember when I was small I
hear her singing that song.

1. A crooning sound. Not words. (MP)
2. In this instance, she is clapping her hands to indicate joy because the lullaby has put the child to sleep. (MP)
3. She is indicating that in real life they would not have left the baby. (BL)

Children's Songs

Let's see now.

Iilak baaiakáate,
ammáaluttuuk.
Itta baleeúuluum,
bálee átchee déek.
Shiilialeekáataa.[1]

That's a children's song and it says,
"Arrow just <u>swe-ept</u> right by us and didn't [touch us]."
That's the song.
They just sing that.
Made words to that song.

Yeah "The arrows which just <u>swe-ept</u> by and they didn't touch us.
And the arrow swept by."
That's the words to that song,
That's a-a-ll [the words] I could remember now.

Let's see now.
What other song?

> Little Rabbits strayed us off.
> I will go.
> Red rosebud berries.
> Red rosebud berries.

That's it. (chuckles)
That talk about them little red berries,
in the brush.
"And they're turning red, they're turning red."
That's the words to that song—kind of short but they sing that.
Made a tune out of it a-a-nd put words in there.

A-a-nd I think that's
all I could remember now.
My grandmother
sang those.
A-a-nd I listen.
A-a-nd
even if they sang it once,
I come to know them.
And I guess it's a long time now since I
still remember them songs.
They're short but
they made a tune and song out of it.

1. The literal translation is "*That young one, this is the one that can be taken. We nearly got shot, but it [the arrow] went over us. Whizzing by again.*" (MP)

The Mother Bear Was Singing

One time my mother said they saw a bear.
Somebody watched this bear.
A man.
Sneaked over and this bear was coming.
Slow, you know how they walk, slow—and two little cubs with her.
A-a-nd on the hillside this bear was digging roots.
Take roots and sh-shake them up and throw them at that little cubs.
They start sit there and eat.
Eat these roots.

Start sitting there,
and she pick up one—this little bear.
The other one
ran over and grab it from her mother,
and took, took the root away.[1]
And the mother got mad—he said the bear, the mother, just
hang over it—knocked the little bear, the cub,
and knocked her down and she laid there.
The little cub.
She laid there.

And this bear took off.
And after a little ways she kept looking back and this little cub was just
knocked out—knocked out the wind out of the bear.
And the mother turned back
and pick up the little cub
and kissed her and start to singing.
Right there—and this man just
sneak in through the grass and he heard it.
Rocked the baby, kissed the little bear a-a-nd the mother was singing there.
Rocking.

Finally it come to and he said the bear

breath,
give a deep breath on the little cub's face—say "piff, piff, piff" like that.
   (blows air out three times)
Give it some air and this little cub come to and then she start to singing.
This bear, the mother bear, rock and kept
this little cub and she set up
and hold this cub in the arms and start to singing.
And this man heard it.

And my mother used to sing that.
And they heard it.
It can sing.
Just like a human being.

I don't know any truth to it but—
guess that's true.[2]

1. As mentioned in the introduction, Apsáalooke language is gender neutral, and elders often use "he" and "she" interchangeably when they speak English. In this story, Lillian used both pronouns to describe the man and the troublesome little cub. To avoid confusion, I made the man consistently male. I made the cub female because Lillian used "she" slightly more often, but she probably thought of the little bear as simply a cub. (BL)
2. Lillian did not witness the events described in this story, but her mother told her when she was young. The date of the original story is unknown. (BL)

Green Beads from a Real Old Lady

When Lillian was a child, an old woman blessed her with green-bead necklaces and the wish that she grow to be a good, big woman (a productive, hardworking adult with a long life). The old woman carried her sacred beads inside her, a form of indwelling sacred power called baachíilape.[1] Such medicine powers can bring health, long life, wealth, or special abilities. The blessing happened around 1910. It was a special memory for Lillian. (BL)

When I was a girl, maybe about
five years old,

my father used to have a lot of people come to
stop at the mill—and sometimes
they call this man *Crazy Man*.
[This is about] his mother,
Child.[2]

That old lady would come around,
and I gave her her dish.
Plate.
Put the best meat on there and my mother said "Give her a good piece of meat."
She'd put the meat on there and bread.
And potatoes and stuff like that too.[3]
I'd take it and I'd spread a
cloth on the floor—they used to sit on the floor and eat.
They don't eat on the table,
so I spread the cloth in front of her.[4]

She'd sit down and I'd set the cloth in front of her and take the dish
for her—I get water for her, I get coffee for her a-a-nd she said that was a grea-a-at honor.
She said "That little girl,
she thinks a lot of me,
and she's good to me—she's ki-i-nd,
she's a kind little girl" she says.
"She's kind to me—therefore,
I'm going to give her a necklace,
this green necklace."[5]

Says "I have some [green beads] in my stomach" she says "and I keep them there.
They're my medicine" she says.[6]
"But you get her a string of green beads
a-a-nd let her wear that,
she grow to be a big,
good woman" she said.

"I want her to have that green beads for necklace."
After that I su-u-re like her.

A-a-nd I don't remember when she died—she was o-old.
Re-eal old lady.
Back then, back there around nineteen ten,
nineteen nine, eight,
maybe-e around nineteen hundred and eleven,
around there we have a lot of old people.
O-old grandmas, o-old grandpas, old people.
But we don't have any now.[7]

I'd like to [hand that down to my daughters].[8]
Barbara's got it.
She was so ki-i-nd to me—she always feeds me good,
and I said "This is Ma-ardell's good friend.
I come to know her through Mardell" I said.
"I'll fix a necklace for her, the green necklace"—that's why she
have that green necklace now—Mardell should have some.
Yes I'll have to make her one.
I'll look for some—I'll find some green beads.

Mary *said so too*—*"You make us one."*[9]
Said "I'll have some good [beads].
Not light green.
More like these [gesturing to her own necklace]—dark green."
I'll make some.
And it's from that o-old lady.
That's why I have these green beads.

1. The word *baachíilape* is from linguist Timothy McCleary (personal communication to Barbara Loeb, 2006).
2. The mill was nearby, so anyone coming there usually stopped by. She is saying that this story is about Crazy Man's mother whose name was Child, much as Swedes would say this is Sven the Younger, son of Sven the Elder. She is indicating exactly who gave her the medicine necklace. (MP)
3. Sharing the food you had was customary. To not offer food was inhospitable. Child was impressed with the little girl running around serving her. (MP)
4. In teepees, Crow families sat on buffalo robes and other belongings on the

ground, and they continued to sit on the ground when first living in houses. Furniture came with influence from Europeans. Medicine Crow (*Counting Coup*, 27) remembered the custom from his own childhood. "In those days, Crow families didn't have furniture." (BL)

5. It sounds like she is giving my mother the right to wear such necklaces, not an actual necklace. (MP)
6. Not all jewelry is medicine, but it often is. These green beads represent medicine because the old woman was said to spit them out of her mouth. They were a part of her body and a medicine to her, so they were sacred. Therefore, Mom's green-bead necklaces are also sacred, and they protect the wearer, giving health and good luck. (MP)
7. Wealth and longevity are supposed to be better now, but we don't have many elders anymore, real old people. People are dying of diabetes, cancer or kidney failure, and other modern-day diseases. (MP)
8. The gift came with the right to make green necklaces for four others, and those four in turn will be able to give the privilege to four others and so on. The beads are part of the family's inheritance. (BL)
9. Mary Hogan Wallace is one of Lillian's daughters. (BL)

CHAPTER SIX

Boarding School

Like many Indian children, Lillian attended a government-run Indian boarding school where they separated her from her parents and tried to reeducate her to white cultural values. Some children went far from home and did not see their families for years, but Lillian's school was in Pryor, so she at least saw her family more often. Corporal punishment was common, so the experience was harsh, and she had bitter memories.[1] If she was six, this chapter must begin around 1911. (BL)

They Put Me in the Boarding School

<u>Then,</u>
they put me in the boarding school.
And that's when I was about
six years old.
If the parents say "No don't take my child,"
they go and report it
to the superintendent,
and the
superintendent says "No.[2]
Just go and
if you have to put chain or padlock on the

people—just take that child and force—force it.
Take it to school, to the boarding school."
That's when we were treated bad.

And when they put me in the school,
I remember right that it was in the fall.
And I got so lo-o-onesome for my mother,
I got re-e-ally sick.
I cri-i-ed and cri-i-ed,
because they took me away from my mother.
And my mother said she always cry, go outside the house and cry.[3]
That's when I got really sick.
Lonesome.

But anyway they put me in the school,
and I finally got over it.
There's a lot of children there.
Some were young children, some older.
We have a big school.
Great big school building, big building.
A-a-nd there was a big boys' dormitory on that east side.
And then on the other side a big dormitory.
And a big partition in there,
and it's upstairs.
A-a-nd a big girls' dormitory and the little girls' dormitory.
And we had beds—nice bed though, nice blanket.

But on Fridays,
Friday afternoon after school, we go home,
with our parents.
Go home and sta-ay home with our parents during the weekend.
And on Sunday evening,
5 o'clock, they're supposed to bring us back to the boarding school.
A-a-nd the employees keep us there.
And that's when I get lonesome, a-a-ah I get lonesome for my mother.
I didn't hardly care for my father though.
He's cranky.

Always cussing and always cranky and you hardly see him.
Yeah he goes and gamble and play cards and other play always.

But anyway I was six years old when they took me in.
I felt bad and my mother felt bad.
Course if my parents say no,
the government is going to, the employee, the agent [is going to put them in jail].
At Crow they had policemens, about ten policemen.
They were Cro-ow!
And they're me-ean too.
They'd go and take some of the boys and girls to school,
a-a-nd if the parents say something these policemen's going to put them in jail.
They were no good.
They were mean.

And when Plenty Coups become a chief he quit that.[4]
He told them not to be mean to the people.
Because,
"They're not mean to you.
I want them to be treated right—I want these schoolchildren, pupils, Indians to be treated right."
He goes to Washington and tells them that there's got to be peace
among the Crow people and the policemen and the superintendent.
"If that superintendent at Crow Agency is bad,
fire him—get him away from the reservation, have a good man in there!"
That's our chief.
Plenty Coups said that.
But that I've heard—I don't know then.
I was just a child and in school and I don't know what's going on but we were told after that.
There's the superintendent,
Major Estep—we call him Estep.
He was bad, he was really bad.
Major Estep a-a-nd Asbury a-a-nd—[5]

Oh I forgot some of the superintendents but anyway I
went through school.
We have a teacher there and bring us
books and pencils—[government] issue.
We didn't have to buy—they'd give it to us.
We'd go to school and we'd go to the schoolroom and they make us sit
  down and,
and the teacher would get a big stick.
If there's any bad boys he
have to punish them.
Sometimes he <u>s-s-lap</u> them hard.
That way we got, all got scared—we daresn't talk back to any of them.
But me,
I'm always good to them and they're always good to me.
The people and all the employees,
they respect me, say I'm a good girl.

A-a-nd sometimes mothers come in with new children.
With a little girl.
Bring it in.
And they hunt me up—if I'm upstairs they call me or if I'm playing outside,
the mother comes to me and say "We heard about you.
You're a good girl.
You're getting big and good girl, good-natured,
and I want you to look after my little girl.
She's sma-a-ll and she's only six years old a-a-nd have to
force her to go to school and she'll be lonesome.
And I'm the mother and I get lonesome too.
But if I keep her home the agency's going to
put me in jail."
And they talk that way—the school employees were mean.
So I kept some.
Helped them.

We have a bi-i-g washroom, whole long washroom—there was sink,
so-o-ap and to-o-wels and co-o-mbs and brushes there.
No we don't have no brush—we had a comb pulls hairs so hurt bad.

And we have toilets.
Let's see now—one, two, three, four, five—
about six rows,
on this room—and on the other there's a partition in there
and another six rows.
There's what
we call the big girls' dormitory and the little girls' dormitory.

But,
we know then we have to obey.
We're supposed to go to bed.
Eight o'clock,
put us all to bed.
And some of them matrons are me-e-an.
They're re-e-e-ally mean.
If you talk back or
even if they tell you to go upstairs and
get ready or do something,
they scold us and <u>slap</u> us.

A-a-nd when I'm about ten years old,
they make the people, our parents, come to visit the school.
They quit that sending us home on weekends.
They quit that and then we kept in school.
But on Sundays our parents come to church—we had a big Catholic church
　right by the schoolyard.
And they make us line up and take us to church.
And after church,
we can visit our parents out on the lawn and they bring lunch.
And we sit down, eat with them.
After we get through we sit and visit our par-r-ents.
But when the ti-i-me,
about four o'clock comes,
they have to go home.
And we have to go inside.
That's when I get lonesome—o-oh my, get lonesome.
But that went on for ye-ears and then-n

the employees got so bad, they mistreated the pupils.

And we had a big garden for the school.
They put out a big garden for the school but they don't feed us them garden stuff.
Sometimes they'd feed us cabbage.
They had lot of cabbage.
A-a-nd sometimes we sneak around.
Slide,
in the ditch—get around until we got to the garden.
We'd pull up carrots—we stole them from the garden.
Carr-r-rots a-a-nd turnips.
And we'd take 'em back to the
yard and
hide in the ditch and break the leaves off.
Wash it good and then we'd steal a knife and slice it and we'd eat it.
Eat the carrots and the turnips. (chuckles)

And we have a big bakery downstairs and we have a big laundry there,
in a big building.
They detail us at work.
And we had about twenty milk cows,
and the big boys bring in milk and we work in the kitchen.
And we wash dishes—we used to have about three big tubs full.
A-a-nd we wash a-a-nd some of them dry-y and put away-y.

A-a-nd when mealtime comes they had about—o-oh let me see, one, two, three, four, five—
about twenty tables longer than this [gesturing to a table about six feet long].
Longer than this.
There's a row of tables over there—they make a-a-ll the boys sit to the table.
And then there's about three tables here—the girls'.
The big girls sit over there and the little girls sit over there.
A-a-nd
they make us eat.

But really somebody have to stand over there,
one over there—
watch the pupils eat—if anything,
a bad boy in the bunch, they
have to go and <u>slap</u> him and make him sit down.
O-or <u>push</u> him out of the room.
Go without supper.
Yeah they're really mean, <u>re-e-al</u> mean!

And
when we were in school—I think this is one reason why they shut that
   boarding school up—teacher used to
say "I don't want you to talk Crow.
Speak English!"
We tried to.
But we don't talk English good.[6]
Sometimes we whisper and if she catch us,
like me, catch me,
talking to another
girl or boy in Crow,
take my name down.
A-a-nd take so many names but at dinner time they have a bi-i-g long hall.
And they make the boys line up in that room.
They line up,
little boys and o-o-on up to the biggest boy.
They stand and here's the partition door.
A-a-nd the girls a-a-a-ll line up.
The big girls and on down.
And then–n-n she takes these names out.

Has a big one of them-m-m soap,
laundry soap—that Fels-Naptha soap.[7]
She take it in a bowl.
A lot of suds and just,
like me she says "This Lillian talk Crow.
And I got her name down.

She's got a dirty mouth.
I better wash her mouth."
So she sticks a finger in there,
in that soapy water and sticks it down my throat and wash it.
"Now she won't talk Crow because I wash her mouth."
And then they—
go—
on down.
Several girls she have to wash their mouth.
And then after that they make us march in the dining room, sit down and eat.
A-a-nd we daresn't say anything.
All them employees were *mean*!

1. For detailed information on Indian boarding schools in the United States, see Adams, *Education for Extinction*. (BL)
2. This was an Indian agent. Superintendents came later. (MP)
3. Crow people did not believe in crying inside the house. (MP)
4. Chief Plenty Coups was noted for managing government authorities skillfully. He challenged a number of policies. For another example, see "Ohchiish, She's a Man Dressed Like a Woman," chapter 7. (BL)
5. These Indian agents were E. W. Estep and C. H. Asbury. The latter became especially notorious for gathering and killing Crow horse herds in the early 1920s. According to McCleary ("Akbaatashee," 45–46) he ordered this destruction of tribal wealth to benefit white ranchers leasing Crow lands. (BL)
6. Most children, especially Mom's generation, did not speak English when entering school. Even my generation had difficulties because Crow was the primary language in our homes. (MP)
7. Fels-Naptha is a strong bar soap that smells like petroleum. (BL)

She Hit Us with That Big Strap

Sometimes they whip us [at the boarding school].
They've got a big strap, rubber hose.
They have a hole in the handle
and hang it on the wa-a-ll right by the doo-o-r and they whip us.

And that day is Sunday [the day of this story].
And I may be about eleven years old.

We went outside on the lawn to visit our parents.
And they said "If you visit your parents don't bring no-o
cooki-i-es o-or <u>nothing</u> that your parents bring."
But some do and I did too.
I had one of them-m sugar waffles.
My mother brought me some—I took some,
a-a-nd
took it down my stocking, push it down there.
Pretend I wasn't holding anything and these other girls did too.
They had some cooki-i-es and or-r-anges—they'd hide them under their arm.
Pretend they don't have nothing but she slap them and find out
they have something.
Like me I got these cookies.
Cookie up here in my slee-e-ve and
one, three, four in my stocking.
And she pulled my stocking down and found those cookies.
She had my name down.

And then that next Sunday she made us line up.
And Julia, Julia Big Hail,
she's my chum.
She was the first one—there was
Julia, me,
Iva—
Iva Bull Tail and Ethel.[1]
Ethel and
Annie Bell Rock,
a-a-nd—now I forgot the two—anyway
they had cookies or crackers or something that their parents brought them.
Hid them in their clothes but she found out we had those.

And that Sunday
she made us come down in the basement and line up.
She had the names down.
And Julia was the fir-r-st one.
She had us line up and she said "Now Julia you step out here."
A-a-nd she walk about a couple steps,

where we line up.
And she just took her by the collar and pull her dress!
They used to have buttons in the back.
Our dresses.
She pull that out and then she (claps hands)—start to
hit her with that big strap.
A-a-nd when they
whip her,
o-oh she's tough—just choo, choo, choo [sound of the hose].

She just
didn't scream—but I was the next one.
She pull my dress, my bare back. (claps hands)
She just slap me couple times and make big mark.
Purple.
(They said "Let's look at it" and it was turned purple.)
A-a-nd
just then I scream.
Ju-u-lia never made a sound but I scream.

I cried—and just then my adopted father [came to the door].
He couldn't get in!
But he took the stick and sla-a-sh the window.
[That was] Red Star.
He was very angry—he was the fir-r-st one at the door.
He took his horse whip and broke the window.
I screamed even louder then.[2]

And this matron
ran away.
And just beat up just two of us.
Didn't get to the other girls—there's about four,
about four more or five more.
She didn't get to them but Julia was the first one.
She give a good whipping and then I was next and I scream,
and that's when my adopted father come to the door.
Took a stick and sla-a-sh a window.

And then-n the parents all, people all, come from
out on the lawn and started talking.

A-a-nd I cried and went upstairs.
And <u>just</u> then my mother came in.
Clenched her <u>fists</u> and look for that woman.
And she asked these people "Where is she? Where is she?"
And they wouldn't—"We don't know! We don't know!"
They all tell her "We don't know."
She looked for her.
She said "She must be upstairs in her room,"
and they said "There's nobody up there."
But we were all scared.
The children-n, pupils, boy-y-s and girls and
women-n and men a-a-ll standing aro-o-und, moving around that hall.
Quite a sight.
And I was crying.

And my mother said "Somebody tell me where that
matron is."
They wouldn't tell her,
'cause we were all scared.
And one, I don't know who,
told her that she might, might be in that dark room.
We have a big playroom downstairs,
and up at the stairway, head of the stairway,
there's a dar-r-k room.
We call it the black room. (slight chuckle)
Dark room.
And we always say there's ghosts there.
And you know how [children are].
We're so-o afraid to go by that door.³

And they showed her the door.
We called it the dark room.
And she-e-e <u>just</u> went a-a-nd
grabbed the door knob and

slammed the door and just tore everything apart and she went in there
   and she
feel around and she got a hold of her.
And took her out a-a-nd
pull her hair up here on top of her head, drag her to the hall.
A-a-nd then men and women a-a-ll come around.

And the policemen was out on the porch.
They told my mother to
let her go.
And she said "No I'm going to take her outside—not in the building.
I'm going to take her outside and beat her up."
So she did—
was just dragging her out and the policemen came and
got her hands off.

But that's when they shut this boarding school.[4]
At that boarding school the who-o-le building stood there for a lo-o-ng time.
And I think it was ni-inetee-en
forty
when they took the who-ole building down.

They'd sent us back to school but
within about a month,
Plenty Coups, our chief,
went to Washington, report how they treating this boarding school.
Says "I want that superintendent [the agent] out of the office."
And they did, they put him out of the office.
And they
shut that school down and there was no more boarding school.[5]

   1. Ethel's last name was McAllister, but the name McAllister is no longer used on the reservation. In another part of the tape, Lillian explained what happened, speaking in Apsaálooke, which Mardell translated. "Ethel used the name McAllister because her father's name was changed. *They [white authorities] said, 'Your Indian name is no good. We will change it to McAllister which you can use.' But it's not their name, and it disappeared. Ethel was the only one who ever used it. She had an older sister, but she got out of school early and married Fred Dawes from Black Lodge. Her name was Alice*, but she don't go by McAllister." (BL)

2. Her adopted father probably came with her biological parents. They all were close and took care of one another. (MP)
3. Mom used to tell me that the school matron put them in this closet or room for punishment. The children feared it. (MP)
4. If Lillian was eleven at the time of this beating, she returned to the boarding school for several more years. She says she attended day school for about six months and was about sixteen when she quit. If her estimates are correct, she quit day school around 1921 and probably left boarding school in 1920. Bradley too says the Pryor boarding school closed in 1920. Bradley also says the school closed in 1912 and reopened from 1918 until its permanent closure in 1920 ("After the Buffalo Days," 329), but Lillian's stories suggest that she attended continuously. The reason for the discrepancy is unclear. (BL)
5. According to Bradley ("After the Buffalo Days," 324–27), the Crow debated considerably in the years before the 1920 closure. Some Crow wanted to continue the boarding school under Catholic direction. Others wanted a day school. Plenty Coups had complained to the Pryor school superintendent in 1918 about treatment of students and conditions at the school, but he too was conflicted. He shifted his own opinion at least once ("After the Buffalo Days," 324–25). (BL)

They're Going to Put My Mother in Jail

When Lillian's mother attacked the school matron, she and another woman were threatened with jail. In this story they ask a medicine man named Fog In the Morning to help them, and they give him quilts and blankets as a customary form of payment. When the lights are out, Fog In the Morning is probably making hand gestures with a fan in order to summon spirits, and when he repeats, "ée, ée," he is listening very carefully to what his medicine is telling him. The word ée *means yes in Apsáalooke. It is also a courteous term that tells the speaker they are paying attention.* (BL)

And they is going to put my mother in jail.
For beating up that matron.
And she said "I'm not scared.
You can put me to hard work.
I can stand it, I can work! I got fists" she says.
"I don't want that woman beating up my child"—she means me.
She whipped me.
A-a-nd my mother said "I don't want that to happen—I don't care if you throw me in jail.
Put me in prison," she says, "I'm not scared of you.

I-I-I'm <u>not scared</u> of any of you!" she said.
"Go ahead, take me to court!"

And they were going to too.
And one day the policeman came and said "Now you are wanted into court.
At Crow Agency."
A-a-nd they took her.
And they said there was another woman helping her [possibly another girl's mother].
"No" she said "there's no-o women was helping me, was all alone—I handled that woman.
I was going to pull her hair and drag her off to the outside and beat her up.
But the policeman got me so I quit" she said.
That's when I cried—but anyway they brought her [and another woman] to Saint X.[1]
Said "Now we have to take you to Crow to court."

And they had her in a buggy.
And come to a house,
this other woman's uncle's.
Fog In the Morning his name—he's a medicine man.
And when they got there that night the
other woman, they say she shed tears.
She said "They're going to
take us to Crow to jail, to court—and they're going to put us at hard work."
And she said "Maybe we can't stand it."

And my mother says "No—I'm not,
I'm not scared.
Let them put me in jail.
I got rights
to protect my child too,
and I'm going to go to court.
I don't <u>care</u> if you put me in prison."
She was mad.

A-a-nd

that other woman, it happened to be that [the] medicine [man] was her
  uncle. She took some stuff, quilts a-a-nd
giveaway [gifts].
Put it down in that man's
front and says "Here—I give you this quilt, I give you this blanket and I'll
  give you some more stuff,
if you pray for us—make medicine tonight a-a-nd,
and not go through this court."
Said "I don't want to go to court."

So,
"All right" this man says.
Clean the house.
Fix up everything."
And they said it was in the night and this is down in Beauvais—they had a
  big house there[2]
And when they come,
he said "Put the light out—make the dark.
Make it dark, put the light out."
And they said they were all sitting around,
and this man start to sing.
Burn incense and then start to singing.
Said they could see, hear, him-m moving his hand.
And then he kept talking and singing—talking a-a-nd,
and he says "ée"—that says "yes."
Says "ée."
"Ee."

Then after awhile he said "All right put the light on!"
They lighted the lamp and there's light.
Light in the house and everybody's looking—says "Tomorrow morning,
I know you're going to Crow to court.
But when you start,
well about halfway to the agency,
there'll be two men coming up on the hill, coming—two horseback riders,
come to meet you there on the road.
And they're going to say 'Turn around and go back to Pryor.

You're not going to court.
Everything is going to go all right.
Everything is all brushed off,
because Plenty Coups went to Washington.
They won't go to all this trouble.'"
See, when the room was dark he start medicine and he see that in the vision.
And then this lady gave him some more quilts.

And so tomorrow they hitch up the horses and the buggy.
They cross the river and come on up the lane, two lanes up that way.
A-a-nd just like this man see in the vision,
there were two riders coming up
to meet them on the road.
She said they stopped them,
these horseback riders—policemen.
Said "Now,
we've come to stop you.
You can turn around right here and go back home.
No more court.
You won't have to go to court."

See how their medicine worked? (chuckles)
Kind of strange isn't it?
So-o they turned around and came back.

1. Saint X was about midway on the old trail from Pryor to Crow Agency. Today the trail is paved highway. (MP)
2. Beauvais is a creek in the foothills of the Big Horn and Pryor Mountains, between Saint Xavier and Pryor, north of present-day Fort Smith. (MP)

Tree, You Got Medicine

This is about Lillian's future husband, George, when he was returning to boarding school around 1895 and his mother was trying to extend his brief summer vacation. The beads in the story serve as a prayerful offering. The location is a park-like stopping point on Sand Creek, about halfway between Lodge Grass and Crow Agency. According to linguist Timothy McCleary, ten enormous cottonwood trees stood there from the late 1880s to the early twentieth century, and the Crow called the place Balapáalapilake. Today, in English, they call the site the Holy Land.[1] (BL)

They say
George was about, o-oh they say he must be ten years old,
and they let him out on vacation in summertime.
Up at the boarding school, Crow.[2]
They took half of the boys, say
when they're—
ten—
to-o-o—
twelve, in that between—they let them go home and stay with their folks for
   a month.
And then they'd bring them back and put them back in school and those
   that
didn't go home, they let them go home too.
Until the school start they have to come back to the boarding school.

A-a-nd George
happened to be home then [at the time of this story].
In Lodge Grass.
A-a-nd one day his mother says,
"Now George" she says "time for you to go back to school.
We gather up
your clothes and we have to take you and I hate to take you.
I want you to be home with us but you have to go—if you don't go,
the policemen's going to take you, and me too, to prison."
So his mother said "All right let's go."
And they hitch up the team and they start coming.
From Lodge Grass.

And then-n way up there,
o-oh about halfways,
they saw ten—
ten trees.

Just like they've
put 'em in line.
A-a-nd his mother Emma, that's Emma, that's George's mother,
she comes and "George" she says,
"Here's some beads.[3]
Here's some beads—when we stop at noon we'll stop at that
ten trees.
We'll stop there for dinner.
We'll cook and eat and then we'll take you on to Crow."

But when they stopped there she said "Take these beads and give them to this tree.
A-a-nd say,
'Tree,
you got medicine.
Now you help me.
When I get to Crow Agency,
I don't want to go to school.
Some reason why you'd rather send me back home.'"
[Emma] said "You wish, you say that to the tree,
and put those little beads right by the root—come back."

So his mother gave him the beads.
So-o, Emma was cooking dinner.
"And now take them beads."
So George took the beads and talked to this tree.
Said he put the beads there by the root and said "Now tree,
when I get to Crow Agency I want you to make them white people there
to excuse me from school so I can come back home with my mother.
I don't want go to school."[4]
A-a-nd came back to his mother and she said "Well did you talk to the tree?"
A-a-nd George said "Yes.
I talked to the tree and I put the beads there."

And then-n after that,
they hitch up the team.

They start to Crow—this is in the wagon.
They kept driving and they got to Crow—it was in the afternoon about four thirty.
Said they stopped there and she said "Well you
gather up your clothes"—they had it rolled up in a sack.
Says "Now take your clothes and I'll go with you to the superintendent [agent]."
A-a-nd George and his mother walk up the stairway and then got to the superintendent.
And that man come out to the door.
Standing around like this he said, George was telling me.[5]
He said "Now,
I've got good news for you Emma."
She say "<u>What</u>? "
He said "You can take your boy back home—he can stay another month."

You know how he gave them beads to the tree and prayed?
As if that prayer was answered—"Came back.
Excused me again to go home with my mother."[6]
That strange?[7]

1. Timothy McCleary, personal communication to Barbara Loeb, 2006.
2. George Hogan grew up in Lodge Grass. He attended boarding school twenty-two miles away in Crow Agency, because one school served both communities. (BL)
3. Emma Chien, eventually spelled "Shane," was the daughter of a Crow woman and French interpreter Pierre Chien. (MP)
4. My father was often beaten about the ears at the Crow boarding school and lost his hearing early, but he was drawn to education and continued his learning at Carlisle Indian School in Pennsylvania. (MP)
5. He may have been standing with hands on hips, a posture Native people associated with white people. (BL)
6. Lillian's story implies that George spent several years in school at Crow Agency, then attended Carlisle and was gone for long periods. She told us, "Sometimes he work at summer, go out in a farm and work for farmers, earn money. He like it, but his mother didn't like it." Snell (*Grandmother's Grandchild*, 31) recalled his history somewhat differently, saying he left for Carlisle at age seven and did not return for thirteen years. She was George's daughter from his marriage to Helen Goes Ahead. (BL)
7. I once asked my mother what she thought might have happened. We concluded that the school was probably full. (MP)

CHAPTER SEVEN

Memories of Youth

These adventures happened during vacations, summers, and other times when Lillian was not in boarding school. (BL)

Them Boys Take Our Bread Away

Girls would come [to my house] and
we'd saddle up my pony and,
and we have a ni-i-ice gentle horse.
Why they always come to me when they want to play—
their mothers don-n't
fix a teepee or-r-r dolls like my mother does.
She fix us a little teepee
a-a-nd just like a sweat bath,
a lodge—make it,
and she tie it up like that.[1]
We a-a-ll cover it with canvas,
and cloth—and she gave us the cloth.
Hand us the cloth and says "All right it's all ready.
Just spread it over your lodge."

And we do, we a-a-ll crawl in there—maybe there's four,
maybe there's three of us.

And we had the pony there—we call it Chubby.
We call the horse Chubby because he's fat and round—not big.
Not big—we call him Chubby.
In English.
[In Apsáalooke] we call him Iischiapaapáshee [Round White Face].
His Indian name is Round White Face—we call him Chubby.
He's aw-w-ful tame.
We lead him around and sometimes we throw our
blankets and quilts and our tents over the horse,
and we all (claps hands sharply) get on him—three of us would ride and one
   was pulling the horse.

And we moved to another place where we could pitch up another tent there
   and we'd build a fire,
and we make little bread.
My mother taught us how to make bread so we make bread.
A-a-nd bake it to the fire.[2]
And when it gets through them boys would come over and fight over the
   bread.
They grab it and take it away from us and
my mother would get after them—says,
"Girls are having a good time,
playing nice and all that till you boys come and take all their bread away
   from them." (laughs)
Oh we used to,
we used to enjoy and kids, seems like they come over to my house.[3]

   1. In the past, little girls had play teepees and small sweat lodges. Agnes Deernose,
      just a few years younger than Lillian, had one (Voget, *They Call Me Agnes*, 91.)
      Pretty Shield described whole villages that she and her friends created in the
      1860s (Linderman, *Pretty-Shield*, 27–28). (BL)
   2. The girls were making pan bread, *baaxawuapáachua*, which consists of flour,
      Crisco, salt, baking powder, milk, and a small amount of sugar, all formed into a
      large, flat, round cake, like a thick tortilla and delicious. It was put in a frying pan
      propped near the open fire and slowly cooked from the heat. The pan can be put
      on top of the fire, but it is better propped. (MP)
   3. We didn't catch this on tape, but she said smaller children would come and play

with her because she played until a very late age. Even though she was older, she liked to play. (MP)

Cree People Start to Making Elk Teeth

When Lillian was a little girl, the Cree did not have reservation lands of their own, and some moved to the Crows', especially around Pryor. These memories must be from between about 1910, when she began to remember events, and 1916, when the Cree received the Rocky Boy's Indian Reservation. She is describing "elk teeth" that the Cree carved of bone and sold to Crow women to decorate their best dresses. (BL)

Our house is on top of the
hill—
hill-like, not too big a hill.
But we have a little creek running,
and on the other side of the creek is
smooth and nice.
In summertime or the springtime,
we even have berries there.
Chokecherries and gooseberries.
That's when I was a little girl.
A-a-nd we seen some people camped there.

And my father would go down there and visit these.
They're Cree people.
They come from Great Falls or up in Canada.
They didn't have no land.
They're not allotted like we did,
so they come over here to Pryor and wa-ander around.
They move camp from there and then they move camp above, *up river.*
And then they usually, most of the time, they camp right
close to our house.
Here's the creek,
our house that's on top of the hill,
and then on the bottom,
they always camp—there used to be about
eight,

eight camps—maybe you'd say eight families, ten or eight.
And they're good people.[1]
A-a-nd they're Crees.

So they start to making that elk tooth—the imitation [carved of bone].
The men
start making those.
They make those,
and they come out perfect.

My mother used to save bones for them Crees,
and they take bones and they dry-y good and dry,
and they take a block,
a-a-nd they chop these bones
the right size.
Keep them and keep chopping, chopping.
And then they make elk tooth.
Them elk tooth you see today on the dress?
They make them ju-u-st the shape of that elk tooth.

And then pretty soon they polish.
A-a-nd they bore a hole in there.[2]
And then they say,
"There's ten [ready to sell]."
They finish ten.
They charge them ten apiece—ten's in a bunch.
"Here's ten and here's another ten.
If you want
twenty pieces or thirty or fifty pieces,
we'll tie them in bunches,
ten in a bunch."
So they start selling them—they make good [they make a living].[3]
I may be about—
eight or nine.
I know it well.
They stayed *quite some time*,
about a year,

and they moved *downriver—they stayed there* among them big trees.⁴
There were quite a few lodges.

And Plenty Coups *said "They're poor but they're good people.*
We should divide up
some of our lands and give it to them.
If we do they can live here."
The Crows said no.
Especially my father.
He got up and said "No!
These people will have children.
When they have children,
this land, Pryor Mountains and on up,
clear pretty near to Billings Highway,
all around there, they will own it all."
The Crows said "Don't give it to the Cree."
Somehow,
the Crows didn't want them in our reservation.
They herd them back
to Great Falls or up there at Rocky Boy,
and they made them stay there.⁵

Now they have housing.
They're well off now—that's good country.
And sometimes we go and visit them.
My daughter-in-law is a Cree.⁶
Her mother's back there,
and we used to go down there—they're good people.⁷

1. Mom used to say they were hard workers. That is probably what she meant by "good." (MP)
2. They carefully bored a hole into the top of each tooth so they could pass a thong or sturdy string through and attach the tooth to a dress. The thong used to be a very long piece of hide that went around the inside of the dress, stringing up the teeth, then tied on the outside on the sleeve, with the thong ends left to dangle from the sleeve in a pretty fringe. Construction is similar today, but long strands of string, sinew, or yarn replace the hide thongs. For more information on attaching elk teeth, see "My Mother Showed Me How to Sew Elk-Tooth Dresses,"

chapter 15. (MP)
3. The industry provided income for the Cree and gave the Crow a way to continue making their prized dresses even as settlers took their land, and elk herds dwindled. The Crow used only the two eyeteeth of each elk, so they would have needed to hunt 50–150 elk for a single dress, an unlikely feat when the herds were shrinking. (Lillian is wearing an elk-tooth dress in figures 20 and 21 and her aunt, Clara White Hip, is wearing one in figure 2.)
4. This must have been on Arrow Creek, the little creek by the road to Pryor. (MP)
5. The Cree were refugees from Canada, and people called them "landless Cree." In 1916 they finally received territory northeast of Great Falls, on the abandoned Fort Assiniboine Military Reserve. Their leader was Rocky Boy, so today their home is called Rocky Boy's Indian Reservation. Stone Child was another name for him. (MP)
6. This is Berneice Day Child, my brother Adam Singer's wife. (MP)
7. Cree were joining the Crow by 1900, mainly in Pryor, and Superintendent Winfield W. Scott described them as industrious people whose numbers reached about one hundred by 1912. He said they sometimes worked for the Crow, receiving payment in horses and cattle. See Bradley, *After the Buffalo Days*, 230. (BL)

Elk-Tooth Dresses

Elk-tooth dresses belong to a sumptuous tradition from at least the 1850s when Swiss artist Rudolph Kurz sketched Crow women wearing them. This account continues the story of Cree elk teeth and explains how Crow women prepared and used them. (BL)

When the Cree got a big bone or one long one,
then they cut it ri-ight in the middle
and break it.
And that's an elk tooth, a set [a pair].[1]
A set there and they'd make another one, another set, another set.
Pretty soon they make ten.
A-a-nd
they string them together in a bunch.
And <u>we</u> buy them,
and start makin-n-ng elk-tooth dress.[2]
We thought that was pretty scarce and
they all want but sometimes
we have <u>re-eal</u> elk tooth.

Real ones.

I know my mother had one [dress] that was made out of black felt—it was
 black felt.
She made that and put beads on—they all put beads
around the neck and make a diamond shape in front and then in back [see
 fig. 21].³
Then on the sleeves and then the dress,
hem it with red.
If it's a black one,
a black material,
they put red trimming
on the hem and the sleeves.⁴
A-a-nd that's when it looks nice.

Then they put the elk tooth on there.
When the elk tooth is done [carved],
you have to put little
color on the root.
Just like the
teeth of an elk.
You know they left a little meat on there [on real teeth] and then dry—and
 then
they make holes on them and they sew them onto the dress.
And that's where we have elk-tooth dress.
Real teeth were scarce,
but they make the dresses because there's Crees around there make elk
 tooth.
And they look like real.
They're experts.

Now we get [bone teeth]
somewhere down in—
o-oh like
a store there, that Buffalo Chip.⁵
In Billings.
He orders

in a bunch, a who-o-ole bunch.
They come in a plastic bag and I don't know where they
come from—where they ordered the elk tooth.
They come
in a bunch, sack them up in a plastic bag—hundred tooth.
Hundred tooth in every bag.
And they sell them.
I think they sell for about,
about $50 a sack.
And there's hundred in there.
All them sacks carry a hundred in there.
And they look like <u>real</u>.
A-a-nd
that's when we
put a little color on them and then we start sewing.

1. She is describing a Cree carver making a matching pair, just as an elk has two matching ivories or eyeteeth that always go together as a set. (MP)
2. Crow women make elk-teeth dresses of rich wool trade cloth and attach curved lines of the gleaming teeth, sometimes in rows almost to the hem. Even today they wear these handsome dresses for parades, dances, and other traditional events and give them as gifts to new brides. (See "They Had a Buggy Full of Dresses and Blankets and Shawls," chapter 12, and other wedding stories.) Yet these are not just pretty clothes. They once symbolized successful hunters and prosperous families; they were so esteemed that fur trader Edwin Thompson Denig valued elk teeth for fifty dollars for one hundred in the 1840s or early 1850s. He wrote, "A frock is not complete unless it has 300 elk teeth, which, with the other shells, skins, etc., could not be bought for less than $200." This was a goodly amount for those times. (See Denig, *Fire Indian Tribes*, 158). Today women have to purchase bone teeth at trading posts and Indian art stores, but the dresses remain costly to make and still represent wealth and prestige. (BL)
3. By the mid-nineteenth century, Crow women had standardized the way they decorated elk-tooth dresses, and they use the same style today. To frame the neck opening, they cut a piece of contrasting wool and appliqué it in place. The main motif is a large diamond that becomes two triangles after the neck opening is cut. One triangle is at the throat and one at the back, pointing toward the waist. (One of the triangles is clearly visible in the portrait of Lillian with her daughters, illustration 21.) Two smaller triangles at the shoulders point toward the neck. Once the piece is sewn into place, most women simply edge it with a lane of white

beads, but they occasionally add a touch of extra beading or a few elk teeth at the throat, especially if they have real teeth to feature (see figs. 2 and 21). (BL)
4. Elk-tooth dresses are made of red, black, dark blue, or green wool. Neck, sleeves, and hem are trimmed in a contrasting color. Dark blue or bright green wool usually trims red dresses. Red is used to trim darker dresses. Especially diligent workers sometimes add beading to the sleeves and hem, but this is rare. (BL, MP)
5. Buffalo Chips is a small store in Billings that sells Native artwork and supplies for making traditional clothing. (BL)

My Father Put Pants on the Dog

My father had a puppy and he raised the puppy and made him mind.
He'd talk to him and said "Sit down" he'd say.
"Sit down, I want to talk to you."
And that dog would sit and look.
Says he had eyes just like a cat he says.
Brown—sometimes they'd turn yellow, sometimes gray he says.
And he'd just sit there.
Sit and look.
Listen.
He had
head like this—listen (cocks her head sideways).
Pretty soon he'd go this way (cocks head other way)—he'd listen.

A-a-nd this time,
he paint up the dog's face—he took some ni-i-ice paint.
Asked my mother for red paint and she had made a buckskin,
sewed a buckskin and had some of that red paint in there.[1]
So she hand it to him—so he paint his face.
Paint his face—he said that dog would just sit there, look on.
And he made red flannel that tied to under his ear
and put the brass [hair ornaments],
dangling on two sides *near the temple*.[2]
He braid that [red flannel] and he stick it onto the dog's ear, under.
And he put a necklace on there and put a shirt on him.
And put the pants on him and he says "Now," (raps on the table)
"you go and look for a woman, a sweetheart.
Now you go to a house and—

and look for this woman.
And that'll be your sweetheart.
Now go on!" he says—so he turn the dog loose.

And this dog go.
I think he went over
to different ones, different houses.
Says he'd come to the doorway.
Just sit there.
Sometimes he wink.
And wink on the other eye.
Just set there—he had this
red cloth up there,
and he'd paint his face—necktie and a shirt, pants, he'd sit there.
And he even had bracelets.
Sit there, look on—go this way. (tilts head)
This way. (tilts head other way)

And they know him—says they call him
Pohpúummaache, call him.[3]
[They said] "He's up to something!
And they even paint his face.
They even put the little brass things on and earrings too and he's up to something."
And one woman said "I know.
He's flirting!"
(laughs) He mind, he knows.

And my father still have that [dog] and one day they went after wood.
In a wagon.
My mother and him.
They went to a little coulee up on-n the other side [of the river].
Here's our house, here's the road a-a-nd the river, and across there.
They went over to haul.
Bring some wood.

On the way,

he stopped and they saw a rattlesnake.
And
that dog, he go for it.
Ran around there and,
and try to get away but this (claps hands) rattlesnake just <u>jump</u> at him and
bit him on the shoulder, on the arm.
And within a few minutes,
his eyes turned—he laid there, tried to kick.
And my father and mother seen it and said,
"Sure too bad he's going to die."

So my father he killed the rattlesnake.
A-a-nd he stood there and didn't know what to do.
So this is kind of nasty,
but he went over,
took his pocket knife,
cut a little piece there in the flesh,
in the dog's arm,
and he said he's just unbutton—"There's no water around so I'll just pee on that."
So he took his belt off and he pee on this
place where the snake bit him.

He's laying there just like dead.
And they said "Poor dog, you just have to die and lay there."
So they left him,
and they got wood.
A load of wood—come back.
To the house.
And here,
next thing you know,
this dog was just
coming home.[4]

That's a tru-ue story and we seen it.
I may be about
ten years old.
And my brother,

he might be about twelve years old.[5]
We seen it.
We seen it [when he dressed the dog too]—we just laugh and laugh.

People all know in Pryor,
so when he had him, the chief,
Chief Plenty Coups, says "Now you train dogs like that.
I'll give you two horses if you'll give me that dog."
And my father's "All right, you don't have to give me the horse.
You just keep that dog." (chuckles)
He gave it to Plenty Coups. (laughs)
Yeh.

Well all the Pryor people,
they know.
He learned.
He can't talk but he sure listen—he understand all the language he tell him.
My father sure taught him. (laughs)
He says "Now you go and find a woman—flirt!
Go flirt to different women—go on!"
Made him go put on necktie. (laughs)
We just laugh and said "You'd better find your necktie."
So,
my brother or my mother or somebody find a necktie,
and he put the necktie on. (laughs)
He minds.

1. The red is probably ochre, a rust-colored, natural earth pigment that has long been a popular color. Her mother was probably using it to decorate a buckskin garment. Women also use it to color the part in their hair, especially when they wear elk-tooth dresses. The paint is worn for its beauty and is not necessarily symbolic. My mother had her family put a red earth paint called *úuwe* on their foreheads to prevent sunburn when we paraded. (MP)
2. He is making ornaments for the ears and sides of the head, in a style that men once wore on dress occasions. (BL)
3. This is a term like "Short Stuff." (MP)
4. It surprises me that Grandpa wanted to save the dog. If a pet dies, the Crow believe that it takes the place of a member of the family, whose life is spared. The death of a pet, then, is not to be mourned because a human life is worth much more. (MP)
5. They were four or five years apart, so she was probably eight to ten and Caleb

twelve to fourteen. (MP)

The Movie Outfit

First thing you know there was a
movie outfit.
From-m California I guess.
They come to Pryor and made all the people take part in this taking pictures.
They want more people,
so we a-a-ll moved to Pryor Gap,
and we a-a-ll camped there.

A-a-nd my father happened to be the chief [in the movie].
They pick him [cast him] as a chief—he'd sit there and hold a pipe and start to talking.
And this lady, the star,
she's May Old Coyote.
She was youn-ng and good-looking and nice.
They pick her and,
and she was about,
o-oh twenty-one years old—she was ni-i-ice looking.
She had braids way down here, big braids.
She was good-looking—*it was good.*

They made my father a chief.
I remember there was a cliff there, not too high,
and they make him sit there
and hold a pipe and start to speaking.
Hold an eagle
feather here and then hold the pipe on the other hand,
start to look up—and
of course a lot of people looking on.
A-a-nd I happened to see him there.
After that, all the acting, they'd take them out somewhere down the road or some hill there.[1]
I don't go there to watch them. (laughs)

1. The movie is *Before the White Man Came*, a romanticized silent film released in 1920. It starred Barney and May Old Coyote, with Bull Shows as a chief, and was filmed at Pryor Gap, an ancient favorite camping place near the Castle Rocks (three buttes in the Pryor Mountains). Lillian completed her first beadwork during the filming (see "You Have to Know How to Bead," chapter 8). Filmmakers also used the Yellowstone River as a location for shooting. (BL, MP)

We'd Go to Crow Fair in a Caravan

Crow Fair is the biggest, most spectacular of all Crow celebrations. Here Lillian takes us to the early years, between about 1910 and 1920, when families spent days traveling by wagon just to get there. Her memories are full of fun, but the story has a subtle political subtext too. The Crow have a long tradition of summer gatherings, and to the chagrin of agents, the districts began inviting other districts for summer powwows. People happily "moved" to the host districts, leaving their farms for long visits.[1]

An agent named Samuel Guilford Reynolds established the fair in 1904, hoping the Crow might stay put if they had a post-harvest, fall celebration to anticipate. He tried to instill agricultural pride, with prizes for the kinds of crafts and farm produce Lillian mentions, but he wisely left room for traditional horse racing, dancing, drumming, and foot racing.

A century after this story, the fair is pure Apsáalooke, and for several days each year the Crow proudly proclaim it the "teepee capital of the world." They devote mornings to parades with beautiful beadwork, afternoons to all-Indian rodeos, ever-popular horse races, and enthusiastic betting, and nights to dancing to the deep sound of drums, all activities that recall the old, nomadic ways of living. Horses share the parades with cars and trucks now, but the agricultural exhibits are gone, and the whole event is in August, much like the old summer gatherings. It is a grand celebration.[2] (BL)

When I was young, my mother done all the work [of putting up camp at celebrations].[3]
We moved, put up our teepee, and
we all look forward [to good times]—we kids play around and
have a great time while our mothers work,

and they invite other districts.
Like Pryor put on a big powwow, they invite the Black Lodge or the Saint X
    people.
They a-a-ll flock over there and they put up a big camp,
and they have big parades and o-oh we look forward for a big parade.[4]

But this Crow Fair,
we didn't have no cars then.
We had to go on just like a caravan.
Somebody leads the
team and the wagon
and their tents and all their belongings—we
travel on to Big Horn valley and then on to Crow Agency.[5]
And on the way,
there's buggi-i-ies and horse rider-rs and dogs. (chuckles)
We used to like dogs—they
follow and bark a-a-nd here we come.

Com-me—
Stop one camp, the first night we'd camp somewhere.
And the horses turn loose—in the morning we'd bring the horses and
harness them—saddle up the horses and we'd go on again and we'd get to
    Saint X,
and we'd camp there again,
because we're on a team and buggy.
Horses.
We'd put out a camp.

Maybe one family wouldn't go,
since they don't have no parade horses or no teepee or no tent.
Maybe one family or two families don't go.
But the rest of the families [do]—there's not too many families.
There's o-o-oh, they may be, when we camp they may be about twenty
    tents up.
Different families.
But (claps hands) in the morning we saddle up again and go—go until we
    get to the Crow camp.

And there all these camps already—teepees up already.
And here we come, Pryor people.
This bunch camp here and the Black Lodge people camp there.
Lodge Grass people, Saint X people, and the Pryor people.[6]
A-a-ll put up teepees—we had l-o-ots of horses, everybody had horses I guess.
We su-u-re like the Crow Fair.

One year—we were teenagers then.
We were
kept at the [boarding] school,
and they won't let us go home.
But during the fair,
the parents are responsible if
these teenagers won't come back or
be on a wild party or anything like that.
Said they'd talk to the parents, [ask] if they can take care these
to the fair and bring them back.
And the parents say "Yes we'll take care of them."

And we [Caleb and I] ride.
We always have a horse and a saddle of our own.
I know my parents used to buy me a horse.
And a good saddle.
A-a-nd my brother has too and all these people, they have horses.
And we go on to Crow Fair.
And gee that's good—we liked that.

But now we have a car, automobiles.
That time we don't have no automobile, no cars.
This is around nineteen—
around nineteen—
hundred and seven,
eight, nine, ten, eleven.
Those years.

And they had what they call exhibit hall [to display crafts and farm

produce].
My mother don't do that.
She take some beadwork over.
She has a table there.
Put names on, put numbers on them and display them.
And somebody have to be responsible there to watch all the stuff.

My aunt, Clara White Hip,
she's Clara May's grandmother.
She went to school at Fort Shaw,
a-a-nd she learned how to speak English.[7]
She's married
and has her own family and we always enjoy visiting her at Crow Fair.
Cause she's my aunt, my mother's sister—and they look ali-i-ike.
And she always bring in some exhibits—
how she make the syrup,
and jelly,
and bread.
A-a-nd she has a table
and bring her exhibit there—sometimes she gets the first prize.

And the different ones [exhibits] are
in a big lo-o-ng hall.
We come in there to look at the stuff.
Some put it on pretty quilt.
A-a-nd [they show] the way they make the elk-tooth dress—they display them hanging up.
We used to go in there, look at everything.
But there's people there that watch all the
stuff where somebody might go in there and steal something.

We like that.
My mother used to
make moccasins—
how they tan the buckskin.
She'd display some moccasins already sewed.

And the sinew—this is a deer sinew, this is an elk sinew.
And this is the man's moccasin, this is the woman's moccasin,
this is a baby's,
young child's moccasin.
She just put those all on exhibit.
She gets paid for them.
Or get the first prize or the second prize.
And we'd break camp and go back to Pryor and we're sad.

But anyway we (claps hands) have lots of fun—we ride horses,
ride around, up the hill, down the hill—we even (claps hands) jump over that big ditch.
Made our horse go run and they'd get (claps hands) on the ditch and jump over that big ditch.
Back and forth.
What if the horse fell down or we
go in that ditch?—but we never do.
(chuckles) Our horses know too.

Oh dear.
I'll never go back to the young
times,
have those times again.[8]

1. The Crow used to "move" from camp to camp when they were nomadic, and even today they "move" for summer celebrations. They set up tents and teepees and build leafy arbors to shade outdoor kitchen and dining areas. They bring tables and chairs, and some families even bring a kitchen stove. (BL)
2. In her introduction to Agnes Snell's life story, Becky Matthews aptly noted that the Crow "came to view the fair as an opportunity to celebrate themselves." See Matthews in Snell, *Grandmother's Grandchild*, 11. (BL)
3. Women were still doing the work of putting up camp, just like nomadic days. Nowadays men do just as much. (MP)
4. When nomadic, the Crow enjoyed parading from camp to camp with themselves and their horses in colorful array. For early Crow Fairs, they did much the same, covering their horses, themselves, and wagons with fine beadwork. They paraded to the accompaniment of Crow drummers and singers. A century later, they still do that, except that cars and flatbed trucks have replaced the wagons. Drummers ride on the truck beds. (BL)
5. Today, Crow Agency is a quick seventy miles from Pryor, on good road. Crossing

the open plains by wagon took three days. (BL)
6. Families from the same district camped together, often claiming the same part of the fairgrounds each year. Similarly, Leforge described close relatives camping near each other during nomadic times. See Marquis, *Memoirs*, 148. (BL)
7. Fort Shaw is a small town in northern Montana, about twenty-five miles west of Great Falls. It began as a military outpost and was later used as an Indian boarding school. (BL)
8. For additional information on Crow Fair, see Yellowtail, *At Crow Fair*; Loeb, "Crow Fair"; and Medicine Crow, *From the Heart of Crow Country*, 119–23.

I Jockeyed

The Apsáalooke have been horse people for centuries, and they gamble enthusiastically, so racing has long been in their blood. The events described in this story happened around 1915. (BL)

We had race horses.
And I love those horses.
All these girls my age,
we don't have no car.
There were no cars around.
[I was] about ten years old,
around there,
and we have to ride horses.
And seems like there a lot of horses—everybody had horses.

And my father raised wheat and he sold the wheat—haul the
wheat over to Edgar and sold the wheat.
And he said,
"This money goes for horses.
We'll buy a horse for
Caleb and we'll buy a horse for her."
And I li-ike it.

And then they bought the horse.
They bought him a
black horse,
with white face.

He was pretty too.
And they bought me a sorrel horse.
A-a-nd I just ride him and ra-ace, practice race, and gee he's a <u>fa-ast</u> horse.
A-a-nd,
sometimes they bring our horses to the school,
a-a-nd we ride to the fairgrounds where all the people have
something doing, either throwing [arrows] or
riding horses—bet on horses and
som-me men all circle around, tell stories and start singing and stuff like
   that—every Sunday.[1]

And they'd take us girls down to that place where they
have races—we'd go there.
And sometimes men in the audience say—
they call me, they say "Her horse is fast.
And we'll get another horse to match."
And said "We'll bet on the horse."
A-a-nd my father'd come and say,
"Undo that saddle—we're going to race your horse."

I didn't like it then.
Say "A-a-ll the girls all riding horses and you take my horse."
"No—them men want to see that this horse is fast."
So they did—couple times on Sunday.
They come and got and make me take my saddle off and took this horse.
And sure enough,
he outrun all the whole bunch. (laughs)
Couple times.

And one time,
when the girls all gathered around the grandstand,
some are off the horse, some are still on the saddle,
and me and some of them moved back
to-o-o some buggies there.
Towards the big ditch.
Kind of line up—buggies.
We went over there for something,

and just then the noise—so people all
went to see what was going on—it's my horse.
Had a run away.

My brother was riding.
He'd take the le-ead and then-n the other horses couldn't catch up with
    him—around the bend, around the stretch,
(claps hands emphatically) he didn't go straight—he come across around the
    bend and they just
go to the big ditch—everybody's watching—big ditch and
jump over that big ditch and went out clear-r up the road.
A-a-nd men was after him—they raced, they couldn't catch up with him.
And that was my horse.
And my father says,
"She-e's the one that run the horse, train that horse." (laughs)

And Walter Chief says,
"She's a jockey" he said[2]—"We put her on and jockey.
We can take her to a fair.
Bridger and Billings and maybe Helena.
A-a-nd up at the Crow Fair and that"—I jockeyed.

By-y goll-ly them horse races are dangerous!
A pony is all right to ride around.
They prance a-a-nd
kick around like
pretty horses but when you ride a race horse,
o-o-o-o.
Ye-a-ah, you might fall off, you might die. (chuckles)
Race horse riding is dangerous.

Ye-a-ah, one time
we nearly took off several times. (claps hands)
Went around the bend and just [as] I got way over here I take the lead.
*No one caught me as we went to the finish line—everyone started hollering
    and whooping.*
It was at Pryor.

And Walter Chief *said "See I told you so!"* (chuckles)[3]

1. They were probably throwing arrows or horseshoes. Throwing arrows is a game the Crow still play. They throw one main arrow, then all arrow throwers try to get close as possible, a game of skill. People gamble at it too. (MP)
2. In another part of the tape, she said she thought she and Walter Chief were cousins by European reckoning. "He was Old Dwarf's son. *Old Dwarf himself*, my grandmother, my father's mother *raised him. He in turn raised Walter Chief. My father was alone, so Old Dwarf took him too. He made them* [Walter and Bull Shows] *brothers. They were all kinfolk anyway.*" (For more on Old Dwarf, see "Uncle Old Dwarf Instructs Me to Live Right," this chapter.) (BL)
3. See Medicine Crow (*Counting Coup*, 49–52) for another horse-racing story, including a humorous account of the first time he jockeyed, at age eight. The horse was the slowest in the bunch but fast enough to terrorize its young rider. (BL)

They Have Dances

We hardly knew that New Year's [Day] before around ninetee-een
ten, ninetee-een—
About 1915,
we come to know, to celebrate the Christmastime and New Year's.[1]
And then they put up a big round dance hall.
Down the creek we say.
Bi-i-g round house, just like the one that's there
in Crow now.
A-a-nd,
I guess we're kind of poor on electricity—don't know how they work it—
lamps I guess.
They put on
dance every night.
And during the day they have dances too-o a-a-nd parade.
I remember there was
one at Pryor, one at Saint X,
and one up at Black Lodge, one at Reno, Garryowen.[2]
That's four dance halls.
I think Lodge Grass have one too so that makes it five.
Round houses.
They have dances in there.

Although we don't have electricity in there. (chuckles)

[They had dances at] Christmas too.
Even it's wintertime, it's snow on the ground,
they [used to] move and put up their tents there.
And I know we put up our tent, big tent,
and put straws right around the
outside,
and the inside to.
Make our bed on there.[3]
And they put a stove inside.
And
we don't know what cold winter is.
Outside there'd be men playing arrow.
"Aa-ii!"—yell and,
and the children all running arou-n-nd, horses all run.
Dogs barking.
Emmm—I'll never forget that time.
And here's supper going on ready or dinner going on ready.
And our home cooking—we like it.
They can camp anywheres.
Timber all around—good camping place.

They still have a big,
long house—they call it the community house.
The Pryor do.
They have dances there, hand games,
feasts.
They have them there.
A-a-nd Lodge Grass has a dance hall there.
And the Black Lodge they have it too.
And Wyola has it too.
The Lodge Grass people have so many powwows there.
Yeh.
They known to be the
outstanding (chuckles)
dancers and stuff like that.

Reno—there's five districts [that have dances]—there's Wyola,
Lodge Grass, Reno,
Black Lodge, Pryor, Saint X—six districts.
They do—they like it.

There used to be no beer, no drinking.
But for couple
seasons they
had people drinking.
They sure don't like it and they put a stop to that.
A drunk can't come in the dance hall.
If they do there's policemen right there and the manager says "Take him back out."
They get a hold of him and take him.
Put him in jail so there's no drinking in the dance.
And they have good times.

And now, the hand games, they have a tournament,
because they're betting.
Bet money on those—they have
different songs too.[4]
A-a-nd the war dance, they have a
different song.
And the owl dance, they have women dance—they have a,
a song different from the war dance song.
They have different songs.[5]
And this Medicine
Dance [Tobacco Dance].
Baasshússuua.[6]
They call it Beaver Dance or Medicine Dance—they have different songs too,
and there pretty words to them.
They nice words to them.

> 1. The Crow celebrate often, and Christmas and New Year's are two of the European holidays they have adapted to their own ways, including drumming, singing, and dancing, as well as generous giveaways, namings, adoptions, and the honoring of accomplishments. The New Year's dances last at least two nights, ending at midnight on New Year's Eve, when dancers form two concentric circles that

rotate in opposite directions, so the people in the inner circle can shake hands with those in the outer circle. For additional details on Crow celebrations, see Wolf, *Reaching Both Ways*, 79–122, and Deernose in Voget, *They Call Me Agnes*, 68–201. (BL)

One year at Lodge Grass, around 1980, the dances were so jazzy, we danced again the night of New Year's Day. At Crow Agency, the dance is bigger because they have "district nights." One night is Big Horn night, one is Black Lodge night, and so on. (MP)

2. Reno is the modern name for the Fallen Bell District. It is located near a store known as Garryowen, so the district is sometimes called Garryowen. It is in the area where the Battle of the Little Big Horn was fought, and is named for Maj. Marcus A. Reno, second in command to George Armstrong Custer. "Garryowen" is the Irish tune that Custer's Seventh Cavalry favored. (MP)
3. They placed straw on the outside of tents and teepees to insulate against cold and used it under beds for cushioning. (MP)
4. Hand games are old-time gambling contests. Many tribes play them. Each team has someone conceal one or more small game pieces in his or her hands. A guesser on the other team attempts to identify their location. The Crow hide one game piece, and each team has a "medicine man" who functions somewhat like a team head, guiding the players, designating who hides, and handing them the game pieces. While the guesser on one side is thinking, the other team sings and jokes energetically in hopes of breaking the guesser's concentration. It is a lively game. The tribe holds especially vibrant annual tournaments in which teams from all the districts participate. Each team wears handcrafted, matching outfits designed by an artistic woman of the district. (BL, MP)
5. The owl dance occurs only occasionally, but celebrations like New Year's dances usually include one. Women ask men to dance, usually husbands of female relatives with whom they have license to pretend to flirt and tease, and men should not refuse. Dancers stand in a circle with arms around each other's waists, stepping sideways to the rhythm of songs and small hand drums. Powwows also include grass dances, traditional dances, chicken dances, jingle dress dances, fancy dances, fancy shawl dances, and so forth. (MP)
6. *Baasshússuua* is the general term for any Tobacco Society meeting, whether a formal adoption or regular meeting. A different term is used when society members gather to plant tobacco seed. See chapter 9 for more information on the Tobacco Society. (MP)

Julia, She's My Best Friend

My chum Julia,
her and I would just go aro-o-und and pick be-erries—pretend we're o-o-ld ladies.[1]
We took cane and we walk like an old lady.

Pick berries and talk like an o-old woman.
And that lady, Julia,
she's my best chum.
A-a-nd she always called me "My dear Lillian."
And me too.

And that Julia she always
suck her thumb.
And she said "Come on now—I'll lay down and suck my thumb.
Try to
take it out."
A-a-nd she'd be laying there sucking her thumb and I'd (claps hands sharply) get on top of her and
push her head and try to pull that thumb and just—
o-oh she's <u>stro-ong</u>!
And sometimes I try to get help.
Somebody would hold her head down and her body down and try to pull that thumb out.
Can't do it.
She's pretty sto-out.

They say her grandpa is
known to be a stro-o-ng man.
And sometimes he even
pulled a buffalo by the tail
and
swing it over [a river when butchering].
They say he's that strong he can
wrap the tail around his hand and
throw him over.
That's how strong—that's her grandpa.
And so she inherits that lifting up anything—she's got strong arms.

She died last—it's been two years ago now she died.
Yeh she's a ni-ice woman.
All the others I don't care to know about them,
'cause they have their own life.
But Julia, I love her.

Sure missed her.
She's my <u>be-est</u> friend.

One time
we were playing, her and I.
Her mother is a medicine.
She has roots fixed up for this occasion,
especially on a woman
giving birth.
She'd be out there and here she goes in the tent
and work on her, help her out.
Here we out there, listen—sometimes we peek in the door. (laughs)
She gets after us.
But we, we want to know what she's doing.
A-a-nd that's why we copy all this when we play—we pretend we got the medicine,
and we're taking care of the woman in labor and
we copy her—we know how. (laughs)
Oh dear, her and I used to have
good times.

And one time,
we were wa-ay out on the hill,
my folks and her folks and some others.
Oh there were about six tents there—people living out there, working in the shearing pen.
They're shearing the sheep.
It's the white man's sheep but they work for the white man and we a-a-ll camp and
we have a ni-ice camping place and tre-e-es and a little stream of water running by and
nice grass, nice camping place—we'd camp there.
And Julia and I, we start playing.
A-a-nd we ride horseback.
And we ride double—a-a-nd here we're girls.
O-oh we may be abo-out—
twelve years old or ten or somewhere around there and Julia said,

"Let's pretend we're big women.
Let's tie something around our breasts and hold our breasts like that
and tie it so it won't shake." (laughs)
Said "Let's tie something around there"—and we did.
Anyway we tie our breasts up like that, tight, and we start to ride horse—
 "Now make the horse
go fast so our breasts will shake." (laughs)
We did.
After we got home we told the mothers and they just la-a-aughed and
 la-a-aughed. (laughs)
Gee her and I used to get around and have good fun.

But other
girls, the teenagers,
they don't play much.
They flirt around too much—they just have the boys and all that, play with
 boys.
Her and I don't do that.
We sure have good times though.
Younger children come and play with us.
Her and I used to take a bunch of kids out.
Wade in the river and swim and
then when we'd get through we'd build a fire and start cooking—o-oh we
 had good times.

When she died she laid in the casket there and I come and look at her.
Emmm.
And I told the
people in there,
I said "Put a little paint on her face."
And they brought some paint.
"Put red, give her red cheeks."[2]
I said "Put some cologne
in her neck and make it smell good"—they did.
She was laying there.
No, I
didn't forget her.

1. This is Julia Big Hail, also of Pryor. Her grandmother called her Dulay because she couldn't pronounce Julia, and that became her nickname. As far as Lillian knew, she did not have an Indian name. (BL, MP)
2. People of my mother and Julia's age did not wear rouge or makeup. Perhaps they were applying red ochre to her cheeks. (MP)

Sham Battle (Julia and I Count Coup)

In this sham battle, Crow men pretend to count coup on their old enemies, the Piegan. Warriors once had to touch an enemy with a gun or stick and escape safely to achieve this brave feat. Clan relatives would proudly parade successful warriors through camp, proclaiming their deeds, singing praise songs, and giving away gifts in their honor. The battle in this story is just for fun, but clan relatives still praise the warriors and distribute gifts. That is why the families have to give things away after the two girls become entangled with the "war party." The Crow men who fought in the sham battle also "gave . . . them Piegan something," but these were gifts to thank them for being good sports and participating. This must have happened between about 1915 and 1920. (BL)

One time we went to sham battle—they call it sham battle. (laughs)
A-a-ll the pe-eople even from Black Lo-odge and
Lo-odge Grass a-a-ll were camping at the Fourth of July celebration.
There at Pryor—there's lo-o-ots of people,
and the-ey start in
at camp, all singing around the camp and then they went on a warpath.
And they went across a ditch and up on the hill.
They had two Piegans hiding in the coulee
there and this whole bunch of warriors are going up there,
to kill them.
Kill the enemy.
And then come back to the camp and they start celebrating.
That was just put on.
So they gave these Piegans something.

And when the men were gone,

Julie and I said "Let's go! Let's go see that battle."
A-a-nd her and I got to the gate and the gate was closed.
We got off and grun-nt and grun-nt and want to take it,
take open the gate—and we couldn't do it and finally we wor-rk and wor-rk,
we kick and grun-nt and finally we got it open, the gate.
And took the horse on the other side and fixed the gate again.

And then, just then, little ways, we want to get on the saddle,
a-a-nd her, either me or her,
pulled the saddle <u>under</u> the horse.
I guess we didn't fix that one that holds the saddle up on the horse, *the belly cinch*.
We didn't get it tight enough,
so it come out under the horse.
And we finally got it off on the ground and then
throw it on the horse again and tighten it up.
And here there was war going, fight going on up on the hill.

A-a-nd we fixed it,
and I got in front and she got behind.
And we start out to a little creek—as we got on the creek a-a-nd start coming up the road—
here they come, a-a-ll a bunch of men a-a-ll on horseback,
singing and waving gun a-a-nd [coup] sticks and oh there was a who-ole bunch.
And here we come. (chuckles)

They stopped for us—says "Oh my, there's two girls come to the war party.
Let's take them in"—says "You girls come over here."
And we got in front.
And they bring the gun.
They even had hair, scalp,
tied to the stick.
"Here, you touch the scalp.
Show the people when you get to the camp.
Show them that they know that you been to a warpath
and war party a-a-nd seen them-m

strike the enemy a-a-nd
kill the enemy, take their horses away,
a-a-nd come back, back ho-o-me,
celebrating."

They said "Now you touch the gun and you touch the stick"—and we did.
We touched the gun and we touched the stick.
And then they start—say "All right.
All have to go now."
And the leaders were about six horsemen leading.
They says "Come right in the middle.
You be one of the leaders too." (laughs)
We were riding double. (laughs)
So we followed the lead
and got to the camp and wel-l-l our
clan uncles got hold of us and lead us around in camp and
o-oh my-y that was quite a sight!

And
Julia's mother don't have nothing.
She got after her.
"We're poor, why did you do this?"
My mother, she didn't care.
How they'd lead us around the camp, around singing and we gave away
   things. (laughs)
That was no good. (laughs)[1]

Julia's my be-est friend, goodness sakes.
I sure missed her.
We just like twins.
And she's a good girl.
She don't flirt around,
have any boyfriends.
We used to just find a catalog and cut those
dresses and just play with them—we'd be so quiet playing way over there,
while the others sneak around corners looking for boys.
No-o-o we never do that.

When she [was older] they made her marry a man.
Just about her size too.
Same age.²
And when they married her off,
their mothers don't like me.
Said "Don't you come around Julia any more.
Don't take her out."
But Julia always sent for me and we sneak around and go together. (laughs)
*They would get after us.*³

   1. On this tape she said she was about fifteen. In another version she said she was about ten. (BL)
   2. This may have been an arranged marriage. My mother later said the husband was Roy Decrane, son of Yellow Bull, but Julia's grandson, Selmer Red Star, said the last name was Old Crane, a different family. Roy and Julia had three children, Alvina, Gretchen, and a boy. The husband died when the children were small, and the son died young. (MP)
   3. Once you married you were expected to act differently. Crow men and their families seem to prefer women cut off friendships after they marry, probably to avoid jealousies. The girls' families usually feel the same way, yet I have seen friends remain friends throughout their lives. (MP)

Ohchiish, She's a Man Dressed Like a Woman

Ohchiish was the last of the old-time Crow berdaches, men who dressed and lived as women. His full name was Ohchikapdaapesh.¹ Crow berdaches were often skilled in women's crafts and respected for their abilities, but Indian agents were appalled, as evident in this account from around 1915 or 1916. Lillian uses both "he" and "she" in the story, and we have preserved her inconsistency to express Ohchiish's ambivalent gender identity. In another story she says, "They don't call him 'him' or 'her.' They just say 'a person.'"² (BL)

Ohchiish [Finds Them and Kills Them],
he was the only berdache left.
Don't know who his relatives were.
We're kids then.

Sometimes he appeared
at the dances—he always come to our house.
Sometimes he sleep there.
He has a team of his own, a buggy of his own.
He can go any time he wants to—come and stay—sometimes he stay at Pryor.[3]
And his homestead, home, a house, is in Saint X.
Right alongside of the road, she has a home.
But she goes around pretty much.
In fact she goes all over
all the districts to
Medicine Dance [Tobacco or Beaver Dance]—she likes that, she has good songs and she
takes part in that.
So she's a good-natured person.
That's all I know.
But she's a man,
dressed like a woman [see fig. 4].[4]

They say
they took him to the superintendent and our superintendent,
E. J. Estep,[5]
he's a hot-
tempered fellow.
He gets after people, so he says,
"I want that man over here in the office."
So they brought her in—all the policemans are mean too—they brought her in.[6]
They say he cried.
A-a-nd somebody told Plenty Coups "Hurry up! Get over there!
At the Office they got that Ohchiish in there.
The superintendent is going to get after him."

So they were in there [Estep, the police, and Ohchiish].
And they said "You put on men's clothes because you're a man,

and you're not a woman.
And stay at your home.
Change your clothes."[7]
And right after he got out he cried.
Say he cried and cried.

So he-e-e-ere comes Plenty Coups just in time.
He went in the superintendent office—he point at his face.
"You're a superintendent—you're supposed to talk nice, be nice to people.
Now if you don't do that, when I get out of this office, you're going to leave!
Within <u>two hours,</u>
(claps hands) you're fired!
(raps on table) I'm not going to have you sit there and be mean to the
   people.
You change your ways and be nice to people like Ohchiish."
Says "In her <u>youth,</u>
she don't go for the men [men's ways]—she dress like a woman and <u>still</u>
she's dressed—I <u>want</u> it that way.
She's ki-ind to people, she's good-natured, she goes to dances
and take part in every
activity" he says.
"You can't be mean to her.
But if you start being mean to her, you're going to get out of this office—
   <u>within two hours</u>!"
Plenty Coups said that.

So he said "All right! All right"—said "Let's shake hands."
He did. (claps hands)
It's all over then.
And they told her—here she was crying out there and they
brought her in and she shook hands with the superintendent.
"All right just keep that way—dress like a woman."
(claps hands) They're satisfied.

So Plenty Coups stood up,
told him, said "You'll be out of this office within two hours.

I'll fire you!
I'll wire to Washington! Get you out of this office!"
And he's a good man, Plenty Coups,
but when Estep turn around and be mean to that Ohchiish,
he gave him some words that
shook him up.
And he come to.
E. J. Estep, he's no good.[8]

1. The name Finds Them and Kills Them, a translation of Ohchikapdaapesh, probably refers to killing enemies. Ohchiish is a shortened version. The letters "sh" are sometimes added to the end of a name when speaking of someone in the third person. (MP)
2. According to Roscoe ("Life and Times," 48), "berdache" derives from the Arabic *bardaj*, meaning male concubine, and the French applied it to men who lived as women. The Crow term is *boté*, half man, half woman. (BL)
3. Having his own buggy and horses indicated independence. People commonly visited each other. Travel was slow, so those from other districts were expected to stay awhile. (MP)
4. Pretty Shield said of Ohchiish, "She looked like a man, and yet she wore woman's clothing; and she had the heart of a woman.... She was not as strong as a man, and yet she was wiser than a woman" (Linderman, *Pretty-Shield*, 228). Denig (*Five Indian Tribes*, 187–88) described a third, neuter gender, evolving naturally when boys showed no masculine inclinations and took on women's clothing and occupations. (BL)
5. This was Evan W. Estep, the agent for the Crow Reservation from 1914 to 1917. (BL)
6. The policemen were Crow but were employed by the agent, so they enforced his dictates, which could be oppressive. (BL)
7. Estep wanted Ohchiish to stay home, away from people, because he was not "normal." He didn't realize the tribe was comfortable with him as he was. He went around visiting and participating in everything, not bothering anyone. Our family considered him a good person, from the stories we've been told. (MP)
8. Other agents also caused trouble for the berdaches or *bodés*. According to Joseph Medicine Crow, Agent E. P. Briskow incarcerated them in the late 1890s, cut their hair, forced them into men's clothing, and made them do manual labor such as planting trees. "The people were so upset with this that Chief Pretty Eagle came into Crow Agency, and told Briskow to leave the reservation." See Roscoe, "That Is My Road," 54. (BL)

Ohchiish Was Taken Prisoner Once

[Once there was a] war party.[1]
I suppose it's [Sioux] from way down in South Dakota o-o-or Nebraska.
The Crow people were around this area.
This Billings, Bull Mountain-n,
Big Horn-n—they all around here.
But the Siouxs came over
and fight,
and they took a lot of prisoners.
Women and children.
And they get home,
they marry off these women.

Ohchiish was taken prisoner [as a boy] *and returned.*
He brought back with him a little girl named
Biilíiche Heeléelash [Among the Willows].[2]
He brought her back.
They say it happened to him.
He returned too!
Who would know about it now?[3]

1. Ohchiish was also a respected warrior. In this story he is captured by Lakota and manages to return, bringing a little girl with him. According to Pretty Shield, Ohchiish, whom she called a half-woman, also fought bravely in the Battle of the Rosebud, 1876, dismounting in the middle of battle to stand over a badly wounded Crow and fire at the enemy. For that fight, he dressed as a man, so the Lakota would not ridicule him if he died and they found his body. (Linderman, *Pretty-Shield*, 227–31.) (BL)
2. The little girl, Biilíiche Heeléelash, lived from 1837 to 1912 and was "a prominent war leader, known for riding into battle in the finest female attire. In 1858 she was one of the leaders (pipe carriers) against the Lakota in the legendary Battle of Rainy Buttes" (Two Leggins, *Apsáalooke Writing Tribal Histories*, 52). According to Lillian, she is an ancestor of the Sings Good family of Pryor. (BL)
3. Ohchsiich apparently showed extreme courage at the Battle of the Rosebud, but most Plains Indian tribes did not force anyone to be a warrior or a wife. If a man had feminine tendencies, he did not have to hunt or go on war parties. If a woman showed more masculine ways, she was left alone too—for example, the famous Woman Chief of the Crow tribe. (MP)

Ohchiish, We Sure Like Her

> *Most of this story recounts Lillian's childhood memories of Ohchiish, who was a family friend, but the story ends years later in a hospital, probably just before Ohchiish's death in 1929. It was the last time Lillian saw this famous berdache. As in the previous accounts, she switches between "he" and "she," expressing Ohchiish's gender ambivalence.* (BL)

Ohchiish sure good to my father and mother.
And when she comes to the house she says "My sister."
She says "I come to stay a night, spend a night here,
play cards,
and I want some of your good cooking" he says.
My mother, she's known as a good cook.
So she says "I'm going to stay overnight.
And I brought some oranges and apples and candy for the kids."
That's my brother and me.
And she gave us a sack of goodies,
and we sure like that—when she comes over we say "There she comes!
There she come, I hope she stay" (laughs)—yes we sure like her.

And he's a good cook.
Umm-m-m-m-m—*gee he's a good cook.*
He'd come and stay and he'd tell my mother "Let me help you.
Let me make some biscuits."
Wash her hands.
Start making bread, making biscuits a-a-nd she start singing.
Always was singing Beaver Dance songs [for Tobacco Society adoptions].
He loved the Beaver Dance.
Once in a while during Beaver Dances,
he would wear his [men's] *leggings* [with beadwork].
He said he'd had them a long time,
but he prized them.
He'd take them out and wear them.
He would wear earrings, bracelets, make himself smell so good![1]

Yes, she's su-ure good-natured.
He was a nice person.
And they say,
folks tell, said
even when he was a young
person they don't call him "him" or "her."
They just a person.

Says when he was a young person,
he dress like a woman,
act like a woman,
talk like a woman.
But his voice, he's got a cracked voice.
It's a man's voice.

He do beadwork,
like women, he sew moccasins,
he tan buckskin,
and he sews own dress.
Cut it.[2]

She dress like a woman.
Wear moccasins, high top.
She has necklaces, earrings—she braid her hair like this. (gestures to her own braids)
But she's a man. (chuckles)
And everybody knows, even kids know he's a man,
but they don't say nothing.
Yeh.

A-a-nd he teases my father a-a-nd [later] my boy Sammy used to get mad.
He said "That o-o-ld wo-oman,
that o-o-ld wo-oman—I don't like him, I hate him because
he's going to take my grandpa away from my grandma." (chuckles)
Says "Some of these days he come over I'm going to hit him." (laughs)
He doesn't know she's a man.[3]

But I remember the time when he was in the hospital.
He was sick and they admit him in the hospital,
and one time I
open the door to see him,
and
he look kind of pale.
And I said "All right, are you feeling better?"—and,
and he said "Yes, some better."
Then,
I think he happened to be going to the bathroom so I hurried out.
Shut the door—I told him "I'll
be back later to see you."
So I didn't go back then,
and I don't know whether he got out of the hospital or whether he was sick or no—I don't know.
After that I never see him.
That's the last time I ever talked to him.[4]
I was married to
Nellie's daddy then.[5]

1. During a Beaver Dance, he would take his leggings and moccasins from storage, put on his jewelry and perfume and then dance Beaver Dance wearing his leggings. That would be as a man, I guess, wearing men's leggings. He'd do that on occasion. (MP)
2. Ohchiish also made two unusually large teepees, one for Chief Iron Bull (Roscoe, *The Life and Times*, 50). Tanning hides for such a lodge and sewing them together was a major accomplishment that would have garnered prestige. (BL)
3. Ohchiish called my grandmother "sister" and teased my grandfather like he was her brother-in-law. This traditional jesting between sisters and brothers-in-law allowed no mercy, but Sam was too young to understand, so he was jealous, afraid that this "woman" would take his grandpa away. (MP)
4. Several old-time berdaches, or *boté*, were still alive in the early twentieth century, but Ohchiish was the last. Baptist minister W. A. Petzoldt arrived in Lodge Grass in 1903 and, according to Tom Yellowtail, subject of *Yellowtail: Crow Medicine Man*, he condemned Ohchiish until his death. "That may be the reason why no others took up the *boté* role after Osh Tisch [Ohchiish] died." See Yellowtail in Williams, *The Spirit and the Flesh*, 183.
5. Lillian and Paul received a marriage license in March 1930, several months after Ohchiish died, but they may have been together in the Crow way prior to the marriage license. That would explain why she said she was married to Paul when

she last saw Ohchiish. (BL)

My Little Brother Had That Infantile Paralysis

Polio, a crippling, deadly disease, reached pandemic proportions worldwide in the first half of the twentieth century. The disease reached Lillian's family around 1920, when she was a teenager. (BL)

I had a little brother [Percy] and
o-oh that little brother is su-u-ure ni-ice little kid.
Sometimes he wants a cake,
a-a-nd there's white people living not too far from our place.
I go over there and ask her to show me how to [make a cake].
I always
favor him because I loved my little brother.
I'd do <u>anything</u> for him.

And he said "Let's go horseback riding."
We have a mo-ost gentle horse.
We call him Chubby [in English].
Iischiapaapáshee [Round White Face] we always call him [in Apsáalooke].
And wherever he is, he'd be eating there or
looking this wa-ay—he hardly
go among the other horses.
And he'd be near and we walk over there.
And when we call him "Iischiapaapáshee!"
He'd just
turn around, look.
"Hold still now—we're going to
rope you."
And we'd go and
he'd just be right there,
where he's standing.

We'd go and put the rope around him.
Bring him to the house and we'd put the saddle on him.

And I'd always have my little brother ride on the saddle and I get behind.
Put a blanket over that [rump] and I'd sit behind the saddle.
And we just go down the roads.
Go up the road little ways and up the little coulee up a ways.
And I'd say "You might get tired—we'd better go home."
Said "No let's ride some more"—so we'd just go up the road, up the country road.
We didn't go to town because there's no highways—there's buggy road used to just
come down by our house, down near little creek,
and cross the creek and turn—and then they go to town.
That's at the road right close to the house.
We just ride up there and back and into the brush and we water the horse and then
talk and come around and
go back to the house—he says he sure likes to ride.

But oh my, when my brother got sick,
sure felt bad.
We used to take him to Billings hospital.
They even
kept him in the hospital.
And seems like
once in awhile he's just about to go in fits,
and cry and kick and fight and all that,
and gee I stand there, look at him—I cry.
And then pretty soon that spell goes away—he'd be so qui-iet.
But he finally died.
He had that infantile paralysis.
Pretty soon he couldn't use one arm.
All dead.
And he was nine years old [seven] when he died.

That . . . that year,
there's epidemic going in Pryor,
and they quarantined the whole Pryor District.
They can't go to Billings, they can't go to Crow.

They know they're quarantined.
And that's about six cases there.
Two died, the others lived.
But after they live,
up to six years,
if they pull through the six year [they survive].
And if not, they get a setback,
and then they die.
They can't cure that.

So one lady lived through.
Her mother and father are there—her father's Indian doctor.
They doctor her,
and she pulled through.
But
her whole side paralyzed and she sure
don't walk very good.
But she has two sons—she got married,
although she pretty near crippled.
Blanche.
Call her Blanche, Blanche Turns Back.
She pulled through,
and she just died.
About six years ago, six or eight years ago.

Now she has two sons living.
Freddie and Roger.
Roger lives down in Lame Deer,
but Freddie he has the house.
Lived there where his parents had the house.
Here's the old house and he built a good house,
alongside of the road—he's living on their place.
Freddie.

[Anyway my little brother] says "Let's go fishing,"
and we do.

And "Shall we
go down the river or down this little creek?"
And he said "The river."
So we'd go down there but I always be afraid of snakes so I wear rubber boots. (chuckles)
Yeh.
We'd go fishing—sometimes we'd catch just one.
(Starts to cry. Quiet pause.)

He loved to horse back.
He likes it and I always take him.
For a horse ride.
Sometimes I just let him ride and I'd lead the horse, take him around the house and
up the hill and up the road and come back.

I al-lways catered to him—sometimes he wants ice cream.
A-a-nd
that lady lived by us, she has a small freezer,
and I learned making ice cream—she showed me how.
So I always go to the store and buy some ice
a-a-nd
crush it in there and make this pudding there,
and then put it in there,
and then I'd turn the pudding in there and
the ice all around there—pound it down,
and then pretty soon I kept turning and he would be looking.
He says "Hurry up, hurry up, it's going to melt!"
And I says "All right"—I kept turning and my father and mother, they said,
"Ni-ice, wonderful thing that you can make ice cream."

But this lady,
they live about . . . o-oh,
about a mile away from our house or half a mile.
Not too far—about just a half a mile.
They lived close to us so I go down there,
and she lend me the freezer

and showed me how to make ice cream.
And
if we want ice cream we have to go to the store and buy ice
and bring it and I know how to make ice cream.
And my little boy would just, he'd just <u>jump</u> up and
go for that ice cream.
Says "I don't want nobody else to
have the ice cream—that's for me!" he says. (chuckles)
[I make] vanilla.
I couldn't make no other kind so I just make vanilla.
It's good and he sure likes it.

But after that, when he got sick,
we used to take him to Billings and we'd stay at the hospital, St. Vincent's
    Hospital.
The old one.
We'd stay there and them nurses and doctors are su-ure good to him.
They'd come a-a-nd pet him on the shoulder a-a-nd,
and help him out but,
no—we couldn't do nothing because he's one of the cases that
took the disease in him.
Can't cure that,
and he died from that.
And he was ni-i-ine years old when he died.

One day he says,
"Dad" he says,
"I want you to dress me up and take my picture.
On a horseback."
And poor little fellow.
Pretty soon he had them convulsions.
Something like that—<u>awful</u> bad.
And pretty soon
his eyes
was cross-eyed,
and he looked pitiful.
And he wanted to ride and have his picture taken.

And we got the little horse, the pony, that chubby one.
Make him stand there,
a-a-nd
we put him on the horse—sit.
He couldn't straighten up—kind of leaning.
Hold the saddle horn like that . . . we took his picture.

I think Nellie still has that picture.
I kept saying we'd better have some more copies of this,
and after that I haven't seen that picture for lo-ong time.[1]

1. This photograph has been lost. (BL)

Horses Run over Caleb

This race must have happened around 1918–1920. (BL)

Since my brother got to drinking and don't take care of the horse,
Father says "We won't have no horses now.[1]
No race horses"—says "I'm too old, not too strong to handle a pony."
But before that we used to have
maybe three on a string.
Maybe couple.

One year,
just one horse.
That horse so <u>fast</u>!
And he out run the who-o-ole—
all the districts.
Reno, Wyola,
St. X,
Crow [Agency].
And we own that horse.
At Crow Fair,
the races,
they go around the track four times,

and he takes the lead.

[He's] a sma-a-all
roan.
It's kind of a roan—
that
grey, white, red.
It's not a pinto.
They called him that Chia Iakáate—called him Small.[2]
He's not a great big horse—he's rather small.
But he's <u>fa-ast</u>!
Golly he outrun the who-ole bunch of race horses.
They go around the circle, the race track, four times—he take the lead.
Emmm (claps hands)—I scream.
(chuckles) I liked that little horse.
Yeh.

One time my brother,
Caleb,
he rode a bay—he was riding for somebody else.
He was riding
a bay horse.
He's a fast one—
we gave [to] this man [Oliver].
Happened that they made Caleb as a brother-in-law in Indian.
[My father] says "Give your brother
this race horse."
My father said that, so he gave that bay horse to Oliver and he owned that
    horse.[3]

So during the Fair,
they train the horse and he's a fa-ast runner—he outrun the who-o-ole
bunch of horses.
And
Caleb was riding
the horse.
Says [to Caleb] "You know how he's kind of spooky sometimes,"

and he said "You know how to handle the horse."
They called him Iiwisheeáho[4]—
Paid
a Big Ransom For the Horse—that's the name,
the name of the horse, the bay.

But we, we own it and we gave it to Oliver.
Oliver Lion Shows.
And he owns the horse and then when the Fair went on,
he run the horse.
And Caleb—
I think this was up at Livingston Fair, 4th of July—
we'd come over there and he rode the horse and he was ahead.[5]
A whole bunch of race horses but he was ahead of all the race horses, Caleb and that bay.
And just then something happened—Caleb fell off the horse.
And all these horses, runners, just came and
run over Caleb.
He's laying there on the track but his horse just kept running and he's leading.
He was the fast runner,
leading the whole bunch.

But they a-a-all rushed over there
a-a-nd stopped the race and they got
Caleb off the track—he was laying there.
And we a-all jump
from the grandstand, run down the track and here he was,
half dead.
And they brought in the ambulance and put him in there and took him to Livingston.
And we all followed.
Take him to the hospital and they put oxygen on him and work him up—
finally he come to.
Gee they all got scared—we thought he was going to die.
He had two bruises back
where the horses step on him. (chuckles)

O-oh my, we was scared—I scre-eam, I cri-ied.
Emmmm.
I was about
sixteen or seventeen.

Yeah we used to own
race horses but we always get the
fast runner.
Yes my father had thoroughbreds,
a-a-nd another one was
Chief—he called him Chief.
A sorrel horse—o-oh he's a pretty horse.

1. See the next story, "Caleb Starts to Drinking."
2. *Chia Iakáate* means Little White (horse would be understood). Mom gave my granddaughter, Montana Sky Scalpcane, her Indian name and gave her *Chia iakáate*, as well as Sorrel Chief, the name of the other thoroughbred race horse she mentions. (MP)
3. Oliver Lion Show's wife was Nina. She was not related to us by blood, but according to my sister Lorena Mae Walks Over Ice, she was a clan sister. That is why Caleb gave her husband a horse. (MP)

   When women marry, their brothers often give horses to their new brother-in-law. They may give him horses on other occasions as well. This includes biological, adopted, and clan brothers. Voget (*Shoshoni-Crow Sun Dance*, 33) describes such gifts as demonstrations of "loyal respect" for the sister. Medicine Crow ("The Effects of European Culture Contacts," 41–42), says that as long as the marriage continues, the women in the groom's family supply fine, Crow-style clothing to their sister-in-law, and reciprocally, the men on the bride's side supply horses and fine clothing to their brother-in-law. See also Lowie, *The Crow Indians*, 12–13; and Leforge in Marquis, *Memoirs*, 37. (BL)
4. Literally means "Expensive" or "High Price." (MP)
5. When the U.S. government outlawed traditional events, many tribes avoided punishment by holding dances under the guise of the 4th of July, Christmas, Memorial Day, New Year's Eve, and other sanctioned holidays. Few non-Native realized they were to practicing their own customs. (MP)

Caleb Starts to Drinking

Let's see now,
around ninetee-en—
oh around ninetee-en—

seventeen,
if I remember right [or a few years later],
Caleb start to drinking.
My father's a heavy drinker.
He hid some whiskey.
And wi-ine.
And beer.
My father took those, he had those—he bought them from Billings I guess.

I don't even know where he bought them,[1]
but anyway he went down the river,
in the brush.
He dig a hole,
and he put that beer and whiskey there—stored them in the cool place
and covered them up,
with a canvas I guess.
He covered them up with a canvas.

He thought nobody know where it was but after he left,
Caleb sneak over there and uncovered that
whiskey and beer in there,
where he stored them away.
In the dug hole.

My father covered them with canvas and then he covered grass over it so nobody'd see it.
And they kept cool.
And Caleb found out where he hid them.
He went and stole them
and sold it to
some men.
And that whiskey was all gone.
And _he_ start to drinking then.

I know that time.
Cause me, I don't [drink].[2]

    1. At the time, it was against federal law to sell alcohol to Indians. (MP)

2. Lillian's family had suffered because of alcohol, and she always had strongly negative feelings about it. (BL)

Uncle Old Dwarf Instructs Me to Live Right

This is about Old Dwarf, the relative who brought Lillian's young parents a dream for horses. A kindly man and devoted Christian, Old Dwarf would have been called an uncle in European terms, but he was a father in Crow terms, fulfilling some of the same the same roles as a biological parent. Here he is instructing Lillian and the other children on proper behavior. (BL)

On my father's side,
I have an uncle that jus-st
told us everything.
How to grow,
how to have a good na-ame and
ho-onor and,
oh everything he'd tell us.
Make us behave ourselves and we used to say,
"There comes the old man, Uncle,
the man with a whip."
He comes in the house—say "Who haven't got a shoe on, who hasn't dressed?"
He'd come in the house like that and kids run around looking for their shoes and
he would get a good laugh out of them.

And [when I was older] we'd laugh when he come up the gate—when he comes to the gate,
and he gets off the horse—he ride a horse.
He'd undo the gate and then them kids—[claps hands to suggest children scattering]—
the kids look down the road—"Here comes the man with a whip!"
And they al-ll say "Where's my shoe?! Where's my pants?! Where—"
go-olly they all run around.

Looking for shoes.
See Caleb's wife died—his children didn't have no mother,
and my parents kept them.
And, (laughs)
and he'd come in and
he had a little whip.
He made a whip and put it on top of the door.
As so-oon as he'd come in the house he'd look around.
Say "Where are the kids—where are the boys and girls?
I want to see who's one that's got
no shoe on,
no clothes on." (laughs)
I used to laugh at them.
And they'd come out and they'd say "See Grandpa—I got shoes on!"
   (laughs)

Yeah Old Dwarf's adopted by my father's mother.
See my grandmother adopted him,
so he's just like a true brother to my father.
And seems like they look alike.
Ta-all and they're not fat but they're tall and big bo-ones and they look
   alike.

He is related to my father.
My grandmother is related to his parents.
She adopted him and took him, raised him with my father,
because my grandmother had no other children.
My father is a twin but the twin, the girl, died.
She died as a baby.
So he really is a brother to my father.[1]

That's the one that's the old man the kids all afraid of.
And he-e-e's a good, honest man.
And he's tal-ll and
yeah I used to remember when I was a little girl I
see him come up the road.
Gets to the gate.

Then I'd have little puppies with me, little tiny puppies.
I hold them and I r-ran down the road a-a-nd here I'd com-me and meet him.
"You want to see my puppies?"—and he's say "O-o-oh my-y-y what a beautiful puppy!
This one is the prettiest"—or "this one"—he kept on saying.

He'd lead the horse—he didn't get on the horse because I was there.
He made me hold the one puppy.
He said "You hold the one puppy, I'll hold one, the other puppy."
And we'd walk and when we'd get to the house he'd say, he'd say "Aa-ii! What a pretty little creature!" (laughs)
He's just say it to make me believe that they're pretty—pretty puppies.

But when I got big and got married he su-u-ure
say "Now you're up to a womanhood.
You'll have a home."
Says "Your brother Caleb,
he won't listen to no advice—we tell him anything he won't take it."
"But" he says "you're a woman that's going to have a ho-ome, some children,
and you'll make good"—and I did.

He says,
"Don't fight."
Says "Live a good life."
Yeh.
"Don't steal or don't fight or don't quarrel."
He always tell us things like this—instruct to live right.
Yeah he's a good man.

He's a Christian man too.
He used to believe he's got the medicine.[2]
But after that,
he become a Christian,
and he lead the singing and

goes to church every Sunday.
His wife goes with him too.
A-a-nd he live a good life.

But when he got too old,
he didn't want to live anymore.
He said "Al-ll our relatives are gone.
They tell us
that there's another place, another land,
and where all the dead people are over there.
They bury their body but their spirit is over there."
And he says,
"I want to go.
Meet my wife."
I think he only lost
two wives.
He didn't lost no,
no other.[3]
Said he wants to go and see his parents.
He didn't mention
the Christian way but he believes in the Indian way.[4]
He says wa-ay back,
after the Creation,
he said he
know that the Indians are here, the white people over there and different nationalities.
But he says "As an Indian,
when we die we go and see our parents.
Our relatives.
And there's a land over there that's where they live better than down here"
   he says.
Said he wants to go.

He wouldn't eat and [says] "I'm ready to go.
I don't want to eat—I don't want to eat, I don't want to drink.
I want to go!" he kept saying.

And we all sit around him, beg him and hold him and
dish something in his mouth—"Ple-ease Dad.
Ple-ease"—we'd al-ll try and make him eat.[5]

And he'd, he'd take about three, four spoonful of soup then he'd quit.
He quit the water—he said "I'd don't want to drink."
Said he'd rather die than to live.
"Eat and drink and put on like that" he says—"I've quit that all."
Says he wants to go.[6]

1. It was common to adopt or "take in" a relative. Perhaps his grandmother wanted to replace the twin girl she had lost, or perhaps she took him in because his mother was ill. Relatives helped by assisting in raising each other's children. (MP)
2. She is saying he used to follow Indian religious beliefs before he became a Christian. (BL)
3. Elsewhere, Lillian said he had also lost a daughter named Sadie who had married a white man and died many years before. (BL)
4. My mother was a devoted Christian, but in the nursing home she too went back to her younger years in her mind, and she would sing Tobacco Dance songs. She would also refuse to attend the church services offered there. I requested "What a Friend We Have in Jesus," one of her favorite hymns, but she refused to go. As she was near death, she did the hand gestures we use in the Tobacco Society dances, and I felt that she was already in the afterlife the Crow know as "the Other Side Camp." (MP)
5. She would call him Dad because he was her father's adopted brother. Our term for uncle is father, *basaakáa*. (MP)
6. In another part of the tape, Lillian said this happened when Mardell was around four years old, so he must have passed away around 1950. (BL)

CHAPTER EIGHT

My Mother Teaches Me to Be a Good Woman

Be Sure You Have a Scissor

This brief and affectionate story is about beading and sewing tools, but it is also a mother's lecture on how to be a good Crow woman—hardworking, knowledgeable, and skillful. (BL)

I like to tell this about my mother.
Says "You're going to gro-ow
to be a woman,
and you're going to have a family sometime,
and you'll get to be old."
She says,
"You learn how to fix these chokecherr-ries
and how to slice me-eat,
how to make those for your family.

And I did—I learned lots of things from her.
She knows how to.
She don't say "Come on, watch!" She don't say that.
She just go ahead and do it and I come near her and watch her.
A-a-nd she tells me, says,
"When you get to your own living,
and when you have chi-i-ld, you have children,
to look after,
a-a-nd you have your own bedding,
your own clothes to look after,
and you do your own cooking, you have to learn a-a-ll those."

But she says "Be sure you have—
have
a scissor
and some needles and some thread.
A-a-nd
keep those.
For your use" she says—"you're going to use those some of these days."

"But a <u>lazy</u> woman
don't have nothing—they don't even have scissor.
Even needles" she says "they don't even have any needle or thread."
"And pretty soon if they want to sew, they run to the neighbors" she says.
"You have any needle? You have any thread? Lend me your needle,"
she says.

"I often see them do that" she says—
"don't you."
"When you a woman" says "have those.
So you can sew."
And I always had.
Learned that from her.
She taught me how to have a needle,
thread,
scissor.[1]

> 1. Women were, and are, admired for their industry and accomplishments because they make their families comfortable. They also produce the beautifully beaded clothing that relatives wear or give away when outfitting brides, a family member's new husband, or Tobacco Society adoptees. Such clothing continues Crow identity, demonstrates love of family, and is a traditional form of wealth. Women who contribute all this bring prestige to themselves and their families. Horse would have wished this respect for her daughter. (BL)

You Have to Know How to Bead

Here Lillian recounts her childhood beading lessons and the unexpected adventure that followed. As in the previous story, she begins with the reasons she was expected to learn. Those same reasons could apply to every story in this chapter because Crow women once depended on their crafts and their knowledge of wild foods to provide for their families and others. When she finished her first beading, she was up at Pryor Gap because they were filming a movie called Before the White Man Came *(see "The Movie Outfit," chapter 7). The film came out in 1920, so this probably happened in the years just before. She estimated that she was ten, but she was probably a little older.* (BL)

My mother said,
"You're going to be a woman now."
I was about ten years old.
Says "You're going to get big and you're going to—
maybe later on when you get older you'll be married,
and you're going to have to know how to bead.
You'll be making things for others."

A-a-nd when I started,
she cut a purse.
She didn't start on a moccasin—she should.[1]
She cut a purse.
Not too big.
And she didn't have no right color I guess,
and she said "You make this flower, outline it blue."[2]
A-a-nd she even took it
and thread the needle.
She says,
"You can bring that needle down
three beads at a time or maybe sometimes if the bead is small you can
come up four beads up.
And follow this line.
Go on this way."

I used two needles
The fine needle and the other one, the bigger needle [for overlay or tack-down stitch].[3]

A-a-nd she always watch me.
Says "Go ahead on the next line,"
and I sit there.
Kept working—I like it.
A-a-nd I thought I was going to learn how to bead
baalaaísshikaatam [a little money bag].
It wasn't too big.
She made it small,
so I could learn how to bead.

A-a-nd she, I remember she put yellow beads on there,
a-a-nd blu-ue be-eads,
and red be-eads and green beads.[4]
She say "All, they a-a-ll match colors—it'll be plain."[5]
A-a-nd she said "Soon as you finish this,"
says "I'll show you how to sew it
and put a bag in there,
so it'll flop over,[6]
a-a-nd attach it onto a belt."
She watched me.
Showed me how to do ev-v-verything.

Pretty soon I had it done.
A-a-nd she show it to the neighbors—we camp at Gap.
That's when they're taking pictures and a lot of people there.
She show it to some of the women there, three or four.
They pass it around, look at my work and said "Oh she's
starting to learn and her first work is re-eal good."
They start to saying that—I like it then.

So pretty soon I put my work away.
And there was a girl,
younger than I am [a child, younger than ten].

She come laughing and sit with me and
she says "Come on let's play, let's go this way, let's go—let's go up, climb
 that hill."
We did and then after awhile she had an excuse
a-a-nd ran down to the tent, the camp,
while I stayed up there.
She went down and stole that purse.
Stole it
a-a-nd put it away, hid it away.

A-a-nd the next day or so,
two girls told me and a woman too.
They told me that she stole that purse.
So-o I came asking,
a-a-nd she said, she start to,
said "I'm going to fight you.
I'm just going to fight you and,
and
I got some girls there's going to help me fight you,
because you accuse me of stealing that purse."
She's always cranky.

So I just went home and I felt re-eal bad.
A-a-nd
my mother did too.
"Don't, don't fret about it—maybe later on I'll ask the grandma
to look for it."
And we never said no more.

And then when she heard we're looking for it,
she took that purse and threw it in the river.
And float down little ways and got stuck there,
under a rock.
And stayed there for about two days in the water,
a-a-nd some girls told me that she did.
"She threw that purse in the water, in the river."
And they told me "It's down there."
Said "Come on, we'll show you where."

I followed them.
Sure enough—I took my moccasins or my shoes off,
wade down the water—the river was swift!
Oh my!
But I went down there and I grabbed it.
Took it out—here was that purse
I finished—it was so-o-oaked, all soaked through. (laughs)

I came back and show it to my mother and she said "Oh we'll dry it and
rub it little bit and we put a new lining on it and it'll be all right."
A-a-nd after that she said "Let me keep it.
Let me keep it where nobody can't see it."
And I never seen it then after that.

She took it (claps hands) and later years,
I don't know how, how it happened.
She might have sold it, she might have gave it away or I never ask—I forgot about it.
But we happened to
go to Cody.
We went to Cody,
fool around there,
and in the mu-useum [the Buffalo Bill Historical Center],
here was that purse,
laying there among the beaded stuff.

And I was with Robbie then [her second husband] and I call him over and I said "Come here and
look at that purse—I made it when I was ten years old,
and someone stole it,
and she threw it in the river,
and we took it back,
my mother and I fixed it, work it over again and I don't know how it got here,"
"but" I said "it's in the museum."[7]
(laughs)
Stra-ange.

1. A girl's first beading does not have to be a moccasin. I don't know why she said this. (MP)
2. Perhaps her mother did not have the colors she liked. There is no significance to using a blue outline. Old time beaders did not necessarily "match" colors the way we do now. If the outline was dark blue, they did not have to make the inside of the flower light blue. They might use a different color. (MP)
3. She is encouraging her daughter to secure the strand with a stitch every three or four beads, so the finished piece will be smooth and tight. This is overlay, or tackdown, stitch. Beaders use two needles for the technique, a fine one for threading the beads and a regular, thicker one to tack down the strands. (BL)
4. Later she said it was a pink flower with a blue outline. The background was yellow framed by blue. The green and red must have been used for details. (BL)
5. She probably means the colors were pretty and went well together. Bright colors. (MP)
6. They lined the inside with cloth and added a closing flap that folded over the top. (BL)
7. The purse is not presently in the museum's collections. Senior Curator Emma Hansen speculated that it might have been on temporary loan from a private collector. (BL)

I Learned How to Make Buckskin

Plains Indian women used to make buttery-soft buckskins with a technique called brain-tanning. In this story Lillian explains the steps her mother taught her. The details are sometimes confusing, but the intensity of the labor comes through clearly—brain-tanning is hard work. The technique was already declining in Lillian's childhood. Most women buy commercially tanned skins today, but they still appreciate a fine hide processed the old-fashioned way. (BL)

My mother showed me how to make buckskin.
She-e dry the hide,
and when it's nice and smoo-o-th,
she scrape it—says "Come on, you take this [scraper] and
do it—don't just hit it down.
Just do it this way, scrape [pull it toward you],
and you're going to learn how to make buckskin.
When you get older you'll have sons and daughters,
and you'll be making buckskin and moccasins for them."

She's got a piece of a scraper [a bone tool with a flat piece of metal attached].
My father made it for her.
So I learn how to scrape the hides.
When I got a little ways she said "All right let me do it."
She scrape all the hair off.[1]

She didn't tell me how she's going to dry this hide—anyway she
put nails up on the house, way high,
where the dogs can't pull it down,
a-a-nd she lay the hide cross way.
She didn't hang it down, the head and tail.
She lay it cross ways "so it won't be close to the ground"—she told me that.[2]
Big nails too—a-a-nd every day she kept turning.

And when that hide is dry,
says "Now we make this *chiiwúsee* [brain solution]."
She said "We make this solution,
and I'll show you how to make it.
Now we get some liver,
and some brains,
and cook that.
When we get the brains you just watch what I do" she said.
A-a-nd she cooked the brains and the liver,
and she made some kind of a grease anyway.
Some grease.
Pour it in there and mix it a-a-ll up good,
and then when this hide was dry she rubbed this mix a-a-ll over.
On both sides.
She dabbed the who-ole thing with that
brain and liver together,
and pretty soon she hung it up,
way up—and every day she kept turning.
And she said "When that's a-a-ll worked in that hide,
it'll soften up and then you'll see how we tan it."

I don't remember the days anyway.
It may be six days or maybe a week or so.
I know she kept turning it around.
And she finally,
one day she said "Now watch me work this."
She put it in the grass,
thick grass, and said "This way that dew,
that damp,
will soften this."
So she rolled it up, step on it,
stomp on it, and pretty soon she'd
turn it over and do it again and roll it up and
put it in the grass
and cover it with a
canvas and put some ro-ocks and i-iron stuff on there where the dogs can't
 get a hold of it.
A-a-nd she'd turn it over in the morning.
Take it and unroll it and turn it over and do it again—just put it in the grass.
Said "That damp a-a-ll cover the hide and soften it."
Sure enough it did.[3]

But when that [solution] a-a-ll work in there right,
couple days after that she soak it.
Said she mix—
o-oh,
I guess it's little lukewarm water.
A-a-nd soap.
Just made soapsuds,
and she put this hide in that,
and every day she kept turning.
She put weight on it,
to hold it down so it won't stick out [of the soapy water].

And she do that,
I don't know how many times—and about the fourth day,
she took it and made a,

a stick [cross bar] tied up to two posts [or two trees] there where it won't touch, high from the ground.
She hung this hide over the stick.[4]
And it was so-oaking wet.
Now she'd
twist it around [wring it].
Put another big stick there and tie the hide to the stick [and twist].
And water dripping,
from that hide.[5]
And then after awhile she turn it around
a-a-nd roll it up and put the stick in there
and tie it [and twist again],
and the water would be dripping out.
Drip, drip.

A-a-nd then when all that water drip out,
she takes it inside and put it inside in the
house where the dogs won't catch it.
And after that,
she [began to] dry it again,
and said "When this is drying,
all that stuff will work in that hide."
And the day come she wring it again
and put a stick in there—twist it and tie it where the water drip and drip till it got dryer.[6]

And then she start to scraping,
and she hold it,
scrape the water off.
Turn it this way and scrape on this side, scrape on that side, kept turning.
Pretty soon it look like buckskin then—
turning [white] color and
when that turning color comes she keep scraping with that iron thing,
a-a-nd pretty soon it was drying [from friction].

She said "I better hurry up and rub it" so she take a piece of wire,
some kind of a wire [or double-edged saw blade]—she

tie it down here in the bottom and tie it up here [securing it vertically to a
   tree or wall].[7]
And she got this hide in between the
piece of—
o-oh it's a lead I guess—it's
hanging there—she put the hide on,
and she start to rub [back and forth].
And as fast as she go,
all that buckskin come out [bits of tissue were flying off].[8]
And she'd stretch it.
Put it down and rub that thing over again and
pretty soon it's buckskin, re-eal white—said "We want it re-eal white."

If you want white,
pretty white moccasins, white,"
she said "we'll put flour on it.
Or shall I smoke it [golden brown]?" she said.
"O-oh" [I said],
"next time you smoke the hide.
This time I'll wear it white."
And so she put flour on it.
Rub it, roll it up,
and put a sack over it—left it there so it'd be white.
And in the morning she rub it again, shake all that flour off,
and it come whi-ite as this [napkin].
Re-eal white and she start to rubbing again.[9]
And pretty soon when that's done she nail it onto the wall and stretch it.[10]
Leave it there for about a whole day and then she takes it down,
and it's just buckskin.
White and pretty.
And that's where I learned how to make buckskin.

1. She has already soaked the hide to loosen the fur and is now teaching her daughter to scrape the fur away. They also had to scrape, or "flesh," the reverse side to remove bits of meat and fat. (BL)
2. She is stretching the hide flat with large nails or large wooden stakes, like the ones they used to stake down tents or teepees. Many women staked hides on the ground, but my mother and Grandma Bull Shows sometimes staked them on the

side of a shed. Lorena Mae Walks Over Ice, personal communication to Mardell Plainfeather, 2008.
3. Dew helps soften the hide. This is an extra step. Not every tanner did it. Lorena Mae Walks Over Ice, personal communication to Mardell Plainfeather, 2008.
4. The water and soap mixture further softens the hide and rinses out residue like fatty issue and meat. After that, she would hammer a stick up between two objects such as trees and drape the hide over so she could wring out the water. Lorena Mae Walks Over Ice, personal communication to Mardell Plainfeather, 2008.
5. At this point, the hide is wrung several times, as you would a wet towel, to squeeze out moisture and brains. While the hide was draped over the cross bar, she attached it to another stick, like a tourniquet, and twisted it until all the water was gone. Lorena Mae Walks Over Ice, personal communication to Mardell Plainfeather, 2008.
6. The dogs would eat the hide if they didn't keep them from it, so they took the hide into the house. It was nearly dry by this step, but they would wring it again to make certain all water had been wrung out. Lorena Mae Walks Over Ice, personal communication to Mardell Plainfeather, 2008.
7. Grandma Bull Shows had a double-edge saw blade with metal edges that she nailed to a wall or tree like a vertical towel rack. It had teeth on both edges. She placed the wet hide between the saw and tree and pulled it back and forth over the edges of the saw until friction dried the hide, turning it white and soft. The saw would bow out from the pressure of the pulling but it was dull and wouldn't tear the hide. If a double-edge saw was not available, she used a wire nailed vertically, much like the saw, and she pulled the hide back and forth over that. Lorena Mae Walks Over Ice, personal communication to Mardell Plainfeather, 2008.
8. What is coming off may be the remnants of brain tissue used to tan. It contains an enzyme that breaks up muscle tissue and looks and smells like elementary school paste. After it is removed, the hide is like velvet. What is coming off may also be the last, loose bits of hide from the flesh side. Most tanners complete this part of the process by rubbing the hide over a wire loop, piece of rope, or other edge to create friction. (MP, BL)
9. For extra whiteness, she rubbed flour on the hide when it was completely dry and pulled it back and forth through the double-edge saw blade again, grasping the hide carefully with both hands so as not to cut the buckskin. Lorena Mae Walks Over Ice, personal communication to Mardell Plainfeather, 2008.
10. The hide is stretched out to allow excess flour to blow away naturally. (MP)

I Learn to Make Moccasins

Pretty soon,
I learn how to cut buckskin.
She showed me how to cut shape [for moccasins].
Said "You cut it around here like this."

She don't know how to make a pattern so she just showed me.
"Cut it straight [along the side] and then around [the toe],
and then this way and this way and get to the heel.
And then-n slice this [the vamp opening],
where you can stick your feet in there" she says,
"and this will be the tongue."

And she showed me
how to make the rawhide [soles]—I like the rawhide.[1]
They keep your feet in shape.
Nice shape.
Leather,
like nowadays,
it stretch a-a-nd go out of shape,
but I like a rawhide.

And she makes [the buckskin],
and the buckskin turn out re-e-eal soft where you can work it, work the needle in there.
A buckskin needle.
You hold the buckskin,
with the rawhide under,
and start to stitch it
around [to sew the buckskin top to the rawhide sole].[2]
And when that comes [right side] out it's just fi-i-ne.[3]

I still do that,
but I use leather because I don't have any hide [rawhide].
But I'd rather have a rawhide for sew.

1. Rawhide is stiff and durable. Tanners follow the initial steps for buckskin but stop before the last steps, which make the hide soft and pliable. (BL)
2. Here she is describing sewing the buckskin moccasin to the rawhide sole. With the pieces inside out, she stitches around the outer edge almost to the heel and then turns the moccasin right side out to finish. (MP)
3. She is saying that when the moccasin is turned right side out, it comes out just fine. The sole is sewn to the moccasin top on the inside, and then it is turned right side out, so you do not see the stitches or knotted sinew. (MP)

I Saw My Mother Make Indian Saddles

Only a few women knew how to make women's sturdy, old-fashioned saddles, and Lillian's mother was one. Although her daughter does not say so directly, she too became a saddle maker. The women's saddle is called an Indian saddle, a tree, or baleeisée, meaning "big wood." It includes a wood frame with tall horns in back and front, where the pommel and cantle would be on a western saddle, and it is covered with white buckskin. The front horn has a prong that serves as a hook. Saddles can be handsomely decorated with beaded pendants dangling from both horns, so women bring the saddles out for parades today, but they used to depend on them when they moved camp, hanging their baby cradles and family possessions from the horns and prong. Strength and dependability were essential, and that is why Little Horse is searching for a tree with just the right shape. (BL)

My mother did lots of beading—she used to make leggings for men, moccasins,
and make bags.
She used to bead.
She does a lot of that and she even makes Indian saddles.

In the Pryor District,
even up today,
there's few women [who make saddles].
[In my mother's time] just three women in the who-ole Crow tribe,
just three women know how to make Indian saddle,
and my mother's one of them.[1]

Sometimes they ask her to make one.
The tree.
The saddle.
I see her.
She takes a thin blanket.[2]
Wrap it around herself,
and then she say "I have to go find this tree.
Cut it and bring it."

"Just don't go with me" she says.
"I don't want no kids to following me—I'll be in the woods,
looking for the tree,
and I'll cut it down and I'll bring it over."[3]
And she said there's no other kind except box elder tree.
And there's l-o-ots of box elder trees at Pryor.[4]

She'd take off.
I guess she wander aro-o-und,
until she find one that she can
wet,
and bend
the way she want to.
Tie it,
and let it dry.
And then after that she
goes over with something.[5]
Dry it and here's the saddle after she finish.
The saddle.

And she cover it with buckskin.
I see her sew it with the buckskin.
Ni-ice white buckskin.
She cover that bow.
The front side [front horn] was smaller—that big, round head was there,
and that's the front side—the hind one
is the bigger.[6]
And the beading—[she did] all that.[7]
She makes saddles.

A-a-nd I remember one time,
a man came over and wanted a saddle.
Said "We know that you're the only one that
can make a saddle."
And he says "I'll give you a horse.
My best one.
And I'll give you a blanket and a quilt."
Said "Make me a saddle."[8]

1. My mother told me a long time ago that each district had at least one saddle maker, usually a woman. In the early years of the twentieth century, they included her mother and another Pryor woman, Uuwutáhosh (Many Irons). Today men also make saddles. (MP)
2. Horse followed the same fashion her daughter favored a generation later. Like most women of the time, she took a blanket or shawl when she left home and wrapped it around her hips, wore it over her shoulders, or draped it over one arm. (BL)
3. She is going to search carefully for the right tree. If she finds a good one, she will be able to take advantage of a natural fork to create the extra prong on the front horn. (BL)
4. She probably cut down the whole tree, selected the part that would make a good saddle, and trimmed it before she brought it home. Saddle makers used box elder because it didn't crack. (MP)
5. She may mean that her mother used something to wipe off excess moisture. (MP)
6. The front horn is smaller than the one in back, but both flare into a flat, round shape at the top. (BL)
7. When they decorate saddles, Crow saddle makers concentrate on the two horns, beading the outer edges of the circular tops and suspending colorful pendants from each. They may also bead pendants for the stirrups and drape the horse with beaded saddle blanket, crupper, and horse collar. A fully decked horse can be spectacular. (BL)
8. I owned the last saddle my mother made but gave it to Myranne Crooked Arm, granddaughter of my sister Lorena Mae. I wanted it to go to a descendant who is culturally active, well brought up, and will take special care of it. I know that Mom would have approved. (MP)

She's the Best Cook

So my mother makes the saddle, she beads good,
and they say she's
the best cook.
She cooks.

And my father
goes and invite people.
He a-l-lways does that!
And my mother says "Here you go and
invite people,
come in and
we don't have much food.

For ourselves.
But you go and think that I'd put on a big dinner for them."
He says "Oh don't care, don't mind about that—we'll get some."
I don't know where they'd get the money—I don't ask them.

But she sure makes ni-ice fry bread.
Nice—she's <u>known</u>
to be a
best
cook—she makes ni-ice biscuits, ni-ice bread.
And she cooks the
bread by the fire outside.
Browned it so nice and then put them on the table.
She sure is a good cook.[1]

1. My grandmother probably made traditional fry bread with flour, salt, baking powder, and warm water, deep-fat fried. Yeast dough is pretty new. My daughter Lorena calls it "white man fry bread." (MP)

Let's Go Pick Berries

Seems like <u>a-a-ll</u> these Indians
like berries.
And my mother tells me that berries
are good for you, good for your blood.
Said "Let's go pick berries."[1]

And I may be aro-o-und twelve years old then.
She gives me a pail and she takes a bag
a-a-nd couple pails.
And [says] "If we get this full we can come back and empty into something
   [a bucket or kettle].
And then by tomorrow I'll be grinding.
Pounding berries to dry.
And then,
if it don't storm,

or rain or
bad weather" she said "we can go out further,
to another coulee,
and pick more berries."

I'm not lazy!
I always want to help my mother—I really want to help her.
Haul water for her, watch her cook and,
and especially when she goes after berries I go help her.
And she give me a pa-ail,
a-a-nd she says,
"We'll pick enough to grind to
pound it and
dry it."
So I help with those.

A-a-nd she usually
pound them up and put them aside—and she gets a whole
handful, both handful.
She start to [squirt them berries into strips].[2]
And she showed me how and I ca-an't ever learn how to
dúchkiituua [squirt].
And they come,
o-oh sometimes they're bigger than this [about the size of hamburger
  patties.]
But me I just take a bunch and
flatten them up [pats hands as if making a mud pie].
She says "You can go ahead and
make them flat" and I
make my little o-old place—we spread out a canvas,
and I put them all in a r-row.
And I'm always careful—I take a
knife, change them when I see that they're a-a-ll dry so they won't get moldy
  inside.[3]

She gets hers dry just fine—she squeeze them, take a handful,
and she squeeze it out.

Another one,
another one,
a-a-ll in a row and they're easy to dry then.
And I sure watch her do that and I can't learn how to do it.
And up to today I can't never learn. (laughs)
I like to do those things for my mother.

1. Later she told us they picked Juneberries (also called serviceberries) and chokecherries in June and July. "A whole bunch of people" would go and would camp at East Pryor. (BL)
2. Women "squirted" the berries from cheese cloths or any similar cloth, rolled much as parchment paper is formed into a cone to decorate cakes. (MP)
3. She is turning them over to dry evenly. My mother's berries were round little patties in a straight row. They were real neat. (MP)

We Dry Chokecherries

Chokecherries are dried like other berries, but they have seeds in them. That is why Horse does so much pounding in this story. (BL)

She dri-ies chokecherries.
She goes out, pick chokecherries and bring them in and
pulverize—pound and pound until they all [ready] and she put them aside,
   make another batch.
They have a big stone.
Heavy.
And low in the center.
And she even have a—they all have,
the Indian women,
they have a little stone that they can pound [with],
big enough to grab hold of that.[1]
They start to pound these chokecherries. (pounds on table)
Pound and pound them until a-a-a-ll [pulverized].
Make a whole bunch, put them aside, [take] some more (pounds on table
   again)
till they get a whole pan full or more and then they start [shaping].

She put a handful in there
and hold, squeeze—
kept rolling in big canvas or piece
oil cloth put there,
And she just squee-e-eze.
All line up in a row—make them look pretty.
All the Indian women, they all do that.
Sometimes some of the lazy ones,
they don't know how to squeeze this way.
And me too—I don't know how to squeeze like my mother does,
so I just (gestures molding in hands)
flatten them—put them in a row, dry them.

That's that dried chokecherries. (chuckles)
My mother sure makes a lot.

> 1. She is describing a mortar and pestle. They used a large stone with an indentation to hold the food while it was being crushed and ground, and they used a smaller, handheld stone to do the crushing. (BL)

Pemmican

> *Pemmican was an important, old-time food that the Crow depended on before refrigeration. To make it, women sliced meat thin and dried it in the sun. Next they roasted it, pounded it fine, and mixed it with fat and berries. Then they formed it into compact, nutritious balls or patties and stored it away. In nomadic times, the Crow used pemmican for traveling and times of scarcity, but the process is time-consuming, so few women make it today. It is a delicacy now, and people may reciprocate with gifts when they receive it, as happens in this story.* (BL)

We [dried berries for] wintertime,
when we're hard up for fo-o-od.
Or sometimes [if] we have plenty of meat,
my mother make pemmican.
We don't have that every day.

Pemmican is something sca-arce,
and this is just som-me special occasion when they
going to have pemmican.
They don't have it every day.

[To make it] she
cook the sliced meat in the oven and turn it around,
until it—
o-oh—
she can tell when it's cooked.
See the meat been fresh when they slice it—put it out in the sun to dry—kept
    turning it around.
And then-n,
when it's dry,
real dry, then she can just pack it away.
And then when the time comes she have to make some pemmican,
she takes some out and put it in the oven.
When it's brown,
she takes it out—sprinkle a little water on it so it won't be tough.

And when it's dry she start to
pound it up.
Put it in a canvas and start breaking it up.[1]
And then she takes a big rock.
A big rock or a short-handled ax—
just the ax, the head part,
and make [the handle] short—cut it short so she can get a hold.
And she start to pound—po-ound a-a-ll that meat.
Turn it aro-o-und.

She do that just
on the ground—she put another
canvas for a pad under where she's going to pound this meat.
She just work there—pound and pound, change
the side, work it around, pound and pound till
it looks good.

And she'd be cooking o-or doing something else—I
grabbed the meat and,
and sort it out and see if there's any lumps there.
And she start in again—po-ound, kept pounding until it's a-all pulverized
   and good.

And says "It's ready now."
It looks, gee it just look like it's black and brown.
When you cook and,
and pound it up they call 'em hash.[2]
And it's su-u-re good—I used to pick some up and put a little salt on there,
eat it. (chuckles)

So she start to
put it in a big dishpan.
Put in all that [hash]—she's going to make a who-ole lot and
she get this pan full and I watch all the moves she makes.
And I help her—I'm right there to help her so I learn from my mother.

And she chop up all the bones off of
buffalo or cow.
They used to issue buffalo.
Kill a buffalo and distribute
to all the districts and we used to have buffalo.
And she
saved the bones.
A-a-nd put them outside.
I remember now there was a wagon.
There was no box on it.
She spread it with canvas a-a-nd put the bones on there so the dogs wouldn't
   get to them.
And she cut up these bones.
Cut them up—my father used to take a
ax and just chop them up and just pile them up.

And she start to boil these bones.
And that's the best grease
to use on the pemmican.

She don't use lard or
nothing except just the fat off of them bones.
She cut them up, pound them up, and she cook and then when the—
the broth boil the bones,
she takes the bones out and then she skim the fat off of the water.
And she put it in the dish.
Kept doing that until she gets a-a-ll the grease off of that broth.
And she save it.

And then she gets this chokecherry ready.
A-a-ll cooked [softened].
When she first pound them,
work them up,
she dries them,
and she pack them away.
And then the day when she want to make dessert or make pemmican,
she takes the chokecherries and cook them.
Boil them and
pour the juice off and take the chokecherries and they all cooked.

And then she puts it in that meat that we call hash—*baannátchiia*.
We call that hash.
She put that in—ni-ice color.
She put the chokecherries in and start stirring.
She just take her hand there—
mix it all up, work it all up till they a-a-ll
mix good.

A-a-nd
she says "Bring the sugar."
Then she puts sugar on there and she
skim all that fat off of the broth of that
meat bones.
And she put the grease in the
meat and start to work it with her hands.
Pretty soon she put more sugar in there.
And then she takes her hands and start to make little balls.
Squeeze them together so they stick together.

A-a-nd
they sur-re good—that's what we call pemmican.
And I say "Mama can I have a piece?"
And she take about a handful, press it together and make it hard and just
    like a ball,
and we eat—they're good.

They're awful scarce and we don't have that every day.
Just when we have plenty of meat she
pack away, maybe [for] Christmas, maybe Thanksgiving.
And they're kind of special.
She makes those and o-o-oh—

A-a-nd if she say "I'm going to give this away,
to my niece or nephew,"
then she makes—sometimes she makes them big balls
a-a-nd medium-sized.
She don't make them <u>too</u> small.
And they're a-a-ll dried together and put awa-ay and when you
take a bite on it, just bite on it,
gee they're delicious.

A-a-nd she gets it ready and
take it to some nephew or niece.
When she takes them they're so thankful—says "O-oh m-my!
We thank you Auntie."
And then before she goes they have to give her a ni-i-ice—
maybe they gave her a brand new quilt.
Maybe a blanket, maybe a shawl, maybe a dress good.[3]
And she says thank you and
she goes off home—and I say "Momma can I have that shawl?" and she says
    "Sure, yes.
And your brother can have the blanket, the comforter.
A-a-nd I'll keep the dress goods."[4]

> 1. Before pounding, they put the meat between large pieces of canvas so none would be lost. I've seen my mother do this. (MP)

1. The Bullshows and Baumgartner families, circa 1910. Standing from left: Dorothy Baumgartner and unnamed daughter, Lillian's brother Daniel Bullshows, her father Bull Shows, and Alfred Baumgartner. Seated in chair: Lillian's mother Little Horse and baby, probably Hulda. Seated on floor from left: Lillian, about six years old, holding puppy, and her brother Caleb.

2. Little Horse's half sister, Clara White Hip, and husband, early twentieth century. Clara is wearing an elk-tooth dress with teeth to the hem.

3. Lillian, approximately fifteen years old, in dress with beaded flowers, circa 1920.

Collection of Mardell Hogan Plainfeather.

4. Finds Them and Kills Them (Ohchiish) in front of his home, 1928.

Photograph by Agent C. H. Asbury. General Hugh Scott Collection, National Anthropological Archives, Smithsonian Institution.

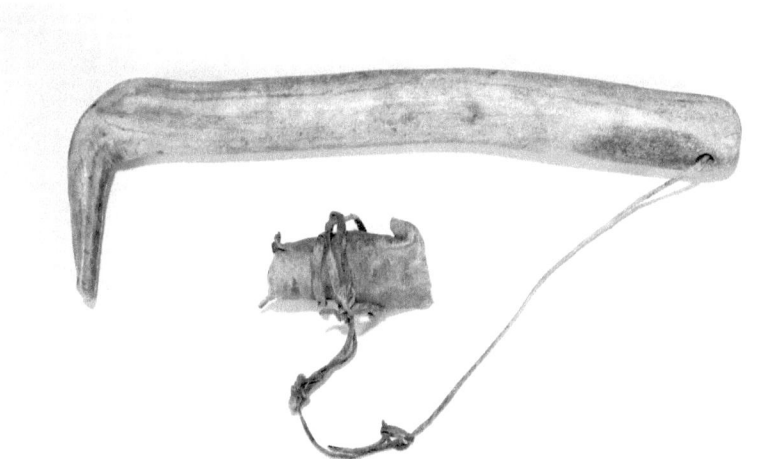

5. Bone scraper Lillian's mother, Little Horse, used to tan hides. Length 13.5 inches.

6. Lillian and her first husband, Alex Plainfeather, at the time of their marriage, 1921. Lillian is wearing an elk-tooth dress from the groom's family, and the buggy is draped with additional wedding gifts.

7. Lillian holding her first child, Samuel Plainfeather, 1922.

8. Lillian's second husband, Robert Yellowtail, with Chief Plenty Coups, circa 1929.

9. Lillian with her third husband, Paul Singer, and daughters Lorena Mae, Nellie, and Rose Marie, in front of the original house in Dunmore, 1934.

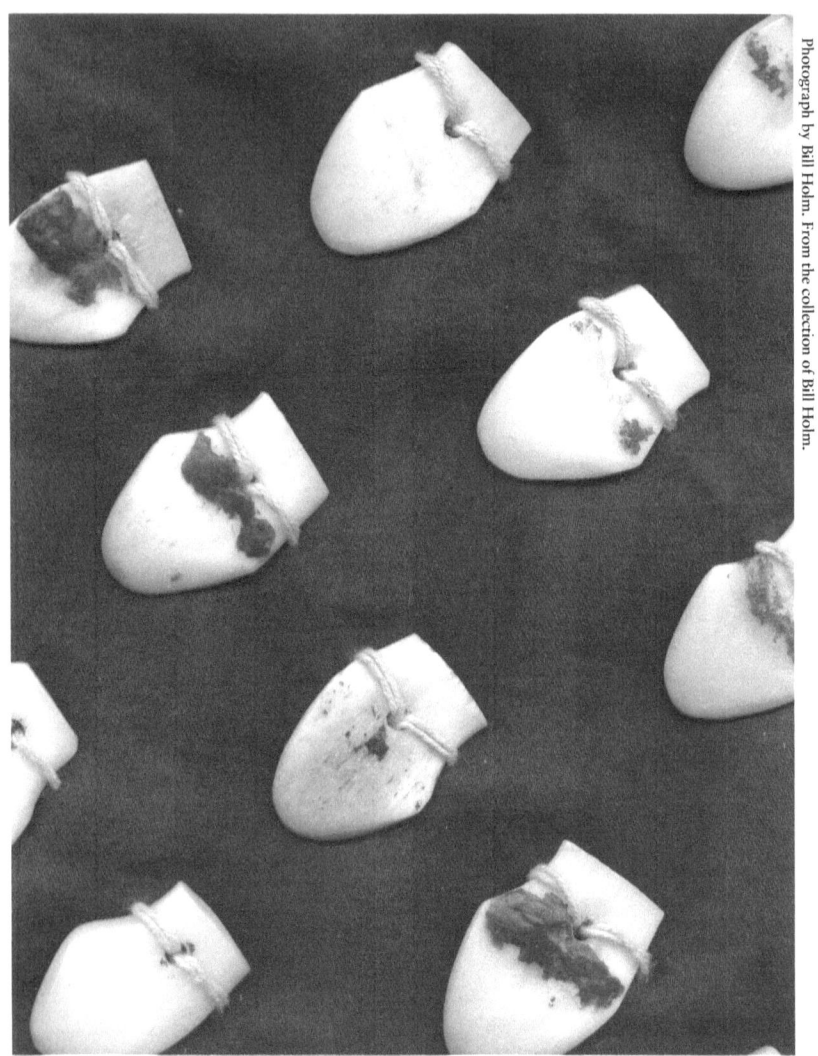

10. Detail of elk-tooth dress, showing the technique for sewing the teeth to the cloth.

11. Lillian's fourth husband, George Hogan Sr. when attending the Indian School in Carlisle, Pennsylvania, approximately age twelve, circa 1897.

Photograph by John H. Andrews. Collection of Mardell Hogan Plainfeather.

12. Lillian's sons, Adam Singer and Samuel Plainfeather, circa 1943.

Collection of Nellie Sings In the Mountains.

13. Lillian's parents, Bull Shows and Little Horse, in front of Lillian's home in Crow Agency, with Lillian's daughter Mary and her grandson Russell, Samuel's son, 1946.

14. George and Lillian Hogan with their daughter Mardell. Taken in Lapwai, Idaho, during a trip with the Church of God, 1951.

15. Lillian with Lady Bird Johnson, Betty Babcock (wife of Montana governor Tim Babcock), and Secretary of State Stewart Udall in front of the old house in Dunmore, 1964. The new house had already been built, so the visitors looked at the old one, then walked to the new one.

16. Mardell, Mary, and Nellie in front of their home in Butte. Published in the Butte newspaper, the *Montana Standard*, on August 14, 1964, with a story of Lady Bird's pending visit with Lillian.

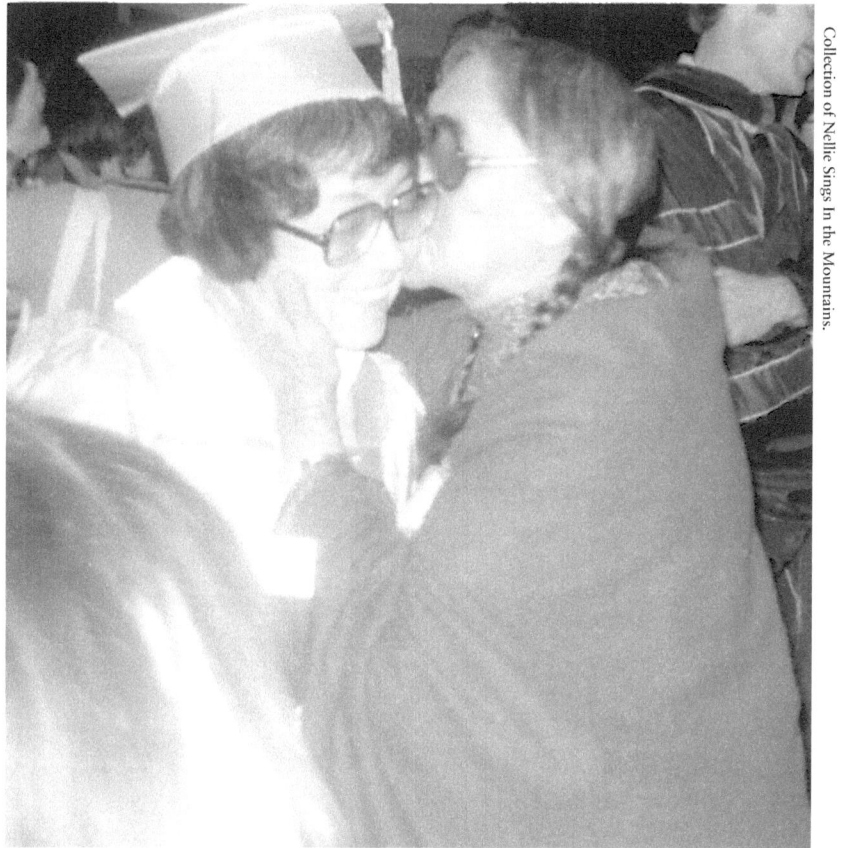

17. Lillian kissing her daughter Mardell when she graduated cum laude from Rocky Mountain College, Billings, 1979.

18. Floral sketches by Lillian for beadwork designs, 1981.

19. Lillian's great-grandson Calvin Walks Over Ice in beaded outfit Lillian designed, circa 1991. During a bleak time in Cal's life, his mother, Sandy, turned to "Grammy" for prayers and guidance, and Lillian told her granddaughter that she would come to her with an answer. She returned with a floral design and told Sandy to bead the outfit Cal is wearing in this photograph. Lillian reassured her that her son would come through his rough period and would wear his outfit with confidence and a new life because she had prayed over it. Cal graduated from Concordia College in Moorhead, Minnesota, and is now with the Social Security Administration. He is frowning here because his horse had almost thrown him, but he is a happy person. He is often complimented, even by strangers, when he wears this outfit.

20. Lillian seated with her daughters and many of her grandchildren, 1976. Back row from left to right: Mary's son Barry Rawn, Lorena Mae's son Carson with Nellie's son Barry Bryan in front of him, Carson's wife Verlie, Nellie, Lorena Mae's son Louis, and Lorena Mae's husband Cedric. Middle row from left to right: Nellie's daughter Merrie Lillian, Mary's daughter Meredith, Lorena Mae's daughter Cassie, Lillian with Lorena Mae's grandson Cedric Thomas ("C. T.") at her knee, Lorena Mae and Lorena Mae's daughter Roberta ("Bobbie Sox"). Seated in front row: Mardell with her daughter Lorena Delrae on her lap, Mary, and Lorena Mae's daughter Loreen. Missing from photo are Samuel and his family, Adam and his family, and Lorena Mae's daughter Cassandra ("Sandy") and her two boys.

21. Lillian seated in elk-tooth dress, with her daughters Mary, Lorena Mae, Mardell, and Nellie, 1976.

22. Nellie and Lillian cleaning buckskin dress behind Mardell's house at the Little Bighorn Battlefield, 1980.

23. Lillian in elder years, probably 1980s.

2. Hash is the pounded meat before it is combined with berries and grease. *Baannátchiia* is the Crow word for ground, dried meat. The word for hamburger is *íiluksaapiia*, which means ground, tender meat. (MP)
3. Material to make a dress. (BL)
4. She is just using this as an example. People gave what they could, and the recipient returned home and shared the gifts with other family members. (MP)

Wild Turnip

And we dig
wild turnips.
We call it wild turnips.
They come in a big bush.
We dig them up and they come,
some come w-a-ay big, about this big around [about three inches].
So we dig those too.

And we
peel them off—there's a heavy
skin on there.
We pull that out,
and it's white inside too, real white and juicy.
We cut it and then my mother would slice it off.
Slice it up and then we'd
lay them on a nice
piece of canvas and dry the weeds.
In wintertime,
when it's good and dried,
she takes it out.
Says "Let's have some of this turnip."
And we did.

Ihé.
That's what she call it—*ihé.*
That's that wild turnip.
And
we cut it up and make a dessert and o-oh <u>my</u>,
the people sure go for that dessert.[1]

And here other women don't care—maybe a few
go out and dig the root, dry it up.
But when it's dry, when it's maked into a dessert,
it su-u-re has a good flavor.[2]

1. I like to eat turnip raw. It's delicious. Sometimes I'd eat so many, my mother wouldn't have much left, and she'd get angry with me. Turnip dessert is a type of pudding. I don't eat it, and I have never watched my mother cook it, but this is my sister Lorena Mae's recipe: Wash and peel fresh turnips and dry them in the sun until they look stringy and the color of spaghetti, probably a day or two. To make the dessert, boil dried turnips in water until tender. Drain and boil again in fresh water to insure that they are clean. Add about a teaspoon of butter to the boiling pot. Continue boiling and add sugar to taste, but do not overboil. Turnips should be tender to the touch. Meanwhile, mix flour with warm water to make a paste (as for gravy) or use corn starch for thickening. Simmer about five minutes. Remove from heat and taste for tenderness. If it is tender enough for you, it is ready to eat. (MP)
2. My mother said that years ago, with more open range and fewer farmers, there were more places to look for wild turnips. There are still some where no one plows. Whatever is available usually grows in the lower hills. When I was young, the few times I went looking for wild turnips with Mom, she and I went over barbed wire to private ground to look for them. I wouldn't try it nowadays. I have heard that ranchers and farmers threaten to shoot Indians who go on "their" property. (MP)

Bitterroot

Bitterroot is a low-growing plant with an edible root, pink or white blossoms, and leaves that resemble grass. Like many tribes, the Crow used the root for food. As Lillian makes clear in this story, they sometimes turned their gathering expeditions into social occasions. (BL)

And now, let's see now—next week,
about next week or so [mid-May],
it's the right time to dig bitterroot.
My mother goes a-a-nd
she has some other women with her,
who always like to
go with my mother and dig the bitterroot.
And I sometimes go with them.

We used to go in a buggy.
Horse and buggy.
Somebody drive and there'd be a bunch of us go.
Go a-a-nd carry lunch, carry water.
Make coffee over there and we'd have lunch there—we start digging.
Dig the bitterroots.
She had me to shake the dirt off of the plants.
I shake the dirt and pile them up and there's a pile there and there's
   [another] pile—pretty soon we
get a who-o-ole <u>bag</u> full and
more than a bag full.

Kept digging and then in the morning she says "Hurry up now.
We can't let them dry.
When they're dry that's when they get so you can't pull the skins out easy."
My mother showed me how.
Open the top—
break it on top.
There's a little heart in there, red,
and in the shape of a heart.
Ju-u-st like a human heart and it's red.
A-a-nd she said "This little heart's
what makes it bitter,
the root—soon as you take this little heart out, throw it away.
That's when the plant is good."

Take that little heart out and then peel it off.
And then when we peel it,
it's a-a-ll white.
And then,
they wash it.
After they peel it they wash it and
spread it out in the
cloth or paper or anything like that,
and we dry it.
Next day we kept turning till a-a-ll that's
dry—and very scarce.

They dry that for dessert.
The people sure like it.
You dry it,
keep it for the winter,
and when the winter comes—when they want that bitterroot dessert,
go and put it in the water like any dessert.
Boil it.
I always put a little grease like butter.
Put a little butter on there, start to boil, boil, boil until tender.
And you put sugar in there.
Put thickening in there.
And after that they dish it out and give it to the people and o-o-oh <u>my</u> they enjoy.
Pretty scarce too.
Awful scarce but they like it—people like that dessert.

But very a few women go out there to dig bitterroot and
I and my mother always be one of them too.
And we carry lunch over there and we eat over there—we enjoy digging them.
And when any feast or
some special occasion,
they make that Indian bitter dessert.
People su-u-re go for it.
They say "I want some of that! I want some of that!"
Pretty soon it's all gone. (laughs)
We sure like it.

CHAPTER NINE

Tobacco Iipche (Sacred Pipe Society) and the Medicine Dance (Tobacco Society)

If She Pulls Through, You Can Adopt Her

After she entered boarding school, Lillian became so sick that her parents thought they would lose her. This is her story of the Indian doctors who treated her and the family's pledge to a clan uncle to join the sacred Tobacco Society if she recovered. Indian doctors gain their knowledge through inheritance, visions, or occasionally dreams. Some employ herbs or touch. Others, like this doctor, use spiritual treatments.[1]

The Tobacco Society is central to Apsáalooke identity. It is dedicated to the health and well-being of the tribe and is named for a sacred plant that is not smoked. Some Crow join by invitation. Others, like Lillian's family, pledge to participate if a sick relative regains health or other endeavors succeed. In nomadic days, they also pledged membership if a relative returned safely from battle. (BL)

I was sick
one time when they,
my father and mother, come up the dormitory.
During the day they come and visit and stay by my bed a-a-nd maybe they rub my feet.
They didn't want to leave me,
and they kept coming and one night
my father said,
"She's getting worse,
and no doctors around here.[2]

I'm afraid she's going to die."
Said "I'm going to take her out.
Now you put her on my back.
A-a-nd get your shawl and tie her,
to my shoulder."³

And there was a lo-o-ng stairway.
I was about—
six years old.
And they always call me Tall Woman, Tall Girl.
I must be tall then.
So,
said "Come on! Put her on my back,
and tie her up.
So I can go down them stairs."
It's a lo-o-ng stairway.

He lift me up,
and I don't know what was happening.
Really I was so si-ick.
And he
packed me on his back and tie me to his shoulder,
and we went down-n slow.
Re-e-eal slow down the stairway and when he got to the bottom of the stairs,
a-a-nd to the door, there's double door—one on the outside and one the inside.
When we got to the door,
my mother was just about to grab the door open,
and he-ere comes the superintendent.
And the doctor.
And the-e lady matron and some of the other employees.
Come and stop my father.
And he said "I'm going to take
my child home—she's about dead.
I'm going to take her home—whoever's going to come near me, I'm going to, just going to
beat them up."

And he had me on his back and I was just about dozing off and I was so
   sick I
didn't know what was happening.
I cried—that's all I did.
I cried a little bit.
And they talk among themselves and they said "All right!"—the doctor says,
"All right Bull Shows.
You can take her."
And "She might die.
You can take her now—we'll get some more blankets and cover her up."
And they tell some of the women, matron I guess.
They got some more blankets and covered
me up and
he got [the blankets] tight.
And they open the door for us and we got
down—took me down stairs and took me where they camp.[4]

And that's when they call these doctors—Indian doctors.
One doctor, they called him,
a-a-nd he said,
he
said "If I ever
doctor anybody, a sick person,
and I know,
in a dream,
that person is
die,
that's when my medicine say 'Quit doctoring.
Your medicine don't work,
so just quit and let her die.'"
And he often done that.

About three left me.
Three Indian doctors
left—they said "She's pretty sick, we can't do nothing for her."
And the last one,
he said he dreamt that up at the Gap, Pryor Gap,

there was a buggy—in this dream,
I was in the buggy,
and the horses ran away,
a-a-nd knocked me off of the seat and I laid on the ground dead.
And he said "In this dream it's bad" he said.
"I can't doctor her any more."

And my father and mother sure felt bad.
So they got another uncle,
a clan uncle.[5]
Daxpitchée Baalapéesh [Kicking Bear].
And
Alasíia Áhush [Shows Plenty] *was called on also,*
and this man he don't walk straight—he's kind of crippled.
Limper.
But he's a good doctor.
He came over.
He said (raps on table five times for emphasis)
—he said "I'm going to <u>stay</u> with this sick girl." (raps on table)

These others
quit.
Left us.
[Shows Plenty] said "My medicine
is going to help me."
A-a-nd I guess he prayed.
Might say "Almighty
is going to help me and this girl will heal
a-a-nd will live."
And su-u-re did.
These others
didn't think I was going to live.
They left us,
except this
old man that heals.

And he had a little rattle,
painted red,
and he start to singing.
Above me,
my head.
Shake it little bit
and start to bringing it,
singing and shaking his rattle.
He done that
I don't know how many times—half of the time I don't know what's going on, I was so sick.

And then this uncle [Kicking Bear],
he came up—see my dad asked him to come and doctor, help doctor too.
And he said,
"You can have this little girl.[6]
She pulls through
and live again,
you can have her and you can adopt her [into the Medicine Dance]."
And sure enough,
I was over it and he adopted me.
It was Kicking Bear who adopted me.[7]

Shows Plenty [cured me].
Said "I'll make some medicine,"
a-a-nd make like if he's making tea.
He says "You make her take it.
Give it to her about four times a day."
The water looked,
o-oh kind of a greenish color.
And he said "Just make her drink it and see that she take it down nice."
And they did.
They always make that and make me take it.[8]

And the [white] doctor says "She's going to die."
And these Indian doctors say "She's going to die."
No.

I pulled through because them two stayed with me,
a-a-nd so my dad said you can adopt her
in this Medicine Dance.
And that's why I was adopted by them,
the man and his wife,
a-a-nd went throu-ugh the Dance.
And that woman is a-l-lways good to me.

1. Of Indian doctors, or medicine men, Denig (*Five Indian Tribes*, 188) says they were thought to "possess superhuman powers to bring about events." Medicine Crow (*From the Heart of Crow Country*, 7) referred to them as both healers and visionaries, "well versed in the secrets of nature through their intensive study and worship of their respective 'gods.'" Frey (*The World of the Crow Indians*, 59, 62) referred to medicine, or *baaxpée*, as a spiritual power, saying it is "more than the power to alter a path, effect a cure, or obtain a job. It is also the power to know which path should be taken." (BL)
2. He meant there were no Indian doctors there. Apparently he felt an Indian doctor would be of more help. (MP)
3. They used to carry babies on their backs in a shawl or something similar, forming a makeshift seat for the child. One end of the shawl went under the carrier's arm, the other over the opposite shoulder. They tied in front, near the sternum. (MP)
4. When her parents heard that my mother was ill, they probably set up a teepee or tent nearby. (MP)
5. Clan uncles (traditionally called clan fathers) come from the same clan as one's biological father, so Kicking Bear must have belonged to the Ties the Bundle Clan, like Bull Shows. (BL)
6. A symbolic gesture. Mom's father is saying Kicking Bear will have the honor to adopt her into the Medicine Dance, the Tobacco Society, if she lives. (MP)
7. See Lowie ("The Tobacco Society," 134) on illness as a common motivation to join the Tobacco Society. The sick person or a relative might pledge membership if one recovers. (BL)
8. She also said that he burned incense. (MP)

Tobacco Adoptions

In a later story, Lillian describes the way she was taken into the Tobacco Society as a young adult (see "They Adopt Me in the Medicine Dance," chapter 13). Here she refers more generally to the four ceremonies and exchange of gifts. New members join the sacred Society through initiation, or adoption, by an established member. They may be taken at any age but are referred to as the children of those who sponsor them. The new "parents" and their symbolically newborn "children" dress each other in fine clothing and give additional costly gifts, and the new members receive songs and sacred tobacco medicines. They will not be raised by these new parents but will maintain a special relationship.[1]

In the second half of this brief story, Lillian is talking about the society's distant beginnings through a sacred vision. Adoptions declined in the mid-twentieth century but have increased again. Only a few are held each year, because of the expense. (BL)

[To join] they have to adopt you
in the Medicine Dance.
And after that,
the adoption, what ceremony they have to go through, after that,
then you're a member with the Tobacco Dance—then
the one that adopt you
give you that tobacco.[2]
You have to give them lots of good things—a horse,
blankets, money, stuff like that.
And then you own the medicine.[3]
You have to be adopted before you can do anything.[4]

Wa-a-a-y back when they didn't have no horses, the
o-old Indians, they don't know that Tobacco Dance.
But later on-n-n,
some men fast.
They go out and fast.
And then the spirit came and give them medicine.
And then from there on,
they start this medicine in the camp,
and then the next thing you know they've adopted one.
Next thing you know,
they can adopt different ones and they start in—that spreads all over.
They can be adopted.[5]

1. For details on songs, dances, and other aspects of adoption ceremonies, see Big Man, "The Beaver Dance"; and Curtis, *The North American Indian*, 64–67. (BL)
2. Today seeds are rare. I did not receive any when I was adopted. I don't know of anyone who did. (MP)

3. "Then you own the medicine," probably refers to both tobacco seeds and other sacred medicines. Although seeds are uncommon today, Medicine Crow ("The Effects of European Culture Contacts," 91) says initiates used to receive a medicine bag of seeds. In the early twentieth century, Lowie recorded the other medicines of several Crow adoptees. Gray Bull, for example, received a black wolf, red feathers, a whip, and two eagle tails. Cuts the Picketed Mule was given special garments and ornaments, a yellow lizard, an otter-skin headband, shells, and two eagle wings, as well as packages of tobacco. Old Dog's medicines included weasel skins, artificial strawberries, and small brass bells that represented stars. Each reciprocated generously with horses and other gifts. See Lowie, "The Tobacco Society," 159–61. (BL)
4. Here is the process I know. The people who want to adopt designate someone to "babysit" the "child" each time we go in, which is three times. On the fourth time, the mother is ready to symbolically have her baby. This is when we get our four songs. The song givers, usually couples, have each been selected by the hopeful parent. They sing the four songs the night before the child (adoptee) is to be "born," then the child selects the songs she wants from each of the song givers. The next day the child will be "born," and we are not in a building anymore. This time we are outside. We begin in a tent where the child is dressed, and she and the song givers have their faces painted. Then we march toward the main lodge, a teepee that is draped with two teepee covers instead of one, signifying two lodges joining. There the "child" gets to dance with the song he or she has selected, along with the people who gave the song. The new parents give their child a medicine. I received a white medicine weasel from Alice Bull Tail, who had adopted Evelyn and George Old Elk, my own adoptive parents. She advised me on how to store it, and I do as I was instructed. (MP)
5. Many attribute the Tobacco Society to a vision that came to Chief No Intestines, or No Vitals, when the Crow left the Hidatsa. Lowie recorded several additional versions of the society's beginnings and evolution, most of them about a single person receiving a vision, including instructions for establishing rituals and inviting others to join or be adopted. See Lowie, "The Tobacco Society," 175–90. (BL)

Time to Plant Tobacco

The tribe used to plant the precious tobacco seeds every spring, accompanied by drumming, dancing, and repetitions of four, a sacred number, and what follows are Lillian's childhood memories of the ceremony. The society has several chapters, and in those days each had a mixer, or planter, who ritually combined the seeds with water, animal manure, and plant matter and soaked them the night before the planting ceremony, but the Tobacco Society, like many Native customs, was condemned by white authorities, so the planting ceremony almost disappeared by the mid-twentieth century, making the following story a valuable record. In recent years Winona Plenty Hoops has been the only living person with the rights of a mixer. She has been working to revive the planting ritual. (BL)

Us Indian-n girls,
we may be around
eight or seven years old,
and that's the first time we ever
knew about [remember] the Indian tobacco.
We see the older people—they keep it so sacred.
They do that once a year.
Plant tobaccos.
And they have nice songs.
And they march [dance in procession to the garden].

They might have about four or five drummers,
and they have the prettiest songs.[1]
And a bunch of women all dress up nice and
put on paint and
a-a-all get ready for the dance and they all look nice.[2]
A-a-nd the people that don't
take part in it—oh l-o-ots of people—stand on the side [of the route],
this side and this side, and here the dancers come.
That's when they call that "time to plant tobacco."
Indian tobacco.

I don't know what kind of seed they are because we didn't get too close to look at them,
but anyway they kept that sacred.
They think you have to do that every once a year.
So the dancers a-a-ll
tie up their hair and handkerchief aro-o-und and tie it.
And they hold up good smelli-i-ng brushes.[3]
They look purple.
These plants look re-eal purple.
They had to hold it in one hand.

A bunch of leaves like chokecherry leaves and stems—hold it, and
when the singers sing,
they stop [in four places, the sacred number] and dance.

They have to sing four times and then,
when they finish the four songs, then they march again,
to the place where they fix a—fix just like fix a garden.
The soil is all dug smoo-oth and ni-ice and they
put down sticks over there and here.[4]
A-a-nd when the dancers come to where the plow
fixed the ground nice, they come and dance right on the edge.
That's when they call that "planting tobacco."
And then the drummers start singing [once again],
and they have to dance about four times, sing it over about four times,
before they get through with that—and they start in where the ground is all
   soft and nice.

They have a big stick, a pointed stick,
a-a-nd make a hole in the ground.
Maybe about six,
six or four,
older people, medicine [people],
that take part in the Medicine Dance.
They have to dance,
and then they hold that seed
and start singing and dancing.
And then pretty soon they get ready and take a step,
on this soil.
And
put a bunch of seed there,
and then leave it there and than another song.
They sing another song. (claps lightly to rhythm)
Sing and sing until they get through, and then they cover the dirt up.
Cover it up,
and that's ready.
In the ground.[5]

Maybe one hill
they put in about—
four,
four seeds to one ground.
Not one person—it has to be
this first person over here,
the second one and the second one and the second one.[6]
A-a-nd no-o-body [else] isn't supposed to get on that ground
where it's worked and nice, ready for the planting.
And when they get through,
now they sing again and dance.

And then a lot of people,
men, especially men,
of course a few women too,
they gather up sticks [for the fence].[7]
Some men have to bring stronger,
bigger sticks,
to fix the fence around this tobacco plant.
And I know my mother says,
"Go to get a big stick."
Before they ever-r
start dancing,
we'd get our sticks ready.
A big one.
We get a stick and
get over,
where the dancers are.
A-a-nd they dance [some more].
Put the corner posts over there—
if it's a big one,
they
put up posts.
And all these people bring in the sticks.
They're building a fence around this garden for tobacco,
so they lean on their sticks.

The more they
put on the sticks,
for the fence,
the more protection for the tobacco, where nobody can't get in.
A-a-nd they sing again and then when they get through,
it's all over.

And then they go out and,
and it's like a picnic—they go in different directions and
sit down with their family and
eat a prepared dinner,
any way they want to.
And when they get through they just leave that garden there—tobacco garden.

A-a-nd with-i-i-n
three weeks or so,
they have to go over and check it.
Look over the garden, see if the seeds are sprouting.
They do,
they come up—they sprout.
Green le-eaves.
And they start growing.
And then they sing again. (lightly claps rhythm)
Sing and sing.
And then when they get through they go back.

And I still remember the songs they sing.
(sings in Apsáalooke)
The words to that is:

> We put in a garden.
> Tobacco garden.
> And in the soil,
> it's a-a-ll growing good.
> And we're all glad.[8]

We sing the song for this occasion,
for the grow of the tobacco.
It's all over—they go home.

And then after that in,
o-oh, during the summer [they harvest].
I never look at this.
They a-a-ll fix
just like a big picnic.
A-a-ll go to this garden.
They built the fence where nobody can't get in there.

And all these tobaccos got big leaves and green and nice.
They grow good,
and everybody is happy.
And so the older people, the medicine
men and women, go and
pull the roots out.
Shake the dirt off.
Put it away, dry it.
And then after it's dry,
they keep that re-eal sacred.
Put it away,
and they pray about it—say
"We going to have
no sickness come aro-ound.
And healthy people.
Children to grow healthy and nice"—and they pray that way.
And then they tie up the
leaves.
Put it away.

But they don't have any [now].
Since all this religion [since] the missionaries come in.
They say that you mustn't worship any plant or any image.
We have to read the Bible, live for God.

So all that medicine is (claps hands)
all gone now.⁹

No, I just know
one person that has
is Winona [Plenty Hoops].¹⁰
She has seeds.
I think she's got some of them plants, tobacco leaves.
They're not green—they're dry up.¹¹

1. Members each have their own songs. Drummers specialize in remembering all of them. One only has to say the title of his or her song, and the drummers immediately pick up the chant and sing. (MP)
2. Several writers describe women playing leadership roles in the ceremony. Leforge (Marquis, *Memoirs*, 190), adopted into a Crow family in 1868, specified that they were the ones who donned their finery, saying "women were the special participants." Lowie ("The Tobacco Society," 164) reported a woman leading the procession to the garden, a position many consider "the greatest office in the society." Several scholars noted that it was the women who danced at the four stops on the way to the garden. See Lowie, "The Tobacco Society," 165; Medicine Crow, "The Effects of European Cultural Contact," 91; and Simms, "Cultivation of Medicine Tobacco," 333). Women also carried the tobacco medicine bags on their backs to the garden and were often mixers, the tradition Winona Plenty Hoops continues today. (BL)
3. The ones I know are willow branches. (MP) Simms ("Cultivation of Medicine Tobacco," 332) spoke of chokecherry branches. (BL)
4. Lowie ("The Tobacco Society, 167) describes sticks placed at opposite ends of the garden with ropes tied between them, defining the sections allotted to each member. Lillian is probably referring to the same stage in the ceremony. (BL)
5. The number of "medicine people" is small, so these are probably mixers, but reports differ on who did the planting. See Leforge in Marquis, *Memoirs*, 190; Lowie, "The Tobacco Society," 168; and Simms, "Cultivation of Medicine Tobacco," 334. (BL)
6. This is unclear. She may intend to describe the planters from each chapter, working side by side to punch holes in the sections corded off for their members. (BL)
7. According to Curtis (*The North American Indian*, 67), young men wove brush and willow branches into the fence when seeking war honors. This would have stopped before Lillian's time, when Plains warfare had ended. (BL)
8. The literal translation of the song is "We've put in a garden. Let us celebrate [or sing praise songs]." In Mom's longer translation, she might have been explaining how glad they felt that the tobacco was in the soil. More recently, I saw this elation at Winona Plenty Hoops's planting. I saw hope in their faces that the tobacco would grow. Everyone knows that as long as we have the tobacco, the Crow will exist as a people. (MP)

9. Several agents and ministers worked to eradicate the Tobacco Society. Agent Asbury, for example, aggressively persecuted individuals for traditional religious practices and "would have Tobacco Society leaders rounded up, bound hand and foot, and displayed in the park at Crow Agency" (McCleary, "Akbaatashee," 46). Yellowtail (Fitzgerald, *Yellowtail*, 24–25) noted that churches do not discourage traditional religious practices today, but he recalled earlier missionaries telling them to burn their medicine bundles. (BL)
10. The position of planter is a privilege passed down through relationship or purchase. Purchase is done with gifts and a request to the owner to carry on the duties. (MP)
11. For additional information on planting, see Lowie, "The Tobacco Society"; and Nabokov, "Cultivating Themselves." Briefer references include Leforge in Marquis, *Memoirs*, 189–90; Simms, "Cultivation of Medicine Tobacco," 331–35; and Voget, *They Call Me Agnes*, 108–9. A film of Winona Plenty Hoops's planting ceremony in 2005 is housed at the Western Heritage Center in Billings, Montana. A second film, of Winona and Barney Old Coyote, 2008, is housed at the Little Big Horn College. (BL, MP)

Tobacco Bags

Tobacco bags (medicine bundles) held tobacco and other sacred medicine powers called baaxpée.[1] *Women carried them to the garden on their backs during planting ceremonies. They were also placed on altars toward the rear of adoption lodges for Tobacco (Beaver Dance) adoption rituals, and they were opened with great care when medicines were accessed. This story describes the respect Crow people show to the bags and the decorations or red cloth wrappings that individual members contribute when they seek extra blessings. It also describes one of Winona's more recent ceremonies. At the time this story was told, many young people were not witnessing the planting, hearing the accompanying songs, or seeing the medicine bundles in use, and that is why Lillian says, "This generation don't know nothing. They ne-ever hear about tobacco." This is changing now, through the efforts of Winona and other tribal elders.* (BL)

They always
make a bag out of buckskin—make a bag
and keep these leaves in there.
And they have to paint this buckskin.
A-a-nd whoever wants to,
they can put beads on these bags.

The bags come about,
let's see—
about ten inches.
A bag about that big.

They can paint it with red paint [probably ochre].
They pray and then dab this paint on,
and some of the women
say "I'll bead, put beads on there," and they put one desi-ign, maybe four designs on there,
and bead and that's a bag.
A-a-nd a piece is sewed onto the top—it laps over [to form a closing flap].
And then they tie it.
And that's where they keep the tobacco plant.

No certain design.
Just to make it look pretty,
because that's a sacred bag.
And they said by doing that they can wish
for a good health,
a good family—all the children, all their family in good health.
They pray that way and then when the tobacco is packed in there, they su-u-re keep it sacred.

But I don't think nobody has any
now except Winona—she might have some.
She's got a bag, buckskin.
About fo-our,
four or fi-ive years ago,
they had some singing.
Some planting there.
She has to sit there,
with red paint on her.
She wears an o-o-old buckskin [from] w-a-ay back
in great, great-grandma.
A buckskin dress
that's painted with red paint.

And she
had her hair all combed and
rolled up and tied up here with some plants—flowers.
And she sit there.
And they were singing.
And she opened this bag.
And we went over to look on the singing, heard the singing.

I used to know the singing.
The songs.
I forgot the songs—I can't sing them again.
I sang just one. [See "Time to Plant Tobacco," earlier in this chapter.]
So that's pretty.
I think that was always nice—now they don't have any more.

I know my mother used to have a bag.
Had be-eads,
and then the string that ties up here [in the middle where the flap meets the
    bag],
and put more beads on there—and they
make it look pretty and
they always keep it inside.
Way up on the wall where nobody can't touch it.
They u-used to keep it outside.[2]

They even say it's holy, sacred.
When they even hadn't open the bag, you mustn't
go in front of that person.
You have to keep quiet and,
a-a-nd see them pack and tie—get ready, pack it away.[3]
They sing too.
Sing and sing and when they get through,
now that's sacred a-a-nd packed away for the family.
They put them away.

The tobacco medicine is in the bag.
A-a-ll packed in there, wrapped up in pretty silk cloth,
ni-ice clean cloth.

Some bring in a piece of cloth and say "Here, put that [the medicine] in—
   wrap it up and,
and wish for good luck."[4]
A-a-nd they wrap it up re-eal nice.
Pack it in the bag,
a-a-nd tie it up,
and you can't open it.
Only once in a while [when] they have adoption,
the Medicine Beaver Dance adoption,
they take one of the bags and put it right in the middle.
Here's the big fireplace here,
and they put it right in the middle [in the rear of the lodge].
But they know that this bag is in there.
They call it *sacred seed*.

But now this generation don't know nothing.
They ne-ever hear about tobacco.
They don't know what,
what that is.[5]
But in my time,
I seen them—we seen them.
Seen them dance, open the bag, plant the tobacco,
dance—and we have to take a stick and
when they build a fence around it [the garden],
we lean [a stick] on there.
And my mother would say,
"When you put the stick down say you want good health.
You want to grow up to be a good person and then
lean on there."
So there might be some truth to it—like this Christian way now.

1. Frey, *The World of the Crow*, 14. (BL)
2. In the past, each bag had its own "house," often a tripod put up especially to hold it and placed outside so there would be no contamination, such as from women's menses. (MP)
3. Witnesses avoid crossing the path of a person holding a medicine bag, even if unopened. They should not move until the bundle is put away. (MP)
4. Medicine bundles sometimes have several cloth wrappings. When a bundle is

opened, a new cloth wrapping might be added. Someone usually offers a cloth as a gift for a blessing. (MP)

5. For a time, young people had little interest in the Tobacco Society, and members were worried, but there has been an increase in young people who consider membership an honor. My husband's uncle, the late Lee Plainfeather, said, "They say you're not a Crow unless you belong to the Tobacco Society." (MP)

When They Open Medicine

Different medicine bags hold different medicines. In this story, Lillian recounts objects she saw as a girl when a bag was opened, as well as some of the rituals she witnessed and the way items were repacked and stored. Other bags might contain different objects. (BL)

The medicine's open and there's a pipe and the feathers.
A-a-nd some cloth, good cloth to cover the bag.
And the plant like pine needles for incense—burn,
smoke—what do you call that?
Baalahkápe [incense].
They burn.
Some tied in a different bag and some of the leaves
tied up in there—and when that is open,
they pray.[1]

They don't look up or either look down or I don't know—we were kids then [when] I seen them.
Pray and
when it's time to wrap,
put it back, pack it back again,
they roll it and pack it, tie it again.
They pray.

A-a-nd some bring in nice new cloth.
Silk or a pretty color.
Put it in there and wrap it up.
The outside has to be r-red.
Thick red flannel—pretty.

And then they put that tobacco
in there, the pipe, and all their incense and the feathers and the
stuff that goes with the plant—they put it in there.
Pray, roll it up,
and then the top cloth comes and they tie.
I guess sometimes they put three ties, on the ends and one in the middle.
And that's a-a-ll packed away,
and nobody can't open it.

Sometimes they put up a teepee.
They always put the bag wa-a-ay up there.
Tie it to the teepee and it look pretty up there.
And I've seen that.
A-a-nd they used to keep it sacred, so
if they keep it in the house,
they don't allow women that menstruating.
They don't want them to come in.
A-a-nd
they kept doing that—pretty soon "Let's put this outside
and anybody, women and all, can come in the house."
So they put this medicine outside
and tie it
outside on the house.
Keep it sacred.
And then when it's not in the house,
women can go in there even if they have menstruating.
They can go in there and do as they please.

So,
I come to know those,
and I seen it.
I seen it.

> 1. This can be sweet sage, braided sweetgrass, bear root, or pine needles. They are not mixed, so these are separate bags of different types of incense. They are used to purify medicine bags or human hands. One always prays while burning the incense. (MP)

They Adopt Us in This Tobacco Iipche (the Sacred Pipe Society)

This is Lillian's story of another sacred society. She and her family were ritually taken in when she was about six, around the time she was pledged to the Tobacco Society, but the two events appear to be unrelated. Sacred Pipe adoptions were rare even in those days and are not done today, so Lillian and her brother were among the last living members. The details she provides are few, but they matter because little has been published on the organization. (BL)

They have a medicine that's different from the Medicine Dance [Tobacco Dance],
and we were adopted.
My father always believe in those doings.
I don't know what made him do that.
I never ask—some reason anyway,
so they adopt us in this Tobacco Iipche [pipe].[1]
Like a stem.
Tobacco stem.
When they adopt you, you have to belong to that.
They have different songs [than the Tobacco Society].

And oh my that was so-o-o sacred—they think it's holy.
A-a-nd they don't do that every year or every day.
Once in a grea-a-at while when this society
happen to adopt somebody—that's when they do that.
A-a-nd I remember when they adopted
my fa-ather and mother, me-e and Caleb,
four of us all together,
and they make us sit there,
And they come, dancing, dancing,
in the teepee [a special lodge].
Make us sit in a row.
And they gave us cor-rn.
And soup.

And then they sing the songs. (claps a rhythm)
How many songs they sing, I don't know.
I was too young to know then.
I may be—
seven.
Seven or six.[2]

1. At a meeting about the Native American Graves Protection and Repatriation Act (NAGPRA), December 1999, Joe Medicine Crow and Barney Old Coyote said Laura Singer was the only living member. I had not realized that Mother was another. (MP)
2. Relatively little is known of this old Society. Lillian called it the Tobacco Iipche (pipe) ritual. Others published slightly different names but seem to describe the same society. Tom Yellowtail (Fitzgerald, *Yellowtail*, 123–24) discussed a "Sacred Pipe Society" and spoke sadly of its demise. He and his wife had been adopted into the society as children, so they too were among its last members. Medicine Crow ("The Effects of European Culture Contacts," 89–90) devoted a paragraph to the "Sacred Pipe Dance," calling it "the core of a society called the Owners-of-the-pipe." He wrote of a four-day adoption ritual ending with the Sacred Pipe Dance. Lowie ("Minor Ceremonies," 335–48) described the "Medicine Pipe" ritual, linking it to the Hidatsa. He focused primarily on male participation, but early scholars often underestimated women's ceremonial roles, so this too may be the society that Lillian joined. (BL)

CHAPTER TEN

We Were Always Hard Up

This sad chapter is marked by Lillian's memories of her father's addiction to gambling and alcohol, and the pain and financial hardship that resulted. Gambling is deeply rooted in Crow history, and horse races, foot races, arrow-throwing contests, and bone games were old-time favorites. Tribal members still like to take a chance on a whole array of games and competitions, old and new, but for Bull Shows, what had been entertainment must have become a compulsion.

   The chapter is also about early reservation people adjusting to a cash economy. Many families received a small amount of "per capita" from tribal resources, as well as rent from land they leased to white ranchers. Lillian's father, Bull Shows, also became a farmer and hauled goods for the government.[1] The first story dates to about 1910–1912, when Lillian was a young child. (BL)

They Don't Have Much Money

Well I remember when I was around about six years old.
I loved my mo-other—I followed her.
Whatever she does, cook outside, I'd be ri-ight there.
And I think I learn lots of
cooking and a lot of sewing from her.

A-a-nd she's not very well off—she's always hard up.
Sometimes she's hard up for fo-o-od.
Like my dad,
he's a gambler—he su-u-re gambles.
And sometimes he'd lose lots of money, sometimes even his buggy and
   wagon and horses and saddle.
Stuff like that—he
bets on those a-a-nd he'd lose them.

And then I don't know of a time that he won lots of money. (chuckles sadly)
He's a gambler—he likes to gamble, he likes to drink.

And my poor mother—sometimes my,
my dad comes home and
gets cranky over nothing and sometimes he
beat up my mother—and I sure cried and I always afraid of my dad.
Always scared of him.

And when we start to go to Billings then-n I must be about eight years
    old then,
and in Indian I say "Father"—I don't say Papa.
I just say "Father, please don't drink—<u>promise</u> me you don't drink.
When we get to Billings we just go and
camp there and eat nice a-a-nd buy-y and
come back."

But
they don't have much money.
Sometimes he hauls
from Edgar, from Pryor to Edgar.
He takes the wagon team and he hauls stuff—
the government ship and unload it in Edgar and then
he goes and load all the boxes, clothing or anything—I don't know.
I'm a child then—I don't know what he brings.
And they pay him.
He's not the only one that hauls.
When somebody wants to make som-me, earn some money, they
hitch up their wagon and go to Edgar and haul stuff to the school.

And that's how they earn money—but once in awhile, maybe
once a ye-ear or-r—
I don't remember—but we get per capita.
All of us.
Say about ten dollars apiece. (chuckles)
And then them times back there,
a pound of butter even cost twenty-five cents.
Eggs twenty-five cents, fifteen cents a dozen.

A-a-nd
sugar, they're not high.
And none of us are wealthy.
And we just work our way.
And I know. [I remember.]²

    1. Per capita is the payment or dividend that each Crow receives from tribal resources such as coal, timber, oil and gas, as well as land leases. It is now paid quarterly, but I don't know how often they received it back then. (MP)
    2. Traditionally Crow women had considerable economic power and managed much of the food supply, including the meat they butchered, prepared, and distributed after their husbands successfully hunted. Lillian's mother seems to have been caught between her husband's addiction and the disruption of the old hunting and gathering system. (BL)

They're Gambling in Our House

My father always has race horses.
He had thoroughbreds.
But he's a gambler,
o-oh my father is a gambler,
and he bets money in this and that—they even have a card table.
At the house.
And men all go down there a-a-nd play cards, play rummy, poker.
He's a gambler.

But I guess I was a teenager or—
I don't remember how old I was but anyway I'm home.
And my mother and I'd go to bed but my mother
fixed potatoes, baked potatoes and stuff like that—put away,
when they're playing cards there, gamble.
A table over there with full of men and another table over there with full of
    men.
In our house, that little house up on top of the hill, that log house.
They'd be gambling in there.

A-a-nd we'd go to bed on the
other
room.

My mother and I.
A-a-nd about before midnight,
my father would go and wake up my mother.
Said "All right they want some food."
And my mother would get up and
fry steak,
potatoes and gravy and biscuits.
She sells them for two dollars a piece, sometimes $2.50.
She makes pretty good money on those.
And she makes coffee.
And sometimes I get up and help.
And sometimes I don't. (chuckles sadly)
So she makes a little money.[1]

After while they quit.
Said we couldn't afford to run a big gambling house. (chuckles sadly)

1. Mom told me her family went from one extreme to another because of Grandpa's gambling—one day rich with winnings, the next day poor because he lost everything. Grandma tried to compensate by selling food, which shows how times were changing for the Crow. Food had never been sold, because the sharing of it was sacred, but Grandma and Grandpa, like others, were learning white people's ways quickly. Gambling, on the other hand, has always been in our blood. There were and still are games that Crows play for gambling purposes. (MP)

Make a Wish

In the second half of this story Lillian sounds like a teenager, but she still seems to be in the boarding school, so these events probably date to the last years of the decade, perhaps 1918–1920.

My mother and I,
sometimes we too poor to have
new clothes.
That's the truth.
My father su-u-re gamble off the money.
A-a-nd he drinks too much.

A-a-nd my poor mother used to work re-eal hard.

I used to think
my father was mean.
But as a father I looked up to him.
I don't say "Daddy."
We don't [say that].
[But I] say "Please don't drink.
Ple-e-ease.
You love
my mother, you love me, you love my brother.
Ple-ease"—I don't say God, I should say [he loves] God.
I said "Ple-ease,
don't drink, don't drink, I beg you not to drink."
He'll say "Yes all right" but then he don't do it.
He dri-inks and he's me-ean.
Sometimes he run away.

My mother say "I love my children.
I know my husband's me-ean—drink.
Gets awful
mean a-a-nd
gamble too much and a-a-ll,
a-a-a-ll the things he
do—go after other women and stuff like that.
But" she says "I'll never quit him.
I'll <u>ne-ever</u> quit him because for my children's sake.
I don't want my children to have a stepfather.
Or a stepmother."
Says "Even if I have scars in my head,"
said,
"from beating me up" she says "I'll never quit him."
And she did—she never quit him.

She has Clara [a relative to turn to],
but she lives up another district—we never see her.
[She's] up at Lodge Grass and we live at Pryor.[1]

That's why—my mother's family used to live around Joliet,
Red Lodge and them places but after she married my father,
they moved to Pryor.
That's when they lived there at Pryor.
And they lived w-a-ay up towards Billings. [See "Medicine Dream for
    Horses," chapter 4.]
They have a log cabin—
a big house.
They have corral, they had horses.
And I wasn't there.
I had a sister and a brother there,
but I wasn't even born then.

And then,
after his parents died,
my father didn't want to live up there that other place up towards Billings.
They moved to Pryor and he,
his uncle and him, built a log house, still standing yet.
That's where we lived.
And that's towards east part of the state.
Now he farm on a low pla-ace and a level.
Most of it is level.

My father was a good farmer.
[He farmed] wheat.
All wheat.
And then in wintertime,
he has to borrow a binder.
And he drives about four horses to that binder.
Two horses ahead, second horse is ahead, a bi-i-g binder.
A-a-nd
he sit on that seat—I used to stand behind, hold on,
because I want to watch where he cut the grain.
He cut the gra-ain and they tie,
in bunches.

His nephew Walter Chief,
he always help him because one of the horses re-eally bad—mean.

He used to run away.
And when Walter and my dad
try to make him behave he says "You (claps hands) whip him up and
talk to him and then
he behave himself."
Gee he's mean.

He wo-on't let no other person drive.
Nobody can harness him, nobody can drive him—except my father.
And he talks to him.
Calls him Pete.
Says "Pete,
you behave yourself or I'll give you a good whipping."
And he does—he must know
the word.
So he behave himself when he talk to him.
But he sure run away with
the wagon and team.
I remember I scre-eam when I watch him run away.
Scare me.

But anyway I was raised,
a-a-nd
I didn't go off
to stay with other people because I liked my mother.
And I thought she poo-or old mother.
"Poor little old mother,"
I used to think—we always hard up seems like.
Not enough money.

Seems like I don't have enough ni-ice clothes when other girls do.
I don't.
And I know [I remember] one time,
we were at school,
and I said "There's the big evening star!"
And there's
a bunch of girls standing around.

One spoke up and she said "You make a wish and it will be true."
A-a-nd "What shall I say?"—and she said "Wish for anything—wish what you want or wish this going to happen and so and so" she said—"just wish for something.
Close your eyes" she said.

And I closed my eyes and I whispered—I said "I know my mother's going to Billings Friday,
and she won't be over for Sunday to visit me.
But during next week, when she comes back, I hope she brings me a bra-a-nd new pair of shoes.
There's going to be a big dance,
next month" I say,
"so I'll have new shoes—I like to dance, I want new shoes"—I wished for that.
"Close your eyes" she said.
Closed my eyes and I said those words—keep on repeating and then after awhile I opened my eyes,
a-a-nd didn't think nothing after that then.

But about a week after that my mother came back from Billings.
Brought me
a brand new shoes, high heels.
And my father said "Now you can dance on the floor like this" he says.
   (laughs)
And I wish for it and it come true.
My poor mother worked for it I guess.
I don't know where they got the money but she brought those new shoes.
A-a-nd that wish come true.[2]

   1. Crow women turned to relatives in times of trouble, but Horse had few to depend on. Her Shoshone mother died young, and Horse's half brother, Bull Don't Show, also passed away. Horse's father remarried and had Clara, but in the days of horse travel, this half sister was too far away to help. (BL)
      To travel from Pryor to Lodge Grass, she would have needed to go by horse or wagon along the trail to St. Xavier and then on to Lodge Grass, approximately sixty-five miles. (MP)
   2. When Lillian went to traditional Crow dances, she wore moccasins, but she wanted shoes for the school dances, sponsored mostly by white employees. At those events, they did popular, couples' dances such as two-step and waltz. (BL)

CHAPTER ELEVEN

The Last Years in School

A Sioux Woman Taught Me to Sew

This is Lillian's story of learning to make European-style clothing. Although she doesn't say so here, this is probably when she first used a sewing machine. She learned from the wife of the boss farmer, who was half Sioux. That is why her relationship to him was uneasy. He treated her well but was also a government authority and a member of one of the tribes the Crow had been fighting only a few decades earlier. This happened around 1920 or 1921 when she started day school. (BL)

I must be about—o-oh,
say about fiftee-een,
and I was growing up to a lady.
A-a-nd
the boss farmer—we always say he's the agent around Pryor—
looks after all the people.
He's the agent.[1]
A-a-nd they're Sioux, he's a Sioux [Sam LaPointe].
And his wife, she is a Sioux too.[2]
They're employees and transfer over here at Pryor,
and he's our agent,
and he looks after everybody.
Goes from one place to another—[if] they have sheep, they farm,
see what they need on the farm—a plow o-or,
o-or a mowing machine or
something that they need on the farm he always brings it—and his wife,
she's good—she don't do nothing but just they got a grea-a-at big house, a
   government house.[3]

They stay there and then pretty soon I got acquainted with them.
A-a-nd she was nice.
They have a boy—they have a boy and he was naughty.
He was about six years old—he was no good.
But after that,
they had a little girl,
and when their little girl was about six months old,
they had me to come a-a-nd
help her out.
Help her washing and help her take care of the baby.
Babysit for her while she run down to the store.
And after awhile when they go to town they always have me stay home with their baby.

I babysit for them—they're Indians too, they're Siouxs and I got to being liking them.
They liked me too.
I got along just fine with them but he's the agent [boss farmer],
and sometimes I have to watch what I say and
I don't daresn't talk anybody or—

I don't know how to gossip then—that time I was too young.
And now I don't gossip.
I don't call other-r-rs,
call them down and cuss them and no I don't, I don't use that language.
And
I hardly did it when I was young.
Maybe I did a little bit but now I don't do those things.
And I,
I get along fine, I enjoy it.
I can talk to anybody—I can
shake hands with
some strangers and they a-a-ll laugh and shake hands with me.
I like people.
I get along fine.

[Those Sioux people speak English.]
They do.

The boss farmer he's a Indian but he's,
he's been through school—he's an employee for the government,
and he knows what to do for the Indians.
And after that,
I never even know when they start to packing and leaving.
She never told me.

I used to make little dresses for the girl and they like it.
That woman,
she taught me how to sew a little dress.
Lay the goods down and she said "Cut this way.
This is the sleeve hole and this is the dress.
The garment is cut down there and you save
some allowance for the hem.
And then if we have to have a yoke,
this piece you cut it wide and gather it and make a small yoke,
and then bring the other piece to it.
And that's a dress" she says.
She taught me how to sew and I know how to make little bonnets,
know how to make dresses.
Little slips, little nightgowns, little dresses.
I know how to sew then,
and I was glad I got acquainted with her.

And after that,
I'm age where I can't go to school anymore.
But anyway,
that time when I was with them Sioux people,
they teach me how to sew.
And sometimes that man would correct me.
Say,
"You speak English, don't be bashful" he says "just speak right out!
And be polite."
Taught me that.
And he's a man that has awful frown on his face and spe-eaks loud.
I used to be
afraid of him. (laughs)
But he, I guess he done good to me.

1. Agents and boss farmers were government employees with different duties. Agents administered entire reservations. Boss farmers worked within local communities to teach farming skills, but they also often tried to direct Crow life, perhaps the reason the Crow called them agents. (BL)
2. I believe this was Sam LaPointe's wife. If I recall correctly, she was not Sioux. Her husband was half Sioux and half white. My mother always talked about this boss farmer. He was not always kind to the Crow because he was half Sioux, but I do hear some good things about him, so he obviously tried hard. During the grand opening for the American Indian Tribal Histories Project in 2006, a young woman came up to me, introduced herself, and asked if anyone on the Crow Reservation would remember her great-grandfather, a boss farmer. It was Sam LaPointe's great-granddaughter. I felt like she was an old friend. I was so pleased to meet her. The boss farmer's wife was not required to instruct my mother, but Sam LaPointe's wife went out of her way to teach Mom to can garden produce and sew the way described in this story. (MP)
3. This is a way of saying the wife was not involved with the boss farmer's duties. She took care of the house and family. (BL)

Two-Step and Waltz

[We used to do]
dance today—what do you call that, two-step?
Two-step and wal-l-ltz.
And they say—
after I get older,
they say I'm a good dancer.
We would dance with the boys and sometimes with a girl.
Sometimes with some good dancers there.
I always want to pick a good dancer—like Carl Masterson,
a-a-nd—I forgot his last name.
Three anyway—they're white.
White people, white fellows—they'd come to our dance we'd put on.

We had a ni-ice floor at the school building,
in the dining room—and the employees put on a dance for us.
And the outsiders can come,
and we da-ance that two-step and waltz is all I know.
A-a-nd they say I dance good.

Ye-e-es—we had fun.
A-a-nd I like that.
So that was when I, I might be sixteen years old.
Around there.

Day School

But anyway I
have to ride horseback when they shut the boarding school.
I had a horse, a pony.
I saddle up my horse—my father doesn't even help me.
I go out,
saddle my horse,
with my coat, a cap,
boots.
Go to school.
In the evening I come back
home, put my horse in the barn.
Start school in the morning.
And pretty soon they
call that day school—they call it public school then.

This was wa-ay back in
ninetee-een—
ten or nineteen twenty, somewhere around there.
I was the oldest in all the pupils.
A-a-nd all the other kids they come from home too.
Sometimes their parents bring them in the buggy
and drop them off at the school and they go back,
and they come after them in the afternoon after the school is out.
But me, I ride horseback and I live about,
about five miles from school.
A-a-nd I saddle up my horse and ride horseback
and come and tie my horse.
Loosen the saddle little bit and take the bridle off and
put it on the post and loose the horse and he'd be eating there,
and I'd go to school.[1]

We have a Sioux, a man Sioux [High Eagle],
come from Pine Ridge, South Dakota,
and he's a teacher.
And his wife is a cook but she's so cranky she won't come and feed the
    children.
And this man would say "Lillian," says "you go prepare a lunch for the
    kids."
And we had about twenty-five.
And I go in the kitchen and start the fire and I make gravy.
And I make biscuits.
A-a-nd
I slice the biscuit and pour gravy over it.
And sometimes we have [a] little bacon.
I put little bacon in the gravy.
I pour gravy over this dish
and pass them around—the kids all come out
to the dining room and eat dinner and go out again and play.
And pretty soon the school bell rings and we all go back to school.

A-a-nd I done that for about a half a year I guess.
And the next year,
I don't know what become of that Sioux.

> 1. Roads were not built on the Crow Reservation until the 1920s, so most Crow children depended on horses. See Voget, *They Call Me Agnes*, and Medicine Crow, *Counting Coup*, for additional stories of riding horseback to school. (BL)

I Grew Up

My brother, he quit school—he was,
oh I think he was about sixteen—they usually let them out
seventeen but he quit at sixteen and he just
go fishing and go hunting and stuff like that.[1]

I don't pay no attention to him 'cause
I go to school, horseback,

a-a-nd come back a-a-nd turn my horse,
tie him up in the barn a-a-nd
pitch couple forkful of hay.

And I come back and
fix my supper.
And then-n-n,
I like to look at magazines.[2]
I used to go to this [dump].
I'm not shamed to tell—there was bi-i-g dump,
dump pile at Billings where people dump all their [trash].
And my brother and I go and gather up lo-o-ots of magazines.
And brush them off—shake them up and brush them off.
Bring them and that's where I get my magazines—I like to re-ead and
look at magazines—sometimes I cut up,
like a pretty woman dressed [pretty], like that.
I cut it aro-o-und and
hold it up—man-n and some more women and girls, cut them up and,
and I play with them—I used to just
make them stand and I'd sit there and I guess I talked to myself.
I sit there—Julia and I used to cut up lo-o-ots of papers—we'd look for a catalog,
and we'd cut up all the women and the men and make them play.
Make it loo-ok like real—we liked that.
I enjoyed playing with those papers.

But after awhile,
I get older—I didn't care for those and
I quit school.
I want to go to Chemawa and my father and mother won't let me go and
  which I wish I did.[3]
I could have had more education and I'm sorry I didn't go.

Gibson Male Bear [was there].
He's a Crow Indian and he's about my age too.[4]
He went to Salem.
Salem, Oregon, [Chemawa] Indian School.

And from there he kept writing to me.
And he says *he was gay.*
And he says "I got a boy, boyfriend for you.
He says he wants you to come to this Indian school.
A-a-nd maybe some of these days you and him will get married,
and you go back to Alaska" he says (chuckles)—so I wanted to do that and I was about,
o-oh—
maybe sixteen, sixteen years old.
And I kept writing to Gibson and he writes to me and says "he loves you" and all that.

And I wanted to go and my parents wouldn't let me go.
The school superintendent went up there from Crow Agency.
Went over there and talk to them and
bring them to the office and talk with them.
No—they just shook their head—they won't let me go.
That's why I have no education today.
I could've went up there to Salem, Oregon, Indian School and I could've made better than this.

But anyway I
grew up and got married.
I was about seventeen or eighteen when I got married and
I quit the school then.

1. He was probably hunting and fishing for food, not recreation. (BL)
2. My mother read lots of magazines. Even in her mid-nineties, she was an avid reader. (MP)
3. Chemawa Indian School was established in Salem, Oregon, in 1880, and still functions as a boarding school today. Like Carlisle, it is an off-reservation school with students from diverse tribes. (BL)
4. Gibson later married Edith Black Hawk from Wyola, and they had a son named Harold. When they divorced, Edith married a Shoshone by the name of Stone. Harold went by Stone so no one is using the name Male Bear anymore. Lorena Walks Over Ice, personal communication to Mardell Plainfeather, 2007.

CHAPTER TWELVE

My First Marriage Was to Alex

They Had a Buggy Full of Dresses and Blankets and Shawls

This describes Lillian's first wedding, in 1921.[1] *Church ceremonies and marriage licenses resulted from pressure from missionaries and other white authorities, but the other events are purely Crow. When Alex asks her to go home with him, he is following their way of proposing. "Outfitting the bride" was (and is) the traditional Crow marriage ritual, publicly sanctioning a union.*

To outfit a bride, the groom's family dresses her in a fine buckskin or elk-tooth dress, a silk dress for underneath, beaded moccasins and leggings, a beaded belt, a shawl, blankets, and even jewelry. Then the in-laws present her to a large gathering, with a professional crier to tell the people why they are proud of her and who outfitted her. If the family possesses praise songs, they may sing them to extol their joy and pride. The costly undertaking requires much artistry, so outfittings may happen months, or even years, after the union, but Alex's family was expecting him to marry, so they were sumptuously prepared, dressing Lillian from head to toe and draping more items on the buggy she rode to the church.[2] (BL)

My first marriage was to Alex [Plainfeather]—I think he's about year younger than I am.
But anyway we got married—he was good to me, real kind.

His mother was Annáhkoo Báakush [Lives On High Ground].[3]
And
my-y goodness they outfit me with
a pretty elk-tooth dress, elk tooth down to the bottom.
And *the hem touched the ground.*
Plainfeather [his mother] outfitted me, and Ruth [Whiteman],

his elder sister,
and then Myrtle too—they were girls then but, oh I don't know who all chip in.[4]
Anyway they had a buggy full of dresses and blankets and sha-a-wls.
They tied them to the buggy—there was a lot of people at the church.
They drove up the lane singing.
They sang praise songs as they came.
They sat with me—they stopped at the church.
When I got off my dress had elk teeth to near the hem—
I had pretty dress, all elk-tooth dress [see fig. 6].

And I guess the people all wait around to see us coming.
We drove up the la-ane to the big church there in the big building—the big school is there,
another big building here and some houses over he-ere,
towards the river.
And there are a lot of people.
And they come up the lane.
And they had me sit in the front,
all dressed up in elk-tooth dress.
And they had the buggy—*it had a cover* and they had the buggy full of
bla-a-nkets and shawl-ls and elk-tooth dresses and they drove and drove till they got to
where the people a-a-ll gathered around in front of the church.
And we got off and we went in the church.
That's when the wedding ceremony went on.
After that we come out the church.
We had a big feast there.
After that everything was over and we went home.

This was on Sunday,
and on Monday we went to Red Lodge,
to get marriage license.[5]
We went to Red Lodge and we
didn't have no cars.
We had horse and buggy.
We camp at Joliet,[6]

and the next day we went on-n.
There's about four buggies—the whole family went.

We got to Red Lodge and we got our marriage license there.
We ate a big dinn-ner [cooked outside] a-a-nd nice.
And came back and camp and stayed there at Red Lodge and pretty place up there.
And we moved back again and we came home.
And that's when I first got married.

It was in, let's see,
about May when he asked me.
He come home—
came home with Caleb, my brother, on horseback.
And Caleb said "You go out there and talk to him.
And I went there,
and my father and mother says,
"You better not rush off and get married."

And I didn't say nothing.
I went out there and he was on horseback—he said,
says "I want to marry you,
and I'll be good to you."
Says "We've been going together for about
a month now" he says—"I want to marry you.
And
if you say yes,
I'm going to take you home tonight—we'll ride double,
on my horse.
And Caleb can go with us."[7]

A-a-nd Caleb came back and asked Alex if I agreed and Alex says "Yes."
So we ride double.
Course Caleb went with us and we went cle-ear up—about six miles is the house from our place.
No, about four miles or so—that's when I married him.

And they had things ready [to outfit me].
They know he's going to get married and they had
elk-tooth dresses and blankets and,
a-a-nd things ready.
And we got married.

1. According to their divorce decree, Lillian and Alex received a marriage license on August 1, 1921, in Red Lodge, Montana (case #DR-2-1923-00001359, Big Horn County Courthouse, Hardin, Montana). The outfitting and church wedding occurred shortly before. (BL)
2. In the late nineteenth and early twentieth centuries, white authorities often failed to recognize Crow forms of marriage. Missionaries and Indian agents actively pressured the Crow to adopt Christian marriage practices and, according to Roscoe ("The Life and Times," 54), jailed some Crow for what they considered premarital sex, common law marriage, or native divorce. Yet the outfitting of brides was a dignified exchange of gifts that honored the families, bound them together, and publicly announced the union, involving more preparation, expense, and ceremony, as well as larger audiences, than many Christian weddings of the time. Many Crow resolved the problem by doing everything, the church ceremony, license, and outfitting, but dressing the bride remains preeminent today. "You aren't married without an outfit." Joy Toineeta, personal communication to Barbara Loeb, around 1980. (BL)
3. Lives On High Ground was Alex's biological mother. According to my husband's aunt, Ruby Plain Feather, Alex was given to a woman named Big Eyes as an infant. Big Eyes told Ruby that she took the baby as a blood son because she nursed him herself. She had given him nourishment from her own body, so to her he was her very own. Big Eyes was wife to Plain Feather, the well-known historian and storyteller who lived over one hundred years. Even I knew him. I believe he died in the 1960s. Some members of the family spell their name "Plainfeather," others "Plain Feather." (MP)
4. Ruth was Alex's sister, and Myrtle [Strong Enemy, née Smart Enemy] was his niece. In Crow, Myrtle would have been his little sister. (MP)
5. The family must have gone to Red Lodge for many occasions because Mom remembered attending dances, rodeos, and parades, and recalled stories of Liver-Eating Johnson. (MP)

    Red Lodge is the small town southwest of Billings that Lillian first mentioned in the story of her father and Henry Russell going to school. Some of Liver-Eating Johnson's claims may be tall tales, but he became known for a lengthy personal war against the Crow for killing his Indian wife, and he claimed he ate the livers of his victims. Johnson later lived part of his life in Red Lodge. His log cabin is preserved there. (BL)
6. Joliet is the small town near the place Little Horse's brother was killed. (See "My Mother Mourns," chapter 2.) It is located on Rock Creek, a tributary of the Yellowstone River, and is between Billings and Red Lodge. (BL)

7. Her brother served as go-between and protector. If her parents got upset, her brother was there, so it was okay. She could also have gone through a friend, a cousin, or anyone close. (MP)

We Gave Away All Those Gifts

Next Lillian honors clan relatives and others by giving them some of her outfits. When some of them respond with more gifts to her and her family, they are continuing the cycle of Crow generosity. When Lillian gives the first outfit to the wife of her clan brother, William Big Day, and he offers a spectacular gift, he is expressing his gratitude and fulfilling the custom of giving horses to brothers-in-law.[1]

We gave the gifts away to my [clan] brother.
William Big Day.
The time I [just] talked about when they praised me [sang praise songs during the outfitting]?
After we got off they unload all the gifts and pile them up on the ground.
And my mother said,
"First thing you do is call William Big Day's wife
a-a-nd let her pick the elk-tooth."[2]
It happened to be *he was a Big Lodge.*
No close [blood] relation.

Annie Big Day [was his wife],
and she came over,
got a elk-tooth dress,
a-a-nd
I don't know what else.
William come up for it.
Wa-a-a-y lot of people there and he had the announcer say,
says "I got two race horses."
"All these peoples know that
my horse is,
my horse is *long winded.*
Little White is the horse's name.

He is great.
No Crow has ever beat him.
He was first all the way till the race was over.
I give Little White to my brother-in-law" he said.
"And *the hísshishiile* [light bay horse]—*both."*
He gave both—they sure liked it.
We moved around to places like Powell, Wyoming, *to rodeos and races—we'd take the horses.*
To Billings too.
Our horse was always first.
He was fast!
Biiammiáhileeishek William Big Day.³

But my mother gave all the other elk-tooth dresses to
brothers and she kept some a-a-nd
I don't know. (chuckles)⁴
I don't know what become of them (chuckles)—cause I don't wear them.

1. When the women in the groom's family outfit the bride (their new sister-in-law), the bride's family usually responds with lavish gifts to her husband, often including horses from the bride's bothers to their new brother-in-law. The relationship includes biological, adopted, and clan brothers. For more on reciprocity between brothers-in-law, see endnote in "Horses Run Over Caleb," chapter 7. (BL)
2. Medicine Crow, in his writings from 1939, states that the bride immediately distributes her gifts to relatives, under the guidance of her mother, and the groom does similarly when the bride's family reciprocates. "This custom is hardly to be called a giving of wedding presents. . . . The families of the couple are the principal concern." See Medicine Crow, "The Effects of European Culture Contacts," 40. (BL)
3. William Big Day was not a blood relative. He belonged to Big Lodge, like my mother, so he was her clan brother and Annie was her sister-in-law. The expression *Biiammiáhileeishek* means that he gave her husband a gift. Thus Mom could depend on William to reciprocate in Crow gift-giving traditions. She had given his wife Annie an elk-tooth dress, and William gave her husband some good, fast horses. (MP)
4. She probably gave the dresses to brothers' wives. Brothers would include clan brothers and blood cousins, as well as Caleb, her only living, biological brother in the European sense. (MP)

We Got Our Divorce

I stayed with Alex
till-l-l—let's see now—
less than a year—maybe I stayed with him about eight months.
Eight or seven months anyway and I left him.
We didn't even get no divorce or anything then—we just separated.[1]

And then after that we went to court in Hardin,
a-a-nd he got divorce,
and I sign it.[2]
And they ask him if he had any child.
"What's your wife's name?" and he said "Lillian."
And "You have any child by her?" and "yes" he said.
"That little boy"—Sammy was a boy then—said "that little boy."
And then
they wrote everything down.
And that's when we got our divorce.[3]

After that I stayed single.
Stayed single for how many years?

1. Lillian and Alex lived together just a few months. Their only child, Samuel, was born in July, 1922. Their divorce decree is dated July 17, 1923 (case #DR-2-1923-00001359, Big Horn County Courthouse, Hardin, Montana). (BL, MP)
2. Since white people frowned on Crow marriages not formalized by a piece of paper, Alex and my mother probably felt pressured to get a license. In the past, they would simply have stopped living together when they realized this first, youthful marriage was a mistake. No one would have thought less of them. Alex married twice after he divorced my mother. Mother divorced one other time and was widowed twice. (MP)
3. Shortly after this, Alex married Rose Plenty Good. Alex and Rose were the grandparents of my husband, Dan Plain Feather. Their children were Leo, Clyde, and Clarabelle, but Clyde and Clarabelle both died when they were young. (MP)

My Mother Kept Sammy

Grandparents often took firstborn children, an old custom with many benefits, so Lillian's parents raised Sammy. The following is from Thomas Leforge, a white man who joined the tribe in his boyhood in the 1860s and lived with them for much of his adult life: "This old-time practice was good for the young parents, it was good for the elderly foster-parents, it was good for the tribe, as it left physically capable young couples free from the worries of providing for their children and thus enabled them to go on producing others" (Marquis 1928, 165). For more information on adoption, see "Red Star and Mary Ann Took Me," chapter 1. (BL)

My mother kept Sammy.
Kept him because they lost a boy.
My little brother [Percy] died at ni-i-ne years o-old.
And then,
when Sammy
was born they said they want to keep the boy—they want to
have the boy.

He's a big man now, has a big family.
He drinks a lot but he's quit now and he's good.
He lives in Pryor.
He's got a house there.
He said "Mother" he says, "if you give me a lot,
where I could build a house,"
he said—"if I could build a house there,
that's for my family."
So I gave him that piece of land and he build a house there.[1]

Now he's got another house,
right in the residence where there
lo-o-ots of houses there—and he owns one there so he lets his son live there.
His son Russell, he's living there.
And Russell he's from Lodge Pole.[2]
Wa-a-a-y, way up north.
He was raised at Pryor and lived at Pryor,
but he married a woman from up there [Benita Fay Bell].

They go back and forth.
They have a big house,
and they've got a
family now and they live up there—but
they're living at Pryor,
in that house [now].
She goes to college.

1. Land distributions under the Dawes and Crow Acts were completed by the 1930s. Today's generations depend on increasingly smaller parcels they inherit from parents and other relatives. (BL)
2. Lodge Pole is a town on the Fort Belknap Reservation, belonging to the Gros Ventre and Assiniboine. (BL)

The Shinny Game

This humorous little memory of Sammy includes a lively description of shinny, an informal hockey game with a ball or block of wood and a curved stick. The story probably dates from the mid- or late 1920s. (BL)

(chuckles)
We used to play that shinny.
It's a game—it's a real game.
And women, sometimes young men, all—
they pick one person and then another one this side—both sides pick—
 "I want him."
And this other one go to call "You come over.
Be in our bunch" and they start to play shinny.

They have sticks [curved] like that.
Re-eal nice.
Shave them up nice, slick and nice—and they,
they can kick. (claps hands)
Hit a ball.
As far as they can.[1]
And this bunch would run for it.
They run—they don't want the other bunch to beat them.

They run-n and run-n and we watch them and the winners
a-a-ll get some
goodies.
We sure enjoy that.

But this time my father
picks sides—the older [people].
<u>Lots</u> of people there,
watching on—it was Sunday afternoon and
we were looking on. (chuckles)
And they said "Now the women.
The older women—no young woman.
The older women and the old men is going to play shinny,
and whoever wins,
they're going to pull their eyebrows out."

So they start to play shinny.
Took the stick and (claps hands)
hit it a-a-nd they fly <u>way</u> over there and they go for it and just
try to knock it off and—and the ball (claps hands) would go.
Somebody would hit it and go back this way and they all hit it and they'd go
    back this way and
they just, they have a good time.
Kick that ball, hit it so it will go this way,
and they would make two flags or something there and
when the ball goes through that, then that's the winner.

So this time the women win.
They <u>kick</u> the ball and (claps hands) they all run for it and they kick and
    kick—it takes about,
o-oh five, maybe three minutes, four or five minutes.
They run arou-n-nd, hit this ball this way and they'd kick it back, hit it
    this way,
and they all run for it—it's just a lot of
<u>fun</u> to look at them play.

So the women win. (chuckles)
And the other men just took off—ran,
hid around the car—and my father, he want to get away, he want to run.
He run for a car.
He run, want to run this way,
a-a-nd
three or four women
was after him,
and we all watch—they
caught up with him and they (claps hands)
got him down on the ground and
one hold him down, they all hold him down and
hold his head like that and they start to pulling his eyebrows off. (laughs)
He kicked and fight but he couldn't do nothing.
After that they let him loose.

Sammy ran over there and he said "You got my father down.
I'm going to hit you."
Hit one of the women.
And my mother says "Oh my goodness—they're just playing shinny and
too bad my boy hit that woman."
Says she caught up with this woman.
She pulled her shawl and "Here.
It didn't hurt very bad but
you can have my shawl for our boy hitting you."
And she took the shawl.[2]
(chuckles)

1. My husband says they generally hit the ball, they don't kick it, but if I were playing and in a tight spot, I might kick it out of the crowd so we could continue the game. (MP)
2. Several early literary sources reference a custom of paying for wrongs with gifts. According to Denig (*Five Indian Tribes*, 151), any misdeed could be paid for except murder. (BL)

CHAPTER THIRTEEN
We're Adopted into the Tobacco Society

They Adopt Me into the Medicine Dance

This is Lillian's story of her own adoption into the Weasel Chapter of the Medicine Dance, or Tobacco Society in the mid-1920s. She had been a young girl when her father promised a clan uncle the honor of adopting her, but she is a young adult in this story. She, her parents, and Caleb are taken in together. Tobacco Society adoptions require four ceremonies and copious food, as she describes, plus considerable preparation and costly gift exchanges, so the process can take years, possibly explaining the delay her family experienced. (BL)

So they believe in this Medicine Dance—that's *baasshússuua* [to soak].[1]
They call it Tobacco Dance and Medicine Dance.
A-a-nd if you
happen to-o-o be a family, and a
member of family get seriously hurt
or sick or something,
one of the relatives they say,
"Now,
when she gets well,
you can adopt her in that society.
Medicine Dance Society."

And they do that.
And they gave me away too.
When I got sick—come out of the
school whe-en pretty near died.
But they had all these medicine men doctor me.
Get well—and my father told one of my uncles,

clan uncle,
he said "Now,
she's your niece
and you're her uncle.
And he says "I'll give her,
my daughter, I'll give you her—you can adopt her,
in this Medicine Dance."[2] [See "If She Pulls Through, You Can Adopt Her,"
   chapter 9.]

They did.
They adopt me in the Medicine Dance.
And that's when I belong to the Weasel Society.
That's when they called me,
and I was adopted—let's see,
I may be about
twenty-one years old when I was adopted
in that dance—so I belong to the Tobacco Dances.

And they take you in four times.
They take you and you sit there and wait and see the dances,
and they bring in lunch for you.
You take it home and give it to your relatives.
And the second time they do that again.
And the fo-ourth time they do that again, take you into this dance.
Has to be in the night.
They go in and they sure dance.
They get up a-a-nd take a weasel and da-ance, or some
otter skin, make it da-ance, just a stick o-or so.[3]
They have ni-ice songs.[4]

So I was adopted in the Weasel Society.
My dad gave me away to my uncle—
one of my cla-an uncles—
so they adopted me.
That's why I belong to this Weasel Society.
And I liked the songs.

[I don't dance with them now.]
When I went to this [Christian] religion,
learn religion,
go to chur-rch and kind of be religious,
I quit that stuff.
So I don't go to them dances anymore.

1. *Baasshússuua* means "to soak" and refers to the way the seed keeper, or mixer, soaks the tobacco seeds before planting. The word is linked to both adoption and planting because "new members were prepared for entrance into the order, just as the actual seeds were soaked in a mud solution for planting." See Medicine Crow, "The Effects of European Culture Contacts," 91. (BL)
2. When Bull Shows promised his daughter, he meant he would allow this respected person to adopt her into the sacred Tobacco Society. Giving a child to adopt is a great honor, but a society member could also invite someone to be adopted. If you see someone of worth, perhaps an industrious young man or woman who seems to seek out traditional ways, you may ask to adopt that person into the society. Adoptions increase membership and guarantee that the Tobacco Society thrives, for that is what makes us unique. (MP)
3. These are stuffed skins. You make them dance by holding them in your hand while you yourself dance. (MP)
4. They also wear nice clothing. Women wear a good cloth dress, shawl, and moccasins until the fourth time, when the adoption officially occurs and the new member is "born" into the society. For this final occasion, the adoptee and the adopting parents clothe each other in new beaded, buckskin garments. (MP)

Caleb Was Better Then

Although Lillian's father pledged the family to the Tobacco Society during her childhood illness, he hoped the ceremony would bring additional blessings to his son Caleb. (BL)

My brother, he drinks a lot—o-oh he's mean.
And my father, he say,
"He better be adopted in the Medicine
Dance and maybe he'll
become a better man."
A-a-nd
he got so bad he beating up his wife and his father and,
and pretty soon we all run away from home and stuff like that.

So my father told him he'd better be adopted.
By an uncle.
He did.
And he did better then.
But after that he start in again.
[Alcohol] it's no good.

CHAPTER FOURTEEN
I Married Robbie Yellowtail

Robbie Proposed to Me

Lillian married Robert Yellowtail in early 1925.[1] This is the story of his proposal. Although she says, "That's when I met [him]," she does not mean met for the first time. This was the night he asked to take her home. For this marriage her new in-laws outfitted her at a big dance, giving their own prized garments. Women might decide to share their own best clothing in this way if a sister-in-law has married a beloved brother or other male relative. Perhaps in this case they were happy he had fallen in love again after being widowed. As Lillian makes clear, though, her parents were less sanguine. (BL)

I stayed single for about
fo-our, five years and then I married Robbie.
I went to a dance there at Saint X,
Christmastime.
A-a-nd
I had some friends with me, ladies,
said "Let's go to the dance"—a-a-nd
they didn't know how to drive cars then.
They said "You're the only one that drives cars"—says "Let's go.
We'll borrow a car"—and we borrowed an o-old-fashioned car. (chuckles)
And we went to the da-ance and that's when I met Lorena Mae's father,
a-a-nd
we danced.

And that evening my parents were there.
I said "After the dance I'll just stay and
go home with my folks."

They were going home.
But after the dance,
Robbie and I got together.
He's one of the drum-m singers.[2]
A-a-nd
he come to me and he said,
"Are you single?" and I said yes—he sit with me and he said,
"I think I'll go with you, I'm single too"—his wife died.
He said "I think I'll
take you home with me."
And "Would you go?"—a-a-nd
I looked at him-m and he was good-looking anyway.
I said "yes"—I went with him.[3]

Dad and Mother didn't want me to—they came after me.
And I just set there and didn't say nothing,
a-a-nd my father and mother said,
"You're young.
He's much older.
His wife died
with four children."
And says "You're going to have some stepchildren,
a-a-nd he's much older than you."[4]

The stepchildren were Joy,
Jiggs,
Marjorie,
Winona.[5]
Winona was just—o-oh I think she was about a year old
or so when her mother died but his grandma always keep her.
She raised her.

A-a-nd
he was a good man—he talked to me a-a-nd
of course he pro-o-posed to me—a-a-nd
I felt for him.
And I said "All right, I'll get married"—but
after I said yes,

Mother and Dad came over.
They said no.
I just set there and said nothing,
so they went back and my mother came back alone,
and she cried.
She didn't want me to marry him.

And Robbie says "No."
Said "I'm going to take her home even if she's your daughter.
I'm going to take her—I ask her, she said yes and I'm going to take her."
And my mother says "Come on, you'd better go home with me."
And Robbie says "Don't you go now, don't listen to her."
So I told my mother, I said "No you'd better go."
Said "I want to marry him."
A-a-nd
we went to Hardin the next morning and got our marriage license.[6]

And the next night,
they was going to give me a lot of wedding presents—[at] a good dance, big dance!
At Saint X.[7]
Goodness sakes you ought to see my wedding gifts.
Bla-a-nkets, brand new bla-a-nkets and shawl-ls.
Sil-lk dresses.
There were pretty silk dresses brought from New York.

Susie-e a-a-nd May Old Coyote, they gave me prettiest [dresses].[8]
"I gave my daughter-in-law the bes-s-t elk-tooth dress in the whole
reservation" said May Old Coyote.
"I want you to wear this one."
And Susie said "No! Hers is not pretty"—says "Wear mine!"
A-a-nd Nellie—Nellie Picket, Joe Picket's wife—had a green one, a-a-ll elk tooth.[9]
"No!" she says "This is colored green and pretty—wear this one!"[10]
And then-n May Old Coyote had me to wear hers.
Elk teeth way down to the hem,
and I wear that one—that's when I got married, that night.

We lived in Crow.
He worked there at the boiler house.
He worked and we lived in the house there,
and he was a good man, he's a good provider.[11]
And that's when I got married.[12]

1. Lillian and Robbie married on either January 2, 1925 (Effie Bull Shows allotment folder, Titles and Records, Bureau of Indian Affairs, Crow Agency) or February 21, 1925 (divorce decree information, case #DR-2-1927-0001001, District Court, Big Horn County Court House, Hardin). (MP)
2. Drum groups provide the songs at traditional dances and other events; their status is one of absolute necessity because most occasions require singing. The drumbeat is considered the heartbeat of the Apsáalooke, so they provide the heartbeat of our tribe. Some men have the gift of singing, and a few special ones can create songs too. Those who remember all the songs, especially personal honor songs, are relied upon to lead groups. (MP)
3. When Robbie asked if he could take her home, he was proposing. Of course, Robbie must have seen my mother before and contemplated it, then asked her when he had the chance. She probably was expecting it. When I was a little girl, I remember people occasionally saying, "He took her home." Usually this was considered the beginning of a marriage. (MP)
4. Robbie was about fifteen years older. (MP)
5. Joy Toineeta, Marjorie Steffes, Winona Plenty Hoops, and Robert Jr., called Jiggs. (MP)
6. Hardin is just beyond the northern border of the reservation. The county courthouse is there. (BL)
7. She tells the story as though the outfitting happened the night after Robbie proposed, but it probably took some time. The Yellowtails, Old Coyotes, and Takes the Guns were all prosperous families with industrious women, so they most likely had things ready, but the outfitting still would have required preparation. He proposed at the Christmas dances, and she says she was outfitted at another big dance. (MP)
8. Susie Childs and May Old Coyote were the daughters of Lizzie's sister, Mary Takes the Gun. Lizzie was Robbie's mother, so Susie, May and Robbie were first cousins in the white man's terms, but among the Crow, they were brother and sisters, because their mothers were sisters. (MP)
9. Lillian spoke of Nellie as a particularly beautiful woman. Later she said, "*Her hair was black and shiny and long. Gee she's pretty. There's no woman even today as pretty as she was.*" About their relationship she said, "Robbie *and Nellie's mother were about* second cousins—the old man Yellowtail *and Nellie's mother were related.* Nellie Scratches His Face *was her* maiden name. *Her father was Scratches His Face* [Akiisé duukáxee]." (BL)
10. The dress was of green wool trade cloth, which was uncommon and would have stood out. Mom always admired the color green, and that may be the reason she remembered Nellie saying this. (MP)

11. The boiler house is still standing by the school, near the Bureau of Indian Affairs housing area. The house next to it may be the one they lived in. (MP)
12. Joe Medicine Crow is the son of Robert Yellowtail's sister, Amy, and he remembers when Robbie brought my mother home as a bride. He was a young boy, and she often played with him as if she were young herself. He said they used to wrestle in what she called "wrestling Indian style," and he said he got strong wrestling her. He said it was fun and she acted real young but sure could cook. Medicine Crow, personal communication to Mardell Plainfeather, 2009.

Owns All Got an Elk-Tooth Dress

Again Lillian gives away part of her wedding outfit but not publicly. This time a clan relative asks for some of her gifts to outfit her own new daughter-in-law, Fourteen. (BL)

Frederick Stewart married Mary—Fourteen was her Crow name.
And his mother *Owns All came and said to me,*
"Your [clan] father has married.
He took a recently divorced woman and
he married her suddenly.
I have nothing to give."

That was after Christmas.
The things I received from my wedding had been packed away.
We lived at the agency.
[We had] a big apartment and we stayed there,
and the pile of gifts [was there],
a-a-nd *Owns All came and told me about my clan father getting married.*
She wanted gifts for his wife—I said "Here they are" and she searched.
I don't know what [she took]—I know she got an elk-tooth dress.
And some blankets—I don't know how many she got.
She took them *home to Fourteen and gave them to her.*[1]

Owns All was from the Ties the Bundle Clan,
my father's clan sister and my [clan] aunt.
Fred and Frank *sure were good to my father.*
Course the old lady too—they're good to him.

His elder brother was Ihchiihpáachileesh [Pushes Himself]—
that was his uncle [by European reckoning].[2]
But he always was at Owns All's house.
They were good to him.

1. Fourteen and her husband Fred were close to my mother. When I knew them, they lived in the Black Lodge District, and she was an avid member of the Church of God, which she and my mother helped found. Fourteen and Mom were close in age, but Mom was the daughter because Fourteen married her clan father. These clan relationships were taken seriously and great care was given to respect. Fourteen was a nice lady. I remember her well. (MP)
2. She calls Ihchiihpáachileesh her father's elder brother because that is how the Crow would define their relationship, and she is calling him an uncle in keeping with European terminology. *Ihchiihpáachileesh* is also the army scout in "The First Watermelon," chapter 3. The details of their relationship are described in an endnote to that story. (BL)

Lorena Mae Is Born

Lorena Mae was the only child of this marriage. She was born in 1927. (MP)

Lorena Mae, she's smart.
Her daddy's smart too.
Her daddy think a lot of her.
Too bad he's [gone].
He died about two years ago now.

Lorena Mae was born at Pryor.
I want to go over to my mother's,
where I could use my mother when the baby is born.
A-a-nd Robert says "I'll do your way.
We'll go over there, live there."
And just about two weeks we live there and then I start.
She was born there at Pryor.
That's the way I want it.
I didn't go to the hospital.

The log house, that's where she was born (chuckles)—yeh.
And Robbie was at the door waiting,
and when he heard the baby scream, cry, he just forced the door open and come in. (laughs)
He say "What is it, a girl or a boy?"
He asks and "It's a girl!"
And he says "*Good!*"

He already had the four children from Clara [Spotted Horse].
Jiggs and Joy-y and Marjorie and Winona.
I like them all.
They like me too.

Cute Cup

One day
we were in the house—I had dinner.
We had just come back from Billings and I had bought a lot of goodies [food],
a-a-nd we set Lorena Mae right there [at the table].
I set there, Robbie set there, the mother and some visitors sit there.
And we had her sitting there a-a-nd we'd bought her a little cup, cute little cup.
Small—just, that cup was so cute.
And Robbie seen the cup a-a-nd brought me over and showed me the cup and he said,
"There's a cute cup—if you want it, we'll buy it."
I said "Oh yes, let's buy that cup."

And when we got home that day,
we set her on the end and her daddy was sitting there and fixing her plate.
And he put that cup there and here she was looking at the cup,
and she said,
"Look at my cup"—she called her daddy.
Said "Bíawakshe" [Summer].
They call him Summer—his Indian name is Summer.

And says,
"You see my cup?
My cute cup?"—and that's the fir-r-st words she talked.
And we were a-a-ll surprised and we a-a-ll laughed and
asked her to say it again and she wouldn't say it.
But that's her fir-r-st words—she said "Bíawakshe.
See my cup? *Bashpáate íkaah* [my cup, look at it]—cute."
And we laughed—everybody laughed.
And we tried to get her to say it again—she wouldn't do it. (laughs)
It was cute!

I think she was about
four years old when I left her daddy.
I kept her but
I didn't want her to stay with Paul—he drink too much, he gets
cranky with her.
Robbie knows about that and took her back.
Sent her to school, kept her—sometimes she's over there with me and sometimes,
sometimes my mother takes her—she went to school.[1]
And then after that she went through high school and finish.
Hardin.

> 1. "Kept her" means they had her live with them for a while. Crow children have many relatives nearby and often move comfortably between households, as Medicine Crow recalls from his own childhood, when he moved between multiple sets of grandparents. "I was kind of a mischievous little boy. . . . But they all loved me, and I learned a lot from each set of grandparents." See Medicine Crow, *Counting Coup*, 30–31. (BL)

A Pretty White Pendleton

> *Lizzie Yellowtail was Lillian's mother-in-law. In this story she is publicly honoring Lillian and demonstrating her affection with a fine gift. Lillian always spoke of Lizzie with fondness.* (BL)

One Christmas evening there are lo-o-ots of people at the church
a-a-nd this Christmas tree in this corner, grea-a-at big Christmas tree.
And they had a pretty white blanket,
a white Pendleton.[1]
It covered the Christmas tree.
The people admired.
"What a pretty blanket" they said—"That's beautiful!" some say.
A lot of people there and I heard them say.
But I looked at it—I know it's pretty but I didn't say nothing.

I was sitting with Agnes or-r Lizzie or-r somewhere.[2]
L-o-ot of people and I was in the audience looking on.
Start singing-g-g—go on with the Christmas program.
After they got through,
they sat around and then Santa Claus came in, gave out gifts,
and took this blanket off and show it to the people.
"Look at this blanket.
Santa Claus brought it from the North Pole" he says. (chuckles)
Held it up so the people look at it.
"And we going to give it to Lillian Yellowtail, Robbie's wife."
O-o-oh my face got red. (laughs)
I went and picked it up—it was sure pretty.

But gee-e-e-e she's a good, ki-i-nd woman.
Lizzie.
I like her.
I <u>love</u> her.
She did, she was su-u-re good to me.

1. The gift was from the woolen mill in Pendleton, Oregon. Many tribes prize these high-quality blankets for gifts. (BL)
2. Agnes, who passed away in 2004, was Lizzie's daughter and my father's niece. In the Crow relationship she was his sister. She married Donnie Deernose and is the subject of *They Call Me Agnes*, in which she referred to my father as "big brother George." (MP)

I Sure Quit Him

Here Lillian recalls leaving Robbie, but she is also describing the way he honored her by praising her hard work and dependability. (BL)

But I sure quit Robbie.
All his daughters, they're good to me.
Marjorie, Joy, Winona.
Winona was just about
two years old then.
Jiggs was
about, yeah he was about two and Winona was about three.
They were still little when I married him,
and they were all good kids.

He is good. [Robbie]
He sure is good to me—one time he went to Washington.
He was the delegate for the Crows—he went to Washington.[1]
"I know" he says,
he told his folks,
"I know she's just like a cowboy" he says.
"She rides good.
She's do all the men's work—pitch hay and feed horses,
and water the horses and put them back in the correl.
She's good at that—you can
let my dad stay home, not go outside.
She'll do the feeding, she'll take care of the horses while I'm off to
    Washington"—and I did.[2]
I used to get up on the haystack, pitch hay,
throw it down and haul it over to the barn and put it in the stall.
Keep two horses in there.[3] (chuckles)
That o-old man used to say,
"Gee this is good" he would say—he su-u-re like it.
Says "We got a daughter-in-law that sure can help us."
Yeah he, he was good [for praising her industry].

Lorena Mae must have been about
six years old
when I left him.⁴
I just took off.
Packed my bags,
went over to town and
got in a train and left to Billings.
Billings Fair going on.⁵
And I never even told <u>nobody</u>!
I left Lorena Mae with my mother.
And,
and my dad know.
"Something's going to happen.
What's wrong with her?"
And I never said nothing—my mother said,
"What you going to do?"
"Nothing, I'm just going to town." (laughs)
I went to town to the courthouse and filed for divorce. (chuckles)

He was going around with other women.
And I never fight over them neither—another woman *was going out
   with him.*
They would disappear together—sometimes I'm over to Pryor.
On business—*I would go to sell wheat or to sign my leases.*
He would take her to Sheridan for a week and stay at the Bull Weasel place.
Some men told me about it.
Bull Weasel.
Bull Weasel *and Sebastian.*
This man's name was Crazy Sioux.
"*You're young*" they said.
"*Don't let him be mean to you, leave him.*"
*So I divorced him.*⁶

1. Robert Yellowtail was a prominent political leader on the reservation. He served on delegations to Washington DC as early as 1913, when he was in his mid-twenties, and he continued to be an outspoken political advocate through much of his life. See Hoxie, *Parading*, for details of Yellowtail's political career. (BL)

2. Robbie is praising her, telling his father to trust his new wife. They can depend on her industrious ways to keep the place going until his return. My mother was always working: cleaning and cooking and baking. Crow men have a saying, *Bía kóok*, which means "It's the woman." They are saying that the woman is the foundation of a home, the strength. (MP)
3. Mom told me Old Man Yellowtail and his wife were kind to her, and she in turn tried her best to be a good daughter-in-law. She said they loved her pies and her homemade bread. (MP)
4. Lillian made a mistake here. By the time her daughter turned six, she was divorced from Robbie and had been married to Paul for two years. Lorena Mae says she was three when her parents separated permanently. (BL)
5. The Billings Fair was held each August. Crows used to put up their teepees and camp there, but they no longer do. (MP)
6. The only divorce decree we located was filed by Robbie in Hardin, in 1927 when Lorena Mae was a baby, but they remained together at least until their young daughter spoke her first words. (See "Cute Cup," this chapter). We have found no official records, but it is possible that they remarried and Lillian filed for the second divorce. More likely they tried to mend their relationship without an official license, and Lillian later confused her stories. According to Lorena Mae (personal communication to Mardell Plainfeather, August 20, 2010), they lost a baby girl who was buried without a given name, and that may have been the reason they tried to remain married. (BL, MP)

CHAPTER FIFTEEN
Paul

Then I Married Paul Singer and He's a Good Worker

This story begins in 1929 or 1930 and ends in 1936. (BL)

Then I stayed single.
And then I
married Paul Singer
and made a home that's where I live now.
We had a home and we work hard—at first we,
we really didn't have nothing, just my bedding and
a few cha-airs and a table and a sto-ove.

We finally work our way—he's a good worker,
a-a-nd we raised wheat and we raised barley and alfalfa and
sell hay and I raised lots of chicken.
The neighbors usually buy eggs from me,
and I had about sixty
chickens.
And pretty soon I had about, o-oh I had a <u>bunch</u> of chickens.
And I raised them—I traded these chicken from Sarpy.[1]
A man and a woman wanted to
trade a harness and a buggy, an o-old buggy.
I trade them off an old buggy and a set of harness for about eighty
chicken.
That's why I happen to raise chicken.
I had lo-o-ots of chicken.
White leghorns.
And I had a few-w Rhode Island Reds.
I had about six of those.

I raised chicken and we raised a bi-i-g garden.
We grow tomatoes and we grow carrots and be-eans and—
a-a-nd watermelon and squash and stuff like that.
Pretty soon people come over to eat watermelon and we're glad to
give them watermelon—but anyway I
canned stuff, put up lo-o-ots of stuff.
Pretty soon we bought
couple hogs and we try to raise them—but
the other one,
the boar,
he died.
He went in another field and we tried to
drive him back a-a-nd from going fast,
I guess his heart stop beating, a bi-i-g—
fat—
pig.
And we didn't want it—the neighbors said "Can we have the meat" and I
    said "Yes you can have it."
They took it.

Pretty soon we had two milk cows.
We raised them.
We had
milk, we had so much milk we bought a separator.
I run the separator—when
he's irrigating I'd be milking
and run the milk through the separator—I had cream to sell to the
    neighbors.
And I keep my money and I make my own butter.
Finally I start canning tomato-oes and be-eans and corn.
And pea-aches and pea-ars.
And we raise our own wheat and take it to the mill and grind it to flour.
We had lots of flour.
And that way we, we made it.

We bought a brand new truck.
A-a-nd we hired Mexicans.

We raised beets.[2]
And we hired about—
eight—
about nine labor people.
We had a labor house there and they come to live there and work for us.

There's my house and then there's the ditch and then
up here right by the fence we call that labor house.[3]
And the sugar company,
Holly Sugar Company,
they told us if we want labor people we have to furnish house, furnish a garden.
We did and brought the family in,
a-a-nd they lived in that house—they su-u-re help us out.
They clean the sugar,
work in the field—they work for us.
Besides that we gave them a bi-i-g garden spot.
O-oh my!
They su-u-re good workers.
They raise watermelon, cantaloupe, different varieties.
Different kinds of watermelon
a-a-nd cantaloupes.
That's why I learned how to work too [farm work].
From that Mexican woman.
She's sure nice.

[Their name was] Vasquez.
That's a Mexican name.
Vasquez.
[They stayed with us] about a year and a half.
And they left.
The daughter got married down in Saint X.
A white man.
We call her Tina.
She got married—I never see her anymore but these Mexican people moved
to some other country and
some other place—I never heard from them anymore.

But anyway we start out
that way and made a home.
The house was his.
Before he got married [to his earlier wife],
his father said "When you grow to be a big man,
you'll get married,
and we'll make a house for you"—and before he got married he build a house, big house.

A-a-nd
he got married and
they say one morning he was sleeping,
and this woman [his wife] came over and start to get mad at him.
And then she left him and never went back to him.
She's still over in Black Lodge.
A-a-nd she's a good woman.
She su-u-re is good to me now, she's a good friend of mine.

A-a-nd
in Hardin his dad came over
and said "He's single,
but he quit his wife but he's still not divorced yet."
He said "I want you to marry him."[4]
That was in Hardin out in the street and I stood there for awhile and I said, "All right, I'm single too"—and I said "If it's okay with him I'll go. I'll marry him."

I used to dance with him at
Reno dance, Black Lodge dance—*I danced with him often.*
I didn't go with him either.
But his father talk us into getting married and we did.
We made good.
He's a good worker.

But when he drinks, look out.
He's m-e-ean when he drinks.
I used to just, when he goes on a drink,

then I just pick up a few stuff and
run away.
I stay away until he sober up—then I come back.

But he started drinking—that's where he died.
They say he come to Billings.
He took a load of cattle.
The boss farmer
asked if he could take a load of cattle
for somebody up at Saint Ann's.[5]
Said yes.
We had a good new truck.
And he had, o-oh there was about eight
cattle.
And the boss farmer said "If you have to make another trip, do that."

And when he unload the cattle,
he start to fooling around there and spend all that money.
He made pretty good.
He made all that money
to drink too much and they say he passed out on the snow.
And our truck was standing out in the street.
He passed out and laid on the snow.
And chilled his whole body.

And when he got home,
my little girl [Nellie] was sick—anyway I was in the hospital with her.
And he came in the door and he was ju-ust r-red in the face.
And I got up and look at him and I says "What's the matter? You've been drinking.
Too much"—he said "No," said "I've quit drinking" but says "I'm pretty sick, I'm sick."
Kept saying that—he set down and I pulled up his shirt and felt him and he's su-u-re hot.

So I called the doctor—he happened to be in the office.
I said "Doctor you'd better come and
check up on Paul"—I always called him Paul.

He came over and pulled up his shirt and start
listen from the back.
And look at him and says "Paul,"
says "you're a sick man."
And he called me over in the office and says,
"You got a sick man.
He's got double pneumonia,
a-a-nd we'd better put him to bed."

Yeah they put him to bed.
And I was in the hospital with the little girl.
Adam was a baby.
Adam was about,
he was twenty-one days old
when his father died.
And I rented a room.
In town in
Hardin—and I
go back and forth to the hospital to see him—doctor says "You going to lose him."
He had double pneumonia and he died.
From whiskey, from drinking.

So-o I had a brand new truck.
I had a shed full of wheat to sell,
barley to sell,
hay to sell,
some cattle to sell.
And the boss farmer came over and said "What you going to do with all your wheat and your barley?"
I said "I'll sell it all and pay the
funeral expenses"—I did.
There was lot of money in it and I paid everything.[6]

1. Sarpy is an area just east of Hardin. A number of white ranchers and farmers settled there. (MP)
2. They raised sugar beets for refining into pure granulated sugar. At the time, sugar beets were raised throughout the Big Horn valley. (MP)

3. This "ditch" is an old irrigation canal. The reservation's irrigation system was designed by engineer Walter Graves in the 1890s but built, financed, and maintained by the tribe. It served large areas of Crow farmland but eventually became too costly to maintain and is no longer functioning. See Hoxie, *Parading*, 274–78, 322–23. (BL)
4. Crow parents did not force marriages, but in the past they sometimes made strong recommendations. An obedient person usually complied. In the pre-reservation period, young men customarily showed their worth to potential in-laws with horses and other gifts, and, in doing so, demonstrated that they could care for a wife. They were not purchasing her. (MP)
5. St. Ann's was a Catholic chapel and day school on Lodge Grass Creek southeast of present-day Lodge Grass, Montana. (MP)
6. Lillian and Paul received a marriage license on March 12, 1930 (case #ML-2-1930-0001648-MA, Clerk of District Court, Big Horn County). According to her BIA allotment file, Paul died on February 19, 1936, when he was thirty-two years old (allotment file of Effie (Lillian) Hogan, Titles & Records Department, BIA, Crow Indian Agency). They had four children. Louis Charles (1930–32) died of whooping cough, and Rose Marie (1932–36), died just two months after Paul, of whooping cough and pneumonia (birth and death dates courtesy of the Clerk and Recorder's Office, Big Horn County Courthouse, Hardin). The other two include Nellie (1934–) and Adam (1936–). Nellie says she was the child in the hospital when her father died. Adam was an infant. (BL, MP)

They Didn't Outfit Me When I Married Paul

Paul had few relatives.
Alice Dawes happened to be his cousin or close relative.
She's the only one—she always calls him "my brother."
I think Alice Dawes and Ambrose's mother are related, some
relations anyway, I don't know—way back.
But she always say "my brother."[1]
And when I married her brother,
it wasn't right away.
About—
couple months or so,
she said "You married my brother.
I should be-e-e giving you a whole outfit,
but" she says "I don't have the things."
She's kind of crippled,
a-a-nd says "I'm not too well,

but I bought a blanket and an elk-tooth dress and some scarfs
and some dress goods.
For you"—she gave them to me.
A-a-nd I was thankful.[2]

And we made a home, him and I.
He has no
too close relatives.

1. Ambrose was Paul Singer's son from a prior marriage. Alice Dawes was Paul's aunt. (MP)
2. Alice Dawes gave what she could but apparently did not outfit Lillian publicly. (BL)

I Worked in the Sewing Project

This is Lillian's story of making a living as a widow and the roles her family took, in keeping with the custom of relatives helping relatives. Her mother took her son Adam because grandmothers were, and are, expected to help care for grandchildren. Kitty and Deernose offered their home because they were clan relatives, and that is how clan relatives treat clan children.[1] At the same time, the story hints at tribal politics. The sewing project appears to have collapsed over internal tensions, notably between Max Big Man and Lillian's former husband, Robert Yellowtail, who were political rivals, especially in the mid-1930s, when Plenty Coups had passed away and prominent Crow men were vying to replace him.[2] The project was originally established by the federal government to provide income for needy women, including widows. (BL)

So he died with double pneumonia.
After that I stayed single.
Yeah made it hard sometimes, pretty hard, but anyway I made it.

I worked in the sewing project.
In Crow [Agency] was sewing project.
It happened so that the supervisor, the agent,

he picks some women
with a sick husband,
or disabled,
some widows,
a-a-nd some single
women.
I happen to be a widow, single, no husband.
And Maud was single, Edith was single.
They were picked from the district.
Anyway they made application—they
admit them to work.
A-a-nd an old lady, Mary Kate, she's alone, no husband—she work.[3]
A-a-nd Mary Humphrey—her husband is an o-old man.
He was not able to work so they put her on this sewing project.
And Mary One Goose, she's alone, no husband.
A-a-nd our supervisor was Cordelia Big Man.
And she sure know how to
sew a-a-nd supervise everybody.[4]

And we sew and make jackets and make pants, make shirts, make dresses.
We didn't put no rivets in there but when they finished the work,
they just come out re-e-eal nice, just like tailor-made.
A-a-nd
the supervisor said "You sew too good."
Said "Your work is
better than any of the women there."
Said "I think I'll put you
just for cutting—you know how to sew but
I don't have nobody to cut.
You cut and give them out to the women,
and that'll be your job.
We buy you—
about four scissors"—a-a-nd my hand got blisters.

Sometimes I just sew-w gingham.
We call that gingham.
And then-n denim too—when we cut denim it was always hard.

I used them gloves to cut—I used to cut
four years o-old, six years o-old, eight,
ten, twelve, fourteen.
Overalls.
And we cut them a-a-nd pass them out, give them to the women.
A-a-ll had sewing machine a-a-ll lined up in there.
We had about ten.
Sometimes ten and sometimes eight.

We gave them out and they sew—a-a-nd
they pay us, the government pay us.
Not very much though.
Gee we get about
fifty-eight dollars every two weeks—that's not much ain't it? (laughs)
Let's see, that's
arou-n-nd ninetee-e-e-n—
nineteen-forty.
About that.
And I thought I was making good.

And William Russell, he's my cousin.
Said "Since you're working good, earning a little money."
Said "I'll take Adam"—he was about,
o-oh I think he's about four years old then.
"I'll take Adam and leave him with your mother,"
a-a-nd
he want to take him—I said "No I don't want him to go."
And I had Nellie too, Nellie was about six years old—she was going to school in Crow.
And I had Adam—he was about four.
And finally,
I sent him to Pryor—my mother took him, took care of him.
I work at sewing—I earn a little money.
And someti-i-mes on Saturday I
buy groceries, lot of stuff like sugar-r, bread, me-e-at, butter, jam.
Stuff like that—get a load,
I go to Pryor.

Ruth.
Ruth she was single too.
Ruth Whiteman, Uuttawaaxpaash [Sacred Weasel].[5]
Her and I usually go together.
We'd take a load of groceries to Pryor.
That way my mother can keep Adam.
And I keep Nellie.

A-a-nd one of my uncles [Deernose]
said "You're living in a tent and winter coming around."
Said "I think I'll move to the ranch and you sleep in my house."
And I did—we made good.
Couple women came over to stay with me—they work in the sewing room too.
Maud and Edith both came to live with me.
And an o-old lady [took care of Nellie].
Mrs. Bull Tail.
Heeleen Asíish—[she] *was married to Simon at the time,*
Simon Bull Tail.[6]
And they were in a wreck and Simon got hurt and he was in the hospital and *the old lady came to live with me* and she babysit for Nellie.
And I worked through.
That was fine—I made good.

And Mardell's dad happened to live the next house.
Donny and Agnes had a house right by Deernose's house.
A-a-nd Deernose *and Kitty* they moved out to the ranch.
And [their son] Winfield, *I cook for him.*[7]
I had Edith
and Maud with me.
And Nellie.
And Winfield's a janitor at the church.
And we were single,
a-a-nd we made good.
We worked in the sewing room.

My we made lo-o-ots of clothes.
We made shirts just like tailor-made.
It goes all to all the districts.
By the age.
And denim *it was*—they make them good.
Denim-m,
about four pairs of pants goes to Wyola and Crow—we call it Reno.[8]
Crow and Black Lodge and Pryor.
And we pack them in boxes—and then the next one
come to fourteen year olds.
They sew and we pack them
a-a-nd distribute out to
the reservation districts.
And we make good.

And Robbie was against that—he was the superintendent,
and he didn't like this sewing project.
Gee he was sure against!
No more jobs and we were poor again.
I don't know [why]
he doesn't like the
Big Man family.
Max Big Man and him used to
have it out
when they have a big council.
He hates
Max Big Man and Max
don't like him.
Anyway I was single then.
Working in the sewing room.

1. Kitty was a Big Lodge, like my mother and grandmother, thus a clan sister. Her husband, Deernose, was also kind to them. The role Deernose and Kitty played in Mom's life comes from the matrilineal clan structure. Children join the clan of the mother for life and consider other members brothers and sisters. They are expected to take care of each other. (MP)
2. For details on this rivalry, see Hoxie, *Parading*, 329. (BL)
3. These coworkers included Maud Whiteman, Edith Black Hawk and Mary Kate Reed. She later added Tillie (Matilda) Pease. (BL)

4. Cordelia Big Man must have been an accomplished woman. Alma Snell said she was "an industrious woman. She could take a saw and a hammer and put up a house like anybody. I think that's how she got her nice big home. It was her doing, and it was goodly built—a strong house." See Snell, *Grandmother's Child*, 59. (BL)
5. Ruth Whiteman was Cree, not related to Maud Whiteman. Her mother married Little Whiteman, a Crow, and Ruth used her stepfather's last name. (MP)
6. Heeleen Asíish is hard to translate. It means something that can be outstanding and easily observed just by sight. (MP)
7. My father built a house just east of the Deernose house. We lived there when I was a child, but Dad sold it to Vernon White Clay. It has since been torn down. Donnie was Deernose's son. He married Lizzie's daughter Agnes, the subject of *They Call Me Agnes*. Winfield was a Big Lodge, his mother Kitty's clan. This made him a clan brother to my mother, who was also a Big Lodge. (MP)
8. Crow Agency is in the Reno District. Wyola is a small town near the southeast corner of the reservation, on the Little Bighorn River and Interstate 90. (BL)

We Went Out to Dig Bitterroot

Lillian remained a widow for four years after Paul died, and she sometimes lived with her parents. She continued to dig bitterroot with her mother in the spring, but their transportation was no longer a buggy. They still went out for enjoyment as well as food, though, as this story makes clear. Lillian had a lifetime of enjoyable memories of working with others to gather, preserve, and share Indian foods, but this particular story must date to sometime between 1936 and 1940. (BL)

When I was single—when Nellie's daddy died,
that two winters, two seasons,
or more,
I came over to live with my mother
and father.
And that's when we'd go out—
in the spring.
We go out to dig them bitterroot.
Toward the mountain.
Like toward the mountain—there's none down the valley.
They have to be up toward the mountain.[1]
We dig.

A-a-nd other women,
like Annie Big Day and Old Lady Big Hail,
and her sister a-a-nd my mother,
all of us go out in the field—we start digging them bitterroots.

One day,
my mother said,
"Let's go up [to the mountain].
You drive the car and,
and we pick up these two old ladies.
They want to dig bitterroot too,"
and she says "You and I can dig."
And we went clear up to where there's a little creek
O-o-h about
four—let's see now, four or six miles from our place.
A little creek—what we call the Fourth of July Creek.
And says "We go down there,
and there's lo-o-ots of bitterroot there."
And she says "We start digging bitterroot."
A-a-nd said that we sure like that—
for dessert.

So Mother and I went—I've got the car, I drove the car and we went and
pick up these two old ladies—o-o-oh they were really happy.
Says "We want to go pick some but we don't have no way.
Nobody would take us up there."
And [my mother] says "All right, get ready"—and they had their wraps and,
and they said "We'll take a little lunch."
They took some bread with them.
A-a-nd they got some water.
There was no water—there was no creek up there,
so she says "We'd better take some water.
Take a jug along and take some water up there."
And my mother said "Yes we got lunch prepared for that."

And my mother said,

"Lillian" she says "she's a-l-lways
helpful and,
and help me dig those bitterroot and
I'd rather have her drive and take us out."[2]
Then we stop and another old lady want to get in.
[My mother] says "It's going to be crowded but if you want to go with us,
three can sit in the back and she'll take us" she says.
"There's no high hills up there.
Oh a little creek but no water there" she says.

We took lunch and we went out there to dig bitterroot.
And when we got off they're just like grass.
They grow among the grass and they were su-u-re spreading nice.
And my mother said "All right, start digging,"
and we just dig in here and there and start and
she went this way, another one went that way and the other.
We start digging bitterroot,
until we got a who-o-ole gunnysack full.
And they did too—they got a bi-i-g sackful.

And she said,
"You just stay overnight at our place,
and we start peeling off the skin."
And we did—we got home, o-oh late in the afternoon, must have been about
five o'clock or so we got home,
and we unload the things.
"We don't want to
let them-m
plants dry up,"
she says—"Keep them in the gunnysack.
A-a-nd
cover it up with a canvas—keep it cool in the shade."
And we did.

So in the evening them two old ladies stayed overnight.
And in the morning we set out there in the open.
And my mother

fix cushion for us to sit there.
Them old ladies set there and start telling stories and laughing.
And oh they had a good time.
We just
cut the top
off, the little leaves off.
And then we start peeling.
And then we break the top off and take that little red heart.
Just like a human heart—red.
Just the shape of a little heart.
Peel it off and take it and throw it away.

And they fixed a table.
My dad fixed a table where we could dry [the roots].
And they look white.
Nice and white.
Sometimes we wash them—
they turn red.
They turn pink color—some red.
And we wash them off and get that
color off and then spread them out and
they dry and
kept turning them around every morning.
Finally they all dried up.

So my mother said,
"Now we peeled a whole lot—we got a sackful,
and that's going to last us.
O-oh we'll fix dessert for some dance or feast."
And we did.
Sometimes they have a Medicine Dance.
My mother say "All right, we'll fix some of that dessert."
And o-oh my, when we fix it,
people always says,
"We want some more of that bitterroot dessert."
They sure like it.
Not bitter.

1. Elsewhere, she said they went toward Edgar, to a place called Small Mountain, to look for bitterroot. Bitterroot are hardy plants that thrive on Montana's sunny hillsides. They need freezing winters and can survive a year-long drought. (BL)
2. Lillian was proud of her mother's praise, which demonstrated respect for her work and other contributions. (BL)

My Mother Showed Me How to Sew Elk-Tooth Dresses

As an adult, Lillian continued to learn from her mother. In this story, she describes watching her mother making traditional elk-tooth dresses and explains the way Crow women attached the teeth, using a single strand of string to anchor a whole line of bones. They still use the same technique today, cleverly securing each tooth so firmly that it lies flat even if the wearer is dancing (something the Crow do often and with great enjoyment). (BL)

There's very few women that
sew [elk teeth on dresses],
A-a-nd sometimes I know they bring [them to my mother].[1]
Like one time, one woman brought two dresses,
and she said "I have to have one for my daughter-in-law and one for me,"[2]
a-a-nd she asked my mother to make them.

And my mother says "I don't have enough string.
You have to find me some string [to attach the teeth]."
And she says "All right, I'll bring it in a couple days."
And I don't know—she might have gone to Billings or Edgar or somewhere.
She got a who-ole big spool of twine
a-a-nd gave it to my mother.
A-a-nd she took paint and
put paint on there and make it red—
the string.
Sometimes they use a re-eal fine buckskin [instead of string].
Cut them,
and put red paint on them,

a-a-nd
start to sew [teeth] on the dress.

For the neck piece they have to use a red material.
They make it red and put beads, white beads, on there,
all around that edge.
And when they get through they put
the red on the sleeve—if the material is navy blue or black, black cloth,
they put that red trimming on there.[3]
The cuff.
It's not [a real] cuff—it's on the sleeve, sewed onto the sleeve.[4]
And at the edge they have to put white.
Muslin.
Make a white trimming on the edge.[5]

And when that dress is ready,
they start to sew the elk tooth.
Sew them on.
You have to bring the needle up [by the tooth],
and that string would be either a buckskin or a twine.
Comes up [through] the
cloth—bring the needle up [see fig 10].
And then
put it down again [through the hole].
Here's the bone—it's got a hole.
A-a-nd take the needle,
put in the middle [of the hole],
through the cloth.
Then they has to come up again.
The needle and the string come up again.
They come up the hole
and then go over [the tooth and]
how many inches [to the next tooth].[6]
They have to line it out,
and they [the rows] don't go straight.
It have to be curved,
so don't have to sew it straight.

Come up [in a curve].
And then the next row you follow
and keep going.

Some wealthy people
get all the elk tooth way down to the hem.
Some just way down to the knee, some down to the—
just the belt, the hip part,
and then the wealthy people—I guess
they got more money and they got more elk tooth,
they just make it until it
get down to the hem.
And they look pretty.

Joanne Bear Below [née Joanne Horn].
She's the only one
in Lodge Grass
that has elk tooth wa-a-y down to the hem.
You don't see it in all the elk tooth.
They just come to the hip or to the knee.
Because they don't have enough bones,
that's why.
But this Joanne,
she's from Lodge Grass.
They kind of well-off people.
And she still have that dress.
She has two!
One that's just cle-ear to the knee but the other one
is wa-ay down to the hem.
And she wears—it looks pretty.[7]

Anyway they hired my mother and she showed me.
She-e
finished a dress.
This woman came over and wanted to make two.
So she
set the-ere and

start to making that and she made me sew,
cause I had a machine, sewing machine.
I sew the neck.
Have to be a ni-ice ne-eat stitches on there,
so I sew that.
It is a kind of yoke.
Diamond shaped there, and then the hole [the neck opening], the collar there [see figs. 2 and 21].
And then
put little beads across,
and if you don't put little beads across,
put some elk tooth there in that space so it look good,
the dress look good.

So that's how we learn.
Needle would come up,
catch that hole, go down and
through the cloth, come up through the hole again.
Stitch it down [on the other side and move the needle] to the other elk tooth.
And you don't have to make a straight line—have to be curved.
And the first row is already there so you have to follow.
That's what makes the elk-tooth dress look pretty.

1. The dresses were made, but the woman did not know how to attach the teeth. (MP)
2. The daughter-in-law is probably a new bride. The woman is assembling fine clothing to outfit her. (BL)
3. For more details on neck decoration and dresses colors, see "Elk-Tooth Dresses," chapter 7. (BL)
4. They appliqué the trim around the sleeve at the wrist. It is not appended to the end of the sleeve like a true cuff. (BL)
5. Wool trade cloth had undyed selvages. Women used to cut dress parts with the selvages at the edges of cuffs and hems, creating off-white trim. Today they often use white muslin for trim. (BL)
6. To secure elk teeth, the sewer starts at the back side of the cloth, the side that will become the inside of the dress. She pushes the needle through the cloth just to the side of the first tooth, loops the string over half of the tooth, and pushes the needle down through the hole in the center of the tooth. This secures one side. Then she brings the needle back up through the center hole, loops the string over the other half of the tooth, and works the needle down through the cloth

at the opposite edge of the tooth. Now both sides are secure, and the tooth lies flat. Next she makes a large stitch from the back side of the cloth and repeats the process with the next tooth. (BL)
7. Joanne's elk-tooth dress has been passed down to her by several generations and is well-known among the Crow. (MP)

They Don't Pay Much on an Indian (I Went to Yellowstone and Saw All These Elk-Tooth Dresses)

Today many Crow heirlooms are in museums or private art collections. In this story Lillian describes dresses that she saw displayed in a store in Yellowstone Park, and she expresses frustration that the treasured garments had left the reservation. Lillian did not normally criticize white people in front of me. She voiced these thoughts only because I asked her how she felt about seeing the dresses there. (We don't know exactly when this trip happened.) (BL)

[Years later] I went to Yellowstone Park a-a-nd
saw a-all these dresses—I think,
I think we counted,
and there was nine
women's dress.
Ni-ine.
A-a-all displayed, hanging on the wall.
And then in the other room there was about six.
And then in that bunch there's two
youth dresses,
one about twelve years old
and one about
four, four years old—a small one.
Pretty.
They're all made pretty.

But I thought it was
terr-rible thing.
Whoever bought those
elk tooth (raps on table),

they don't pay much on an Indian—they either bought those from the pawnshop
or directly from an Indian.
Couldn't be [from an Indian] because they treasure that dress—they won't sell it cheap.
A-a-nd,
I don't know how in the world the
store up there
bought them dresses—I wonder if they're still there
and hanging up—oh they were pretty.

Kind of a dirty shame.
We were short down there in the reservation.
Here there were about eighteen dresses hanging up on display up there in that store.
I wonder if they're still there.[1] (chuckles)
I suppose you can't buy one.
If you buy one it'll cost about thousand dollars.[2]

1. We later looked for the store, but it no longer exists. (BL)
2. Nowadays you can see many dresses in pawnshops in Hardin and Billings, as well as premade dresses sold in local gift shops. (MP)

CHAPTER SIXTEEN
George

Then I Married George Hogan and He's a Good Christian Man

Anyway I,
I was single,
and I married Mardell's dad, George.
I worked in the sewing room then,
a-a-nd I was single,
and her dad came over.
And Mr. Bentley [the minister] said,
"You're going to make a good mate" he said.
"He'll be good to you."

And I set there thinking and I said,
"I'll ask my parents."
And my dad says "You're lucky to marry a man like him."
He says "He's much older,
and you're going be old too."
He said "You got children to support,
a-a-nd he'll look after you."[1]
So I married Hogan.
And he's a good man, he's a goo-o-d Christian man.
I married him and we had a house, we have a home.
Pretty soon we had a car
We had leases coming in and we bought a car.
We made along good.

1. Lillian married George Hogan in 1940. According to the family tree in *Grandmother's Grandchild* (Snell, 189), George was born in 1881, but he wrote 1885 on his daughter Mardell's birth certificate. In the former case, when he married

in 1940, he was twenty-four years older than his new wife, in the later case nineteen years older. (BL)

Lizzie Outfitted Me

Lizzie [outfitted me].
And May and Susie-e and Nellie.
It was about, o-oh about four months after that [after marrying George].
Lizzie gave me-e-e couple blankets and
an elk-tooth dress.
She sure was good to me, Lizzie was.[1]

1. The same people outfitted her when she married Robbie and when she married my father. Lizzie Yellowtail was Robbie's mother and my father's sister, so first my mother married Lizzie's son, Robbie, then years later, her baby brother, George. When married to Robbie, Lizzie was her mother-in-law. (See "A Pretty White Pendleton Blanket," chapter 14.) With this new marriage, Lizzie became her sister-in-law. (MP)

Sun Dance

The Sun Dance is sacred to all Plains tribes. It is held in a ritually constructed, roofless "lodge" where participants pray, dance, and fast from both food and drink for three or more days. In the past, the sponsor was often motivated by revenge, seeking a spiritual vision to aid him in avenging the death of a loved one by enemy hands.[1] *Today participants often seek the health and well-being of family members or other important, favorable outcomes. Europeans tried to crush the ceremony in the nineteenth century and outlawed it outright in 1904, a law that remained in place until the Indian Reorganization Act of 1934. The Crow occasionally joined the other dances, such as the Cree event Lillian's mother entered in this story, probably in the early twentieth century. The tribe stopped practicing their version in the 1870s. It would be more than sixty-five years before the Crow once again sponsored their own.*

This is Lillian's story of the Sun Dance's return to the Crow Reservation in 1941, when the tribe had forgotten details of the ritual and turned to a Shoshone religious leader for guidance. Historians have recorded William

Big Day's role in retrieving this old and holy ceremony, but others contributed too, including Lillian's brother Caleb, whose personal reason was his sister's health.[2] *Lillian did not enter the ritual herself because of her Christian beliefs, but she was proud of Caleb's role and supported him. She makes that clear in this story.* (BL)

My brother was one of the first ones that brought in the Sun Dance.
One season—I think it was nineteen—
thirty-five—somewhere in there,
he went to see-e the Sun Dance in Wyoming.[3]
A-a-nd
I know all about that.
He came over and he said "I want to go to see that Sun Dance at Fort Washakie.[4]
They say they always put on a good Sun Dance,
and men fast,
dance and that—I'm going to go and watch it.
"Will you let us use your tent?"
And I said "I'll let you use the small tent"—I have one small tent.
O-oh it's pretty-good-sized tent.
I said "I'll let you take the small."
"And if you'd buy us a few grub" he said.
So I did.

Caleb went over to Fort Washakie to watch the Sun Dance.
That's ever the first time a Crow Indian went over to watch the Sun Dance.
They watch
them dance.
And then Caleb
went to the head man
and told him that "Will you bring this dance
to Pryor next year,
if I
put up the teepee [the dance lodge], do the work,
all the work? Men there will help me."
Says,
"Will you?"

And this man
says "Yes.
That will be the mo-ost wonderful
thing that happened to Pryor people."
Says "We'll take the dance over there."
So he's one of the first ones.

I was re-eally thin.
I had lo-o-ow blood pressure.
So my brother, I guess he prayed "that
my sister gets well from this sickness."
He says that "my
sister gets well,
I'm going to bring this Sun Dance to Pryor"—he did.
And the people all wondered why they
started the dance at Pryor.
[One reason was because] my brother prayed that way.
Says "I want you to pray for my sister, that she gets well."

And I got all right—I was anemic.
I was so-o-o thin and pale and about three doctors took care of me in
    Billings.
And Dr. Movius is one of the good doctors in Billings.[5]
Dr. Movius and his partner, they took care of me.
Found out that nothing wrong with me except anemic.
And I got all right.
They got medicine for that—they gave me medicine.
That's [one reason] why they brought the Sun Dance
to the Crow Indians.

And George and I didn't believe on it but
I took lots of grub over there for the feast.[6]
They had a big feast after the dance, after the dancers come out—three days,
    and the next day, the fourth day, they had lo-o-ots of people [when the
    dancers came out].
Because that was the fir-r-st dance they had.

A-a-nd the Big Horn people and the Lodge Grass people a-a-ll flock over
   there.
Big
campground, lo-o-ots of people.
I know we went there.
I left George at home.
I just took the kids and we camped with my mother.

But the second year,
we put [up] camp and we attend it all.[7]
After that different ones
say "I'm going to have the Sun Dance next year."
They announce it and they have to have it there.
I don't know about this year—I never heard who's going to have the Sun
   Dance.
I never heard.

[When I was a child] my mother danced one time at Pryor
when the Crees came over, put on the Sun Dance.
They were just
four women dancing, four men dancing.
And they [built]
round—
oh I don't know what they call that [in English].
That round dance [lodge]—put trees and barks on there and make
ashkísshiluua [lodge dance].[8]
That's the Sun Dance house.
So they made that and my mother danced.

I don't know why she danced but I was about
eight years old.[9]
A-a-nd,
one morning we got close to the
dance arbor—you can't come in or you can't get too close.
So we got near and she make motion at me.
A-a-nd,

I did—I went over there and got to my mother,
and she was, o-oh she changed in her face.[10]
But anyway she said "I have to comb my hair for another [day].
The whole day and then tomorrow we'll get out,"
she said—"but they passed around these berries
for next year's berry picking.
Say 'we wish forward for
next year's berries'"—and she said "Here.
Hold these in your hand and pray" she said—"Take it home and eat it" she said—"Eat the berries."

A-a-nd said "You'd better go back to the bunch now—you can't fool around here."
Said "This is holy ground."
Says "Just go right back to the girls"—and I did.
I took them berries—there was just four.
Four berries.
And I took them—I ate them. (chuckles)
So,
that's all I know about Sun Dance from the Crees.

The Crees had their Sun Dance but
quit [having them on Crow land]—never had any then for about twenty
    years or so, when my brother went to Shoshone,
and he invited the people to come and dance.
Now they do that for celebration and camp and they have pretty songs and sing—they say that's holy.
So I suppose it is.

   1. As stated by Medicine Crow ("The Effects of European Culture Contacts," 92), the Sun Dance of the past "was held only when a mourner was enraged enough to declare vengeance in such a sacred manner." For detailed information on the old-style Crow Sun Dance, see Voget, *The Shonshoni-Crow Sun Dance*, 77–128. For a lengthy account of Big Shadow's quest in 1844, see Curtis, *The North American Indian*, 67–83. See also Fitzgerald, *Yellowtail*; and Frey, *The World of the Crow Indians*. (BL)
   2. Caleb's participation is briefly mentioned by Voget, who describes him as William Big Day's best friend. See Voget, *The Shoshoni-Crow Sun Dance*, 132, 134. (BL)
   3. According to his obituary, Caleb entered the Shoshone Sun Dance in 1935 and

returned in 1938 and 1939. In 1940 he went with William Big Day and in 1941 helped bring the ceremony back to the Crow (*Big Horn County News*, September 18, 1991). When recounting the story, Lillian originally said 1970 or 1975, but she was confusing two events. She had also assisted Caleb in the 1970s when he attended a Sun Dance in Idaho. Her daughter Nellie drove, and his granddaughter Brenda went with them. (BL, MP)

4. Fort Washakie is a small Shoshone town on the Wind River Indian Reservation in Wyoming. It was established as a military fort in 1878 and was named after an Eastern Shoshone chief. (BL)

5. Arthur J. Movius, founder of the Billings Clinic. Information courtesy of the reference librarians at the Parmly Billings Library. (BL)

6. My mother came from a traditional background, but was conflicted about Crow and Christian ways of worship. All of her family belonged to the Tobacco Society, and her brother, Caleb, believed strongly in the Sun Dance, as I suppose she and her parents did. However, my father, George Hogan, had attended school in Carlisle, Pennsylvania, where the founder, Richard Pratt, pursued the motto, "Kill the Indian but save the man," wanting Indian children who attended Carlisle to discard their Indianness and become imitation white people. Father returned to the Crow Reservation a Christian, and, when he married Mom, forbade her to participate in Crow religious ceremonials. She had been involved in Pentecostalism when married to Paul Singer, and they lived in the Black Lodge area where Pentecostalism had its roots, so my father's beliefs were no hard transition for her. She never entered the Sun Lodge as a participant, but she verbally supported her brother's involvement and was proud of his participation. She often bragged to me of his role in bringing the Shoshone-style Sun Dance to the Crow. (MP)

Many Native people have experienced conflict between their traditional and Christian beliefs. See Medicine Crow (Counting Coup, 54–57), for one noted Sun Dance leader's efforts to synthesize these religious views. According to McCleary ("Akbaatashee," 47–49), Pentecostalism became established in the 1920s at Crow Agency, just a few miles from where Lillian and Paul lived. It provided a safe haven when Agent Asbury aggressively prosecuted traditional spiritual practices. (BL)

7. Sun Dances are usually held in isolated places, and families camp around the perimeter of the lodge. Campers are usually relatives of the dancers but may include the sponsor, his family, the singers, and anyone else wanting to benefit from prayers. (MP)

The lodge is a large circle of saplings and brush. It surrounds a center post and is open to the sky, except for slender saplings that link the center post to the sides, like the spokes of a wheel. Within the embrace of this lodge, dancers pray, fast from both food and drink, blow through eagle bone whistles, and dance to the rhythm of drums and Sun Dance songs. The Crow version of the ritual lasts three days, during which family members camp at a respectful distance so the smell of cooking will not discomfort the fasting dancers. A new lodge is built for each dance and is left to the elements after the ceremony. (BL)

8. *Ashkísshiluua* means "lodge dance." The Crow word for the sun lodge can be translated as "the big lodge," and the dance was referred to as the lodge dance. (MP)

9. Today men and women both participate, often for the well-being of family members. They might, for example, spend their time in earnest prayer for a sick relative's good health or a child's education. It is not a ceremony to worship the sun, but dancers do face the east and dance at sunrise. Perhaps that is the reason white people applied the name "Sun Dance." Now three or four are sponsored every summer. (MP)
10. She is indicating that she went close enough to the lodge to watch but maintained a respectful distance, as required, until her mother gestured to her to approach briefly. The change in her mother's face probably reflected the strain of fasting. (BL)

I Had Mary and Mardell

So I had Mary—Mary was a twin,
and her twin sister died,
but she was a nice little girl in our family.
Mardell come along.[1]
And she made good, good education.
Mary had a good education.
They all made good.
Make a living on their own,
and I'm proud of my girls.[2]

1. Lillian and George had three children, Mary (born in 1941), Mary's twin (who died at birth), and Lillian's last child, Mardell, born four years later. (BL)
2. This is pride for all her girls, not just Mary and Mardell. (BL)

I Beaded Moccasins, Purses, Belts, Gloves

When Lillian was young, her mother had admonished her to learn to bead because she would have a family and would be making things for others (see "You Have to Know How to Bead," chapter 8). That is indeed what happened. During her life, Lillian beaded many pieces for others. This story lists just a few. (BL)

When I was young,
I said "I'm sure going to learn how to do that [beading],"

and I start beading moccasins—I made
moccasins,
and I made purses.
I made belts.
I never made any leggings.
I never did—they must be easy but I never made any.
I made purses, I made
two belts [and a child's belt for Carson Walks Over Ice],
I made gloves
for my brother and I made pants.[1]
But I never made any leggings.

   1. Belts are worn by both men and women. They are several inches wide and solidly beaded, so require considerable effort to make. Gloves are dress versions of cowboy work gauntlets, with wide, flaring cuffs, and are often decorated with flowers. Men wear them for parades. Purses may be rectangular handbags carried by women or small pieces that both men and women wear in front of their belts, concealing the place the two ends of the belt tie together. Men no longer wear leggings, but women do on dress occasions. These are large and solidly beaded, so their construction too is labor-intensive. (BL)

A Belt for Lorena Mae

This humorous memory must have happened around 1943 or 1944 during Lorena Mae's last years at home. (BL)

I only made two belts.
One was for Lorena Mae—a big one.
I finish that.
And you know,
she went to high school then,
a-a-nd when I made it,
I put dark green beads on the leaves.
This was the leaves
attached to the flower.
And I outlined
dark green
over [around] these leaves—so it show plain.

And I put some light
green
inside of this leaf.
And I finish one leaf,
and she come back from school—"How you getting along with the belt?"
A-a-nd [I said] "You want to see it?"—and I show it to her.
I took it and she looked at it.
She pushed it to the side
and said "I don't like that leaf.
The color on there looks like somebody
poop on there." (laughs)

Yeah George,
George got after her—he said,
"You're not right—you'd better not say anything about your mother's work."
So the next day I ripped that color off.
Made it a different shade.
So she was well pleased. (chuckles)
She said it look like that.

Lorena Mae Said "Mama, Cedric Wants to Marry Me"

Lorena Mae married Cedric Walks Over Ice in 1945. They would be together until Cedric passed away in 2004. (BL)

Cedric and Lorena Mae were going together.
I remember,
they run aro-o-und to dances and stuff like that and he'd bring her back.
Or they'd be fooling around in Crow with a whole bunch of kids.
They were dancing out there in the yard and all that.
And I didn't care but the father gets mad because he's the superintendent.
Robbie was the superintendent there in Crow,
and he gets after her and
he didn't want her to stay with me.
She would go to school in Hardin,
but right after school,

arms full of books,
she don't go home to her daddy's house—she'd come over to my house a-a-nd
e-eat a-a-nd pla-ay and foo-o-l around till
sometimes by night time her daddy comes after her and she'd go over there.

A-a-nd o-one fall-l weather,
o-o-oh it was sno-owing hard—wet sno-ow, snow getting deeper, deeper,
a-a-nd poor Cedric he,
he was going back home to his grandmother.
Grandmother lived about
three miles from Crow and he's walking because his mother has too many children besides him,
and he stays with Grandma—his grandmother, o-oh his grandmother she-e's so goo-o-d.
And she kept Cedric.

[His grandmother's name was] Sarah Stewart.
That's Josephine's mother.
Josephine [Pretty Weasel] is half sister to Elizabeth.
That's Cedric's mother.
She-e's pretty.
Emmm, Elizabeth's pretty—Cedric's mother.
But she married and
her husband died.
Louis.
A-a-nd
let's see now—she has
Cedric,
Billy,
Theresa,
that one—
let's see now—she's Mrs. Yarlott now—she's Mrs. Yarlott [Delma Jean].
A-a-nd—
what's that one lives in Reno?
O-oh I forgot.
When I forget, I just forget.[1]

She's a good woman—she su-u-re is good to me.
She's so ki-i-nd, just like her mother.

But Elizabeth is known as one of the prettiest women in the reservation.
She's pre-etty!
She's pretty.
She has Cedric,
Billy [and the girls].
And then after that she married again—
she had three more boys.
She has six—I think she has six.
If I remember right. (chuckles)[2]

Yeh Elizabeth sure is a good woman.
I like her.
I sure missed her when she died.
She drinks too much.
She didn't want to live.
She told me she didn't want to live.
Said "I just drink and drink and drink."
She said she
missed her husband Louis and,
a-a-nd she married
another man and she got three sons from him.
After that,
I think she quit this man—Bernard [Tobacco].
She quit him and she stayed single for awhile and then she died.
Too bad she died—she's such a good woman.
But she drinks too much.
Drink, drink, drink.
She wanted to died—she said she didn't want to live any more.
Too bad.
And she's such a good woman—I sure missed her.

Anyway Cedric and Lorena Mae,
they went around together for long time and one night
he brought her home,
a-a-nd they were on foot—he didn't have no car.

They were on foot.
And Cedric was ju-ust—his foot was so-o <u>wet</u>, his shoe's wet and
pants is wet and Lorena Mae was too,
because they were on foot running around—they both got wet and, and this
   was o-oh aro-o-und 6:30.
They come in a-all <u>soaking</u> wet.
Says "Mom" she says "will you start a good fire so we can dry our clothes,
so Cedric can go home?"
He walks home because he don't have a car.

Anyway they both come in <u>w-wet</u>.
Cedric was a-a-ll wet and she did too and they start to dry
their clothes—wring their socks and
put their sho-oes in the oven.
Put some boards there and put their shoes—try to dry them.
And we had a little pickup,
and I said,
"Take him home in the pickup."

And she said,
"Mama" she said "Cedric wants to ma-arry me-e and we've been going
   together for about
four months or more."
She says "Poor fellow—he has no place to go except his grandmother,
and oh" she said,
"Cedric's already proposed to me but what shall I do Mama?" she said.
"Can he stay tonight?"
A-a-nd,
"He likes to stay but we have to ask your permission if we can get married
   tomorrow."

"Yes" I said—I feel sorry for him,
and I said "I want you to get married."
And this was in the night so I said "He can stay now."
I fixed them a nice bed and
in the morning I gave them
twenty-five dollars—I said "Here's the car."

I said "Go get the marriage license and then
when you come back, tomorrow you go to the priest
and get married."

The day they got married,
I gave Cedric twenty-five dollars—I said "Now go get married"—they did.
A-a-nd they
married ever since.
They got—let's see,
Carson,
Sandy,
Loreen.
Louie.
Bobbie Sox.
I think Bobbie Sox
is the youngest.
Bobbie Sox is down in Hawaii,
and Louie's home.
Louie's single.
I don't know how old he is but I know when he was
a baby I took care of him and all that—help her out.
I always buy baby clothes for him,
because Cedric is a heavy drinker.

I even got a truck for Cedric.
I said "Cedric has been on foot."
I said " I hate for men to
be doing that"—I said "I'll get him a car."
Cedric said "I never own a car.
I'm always on foot because I'm too poor and my poor mother is always
　　single and poor.
Too many children.
Now I come to a family that can help me out and I'm ready to marry you."

And I gave him twenty-five—I said "Now you go get the marriage license
and go to the priest and get married."

But after they got their marriage license and came back,
he says "Let's go to the priest,"
and Lorena Mae says "No I don't want to go to the priest.
We just use that marriage license to get married—that's all.
You're crazy and I'm crazy too—we might
divorce—we might separate and divorce and you marry another woman, I marry another man."
Says "Let's not go to the priest, the holy part" she says—"Let's not go there." (laughs)
But Cedric said "Your mother gave us this money to get married." (laughs)
So finally she married him.
That was nice.[3]

1. Elizabeth's other daughter is Regina Goes Ahead. She married Paul Singer's first son, Ambrose (Singer) Dawes, who was raised by relatives. Regina and Ambrose were married for years but were childless. After Ambrose's death, Regina married Clem Goes Ahead, and they had several children. She is a real nice lady. (MP)
2. Elizabeth had ten children. Cedric's sisters are Theresa (Gun Shows), Mary (Black Eagle), Regina (Goes Ahead), and Delma Jean (Yarlott). One of his brothers is Billy, who took the last name Stewart because he was raised by his grandmother Sarah and her husband Tom Stewart. Another is Arthur Fitzpatrick, who used his mother's maiden name because she was not married to his father. After Elizabeth married Bernard Tobacco, she had three more sons, Dana, Larry, and Joe. (MP)
3. Lorena Mae married while my father was still alive. Robbie was his nephew, so Lorena Mae was his niece. They got along very well, and he loved her very much. (MP)

My First Grandchild

Carson's my first grandchild.
Lorena Mae's boy,
Carson.[1]
I was crazy.
Mary, that's Mardell's aunt,
Mary Takes the Gun,
her, she had a string and a scissor ready.
And we was taking Lorena Mae to Billings [to the hospital].

We were up at
Lodge Grass or Crow and she said "On the way she might have the baby.
You better catch up with us"—I had Mary [in the car].
And she says "I better take a string ready and when the baby's born I'll tie
   the navel,
and use the scissors to cut the cord and tie it with the string."
That's what they do.
But she didn't have it on the way—she hold it. (laughs)[2]

   1. Lillian made a mistake here. Her grandson, Carson Walks Over Ice, was born in 1946, but her son Samuel already had two children—Russell, born a few months earlier, and Jason Shane, born before Samuel married Adeline. Lorena Mae was the first daughter to have a baby, though, so this was probably the first time Lillian attended a grandchild's birth. Perhaps that explains her mistake. (BL)
   2. Carson was born in April 1946, so he is seven months younger than me. (MP)

My Mother Had Cancer

   Lillian lost her mother in 1948. (BL)

George and I
moved to Pryor when my mother was sick,
but after that George took the girls back [Mary and Mardell] and I stayed
   home with my mother,
father and mother—and I took care of her.

And my brother was ne-ever there.
You know when my mother was
living and my brother was living,
my brother a-l-lways go to Billings and drink and never come back.
But yet they favor him more than me.
I hate to say that but they know it.
"Your brother-r, your brother-r."[1]

But
I was there with my poor old mother.

A-a-nd
before
I came over I had
made
some silk dresses.
She bought herself some pretty material [for] silk dresses,
and I sewed them up for her—she said,
"When I get well,
get well again, I'll wear these
to go to Easter parade or
some special occasion"—she said that she'd wear those dresses.

And I got her two mufflers.[2]
Real pretty.
See we get our mufflers from either Germany—
they have a factory down there that
make pretty scarfs like that
and we get that—or either down in Japan.
They're pretty!
A-a-nd I bought two,
and she'd look at the other one and she'd hold it up like this and say "O-oh my—it's so pretty.
They make beautiful mufflers now-a-days"—and she said "This green one,
I'll wear that after I get over this sickness.
I'll wear this muffler.
This is so pretty—you bought it for me and I'm going to wear it for
some special occasion."
A-a-nd says "I'll keep that."
Says "As lo-o-ng as I live" she says "I'm going to keep this muffler."
And she liked that green.
She didn't talk about the other.
I think it was red and,
oh different colors—pretty too but she didn't care so much about the other one.
But she like this green one.

So-o,
I stayed there with her.
Sometimes I'd take her outside and fix a ni-ice seat for her.
I'd take her out and I sit right by her and
she'd just doze off.
Go to sleep and wake up and look at me again.
Pretty soon she drop like this [head forward]—I set there pretty near half
   a day.
And when the wind is cold I cover her up and then I say "Mama."
"Mother" I say—we don't say Mama.
I say "Mother."
Said "Let's go inside."
[She said] "All right"—and I put her slippers on.
I made her wear slippers.
Put them on and I'd take her inside.
Put her to bed again—she don't want to walk or she don't want to get up
and do anything—she couldn't do it anyway if she wanted to,
'cause she was too sick.
But she think about getting well.
Says "When I get well."

She had cancer—she died with cancer.
But I was there a-a-ll the way through.
So she kept saying,
about my brother,
says,
"Where's Caleb?"
She wants to know where Caleb is—I said "He'll be over some day.
He's running around Billings and
having a great time" I'd say.
"He'll be back, he'll come to see you" but he never did.
He doesn't know that his mother was dying.
Doesn't even know it.

And then my nieces are there—that's Caleb's daughters.
I had two there, Iris and Grace.

And I,
sometimes I buy for them.
Shoe or socks or maybe a blouse or pants.
And Caleb doesn't even know how to buy nothing for them girls.
Just drink, drink.
Doesn't care.
No.

When my mother died,
Clara came over and stayed with me.[3]
For about four or five days.
And she said "I'd like to keep some of my sister's belongings."
And she said "I wonder if she got any moccasins" and I said "Yes. I'll show you her moccasins."
And I took a little trunk there where she always keep her dresses and moccasins and stuff.
I open it and there was two pairs and one was kind of ripped.
Was fixing it and it ripped—she didn't care about that [pair].
But she got the second one, beaded moccasins.
Said "This is going to be a keepsake."
So she got the moccasins.
She just stayed with me about three days and she went back to Lodge Grass.
And this is at Pryor.

I had Mary and Mardell then.
So that must be around nineteen—what?
I can't go back.
Right around there [1948]—that's when my mother died.
And
George stayed home with the girls.
Nellie and Mary and Mardell.
He had them start
to school,
and he stayed with them in Crow while I stayed at Pryor with my mother,
but when my mother died they all came over and they stayed about a week.
Then after that I went back [home].[4]

You know,
when a person died,
when dress and prepare to take her to the mortuary,
they don't want them to go out the door.
They open the window, raise the window and take the body out from that.
If they take her out the door,
there might be one of the families
who go.
Die.
So they believe in that,
taking the body out—just raise the window and
get them out of the window.
So they don't take them through the door.
That's the old people's belief.

So I remember they took her and
put her in a,
a coffin,
and we took her up to the cemetery.
And I still, every year I go down there,
to the grave and decorate it,
and see where my mother is.
Lays there and then my father.
And my two brothers,
they're buried over there,
just a ways.
There's my father and mother right here a-a-nd there's babies.
And Caleb's—they lost about three babies.
They're there—and then my little brother Percy's there and then Daniel.
And they're all in a row.[5]

1. Lillian spoke on other occasions as well about her parents favoring Caleb, a seeming sorrow in her life. (BL)
2. By "muffler" she meant a scarf. Crow women folded square scarves into triangles and wore them over their heads, tied under the chin. A few older women still follow this fashion. (BL)
3. This was Clara White Hip, Lillian's mother's half sister. (BL)
4. After my grandmother's death, my mother came home to Crow with us, but every

summer we stayed with Grandpa Bull Shows in Pryor. This was Mom's way of "taking care" of her father without abandoning anyone. I cherish my memories of summers there. I heard Johnny Cash and Elvis Presley songs for the first time one summer at my grandpa's house, when my cousin, Iva Bull Shows, played some records. The Bird Hat girls taught me how to play the tambourine. (MP)
5. My sister Mary had a twin sister who died at birth. She is also buried near Grandma and Grandpa Bull Shows. My mother is buried in Crow Agency, a row away from my father. (MP)

Somebody Took All the Medicine

My mother had two [medicine] bags.
And she put the one up on the wall,
and she put the other one in a trunk, pack it away in a trunk.[1]
But when she died,
at the burial we took her to the grave,
and we were a-a-ll there.
The family is there.
But someone
sneaked away and they say he says "Come on.
Before the crowd
ends up and go back to the house,
let's hurry and get in the old lady's trunk
and get all that medicine and take it.
And I'll pack it away somewhere where nobody can see.
And later on we can sell it."
They done that.

And we a-a-ll sad and came home, back to the house after the burial.
We a-a-ll sit around and
talk and a lot of families come aro-o-und.
Som-me fixing lunch for us and we sit around.
We never have no intentions to go and open the trunk and
look who took all that medicine—we never do.
We thought they were all in there—but a relative,
he took all of it and stole it and took it somewhere.[2]

A-a-nd in about a week or so,

he took them to a man in Billings, a white man—he sure believe in medicine,
    Indian medicine.

They take it

to that man and he give good price for them.

So they take all that medicine over there to that man.

But that man is dead—I just wonder where all that medicine is now.

His name is Wildschut.

I interpret for him

and my mother and father.

And he's a good man-n.

He even says "Now I'll go and bring a big feed."

He goes and picks the best m-e-eat.

Bread.

Cake.

Chicken.

A-a-ll the goodies.

A-a-nd bring them over to the house.

And

lay it there after the medicine's open.[3]

1. According to Frey (*The World of the Crow*, 24), women were the caretakers for medicine bundles. He describes the bundles as "the most cherished and protected family possession." (BL)
2. This is an example of family heirlooms going from Indian hands to museums and private collectors. That process intensified on the Crow Reservation in the late nineteenth century. Sometimes individual family members secretly removed items for personal benefit, as in this account. Some families let go of them when they began to doubt their own traditions because of the teachings of agents, religious leaders, and boarding school staff. Others sold family possessions in financial desperation when the old economy collapsed. Occasionally collectors stole them directly. The process happened all over the plains, so few of the old artworks remain on the reservations. (See "The Don't Pay Much on an Indian," chapter 15, for another example of Crow heirlooms leaving the reservation.) (BL)
3. The collector in this account is William Wildschut (1883–1955), a Billings businessman who was well regarded by many Crow. He also authored a manuscript on Crow beadwork, later published by John Ewers. Lillian praises him here for feeding people generously, a culturally respectful way of doing business in Crow society. She is not suggesting he instigated the theft. (BL)

My mother probably interpreted English to Crow for her parents. It sounds as though Wildschut approached them before Grandma's death, but no one had any medicine bundles for him. After her death someone took the bundle and sold it to him. I have seen Bull Shows's items in New York and wondered how they came into the collector's possession. (MP)

George Went with My Father to Make a Will

When Congress passed the Dawes Act in 1887, they began dividing the reservation into homesteads, or "allotments," and turning communal land to private property. Now Crow elders needed wills to distribute their land. In this story, Bull Shows makes a will, probably between 1948 and 1951, but needs assistance with English.

When Lillian explains how she got her own land, she is telling us she received a homestead under the Dawes Act, a second allotment of grazing land through the Crow Act of 1920, and smaller parcels inherited from her parents. When she says, "Our children don't get any. They're not allotted," she is talking about the impact of the Crow Act. In the early twentieth century, outsiders tried to open "surplus" reservation land for white settlement. Tribal leaders negotiated the Crow Act, which divided remaining land among individual members and prevented reservation homesteads for non-Natives, but she is explaining that no land was left for younger generations of Crow. "Unallotted" descendants receive no reservation land unless they inherit it, and that is why Bull Shows wants his will to include land for Iris. (BL)

My father and mother, they never been to school."
A-a-nd
no they don't know <u>how</u> to speak English.
They don't know a word.
But they buy—they know how to use money.
And then they were allotted.
The government was good enough to
give us land—give us a piece of land,
in our name.

Like me.
I'm allotted a homestead.
Gave me a lot.
Says "Build your home there and that's a homestead."
But you can't sell it.

And
I think it was nineteen—
nineteen thirty-three,
they got lots of land that's not allotted.
So some of this land we were allotted [before]—
one hundred and sixty acres of land for our homestead.
And then what was left was
a big piece of land and they say "Now,
we'll give you about
another hundred and sixty acres for grazing land."
And see they add that grazing land for us.
Therefore now that's ours.[1]

But our children don't get any.
They're not allotted [because no land was left].
And now, say about nineteen—
eighty or nineteen ninety,
this generation would say "We want that land allotted to us."
Some of them ain't even born [during allotment],
and some are young—they don't know what their parents are doing.
But they will inherit our land.
Like me, I made a will.
Give some to Mary.
Give some Mardell, Adam, Nellie.

When my mother died, I inherited her land.
When she passed away she didn't make a will.
She just kept still—didn't know how.
And we don't want to tell her to go ahead and make a will.

But my father did.
He went with my husband to the office and he set down to the
secretary, the clerk there in the office, and say,
"I want to leave this piece of land to Lillian."
(Always call me Lillian.)
"And then the brother Caleb.
And Harry."
Harry, that's my nephew [Caleb's son].
He's the one that
talked into my father—he says "Now,
you go to the Indian office
and will a piece of land to Iris
because you say you adopt her, adopted her in the Indian way.
She says
she calls you Father.
She calls you Father and the old lady Mama.
So therefore you adopted her so she's just like a sister to Lillian.[2]
Now you go to the office, make a will and give her a piece of land."[3]

So my father did.
Gave her a piece of land wa-a-a-y up at East Pryor.
So,
then
my brother never said nothing—he don't know.
He doesn't say <u>nothing</u>.
And he didn't know
my father make a will—but I know because he took George.
Called him one day—he said "Now,
get me over to the Indian Office so I can write down,
have it in writing and write down in the Office.
I want to make a will."

So my husband went with him.
And when George came back he told me.
He said he done pretty good.

He [my father] said,
"My land
and what I own," he says, "all go to Caleb and Lillian.
But I want to give Iris
a piece of land,
way up to East Pryor."
About—let's see now—I think it's
one hundred and fifty acres.
"Grazing land.
And I want to give her that."

But Harry,
he talk him into it.
Told him to do that.
But I said "It's all right.
What I'm getting, my own land,
that's enough" I said.
I don't go and say "I want this and that and I want all the land
that belongs to my father and mother.
I inherited that and I want more"—I don't say that.
I said "That's all right, let him do it."

So Iris got some of our land.
Wa-a-ay up on the mountain.
She has
three boys,
two girls.[4]
Let's see—she never got married but she has all these children.
She never got married.
So that little piece of land [is] all them kids will inherit.
Her land
that my father gave her.
It's a ni-ice piece of land wa-a-ay up to East Pryor.
So,
that's all right,
she have a piece of land.

1. The Crow Act was drafted by Lillian's second husband, Robert Yellowtail, and other educated Crows, after considerable debate. For details on the process, see Bradley, *The Handsome People*; and Hoxie, *Parading*, 261–63. (BL)
2. Being adopted in the Indian way happens without formal papers. Grandma and Grandpa Bull Shows just took Iris, raised her and considered her their own, much as they did my mother's first child, Samuel (see "My Mother Kept Sammy," chapter 12). Because the grandparents raised Iris, my mother always considered her a sister instead of a niece. (MP)
3. In 1931 Congress passed an act requiring adopted Apsáalooke to have state-approved papers to be recognized as heirs. Since Crow adopt frequently, and children move between households, recognizing multiple sets of parents, adoption papers are usually inappropriate. Most, like Iris, wouldn't have them. Bull Shows needed a will to legally specify that he was leaving land to her. (BL)
4. Iris's sons are Samuel (named after my brother Sam), Darwin, and Victor. Her daughters are Brenda Fighter and Iva. (MP)

My Father Died There in My Home

Bull Shows passed away in 1951. (BL)

My father was,
I think he lived to be ninety.
He says he's ninety-one.
And some of the relatives,
they say "You're not old, you don't look—you're only fifty, you're only sixty."
And they said "You're not up in seventy or ninety." (laughs)
They used to tell him.
He says he's old, he's up to ninety now and some of the relatives say "No you're not eighty!" (chuckles)
Mardell and Mary, they get to see their grandfather.[1]

A-a-nd
he said,
"When I die" he said,
"don't let me wear my Indian clothes."
He said he's going to see the white man
when he died—he means God.

Said "Let me wear my civilian clothes.
Don't put no Indian clothes on me."

So when he died,
I stayed with him.
This is no story—it's a sad story.
But the la-ast days,
he was at Pryor with my niece and my brother but my brother's not there.
He said "I'm sick,
and I can't live
too much longer,"
but he said "I want to go to my daughter's house.
She'll take care of me—she'll feed me, she'll take care of me until my last
    breath" he says.
"I want to go live with her—take me there."

And I remember the day they brought him to the house.
He ba-a-arely walk.
Somebody have to hold him.
He drag his feet.
They got him to the house.
And I cried—he said "Don't cry.
Don't cry."
But he said he wasn't going to live
very long—he said,
"I want to die in your home.
Don't take me to the hospital."

But George and I said we'd better take him to the doctor,
where he'll have better care.
We took him there and they gave him medicine—they know he was going
    to go.
So he said,
"Ask the old man if he wants to stay in the hospital or go home with you."
And they ask him
if he wants to be admitted in the hospital.
He said "No, no! <u>No!</u>" he says.

"I want to go back with my daughter,
and she'll take care of me and [I can] die at her home.
I want to do that."
So the doctor says "All right.
Just take him home—do what he says.
He may last a week or maybe four or five days."
He had kidney trouble.

So we did—we brought him home, fix him a nice bed.
He died there.
At my home.
Everybody went to sleep—it was late.
That day I kept sitting with him and
tell him some of the Bible verses and
we set there for long time.
George and them come and sit by him and brush his hair and,
and then that evening we put him to bed.
A-a-nd there was Iris and Grace a-a-nd Nellie and
Adam and them—they all went to bed.
Says "You kids go to bed—I'll stay up with him."

And I did—I stay up
till his last breath.
He, o-o-oh he never struggled—he just laid there.
He had his hands fold and he laid
on his side and he'd look up a little bit and he'd close his eyes.
And his foot
over one foot and he'd say (sound of clearing throat)
—he'd do that.
I'd look at him.
He'd look up a little bit and close his eyes.
Pretty soon he just
lay there re-e-eal still.
I pull a chair right by him now, holding his hand—sometimes I feel his face.
Set there.
Sometimes I feel his
knee and foot—I cover him up good.

George would come and
see how he is and then he'd go back to bed again.
Watched the kids—there was
Nellie and Adam a-a-nd Iris and Grace and them all sleeping.
In the other room.
But I touch his foot and it was re-e-eal cold.
And I kept touching his body and then
I'd cover them up again.
Pretty soon his hands got re-e-eal cold.
But he's still look up a little bit and close his eyes—he'd say (sound of
   clearing throat)
—he'd do that and lay still.

A-a-nd I set there holding his hand—pretty soon,
about one o'clock, I felt his face,
and his nose is cold.
His whole face is so co-o-ld!
So I went and woke up the girls, woke up Nellie.
I said "If you want to
see your grandpa,
he's going to pass away maybe within half an hour."
Said "You want to see him,
get up, dress up, dress and sit up.
Cause he's going to go pretty soon.[2]

And George came up.
Put blankets over the kids and made them sit there way over there.
And George came over, sit on the other side—I sat on the other side.
Never move—he opened his eyes a little bit, he say (clears throat)—do that.
Pretty soon he opened his mouth.
Once.
Second time.
Couldn't make it.
It was all done—he was gone then.
And George and I set there looking and the girls came over.
Poor girls—they came over screaming.
I remember that sound. (starts to weep)

So I went over to the church.
That's,
that's Baker [Pastor Lee Baker],
the Church of God.³
George and I went over
and telephoned to the mortuary,
and they come and got his body.

My mother didn't want to go there—said "Never, never take me to the mortuary."
Says "I don't like it there!"—so she stayed in [the house].
We didn't take her there—they just took the casket to Pryor.
And we all took it.
Buried her up in the cemetery.
She don't want to go to the mortuary there to Bullis.⁴
But my father says "Take good care—I'll do whatever you want" he says.
So I had called a mortuary—Bullis, they come and took him.
And the girls
sure scream and cried. (weeps)

1. She is telling us that her father was still alive when Mary and Mardell were children, so they knew him. (BL)
2. Grandpa Bull Shows died when I was six. I remember it so very well! I was scared because I had never seen anyone die, and I didn't want him to die. Dad was sixty-three when I was born and had already lost his parents, so this was the only grandparent I knew. (MP)
3. The Church of God has been closed for some time, but Mom helped build that church. Quite a few neighborhood women helped too. Some of the other founders were Alfretta Fitzpatrick, Florida Fitzpatrick, Florida Big Medicine, and Caroline Other Medicine. I was a little girl, but I put in a few nails myself. (MP)
4. Bullis Mortuary in Hardin. (BL)

Dave Haun Wrote a Check

They said Caleb,
he was around Billings drinking.
And somebody stopped him and told him that his father died and he was
in Hardin at the mortuary.

So,
he was half shot I guess—and he said "I'll go now."
So he took off—he walked
to the highway,
and walk up that
road, the highway.
Went over the field, went over the hill,
all them curves.
He walk—nobody picked him up.

But when he got down to
just before Pryor Creek,
he was walking, a car come along.
The driver was going to
up on the hill.
But he saw this man walking on the road.
He turn around and passed and stopped for him.
Happened to be our lessee, Dave Haun.[1]

He said "Caleb."
He says "Where you going?"
And Caleb says "My father died,
and he's in Hardin,
and I want to go see him."
"All right" he says—"you get in there—I'll take you over there."

So he get in the car and took him over there—before he got off,
he wrote a check out.
Twenty-five-dollar check—"Here, I know you have no money."
Said "Here's twenty-five and
here's another twenty-five.
Effie's in there"—says "You give that to Effie."
That's me.
Says "You stay by your sister a-a-nd
all the way through—that twenty-five might help you out."
Caleb said he was su-u-re nice
to haul him back.

So he gave him twenty-five and we were in there.
And Caleb come in there and seen us and hand me that check.
"Here's a check for you now, twenty-five—and
Dave Haun wrote out a check for me."
So he was there.
But he walked.
[Until] Dave took him over there.

   1. She called Dave Haun their lessee because he rented farm or grazing land from them. (BL)

Lorena Mae Moved to Arizona

Lorena Mae and Cedric live in Phoenix [after] she married.
Cedric was an employee who worked for the government.
He was transferred to Phoenix [in 1952].
He left alone.
He didn't take the car—he left it with Lorena Mae,
and we traded the car for a big Ford—Ford two-door, four-door—big car.

[By then] she has Sandy,
so-o,
they moved to Arizona,
and they had the two children [Carson and Sandy].[1]
Lorena Mae went to college in
Glendale, Arizona.
There's Phoenix—big
city, this Phoenix.
And joining that there's
the campus,
there in Glendale.[2]
[She studied to be a] secretary.

I went down there for the graduation.
I got me a new Ford,
and George was living at the time,

a-a-nd me a-a-nd Mary a-a-nd Nellie,
they were young.
We all went down there for the graduation.
I never forget that time—it's sure nice.
Yeh.[3]
A-a-nd
then she,
she went to work at the Office too—where Cedric worked.

1. Lorena Mae moved to Phoenix in 1952, after Cedric graduated from Haskell Institute in Lawrence, Kansas. My father accompanied her, Sandy, and Carson. Louis, Loreen, and Roberta (Bobbie Sox) were born years later. Before that they lived in a small house behind Cedric's uncle, Mike Fitzpatrick. Mike was the brother of Cedric's mother, Elizabeth, but he was raised by Sidney Black Hair so he is sometimes called Mike Black Hair. (MP)
2. Glendale is just west of Phoenix. (BL)
3. We went to Arizona for graduation in 1954, and my mother dressed in modern clothing and wore a bun because she didn't want anyone to stare at her moccasins and braids. (MP)

I Beaded Pants for Carson

In this story Lillian tells us how some women watched her make buckskin and how she later used the buckskin to make pants for her young grandson so he could parade. Her daughter-in-law, Adeline, was one of the women who watched her, and she later helped Lillian bead, a common Crow custom. Crow women often help their relatives, especially with beading projects, which are time-consuming. The woman who initiates the outfit claims it as hers, but other women in the family may assist.[1] (BL)

[One time] couple women [watched me tan].
Annie Big Day look on,
and Adeline [Samuel's wife] *and her mother Julia.*[2]
We camped across the river—that house used to be in Crow.

I did it outside.
So the three women set there and watch us,
and [the hide] turn real whi-ite,

a-a-nd Annie Big Day and Julia said,
"Goodness sakes this buckskin is so so-oft, just like cloth.
I wonder how you
done it so nice.
Our old lady"—that's Annie's mother—
"showed us how and we tried it—ours don't come out.
When it come out of the water a-a-nd the water dripping out and we rub it down,
as soon as we rub it, it gets hard and tough." (chuckles)
That's Annie said that—"You better show us how to make it."
I said I would and they never come around and I never went around there.
I never showed them.

Anyway I *scraped and stretched*.
Mine come out re-eal white and George helped me
stretch it.
And you know,
the ver-ry night,
I said "Carson is going to parade.
[Let's make some pants for him.]
And let's put some beads on the pants
and sew them up."
A-a-nd
Adeline [my daughter-in-law] helped me.
She put just one flower there and I put one flower there and the leaves,
and that very night I start to sew it on the machine [sew the pants together].[3]

And it was Crow Fair—we were going to move camp the next day.
Lorena Mae and Carson, they're down in Arizona and they come for the fair.
We didn't have no horse then—I went to my lessee and I said,
"Can you lend me a horse, a pony?" and he said "Yes,
sure, if you take that white horse, re-eal gentle.
You want a saddle?"—I said "No we got a saddle."
So we went back to the tent.

The next morning Carson parade.
Wore that pants.
I was so pro-oud of it. (chuckles)
I think he was about—
eight or nine. (chuckles)
We got the picture.
But I don't know what become of the pants.

1. For further information on beading and the contributions of multiple women, see Loeb, "Crow Beadwork," 58.
2. Adeline and Julia Rock Above. Adeline married my brother, Samuel Plainfeather. (MP)
3. Crow women often bead garments before they sew them together. If the garment is in pieces, the parts are easier to handle and other women in the family can take sections home to work on. (BL)

Wood, Coal, and Electricity

We burn wood.
Mardell's dad, he su-u-re is good at
loading the wood,
and we used to ask,
"Who's going to go along" and this and that—and the neighbors
said "We'll go!"
And they get a truckload, we get a truck.
And we make a picnic.
We have a big fire started and we cook meat on there and
o-oh we enjoy that.
A-a-nd we had
goodies with us, coo-o-kies and fruit, banana-a-s,
and the kids all run around and they sure like it.
A-a-nd we used to,
several families a-a-ll bunch up and go after wood.
We'd get a load.[1]

Now after that,
we quit doing that a-a-nd George and I used to go.

We'd say "We go ear-r-ly in the morning a-a-nd make a big load."
A-a-nd sometimes we'd take his sister along.
Mary, Mary Takes the Gun.
And she picks wood and pile them up.
We'd take a load, our load,
and unload it at the house at home in Crow,
and then we'd take hers in the afternoon.
We'd take two loads.
And we liked to do that.

The dead trees, we'd cut them down.
But the ones that's laying around,
we'd saw them up—even if it's a big log laying there.
We'd take the saw and cut them up—chop them up.
We didn't have that [power saw],
so we used to just use hand saw.
We counted to about seven
loads, big logs.
If they're just sticks and,
and pretty-good-size wood,
we take a <u>big</u> load and should last us about—
seven loads should last us about—
whole winter.

And we'd haul coal too—we buy coal,
a-a-nd we buy a sack full.
Take a gunnysack,
even to Sheridan [Sheridan, Wyoming].
When we'd go to Sheridan,
we'd take two gunny sacks
and fill them up with coal.
They only cost—
let's see that time I think they cost about three dollars a sack.
Coal.
That's quite high ain't it?
A-a-nd tie them up and put it in the car and we'd take them home.

And we have a little coal shed—put our coal in there and
Mardell's dad used to be awfully careful how he break the coal.
Take it nice and easy—crumble out and
sometimes he make big chunks and small chunks,
fine stuff.

Even when I was staying up there at the Battlefield, the apartment,
Mardell go to work,
and I haul coal.
Sometimes we haul in big chunks a-a-nd
put them in the garage in the pail,
and we can just start the
fireplace with great big chunks of coal and big logs
a-a-nd keep that fire going all night.[2]
Sometimes I chopped and someti-imes Porky [Mardell's husband]. (chuckles)
But [past] times her dad,
he chops wood—he's real good.

(Laughs) [The kids helped.]
Nellie said "This is going to balance and this going to fall,"
a-a-nd make Mardell sit—said "You sit there.
Hold a log down."
And she'd sit there and they'd start to pushing it. (laughs)
We liked to do those.
We thought that was our job and we had to do it—we like it.
It was fun.

And then pretty soon we haul a armful.
Armful of big kindling.
We call that kindling.
We haul that in,
covered it up.
And we have a little shed
to put our wood in there for the winter.
And we well fixed,
if you have enough wood for the winter. (chuckles)
Yeh.

I can cook on [wood stove, range, or open fire], all of that—I learned.
I like all of them.[3]
In the house,
cooking on the range,
slow process.[4] (chuckles)
Mardell remember all those because she lived right on the farm.

A-a-nd we do all those things.
They help.
Yeah we enjoy all that—we don't say it's hard work.
We just go at it and just finish it.
We like it.
Yeah but that, I can't do it now.

We got a ax,
a big a-ax, a good a-ax.
O-n-ne
head—we always say head—
and a good ax with two blades on.
And George always take it to this blacksmith in Hardin, have it sharp,
and they sharpen it on both sides,
and he says "Don't let the kids touch
this ax."
And we always said "Don't touch that ax—it's sharp, it will hurt you."

So we had those things around—we don't now.
We just push a button-n and fire goes.
Yeah this is different.
A range like those is good,
but way back in nineteen ten,
nineteen eleven, nineteen twelve, around there [when I was a child],
we used just a
black,
cast-iron stove with a oven on.
Sometimes there's just two lids.
Sometimes there's four lids.
And we cook on there.
So we liked that too.

1. Preparing for winter was an annual event each fall, right after Crow Fair. Dad and Adam sawed and us girls sat on the logs to sort of hold them down. The log was put over a sawhorse, with one end sticking out for Dad or Adam to saw off. The main part of the log was between the x's of the saw horse, and that is what we sat on to balance or steady the log. Sometimes Nellie and Mary sawed too. We all had responsibility to put the sawed and chopped wood into the woodshed. (MP)
2. Between 1979 and 1990 I had a house at the Custer Battlefield, now the Little Bighorn Battlefield National Monument, and lived on the grounds. My house had a fireplace. (MP)
3. In summer we used to take our woodstove outside so Mom could cook without heating the house. Seems to me like those biscuits were better. (MP)
4. She always complained that modern ranges didn't heat fast enough. (MP)

A Car Hit Us

One day we went after water.
I was driving,
and we had our jugs in the back.
We had a little pickup.[1]
I was driving and George was sitting there.
A-a-nd we went in the
parsonage where we usually get water.
We drove in—just as we turn, a car hit us.
A Wyoming car hit us and we (claps hands) both shook up.
A-a-nd turn us around.

Both of us
hurt our neck,
arm and shoulder.
[Especially] him!
They took me to the hospital.
They gave me a shot and made me lay down a-a-nd,
finally,
I said "I'm all right—I want to go home."
But him,
about three nerves pinch.
In the back.
Pinched nerves in his backbone,

and they can't operate on him because
on account of his age.
And that's why he died—from that.
Nerve pinched—he couldn't use his hands.
His head was hanged down like this [chin on chest].
Couldn't lift up his head.
A-a-nd doctors couldn't work on his neck.
Said if they did,
he will die.[2]
He lived for about
six years after that.
And he died.

Worked in the Forestry [BIA Forestry Department].[3]
[And] he work in the Office [BIA].[4]
He work in the Office,
and he quit.
The boss called him over one time,
and he said "George you'd better quit your job.
Retire now—you're of age you should retire.
I heard some men that's talking against you.
They're going to fire you,
and you're going to go without a job."
And said "I think it's about time that you quit."[5]
It was Harold Stanton's father.[6]
So he quit his job and
he retired and he draw pension.
And that's why I'm drawing pension now.
From him.
Widow's pension.

So-o,
yeh he did—he wasn't sick.
He just couldn't use his hands anymore.
They told me, the doctor told me, some of these days he can't use his hands.
From that pinch.
And he did.

That was
where that car knocked us over and
all shook up.
Sometimes my neck don't feel good—like yesterday,
my neck hurt
coming up that road [to Big Sky, Montana].
So I still
carry
on.

1. They were living in Crow Agency in a house without running water, and they were hauling water by pickup. They were driving to the Baptist church in Crow Agency. (MP)
2. The damage came later, not suddenly as it sounds here. (MP)
3. My father worked at Lookout Point in the Wolf Mountains, and he often said he was not afraid to be alone up there because of his Christian faith. Later, around 1955, he named a child for this. The child was the son of Lee Baker, the minister of the Church of God, and the name he received was Not Afraid to Be Alone. (MP)
4. In the Office he was clerk of court for the tribal judges. (MP)
5. This probably had something to do with tribal politics, which were getting vicious about then. (MP)
6. Harold Stanton is a lawyer in Hardin. He seems always to have an interest in Crow politics and affairs. (MP)

We'd Better Go Back to the Farm

Damage from the accident developed slowly, so George lived for several more years. It was during that time that they decided to move back to Lillian's old home in Dunmore. (BL)

We made a nice home,
and we lived in Crow.
We build a big house there,
and all our kids going to school and George said,
"Lillian" he says,
"I think we better go back.
To your farm—your house [in Dunmore].
This is no place to raise children."

Said "They're among the children—they go out every night, play,
out every night, they come back late."
Says "This is no place to raise children."
Says "We'd better go back to your house."
So that's why we're living at that place now.[1]

>   1. Lillian and George moved back to the home she had shared with Paul Singer. Later, after George passed away, she tore this house down and built a new one on the same property (see "We Ordered a House from Minneapolis," chapter 17). She stayed there until she moved to assisted living a few years before her death. (BL)

George Passed Away

> *George Hogan died in 1958. At that time, Lillian was about fifty-three years old. Ferole Mae Pease is George's daughter with his second wife, Marjorie White Hip.* (BL)

George, when George was sick,
he was at home and it happened to be
Nellie's birthday and we ate a birthday dinner.
And I gave him, bring him supper—a plate,
to the bed—and I said "I'll feed him."
"All right—feed me just little bit."
But he said "If you'd rather take me to the hospital,"
said "take me right away."
And we did—within couple hours he passed away.

And [his daughter] Ferole Mae
was in there with him.
Ferole Mae Pease.
I called her and she came over—she happened to live
not too close from the Office.
They both work as an employee there.
So I call her and I says "You get over here before your father passed away."
I said "You'd better hurry"—"All right, I'll be there right away" she says.
She came over and was there.

I called the minister, Mr. Bentley,

and said "Get over here Mr. Bentley."

I said "Get over here—George is going to pass away within an hour or maybe half an hour.

I wish you'd better hurry up and get over here."

And Ferole Mae was in there,

and I was out in the hall,

and she come out crying,

and she said "I saw my daddy

take two breaths and passed away."

And I wasn't in there when he passed away but Ferole Mae was there—I was in the hall.

Yeh.

Mr. Bentley and I walked in there and he was gone then.[1]

But I saw my father take his last breath.

Su-u-re made it hard.

My mother too.

Yeh.

1. When my father was dying and Ferole came, Mom escorted all of us to the Church of God in Crow Agency, where we kneeled and prayed for him. By the time we returned to the hospital, he was gone. He passed away on April 27, 1958. (MP)

CHAPTER SEVENTEEN

The Kids Are Growing Up

Arizona and the Grand Canyon

These events happened almost immediately after George's death, when Lillian moved everyone to Phoenix to be with her daughter Nellie and with Lorena Mae and her family. (BL)

[Lorena Mae got pregnant with Louie],
and then from there she had Nellie come over.
Nellie go to school in Arizona
where she can babysit Sandy and Carson
while Lorena Mae goes to work—she did a-a-nd
Nellie got so lonesome she wouldn't e-eat, she wouldn't slee-e-p.
She went to school and after school she come ho-ome and
go right into her bedroom and shut the door and wouldn't talk to n-nobody.
And she won't eat.

So Lorena Mae called home and she said,
"Mama you got to do something,
about Nellie."
She told me "She won't e-eat, she can't sleep, she cri-ies and,
and" says "I can't make her to understand me.
But she cries too much and she's getting thin" she says.
"She looks so pa-ale,
and you got to do something—come and get her o-or
you come over and live over here."

This was at Christmastime.
So I asked Mary—I said "What shall we do?"
Nellie's over to Phoenix,

with Lorena Mae,
and I asked Mary what to do,
and she said "Let's go."
We pack up and we left there.
We-e
nailed the doors and nail the win-ndows, board them,
a-a-nd had my lessee watch the house,
and we took off Christmas Day—had our turkey ready in the roaster.
(claps)
That afternoon the girls were so in a big hurry!
They want to leave—they want (claps)
to pull out![1]

And I remember that we just travel all night till we got to
that George's Town or George's Ci-ity,
down in Utah.[2]
We stayed there and the next morning o-oh it was snowing hard.
Sno-owing a-a-nd lots of snow there,
a-a-nd I said "Let's turn back.
We're going to hit some bad roads."
And they said "No, no, no!
You're always afraid of highways, slippery roads.
We're not afraid—we'll get you there."
So we did—took off,
got to Phoenix.
We got to Lorena Mae's house,
and o-oh she was happy.
She's really happy and Nellie,
Nellie got all right too.

So-o,
I said "Lorena Mae" I said,
"we can't live in one house,
your family and my family."
I said "We'd better
get an apartment or house, rent a house."
Said "That's fine" she says.

"Just so you don't live too far
out of town."
So-o took us I don't know how many days—maybe
couple days or so—look for a house and
we found a bra-a-nd new apartment they just got through building.
Nobody lived there—haven't rented out yet.
We got that apartment.

And I didn't bring no furnitures.
So-o Lorena Mae said "Oh if you want some furnitures,"
she says "Mama you've got enough—you've got lots of money."
Said "Let's go shopping for furnitures."
So we went
to the store—anyway I forgot where we went.
Town somewhere.
I got me a bedroom sui-i-te, a dining room sui-i-te, stove,
and refrigerator—well everything.
A-a-nd we moved into the new apartment and I bought a-a-ll those stuff.

A-a-nd I make the kids go to a mission school.
Nellie and Mary and Mardell.
They put them in a mission school,
and I kept one of my niece's daughter.
My niece died [Grace Bullshows].
I kept her little girl [Davene Bullshows],
and she was about seven years old.
I had her with me at the house but these girls, I put them in the mission
    school,
South[west] Indian Mission [boarding school].
They go to school over there—I kept this girl,
make her go to school up in the public school where I lived.[3]

And Lorena Mae lived right close.
She had a telephone installed.
Adam went to work in the lumberyard.
And I had a brand new car.

Before we left Hardin
I bought a new Rambler—white one.
We come in that.

So I made the girls go to school in the mission school.
I put this Davene in the public school close to my apartment,
a-a-nd on weekends I go after the girls and bring them home.
They'd be home during the weekend but I'd take them back Sunday night.
I'd drive.
And I used to drive downtown.
Shop around.
We lived there for the who-ole
year—they went to school there.

A-a-nd about
in May,
just before the school out—
no it was in June—
my eyes got bad.
So I left the girls with Lorena Mae to go back to Billings for my eyes.
Adam and me and Davene,
in my Rambler—and they got a grea-a-at big trailer
full of stuff.

And I brought
a Cheyenne.
He went to a college there at Phoenix.
He was going back to Lame Deer[4]
so I, I lend him my small trailer.
I got a U-Haul trailer and <u>loaded</u> with furnitures.
Went back home.

And the day we left we made Grand Canyon.
We want to see the Grand Canyon so
we stop at the camp,
camping grounds—o-oh that was <u>cro-owded</u> with people!
We finally squeeze in—Adam slept in the pickup.

There were mattresses and everything in there.
Had a big trailer.
He just sneak in—open the trailer door and he sneak in there,
and the mattresses are there—he slept in there.
And Davene and I slept in the room.

And the next morning I said "We'd better get a early start."
And they said "We want to see the Grand Canyon."
And I said "I don't want to.
I want to get home."
But anyway we got to the Grand Canyon
about eleven o'clock,
and
Adam and Davene, they walked down that trail,
and they said "We won't go down the valley.
Says "We won't.
We'll just walk down the trail for about
couple hours and we'll be back."
And I guess they did.

I said I didn't want to go.
I just stayed up on top.
Looked do-own and look at the pe-e-ople and I'd go in the curio stor-re.
Eat lun-nch there and look aro-o-und.
I'd go back and look and they're not back—I'd go back to the car and
    waited and waited.
They went down there about eleven o'clock.
They never got back till two o'clock.

So we started,
and "Let's try to make
Lander, Wyoming" and we travel a-a-ll
day and all night and we got to Lander, Wyoming.
I got relatives there.
Shoshone.
A-a-nd we stayed there that night.[5]

Adam slept in the car.
Davene and I slept inside.
She fix a nice bed for us.

And the next morning we got up at about five o'clock,
and we got up and (claps)
we took off.
The lady fixed coffee—when I was up,
she had coffee all ready.
We got up at
five—we left about
sometime after six.
And made home about four o'clock in the afternoon.
Dunmore. (chuckles)

1. Nellie went to Arizona in 1958. Then my father died, when Louie was two months old, and we all moved to Arizona shortly after. I graduated from the eighth grade there in 1959. (MP)
2. Probably St. George, in the southwestern corner of Utah, on Interstate 15. (BL)
3. During our time in Arizona, we lived in Sunnyslope, a suburb of Phoenix. (MP)
4. Lame Deer is a town on the Northern Cheyenne Reservation, just east of the Crow Reservation. (BL)
5. The relative she stayed with was Suzette Wagon, on the Wind River Reservation. Mother's maternal grandmother was a Shoshone and Suzette must have been a descendant of one of those Shoshone relatives. I met Suzette just once. My sister Mary knows her better. (MP)

The Girls Got Home

Anyway I left my
daughters—Nellie,
Mary,
Mardell,
with Lorena Mae and Cedric—I said "Make them go to school."
A-a-nd this was in May,
a-a-nd she said the school will be out in about three weeks.

So Adam and I hired a U-Haul trailer.
A-a-nd my old trailer,
I lent it
to this Cheyenne.
He's going back to Lame Deer—he was going to college too,
but he is going back for the summer.
So he—he asked me if he could take the trailer and I said yes.
"I'll give you some gas money."
I gave him some gas money and I
gave him my trailer—I said "You can have the trailer,
but the stuff in there,
the furnitures in there" I said,
I don't give that to you"—I said "I'll give you the trailer."
"Ye-e-es!" he said—"I want the trailer." (chuckles)
He hauled a loaded trailer of stuff back home for me.
But I pulled a
U-Haul trailer home
with a load of stuff.
A-a-nd that afternoon got home.

When I got home went to the doctor about my eyes,
and I was treated—they were all right.
A-a-nd in about a month,
I sent the fare for the kids—for the girls.
And Nellie,
or Mary or Lorena Mae,
load them up in the bus,
and they got home—they got to Billings.
I was waiting there when they got home.
And they've been home ever since.[1] (chuckles)
I enjoy all that time.

  1. Most of her children left for short periods for school, employment, or military service, but they have otherwise remained on the reservation or in nearby Billings or Hardin. (BL)

I Stayed in Nespelem, Washington

But anyway Lorena Mae and Cedric lived in Arizona for about five or four
  years,
and they moved to Nespelem,
Washington—transferred.[1]
When she got there says "Mother,
I want you to come over.
We have a house.
We haven't got no dishes,
no plates, no kitchen utensils or nothing,
because they're coming with a load of our furnitures.
They'll be here in a week or so,
from Phoenix to Nespelem,"
she says,
and we don't know how long that's going to take" but she says,
"I wish you'd come and stay with us."
I went over there and stayed with them,
a-a-nd we went and bought some dishes and bowls and kettles and stuff.
At first she was using paper plates to eat. (laughs)

I stayed about
two months or so.
A-a-nd Mary and Nelson were married then—they went after me,
and I went back.
They have a car and they had a pickup and they have a house there,
and they're well fixed so we just left.

So they live in Washington about four years.
A-a-nd one time she called,
and she says she was mad at Cedric.
Said "I'm tired of this.
I'm going to leave him."

"I won't leave right away because I'm going to work in the Office too."
Says "Would you pick up the kids
and put them in school in Hardin

while I'm over here?"
A-a-nd I said "Yes,
I'll pick them up—if you want me to go after them I will too."
She said "That's too much for you Mama" she says—"I'll just send them in the train,
and you pick them up in Billings"—I did.
Soon as I got them
home I made them go to school in Hardin,
and I lived with them—I took care of them.

And then pretty soon Lorena Mae—
she didn't want me to tell this to anybody—
said "Keep this to yourself"—says "I want to leave Cedric.
I want to go home."
A-a-nd,
"Get a truck and get over here and haul my stuff."
So I got a truck,
a big truck,
and I sent Adam and my nephew,
to Nespelem.
And they unload a-a-ll Lorena Mae's stuff,
and they came [home].

A-a-nd they took a wrong route.
They went to Great Falls (chuckles) without going to Hardin.
They took another route with the truck there and here Lorena Mae got home,
and we have to look for them—finally we found [them]
with a load, a truckload of stuff.
Finally found them.

Lorena Mae [used to] get mad at Cedric but they get along good now just fine.
Cedric is an o-old man with grandchildren.
He's good to his grandchildren—he's good to Lorena Mae.
And they have
built a big house.

And she bought that place—that land.
About—
eighty acres.
That land belonged to Cedric and his sisters,
and Lorena Mae bought that,
and she build a house there, that house that she's living there now—she bought the land.
Paid the family and she build a house there.
"And when I die" she says "all go to my daughters."

She start in
buying horses—they got lots of horses.
Yeah she has pretty horses now.
Let's see now—she bought one for [her daughter] Lorene,
a-a-nd the mare, she gave about two colts now,
and one about a year old.
Past pretty near two now a-a-nd she had the one-year-old colt now.
And I believe she's going to have another one—the mare.
But Lorena Mae has these others.
About five
parade horses.

A-a-nd
Lorena Mae's smart.
She's just about run the family,
and Cedric just keep qui-i-et and smi-ile and
he doesn't talk too much.
He just sit there with no shirt on and big fella,
and pretty soon visitors come and he put on a shirt.
Course I don't go there every day or nothing like that—I just visit them.
A-a-nd she seem to be always glad to have me come and visit her.

1. Nespelem is on the Colville Reservation in northeastern Washington. According to Lorena Mae, they moved there around August 1959, so they had been in Phoenix about seven years and must have left a few months after Lillian and the girls returned to Montana. (BL)

Buying Hopi, Our Last Pretty Horse

Lillian probably purchased Hopi in the late 1950s. (BL)

Fair time is what they all look forward.
They want to prepare—
get a good-looking horse for parade horse.
We do that too—one time I went to Miles City.
Look for a parade horse,
and I got one.
It's pre-etty.
Spooky.
And Adam and I took the trailer.

I bought that and I bought two in Billings.
I bought three parade horses.
Mary rides one.
And then Carson—he still was,
o-oh he may be
twelve years old.
And San—we make [have] them ride those horses.[1]

Now I don't have no horses—I
turn them loose to the range.
And I said "Me and my poor horses.
I don't have enough pasture.
They can just take off and the horse buyers can come and take them away."
I said "We don't want no horses anymore.
We've got such a small pasture,
and if you want any more horses, we have to lease a big piece of land to raise horses."
So I said "Let's not have any more horses."
We used to have a big corral right by the house, alongside of that big ditch there.
We used to have a stack of hay in there.
A big corral—I made them take it all off.
I said "Get rid of that corral!

No more horses." (chuckles)
So we quit having horses.
But I like them.

One time when I bought a horse from Billings,
I said "I'm going [to a] horse sale today."
I said "I'd better go over there and buy a parade horse."
So Adam and me and Nellie and the girls all went over there to the horse sale.
And there's big grandstand.
Big room and under there they bring in the horses in the arena,
and they take them out to see.
They bid them.
The highest bidder gets the horse.

So they brought this sorrel horse.
Kind of a spooky—oooh it looked pretty.
And somebody over here [bid] a hundred and twenty.
And then another one over here offer hundred and thirty.
Forty.
The fellow over there bid on it.
I think he bid about a hundred and fifty.
"Hundred and fifty."
And it got to two hundred,
and then I said "I'm going to bid for that."
Pretty.
So, big [place], lots of people.
I waved and they look and said "What?
How much you bid on this?"—I said "Two hundred."
And (claps)
they quieted—the others didn't bid on it anymore, they didn't say their number.
So they said "That lady gets the horse."[2]

We call him Hopi.
Gee he's pretty.
Spooky and he'd turn around and pra-ance.
Gee he's pretty.

Yeh.
They sure liked that horse.
They always say "Hopi."
They all know the horse.

Train run over him—kill him,
right by where we live.
O-oh Nellie and I and Adam, we used to go over there
and look at him—but Nellie
took a pair of pliers
and my knife
and had Mugger with her.[3]
Said "I want you to take the teeth [for a medicine]."
And they did.
I wouldn't look—I said "I'm going to stay in the car—I don't want to look."
So they went up, climb over the
railroad track and he was laying on the other side of the track.
And they went and cut the tooth out, the front tooth—Nellie has them.[4]

That's our la-ast pretty horse—Hopi.
I think Mary,
Mary and Mardell name the horse.
Hopi (chuckles)—he was pretty.[5]

After that I never want to buy a horse.
Adam lives in Billings.
Nobody care for the horses and I don't want to turn my horse over to
    Lorena,
because they got too many horses.
I don't want to.
I said if I do,
I'd pay them,
but sometimes she
has her own way about everything.
She's the boss. (chuckles)
And I know she wouldn't want to take care of our horses.
So I quit buying horses now.

And now especially, I'm o-old.
And here Adam is living in Billings.
Mary living separate now, Mardell is over there [in Oklahoma].
We have no corral, no pasture.
I don't want to buy a horse.
Yeh—I like horses though.

1. San is Sandy (Cassandra) Walks Over Ice, Lillian's granddaughter and Lorena Mae's daughter. (BL)
2. In the late 1950s, two hundred dollars was a high price for a horse. I remember the sale very well. We all fell in love with him because he came into the arena prancing. The salesman told us he was a cutting horse, used by cattle owners to single out particular calves or cows from a herd. He was extremely lively and spirited. He bucked me off twice! (MP)
3. Mugger is our family nickname for my cousin Samuel Bullshows who Mom also raised. (MP)
4. Our family has the "right" to wear the eye teeth of horses. Horses became my family's medicine after my mother's grandfather or great-grandfather captured a crippled white horse from the Lakota. When he cleaned its hooves, the horse proved to be fast and saved his life by outrunning the Sioux. (MP)
5. I named him Hopi. (MP)

I Bought My Children Cars

And I bought Mardell a car one time, one year.
I think it was Christmastime [1961].
I got a car
in Hardin—I bought it and paid for it and
brought the car and
parked it at the neighbor's yard.
I said "I don't want her to see it,
a-a-nd I don't want her to know that I bought this car for her."

And I think it is a gray Ford.
I brought the key and put it on the Christmas tree.
A-a-nd when they distribute out gifts,
we hand her the key and she just <u>jump</u> up! (laughs)
Yeah,
it was quite a sight when we a-a-ll jumped for joy.[1]

First time she had a car and from there on I guess she trade.
Make way and now she's got a car of her own.

Yeah I like to help them out.
I got
a-a-ll the children a car.
If they have to pay the balance,
they have to—like Nellie.
I bought her a car and I said "Here's your car now.
If the payments come up you have to make."
There wasn't much anyway.
There was about $75 a month and she went for about
half a year—she paid for it.
Said "Thank you Mother" she says—"If it wasn't for you I'd <u>never</u> own a
 car." (chuckles)
And Adam, I bought him
cars too—but I never help Lorena Mae. (chuckles)
She's well off—she don't care.

1. I was sixteen years old, and it was an old jalopy that cost her four hundred dollars. She was tired of me riding around with other teenagers, and she wanted me to have my own so that things would be safer for me. (MP)

I Had a Houseful

There had always been people at Lillian's house, but she took in more after her husband died, so her house was filled with her own children, some of her relatives', and others. Although she doesn't mention it in this story, she also took in foster children. Sharing child-rearing responsibilities is an important Crow custom, and Lillian was proud of raising so many. (BL)

Pretty soon I got lonesome (chuckles)
and I had some kids [living] with me.
I brought in the boys, two nephews.
And two daughters.

One time I had a houseful [of] teenagers.
Some white women, Betty, Bunny, and all them lived with us—Vista
    workers, I had a bunch of those.[1]
I had a trailer outside where they stayed.
And I had all my children.
And I even had [my step-granddaughter] Colleen.
And Blue,
she was young then, she was the youngest one.[2]
Oh I had about six anyway,
of my own—beside the Vista workers.[3]
(laughs) We sure had a lot of good times.

1. The Vista people came around 1962. They lived with my mother when she was lonely, after Dad passed away. Carlene was another Vista worker. She came from South Carolina and married a Crow, Dan Old Elk. (MP)
2. She kept some of my Bullshows cousins, as well as Colleen Old Elk (my sister Pearl Hogan's daughter) and Blue (Roberta Little Light) who lived with us for several years. Pearl gave Colleen up years before, when she was divorcing, because she couldn't take care of all her kids. Colleen's paternal aunt had raised her, but she died. Colleen and I became friends, and I wanted her to live with us, so she did for a year or two. Then she went back to her mom. Blue's mother was dead, and her father asked my mom to care for her. Mom also earned extra money by taking in kids for the welfare department, Social Services. The Crow Agency Social Services often asked to her keep a child or two. (MP)
3. "My own" refers to Nellie, Mary, and me, as well as Blue and her step-granddaughter Colleen. (MP)

Piiláako Wanted to Go Hunting

As this story will make clear, Lillian continued to enjoy "Indian" foods and the fun of gathering them. (BL)

We'd go in a bunch and say "Let's go after berries."
We go after berries—chokecherries.
And we go to Juneberries—there's no Juneberries in the valley.
They're up in the mountain.
And we go all in a bunches—we carry our lunch,
stay overnight, camp overnight.

A-a-nd especially we like to take Adam along
because if we see a bear, he sure can kill him.
He has a good gun.
I had a gun too so we're ready.
We'd go to East Pryor,
and there's <u>bea-ars</u> around!
[I never killed a bear]—I'm afraid to. (laughs)
That gun would kick me off. (laughs)
But still I—I bought a gun.
We always go hunting and
they all had guns—I said,
"I'll buy me a gun.
Show me how to shoot."
And I went to the hardware store
and all line up on the wall.
I said "I want a good one.
I want a <u>good</u> gun so I can shoot
a bear or a buffalo" I said.
This man laughed and
he gave a Winchester Seventy I think it was.

These kids were growing up then.
We were right at the house [in Dunmore].
And we go-o hunting up to Sarpy,
up to East Pryor—I had a big station wagon.
After that I said "This station [wagon] is not good for rough country."
I said "We'd better get a pickup"—we got a pickup, one of them big ones.
A-a-nd we get a load [of people].

One evening I had to laugh.
We were going hunting.
This [one] want to go, they want to go—and I said "We're all loaded [full]."
I didn't take Mardell or I didn't take Mary or none of the girls.
But anyway I took A-a-dam and me-e and his wi-ife,
a-a-nd Sa-amuel and Jo-ohnny—and Piiláako,
an old lady wanted to go—Amelia Passes.[1]
She's older than I am.

Yeah I guess she's
one of my cousins—anyway she want to go.

And we had a big pickup and we rolled up our bedding and put it in there.
We got to East Pryor,
and it was getting dark and we build a fire.
A-a-nd we made some coffee and I had sandwiches ready—gave them all coffee.
I said "We're going to pull out early
in the morning before sunrise so we can kill some deer."
Said "You all go to bed—we a-a-ll sleep in that pickup."

And I remember Amelia.
We shut the gate [on the pickup]—we had a big gate,
slide up and down,
a-a-nd we put her at the gate,
and she said "All right you put me at the gate."
And she said "I'm the strongest and the smartest
one in the bunch" she said—"put me there" and we put her by the gate.
And she all wrapped up and went to sleep.
Boys all curled up and wrapped up, they're all rolled in that pickup.

Ear-r-ly in the morning,
Adam got up and says "Shall we have breakfast?"—I said "No.
Let's just go—get up a-a-nd go and get to a good spot,
and we'll build a fire and have breakfast."
So we did—before we got to the spot, they killed two deer.
That was
lucky and Amelia says "The-ere—see I told you." (laughs)
She thinks she's the lucky one.

She's old now—they put her in a
nursing home.[2]

> 1. Amelia Passes was a relative and long-time friend, the one that everybody called Piiláako, meaning Brings Back Ten. I don't know if she was named by someone who brought back ten scalps or ten horses, but everybody knew her by Brings Back Ten. (MP)

2. At the time of this recording, Amelia was still alive. The two women had remained friends, and Lillian had some dresses she was planning to take to her in the nursing home. (BL)

We Ordered a House from Minneapolis

We had the old house all torn down,[1]
and I build this house with my own money.
I saved about eight thousand,
and then the rest,
the government helped me to get a loan.
They helped me to build the basement.
And Nellie helped me.
When I wanted the basement I didn't have the money,
a-a-nd
she says "Mom" she says,
"we should have a basement."
She says "I'll give you some money."
She must had some money then.
She put in three hundred, gave me three hundred.
A-a-nd I went to the Office
a-a-nd got a loan,
and that's how much loan I got.

Her and I start building that basement.
And I had the foster children.
I had about six,
and they're growing up too—they help us build a basement. (chuckles)[2]
That's why I have a basement now.
Adam haul the gravel in
a-a-nd make the cement—he knows how to mix it up, build it.
And
we start building that basement.
Nellie and me
and the kids.
And I had carpenters
build the house.

Indian carpenters.
We picked a good one—Nellie, she's the one
had it all planned out.

We ordered this house.
Capp Homes,[3]
in Minnesota.
There's a company back there.
There's a big catalog this house is [in] where you can order,
and we ordered that home,
from the catalog.
We order from that catalog and
that's where we have my home now—it
come from Minneapolis.
They haul the lumber
over and put it there and then I got the carpenters.

Nellie [picked it]—I didn't do it myself.
Nellie knew
how to do it.
She made me order that house
in the catalog.
A-a-ll paid for [now].
She put in about three hundred
for the basement and then the rest I put in.
I get little lease money,
so we finished the basement,
her and I and the children.

But we didn't have no floor.
Our preacher, our minister,
said we need a floor so he came over and
I said "All right I'll pay you"—says "You don't have to pay me."
He's our minister and he build that basement—the floor.[4]
And then we start in the sides.
Nellie planned everything for me, and she even made me order that house
    from Minneapolis,
and she never lived there.

1. The "old house" was the one in Dunmore that she inherited from Paul Singer. (BL)
2. They helped with labor, not money. (MP)
3. We are unsure of the exact spelling. (MP)
4. The man who assisted them was named Hammon. He was the minister at the Church of God. Nellie Sings In the Mountains, personal communication to Barbara Loeb, 2009.

The First Lady Came to Visit Me

This visit and the gift of the green-bead necklace were treasured memories that Lillian spoke of several times in our recordings. The visit occurred in 1964. (BL)

We were at the Billings Fair, Midland Fair in Billing.
And we a-a-ll camp there—a big camp, lo-o-ots of Indians.[1]
And we went to the grandstand, watch the horse racing and
the rodeo and stuff like that—we set there and watch and watch.
After we got through we'd go down to the midway
and buy hamburger-rs, sandwiches or go into some games and stuff like that.[2]
Anyway we're down there.
Take in the fair and the races and we came back to the tent.

And a car had come and stop.
A big car, a government car.
A-a-nd they said "They were looking for <u>you</u>."
And they said they want Effie,
Effie Hogan—they're looking for Effie Hogan.
And said "they had looked for you all day long,
and they don't want to give up until they see you."

And I said "What for?
What'd they want to see me for?"
And said "Lady Bird,
president's wife, is going to come and visit you.
For a guest.
Said "Would you accept the invitation?"

And I said "Su-u-re enough! Su-u-re!"—I said "I'd be glad to do that."
"So you'd better get ready."
So I said "All right mister! I'll break camp right now!
And get to my house and clean up, get ready for the
day when she arrives."
And that was a wonderful sight.

So we all ran over to the tent and start to packing.
We had a truck there, our car there too—Nellie and all of us start to
packing up and Ferole May, Mrs. Pease, was clear up to Browning,
    Montana, and
somehow she heard and let's see now, yeah let's see—how did it happen
    now?[3]

We went to the
camp and break—just pack
all our stuff in the pickup a-a-nd
people around there say "What's happened? You have to go? What
    happened?"
And some of them want to know and I said "The president's wife is going to
    visit me.
Come to my house and
see me and go on a tour."
And they said "What a wonderful thing is going to happen to an Indian
    woman."

So they said these boss farmers, the agency,
they talked around and they said they picked me
[as] one of the best housekeepers, one of the best Indian woman in the
    reservation.[4]
Said "We'll pick her,
a-a-nd we'll have the First Lady visit her home."
So they picked me that day so I went over, washed my windows and cleaned
    the yard and,
and <u>oh</u> we worked hard.

And the da-ay they arrived there was e-eight Greyhound buses full of people.
E-eight Greyhounds full of people and there were secret police
a-a-ll around—I don't know, ten or eight,
a-a-ll hiding around the house, behind the house, behind the barn,
see if anything happen to the
president's wife—secret police,
all hid in the weeds.

And then she came in [the yard] [see fig. 15].
Got off the bus
and came in and shook hands with me.
And we went to the table and start
and were standing around talking and here the telephone rang.
In the house.
And I said "The telephone's ringing."
And Lorena Mae ran in—said "I'll answer it!"
She ran in the house and telephone,
and she said it was the president and he wanted to talk to Mrs. Johnson.
And she called "The president wants to talk to
Lady Bird Johnson."

So they got her in the house,
and she talked—I don't know how long it was, maybe a couple minutes
   or so,
and then she come out laughing a-a-nd
we all got around the table and we had fry bread there.
She took one and she [said] "We have to go Mrs. Hogan."
She says "We have to be at the park,
and people are waiting there for me—I can't stay long,
which I'd like to do" she says—"I'd like to
meet you and I'd like to visit you and all that but we have to go."
There were e-eight Greyhound buses full of people waiting.[5]
All got off but they have to get in the bus again so they took off.

That's a thing that I can't forget.
So after that we
just feel happy. (chuckles)
Yeh.
I don't even remember what year that is.
Lorena Mae would know.[6]
And Ferole Mae.
She was up at Browning and she heard it,
and they come all running over here.
They were all there.
I don't know how it work in.
Mary was going to college in Butte.
And Mardell.
And Nellie was there to babysit for Mary—there was
Meredith—[Mary's daughter] Meredith was about two years old.
And Barry [Mary's son] was three years old.
A little boy.
Meredith was just crawling.
She didn't walk for long time.
Even she was about a year and a half or so,
she would crawl—she never start to walk for long time.

But anyway they were there [in Butte],
and they heard the news,
and they all piled in the car—I got them a car, I got them a brand new car.
And they came on over—and Ferole Mae was up at Helena.
She heard the news say
that Mrs. Lady Bird Johnson soon be the guest of Effie Hogan and Ferole
 Mae said
they were washing dishes and they were drying the spoons and she said,
"Let's throw away all these spoons! Let's (claps hands) pack up and go!"
 (chuckles)
And they were over here
at the house
before the whole crowd came in.
Emmmmm, that was good—quite a sight.
Yeh.

Anyway it was in the newspaper where the girls, the three sisters,
Nellie, Mary, Mardell—
made them all stand up their house in the porch.
"The three sisters are going back to their mother for the visit of Lady Bird
    Johnson."
They had that in the newspaper [in Butte] and I got the clipping with
    me now [see fig. 16].
Yeh.
I have that.

1. Families used to set up their teepees and tents at the Billings Fair, just as they did for events like Crow Fair and Sun Dances. (BL)
2. The midway was were the carnival rides were. (BL)
3. My sister Ferole's husband, Bill Pease, worked for the Realty Division of the Bureau of Indian Affairs, and they were living in government quarters in Browning. He had been at Crow Agency for years, then transferred to the Shoshone/Arapaho Wind River Reservation in Wyoming, and finally to the Blackfeet Reservation at Browning. Later he retired to the Crow Reservation. (MP)
4. There were no longer "boss farmers" in the 1960s when this happened. I believe my mother was talking about Howard Morton, the Big Horn County extension agent, a nice man, friendly and helpful. During LBJ's administration, Lady Bird developed a project to beautify America. The tribal chairman, Edison Real Bird, asked Mom to host her visit because she had the new house she built next to her old one. The government had purchased Crow lands to build the Yellowtail Dam, and proceeds from this sale were to be used to improve our lives. Though Mom used mostly personal money for the new house, her "dam money" and ours were used to pay it off. We each got approximately $1,600—$600 cash plus $1,000 that required BIA approval to use. (MP)
5. I was impressed at meeting Morris Udall, the environmentalist. He and the governor's wife were both there. (MP)
   Udall was secretary of the interior for Lyndon Johnson. He supported civil rights and was an advocate for Native Americans. (BL)
6. Lady Bird Johnson visited the Crow Reservation in August 1964 and was ceremonially adopted by a Crow family. (BL)

CHAPTER EIGHTEEN

Sacred Experiences

I Come to Know the Bible

I went to the Catholics—I'm a Catholic.
A-a-nd I believe in it
pretty strong—they're religious,
and they pray for us—we want to be prayed for.
Live better, better life.

Course I don't drink.
But when I was a young girl,
I ran around with some boys.
And I'm a divorce [sic]—I divorced my husband and married another one.
And stuff like that.
But I don't put on a drinking party or anything like that.
I don't drink.
So-o,
that's a good life if you're not drinking.

The missionaries come to the reservation—start.
Teach it—now there are too many missionaries in the reservation now.
There's the Catholic.
I know the Catholic—they're good people.
That's the truth.
Teach us everything.
But there's the Baptists.
And Pentecostals [Four Square].
And I don't know what the others are but anyways there's
about seven or eight churches in Crow and in Hardin.
Different denominations,
so therefore I don't know [those].[1]

But I believe in God.
I come to know the Bible—I'm not no expert but
I think it's holy.
I read the Bible every day,
but my Bible's big and heavy,
Last night I come to think I didn't bring my Bible [to Big Sky].
I said "I should borrow somebody's Bible—I should be reading."

Yeh I believe that.
We go to all the church meetings—we like it, we enjoy it.[2]

1. She means she doesn't know much about religious differences, including different denominations. To her it was the same. (MP)
2. My mother enjoyed church immensely and was a devout Catholic. When she married George Hogan and moved to Crow Agency, he attended the Baptist church, but this is when she and several other women established a nondenominational church called the First Church of God. It was near our home, and she was an active participant. (MP)

I Want to Pray Like My Mother

Lillian and her mother were both devoted Christians. This account describes their prayerful fasts, which use Christian prayers, Bible reading, and, in Horse's case, the use of a church, but they also echo the much older Crow custom of fasting and praying in an isolated spot, often in search of a vision. (For examples of meditative traditional prayer, see "My Mother Mourns," chapter 2, and "Sun Dance," chapter 16.) (BL)

My mother is Catholic.
She su-u-re is a good strong Catholic.
She used to go and fa-ast.
Says "I want to fast.
I'll go without water—I'll go without eating for three days."

She used to do that.
I remember [one time] it's before Easter.
Before Good Friday comes, she goes.

Says "You take care of the kids.
I have to go
and stay at the church."
And my father want to take her—and "no" she says.
"I want to walk."
And we live about, about a mile and a half,
to the church.
Walks over there—she takes a
couple blankets,
muffler [head scarf],
a little pillow.
She goes to church.
In there.

And the father [priest] knows that
she wants to fast.
He shut the door
and pray for her and go.
And she stay there
a-a-ll night,
a-a-ll day,
another night,
next day,
and then by evening,
my father or,
or the priest,
go after her and tell her to go home.
Then she does.

That time she wasn't sick.
She wasn't sick.[1]
She pra-ays—she's good, want to be a good Christian I guess.
And I,
sometimes I want to copy her way.
When I'm at Crow,
at home,
I say "I have to go do like my mother did."

One time I
done that and Nellie came and stayed with me too.
We go out, up on a hill.
I said "I want to go up on the hill."
I'd take my Bible,
and a pillow and a blanket.
I'd go wa-a-a-y up on the hill
and pray like my mother.
I'd just copy her ways.
I guess the Lord gave me
strength to do that.
I enjoy it.
Come back and they all know that I've been praying for them.
They like it—my family.

One time when we live in Crow—we had a big house,
and I told George, I said,
"There's plenty to eat."
I said "You just eat your supper—I'll be back sometime before night."
I took off—I went up on the hill,
and I got to the highest part of the hill.
Fix my cushion.
Set there—start to praying.
Open my Bible—start to praying.

In that sa-ame spot,
the next morning I came early.
This time I went early to that same spot where I prayed.
It's high up the hill.
I went and parked the car
at the foot of the hill,
and I walked up.
And when I got there early,
the who-o-o-ole grass, maybe about
forty yards or twenty yards,
on the grass there was asbestos.

A-a-a-a-a-ll over the ground—<u>shining</u>.
Sparkle.
Shine—I just stood there and looked at it.
Emmm.
Looked up and then looked down and here it's pretty!
A-a-ll over that hill.

So I went.
Just pay no more attention to it—I went on top of the hill, I prayed.
O-o-oh I must have stayed about three,
maybe couple hours or so.
When I got through I was coming down.
I look at that where it was all shiny with asbestos.
Was all gone.
And I told some people.
And they said "Them's asbestos.
A lot of money in that."
They said "If you ever tell some of the authorities,
they want to attend to that" they said.[2]
But I never did.

What are they?
I don't know. (chuckles)
Just like it's plastic.
It spread way out there and just shiny—sparkle.
Pretty.
I couldn't tell you what it is.
And after that we looked for it and we can't find it—never came out.
The only time I seen anything stra-ange.

1. Her mother later became ill and passed away, so she is saying this happened before she became sick with her illness. (MP)
2. They guessed that she was seeing asbestos because it was mined in Montana and was sometimes shiny in its raw form. (BL)

I Always Sing the Songs

Because George was so devoutly Christian, Lillian promised him she would not participate in Sun Dances, Tobacco Society ceremonies, or other sacred Apsáalooke rituals. She honored that promise for the rest of her life but attended the events to watch. She also continued to sing Tobacco Society songs, as described in this story. (BL)

I quit going [in Tobacco Society dances].[1]
I don't—but
if I have to si-ing the song, I know them and I sing it.[2]
Like Lorena Mae.
If she go to take me to Billings or to Sheridan,
just her and I,
coming back she say,
"Now Mama, I wish you'd sing some Indian song.
Tobacco Dance song."
I do and she said "O-oh my that sounds beau-u-tiful!"
"I like that song" she'd say—"Sing some more."

I start to singing Mary's song.
And then after I got through, says "Sing it again." (chuckles)
Yeah we did again.
Sang it.
And I always sing my uncle's songs.
My uncle has nice songs.
Mary.
Mardell.
Mardell, I only remember one song.
And Mary,
I only remember one song too. (chuckles)
And me,
I remember one song.

This is Mardell's song.

> *Weasel, I go along into the ground [the earth].*
> *Chanting Weasel, I go along into the ground.*[3]

That's Mardell's song.

And Mary's song, let's see now.

> *I have just arrived from upriver.*
> *(Chant)*
> *I am looking for ways of good fortune.*
> *(Chant)*

And that's Mary's song.
Says "I'm trying to find my luck."
A-a-nd Lorena Mae sure like it.

And my father's got some songs that we're not supposed to give away,[4]
a-a-nd they said,
"When you're hard up,
where you're sad,
sing these songs and they'll brace you up."
So we used to do that.
I don't do that any more.
My voice.
Don't sing so nice. (chuckles)
Yeh.

1. She would not participate in Tobacco Dances but attended several with Mary as an onlooker and would have been displeased if Mary had not taken her. She was at my own final adoption, and I remember how happy she was that I was finally a member. My brother Sam and family are also avid participants. (MP)
2. My mother always thought Tobacco Dance songs were the prettiest of all Crow songs. Every time we traveled, she would sing one and say, "That was [so-and-so's] song." She knew quite a few, and I remember her singing them even from my earliest childhood. Much to my regret, I never recorded those songs. (MP)
3. Could be a reference to tobacco seeds. (MP)
4. Her father had some Tobacco Society songs that he did not want given away. He would have received four personal songs like all adoptees, but as a member he could later purchase additional songs he admired. (MP)

CHAPTER NINETEEN
Traditional Healing

I Have Other Necklaces from Older People Way Back

This story describes family necklaces. Her father's included a red one, a pale blue one, and one combining red and white beads. Her mother's was red and white, probably with a horse tooth because she calls it a "horse's necklace." As mentioned in "Buying Hopi," Lillian's family has possessed the right to horse medicine for several generations. All of the necklaces were imbued with medicine powers much like Lillian's green bead one. (BL)

My father says
he was a twin and the twin, the girl, died.
A-a-nd the mother and the father, oh they
think a lot of him.
They don't want him to die—they go and get
some older people to pray for him
and give him the blessing a-a-nd wish him good luck and all that stuff.
That's why my father lived to be old.

A-a-nd he says it's been a long time ago,
when he wasn't even sick.
He says "When I was young,
re-eal small,
I was a twin,
and the twin died."
And then from there the parents afraid that
he'd die too,
and they gave things to older people and have them pray for him—all that
 he says.

"And they always give me different colors of necklaces,
like white and red,
with elk tooth in the middle.
And that blue pale beads
too—you wear that
and put little shell on there, that's two [necklaces].[1]
And wea-ar
red beads.
Don't mix it with white" he said.

"There's the three necklaces I have—
I'm-m given by older people way back" he said.
"And I'll give it [them] to you,
because I don't want to give it to your brother because
your brother don't wear necklaces—no beads" he said.[2]
"You're a woman.
You're supposed to wear a necklace,"
he said.
"I'll give you all these beads."

My mother gave me the red and white too.
She said "That's from the horse—horse's necklace."
Said her grandfather
made the necklace for her and she passed it down to me.[3]

But this green necklace,
another different lady, o-old, re-eal old lady,
she's the one that gave me the green beads.[4]
No relations to me.
But she looks pitiful.
She's o-o-old and I used to
tell my folks to go bring her and feed her.
Bring her and make her stay with us a few days and fix her a ni-ice bed.
And she says "As a child,"
she says "she su-u-re is nice to me.
Feed me good,
cut up my meat for me,

give me water to drink,
and she's kind to me" she says.
"I want to give her a necklace.
That green beads is my medicine.
I have some in my stomach.
Keepsake" she says—"They're down there."
So she must have some beads in her stomach. (chuckles)
Says "They're my medicine" she says.
"I give this little girl the green beads to wear."

That's why I always wear green beads.
But I have those other necklaces.
Father gave me some.
Mother gave me one.
That old lady gave me the green one that's my favorite.
The green one's my favorite one. (chuckles)

1. This pale blue is an old bead favored by Crow artists. In the Crow language, it is called *chiichíashte*, meaning a light blue so pale it is almost white. (MP)
2. Some Crow men still do wear special necklaces. Dennis Holds, personal communication to Barbara Loeb, 1993.
3. This horse necklace is worn by our family and the Whitehips, who descend from Mom's Aunt Clara White Hip. Some of the family still use two words for their last name, as Clara did. Some use one word. (MP)
4. See "Green Beads from a Real Old Lady," chapter 5.

Medicine for Swelling

Lillian's ancestors received the right and the knowledge to heal with a medicinal root, and the family considers it part of their inheritance. Apsáalooke doctors often specialize in specific conditions such as this one or the midwifery Lillian recounts in the next stories. Patients reciprocate with gifts because that is the traditional form of payment. (BL)

My mother
has a medicine,
was given to her,

by some relatives way back,
a-a-nd she can cure swelling.
Get's too bad,
and doctors can't cure it,
she go and work on them and cure—heal them in no time.

They said a man—Austin,
Austin Stray Calf, lives in Hardin.
Close to Hardin anyway.
They say his foot,
from knee to the ankle,
swell up.
Sometimes it break out and
blood come out and swell up.
He couldn't hardly walk—they take him to the peyote.[1]
They take him to several doctors—can't do nothing—they can't heal it.
Gave him medicine, they can't heal it.
They had peyote meeting up at his house too.
That didn't cure him.
So they said they better take him to Arnold Costa up here at Pryor.
"They'll put up a teepee and they'll
doctor him with peyote,
and he'll be cured."
A-a-nd they brought him over to Pryor.
They brought him over and they
went in the meeting and that night they
stay awake all night, singing, singing.
All night.
But after that it didn't heal up.
They say it got worse.
And he said "If I see another doctor they're going to cut my leg."
"They might!" he said.

A-a-nd it was Simpson [Sings Good]'s mother said "There's an o-old lady
    down here [at Pryor]
that can cure that swelling."[2]

And they asked "Who?" and they call [name] my mother.
[Austin] says "Go get her!
Go get her so she can doctor me."

So they went after her.
And she said "I don't have any of that medicine any more.
But tomorrow I'll be over.
I'll be over
to doctor—I'll find some of that."
There's some root down in our spring, down there.
She told my dad to go dig some—he did.
He washed it up good.
A lot of it.
And she went to that place the next day,
to doctor that man.

She said he couldn't move his feet, leg.
The swelling got worse after they went in the peyote meeting.
Said "I'm afraid he either die from it or
they cut his leg off."
And the swelling got worse.
A-a-nd she said she doctored that,
and it all healed up.
And he can get up on his
foot and stand up.
Said "I belie-eve
that old lady has the re-eal kind of medicine for healing."

But you have to pay [with gifts].
They said when you don't pay,
you won't get no result.
So they did.
It come from the family and they gave her
quilts and money
a-a-nd stuff,
because she healed that swelling.

She keep that up.
Now we have it [the knowledge and right to use it].
When she died she told us what it is.
"Any sore throat or any swelling,"
said "use that root."
We have it.

One time [in] Lodge Grass,
it's my, it should be my nephew I guess.
Jerome.
Jerome White Hip.
Their little boy had
swell-ling.
His face all swelled up and his eyes just close—he can't see.
And his ears is all swell up, stick out like that.
And they took him to Hardin doctor, took him to Sheridan doctor, took him to Crow doctor.
They put that purple stuff on him a-a-nd didn't heal up.[3]
Bu-urn and itch, kept swelling.
They couldn't do it, couldn't do nothing.

So,
Lorena Mae told him that "My mother can heal that sickness."
And I stayed with Mardell at the Custer Battlefield.
They came and said,
"Will you doctor that boy if we bring him?"
"What's the matter with him?"—and he says "he's swelling.
Take him to Billings and Sheridan and doctor in Hardin and a government doctor.
They can't heal that swelling."
He said "That's poison ivy.
Must have caught.
Throat all swell up, face all swell up—he couldn't see, his eyes closed.

"All right" I said—"I've got some of the medicine."
So I doctored him right at Mardell's house.

I made some of that solution and I doctor him and said "Bring him back
   tomorrow."
Next day his eyes open—all swelling went off.
Next day it's all right.

And then the <u>next</u> year,
said "Take me to that old lady—the little o-old lady
so she can doctor me." (chuckles)
They did.
And they gave me a bi-i-g watermelon (chuckles)
—and five dollars.
They paid for it.
So I doctored him again—the next day he was all right.

So we still have—I want Mardell to take some home.
Last year Lorena
got sick real bad [from chigger bites].
Swelling.
Her face.
So Mardell called [from Oklahoma],
and we went to Lodge Grass and digged a whole lot of it.
And washed it good and dry it—now they're here [visiting].
So she better take some home. (chuckles)
Sure fix sore throat.
Swelling.
Su-u-re
do the medicine.

And Nellie!
O-o-h my—never saw such swelling in my life.
Both her legs swell up,
clear up to her knees—kept coming up.
She couldn't walk then.
I said "All right I'll doctor that"—we happened to
come up to Red Lodge.
And I drove—she's my chauffeur,
but she couldn't use her leg, her legs swell up so bad.

Stiff and she can't stand up—she can't bend her legs,
swell up so bad.

So we got at the camp in Red Lodge, youth camp,
and she said "Mama" she says,
"if this keeps up tomorrow, just cover me up a-a-nd go" she says.
"I don't think this will ever heal up unless you doctor me.
Unless you put some of that medicine on me."
I said "All right."
So that evening I went to the kitchen.
I said "Will you give me a big can?
One of them gallon cans,"
I said "and a butcher knife?"
Said "What you going to do with it?"
They kept asking—I said "No.
I'm going to make something out of it"—said "Don't ask any more."[4]

So I took the knife and I took,
I took stick—walked for about half a mile before I found some of that root.
I dig it up with the butcher knife, came home.
Went to the river and wash it re-eal good, scrub it.
And I cut it up and put it in the
can, that gallon can—boil it.
Boil it real strong—I said "I'm going to make it stro-ong!"

She couldn't get off—she couldn't straighten up her legs.
I had her in the car—puff up pillows and I went to the prayer meeting.
I said "When I come back,
I'll take you
up to the dormitory."
I put some on there before I took her to the dormitory.
Wrap it up good, wrap her up with some of the leaves there.
She could har-rdly walk.
And that was the fir-r-st time I
put some of that
medicine on her.

A-a-nd she said she quit itching.
Burning.
And then-n I walk her up.
She said "Wait till everybody goes to bed—take me up."
So we waited in the car—we slept I guess.
It's wa-a-a-y late, around ten o'clock or so.
I took her up to the dormitory—we walk re-e-eal slow.
And I got two beds close to the door,
and I made her lay on the one bed and I lay on the other bed.

And fi-ive o'clock in the morning,
she was right by me—she just got up and shook me.
"Mama, Mama!"
I got up—"<u>What</u>?"—I got scared.
"<u>What</u>? <u>What</u>?"
She's "Get up and look at my legs!"
And a-a-ll that swelling went off—they looked normal.
"All right, get up Mama—let's go up to Mockingbird Hill"—
there's a toilet up there, up on the hill.
Said "Let's go up there "—so her and I walk up that hill.
And that's healed up in no time.

So we still have those [rights].
My mother has that medicine—now she gave it to us.
We have that medicine.
And Lorena Mae said some nurses somewhere said,
"Give us some of that medicine."
"No sir-e-e-e!" she says—"We don't give you no medicine!
We inherit it down from my grandma—they gave it to us just for the family.
We're not going to give it [the right] to you." (laughs)

It's for swelling.
[A relative] gave it to my mother and my mother gave it to me—now I gave it to the girls.

   1. Peyote is a Native religion with songs and prayers as in any worship. Austin was a member and was "doctored" or prayed for in the ceremony. (MP)

2. By calling this woman "Simpson's mother," she avoids speaking the name of the deceased. (BL)
3. The "purple stuff" was a salve from the Indian hospital, possibly a form of calamine. (MP)
4. We were at a church youth camp. The white people were curious. (MP)

Midwives

There *are* Indian doctors.
A woman is
carrying a baby,
and when it's time to,
there's Indian woman doctor.
Just like a doctor—as you say it's a nurse but I say a doctor.
They'd be right there burning incense.
Make them
touch, heat,
a-a-nd stand over that
incense a-a-nd make inhale that.
Pretty soon the baby starts
to going. (claps hands sharply)
Pretty soon—born.
And then they're right there to cut the navel
and wrap it up.

And they do that—the Indian women.
So they know how.
I guess
from way back they
carry that on—but they use medicine.
I heard about that and I seen them there.

A White Woman Was Going to Have a Birth

The events described in this story happened sometime before 1950, when there were still elderly Crow women who did not speak English and when Theodore Benson was still practicing medicine. (BL)

One time there was a woman. (chuckles)
One woman was going to have a birth.
It's a white woman,
and they happen to live by close to Indian house.
And she start her pains and the man
was ready to take her to Fromberg.
Up here at Fromberg, Montana.
There's Dr. Benson over there.[1]
So he says,
"Get dressed now—we'll take you to Dr. Benson."

Says "I <u>can't</u>.
I might can't hold the baby.
It's going to come any time now."
A-a-nd she says "Go get that Indian woman that live close.
The neighbors."
Says "Go get her! Get that old lady."
So he runs over there—"Come on! Come on!"
And this old Indian woman don't speak English—say,
"Come on, come on.
Come, come—come on, come on." (laughs)
I guess he just [gestures]
big stomach and baby's going to come. (laughs)
And she understand him.

So they come to the house
and point at her and she laughs.
Says,
"You sit here.
Sit here, watch her while I go get the doctor" and the woman said "No don't go!

Don't go—I'm going to have the baby now."
A-a-nd sure enough.

She's a doctor herself, that old Indian woman.
She just laughed and says "All right—you [husband] get out
Get out and me see" she says. (chuckles)
So this woman
start to
making some tea.
Making tea—medicine.
She rushed around and
made that
medicine and make her take it.
Says "Hurry up! Take it."
And this man is outside—says "You go outside."
While she's with the woman.

A-a-nd that woman laid down on her side a-a-nd don't want to get up,
but she made her get up and kneel down.
Hold onto something.
And she fixed up something to hold here and hold on this side.
A-a-nd she made her burn som-me incense.
Says "Now you pull your dress like this.
Stand over that.
When you get through doing that now take this medicine."
And she drank this medicine.
Pretty soon "Hurry up! Hurry up!"
And—and she made her kneel down and hold this post.
And she was there right behind her and she took her hand—re-eal slow.
Just then the baby came.
Screaming!

A-a-nd she took the baby aside,
a-a-nd she cut the navel and tied the navel,
and then had the man come in.
"Now, no doctor." (laughs)
She sure was there—after that them couple
su-u-r-r-re like Indians.

Said "The Indian woman was sure kind
to help us out."
Sometimes he says "I'm going to help her a-a-all the time.
Every day even I can give her something."
Then they—they want to pay her and she says "No, no.
No money." (chuckles)

Yeah she was right there.
[Her name was] Stays on Top—
the House, I guess—Asshee Aakeennáhkush.[2]
That's her name, Indian name.

   1. Fromberg is a small town twenty-four miles northwest of Pryor. Dr. Theodore
      J. Benson opened a practice in 1907, during the town's homestead period, and
      retired in 1950. His home is on the National Register of Historic Places. The
      Colonial Revival–style building originally housed both his home and his medical
      clinic. (BL)
   2. I would interpret the name Asshee Aakeennáhkush as Stays on Top of the
      Lodge. (MP)

My Mother Give Birth

I know some times my mother give birth to a little [baby],
she didn't have no doctor.
My father went after some couple women
to come and stay right by her,
when she's in pain.
But he stayed outside.
And
some of the kids
are with me so we all stayed outside.
Just wait.
Wait—pretty soon the baby was born.[1]
And they cut the navel and,
and wrapped him up—I don't know what all the rest that they done.
Wrapped him up.
Fixed—and then my father went inside,
and all of us went inside to see my mother.

Here they'd fixed her
a good bed—she laid down.[2]

But I go to the hospital.

1. "Pretty soon" means after a while. It does not necessarily mean a fast birth. (MP)
2. Her parents lost a number of children. This story may describe the birth of a baby sister mentioned just prior to this story or the birth of Percy, a little brother whom my mother loved dearly (see "My Little Brother Had That Infantile Paralysis," chapter 7). (MP)

Yellow Mule Was So Sick

In this story, Lillian helps Yellow Mule, and he later thanks her with small gifts of money when he sees her. This is an Apsáalooke way of showing appreciation. Lillian thought these events happened about 1970. (BL)

Yellow Mule,
he was so sick,
the doctors gave up—gave him up.
They said—they told his wife,
said "If you want to take him home
to pass away at home,"
they said,
"do that—or if you want him to just stay here
and die [he can] pass away here in the hospital."

A-a-nd
there were people around there, relatives.
He happened to be a nephew.
In the clan way.
So I said "I'd better go see that man.
He's my nephew, he's my son—in Indian way I call him my son.
Said "I'd better go visit him."
I went in there—there were relatives in there.
A-a-nd

his wife [Dorothy] was sitting right by the head part and
holding his head and hand and all that.

I went in and talk to him.
"I bet you feel better now—you look good."
And he look at me and
just shook his head.
Didn't talk.
I felt his foot.
Said "I'll hold your foot a little while,
under the sheet."
I felt his foot little bit.

There's other people around,
and I said "Oh you'll feel better tomorrow—you're looking good, looking
    better,"
I said, "but I want to pray for you before I go.
I been wanting to come and see you but
was so busy I didn't come but I'll come again.
I'll pray for you now and go home and pray."
And so we all start—I said "All of you pray too."
I touch his foot, hold his foot—I start to pray.
Pra-a-y and pra-a-y—it wasn't even a long prayer either.
Pra-a-y and pra-a-y and then pretty soon,
over.

And then I said "All right,
my son" I said.
"You're going to be all right.
The Lord will help you."
I said "You'll be all right.
And Dorothy too, you'll be all right, you'll be happy."
I said "I'll come again some other time—I'll see you again."
And then when I went out,
they say he closed his eyes.
And they ask him "What's the matter, you're closing eyes?"
"Something in that old woman

that touch me and pray for me.
I don't know what it is but there's something happen."

So after that he got well.
Went home.
About a
couple months after that he got home, start driving the car.
He'd meet me in the store and
dig in his pocket and says "Here—buy you some goodies.
Buy you some meat."
Give me ten dollars.
I said "O-oh dear.
Thank you—I'll have a big feast." (chuckles)
And couple times he gave me
dollar—says "Here, get your lunch."

He's dead now.
Yellow Mule.
His wife is still living.
Dorothy.
That was
about twenty-five years ago.
And he said,
"Something in that o-old woman.
When she prayed for me I feel something.
Something in that old woman"—when I went out,
he told his wife and the people in there.
And after that, o-oh about three or four months after that, they told me what he said.
About me—and I said "It's not me.
It's the Lord.
He answered the prayer—he got healed."
I said "It's the Lord's hand, not me."
I said "It's not me."

So he knows—after that he was so-o-o good to me.
Dorothy still is good to me.

CHAPTER TWENTY

I Gave Indian Names

I Named Cal "Good Dancer"

Around 1975, when Lillian's great-grandson Calvin was four, she gave him his Indian name, Good Dancer. What she is describing is not the naming itself, but the dance contests that explain the name's background, probably the same stories she relayed to listeners the day she named him. She ends with a Christmas dance years later, when they played a special song for Cal and had him dance alone before the crowd. When Lillian stood at this gathering to retell the history behind his name and to have him give away money and gifts, she was publicly conveying her pride in his accomplishments. Her great-grandson had become a skilled and graceful dancer, a talent the Apsáalooke admire. (BL)

I was a good dancer—I got four prizes.
Four times they chose me for good dancing.
Push dances.[1]

The school put on a dance for us, and they asked outsiders can come.
It must be Fourth of July or som-me
big celebration—lo-o-ots of people camped.[2]
Fairgrounds *we called it*—we could see
about, o-oh about a mile and a half,
and you could look out the window and see the tents and the teepees.
And that night they put on a dance [and people came from the fairgrounds],
a-a-nd we da-anced and da-anced—I da-anced.
A-a-nd all the other couples,
make them sit down and there's just four partners dance around the floor.
Emmmm, we're sailing along. (chuckles)
I'll never forget that.
That's when I was picked for a good dancer.

I always pick a good dancer—
partner—
and we su-ure dance.
And I know the good dancers [to pick].
[They say] "Get your partners!"
And the men's turn,
the men usually come and pick us out.
And then if it's a women's,
"Ladies get your partners" and then we'd get up and run.
To the men.
And I always get a good partner—that's when I learned to dance.
Emmm, they say I was a good dancer,
so I have that in me I guess.

This was in school.
Then after we grow up, I got married a-a-nd
quit [divorced] and I stayed single a-a-nd
went with Maud and Edith and them and we'd go to dances.
We did them push dance.
At Reno Creek and Lodge Grass and Black Lodge.
We would dance there around Christmas—a dance in Pryor,
we would go dance there.
That's when they say I'm a good dancer.
A-a-nd one occasion they
pick out all the good dancers—four.
Four partners—this lady has a partner, one, two, three, four [couples].
They make us dance around the
circle—everybody [else] sit down.
We da-anced and da-anced.
My partner was Lester Jefferson. (chuckles)
Good dancer.
Push dance.

Then again at Black Lodge.
Frankie Medicine Horse.
Good dancer too—he was my partner.

And another time *they had a dance at Reno—I danced with a white man.*
Named Campbell.
I was married to Robbie at the time,
and Robbie says "Go—go pick."
He said "Go pick him."³
So I went and danced and
we got the first prize. (chuckles) At Reno.⁴

That's why I named Cal.
Said "Good Dancer."
[Years later] up here at Christmas dance,
had a special song for him and he danced alone,
a-a-nd everybody look on and o-oh I was thri-illed
to see him dance—he su-u-re is a good dancer—I named him.
So when I got up,
I had stuff.
Giveaway.
And everybody watching.
I gave him twenty-five dollars—I told the announcer to tell.⁵
I said "This boy is a good dancer because I named him.
I named him Good Dancer because I was a good dancer.
I named him—I'm glad" I said.
"I want him to give away this twenty-five dollars
to somebody that he knows."
So he gave away twenty-five—had lot of stuff to give away.

1. Push dance is a social dance, with the male leading or guiding his partner, pushing her in a circle around the room. Most of the dances she describes were Indian social dances like the push dance, but she liked "white man dances" too, and mentioned doing the two-step at "white man dances" in Cody and Red Lodge. This probably was just a few occasions, so she never forgot them. (MP)

    For traditional Indian dances, small children may hold hands with their mothers or others they know well, but Crow adults do not have partners. They dance alone or beside friends and relatives of the same gender, facing forward and moving counter-clockwise. Most prefer the slow Northern Plains traditional style, but modern young people may do showy and athletic "fancy" dances with spinning, complicated footwork, and brightly colored regalia. When not doing white man or push dances, Lillian was a traditional dancer. Cal became a fancy dancer. (BL)

2. Crow use any special occasion, including white people's holidays, to camp together and dance. (MP)

3. Women cannot dance with their male relatives or their own husbands, so they usually dance with their husbands' relatives. Robbie is encouraging her to dance with a white man because he is unrelated to her. (MP)
4. The six districts each have a hall for meetings, hand games, and dances. Reno District is where Crow Agency is located. (MP)
5. An announcer is a "crier" with the right to address a gathering. You can approach an announcer during any occasion and ask him to speak publicly for you. Mother was a crier too, a right she received from Big Ox, but she only used it once when she absolutely had to. She passed this right to me after I became an interpreter for the National Park Service. (MP)

I Named Her "Lady Bird"

> *To name her great-granddaughter, Allannah, Lillian focused on another milestone and again recounted the history behind the name. She named Allannah in infancy, in 1990.* (BL)

For a long time [my grandson] Barry Bryan didn't get married,
but then all of a sudden,
he brought that girl, his wife now.
She's single too,
and I guess he went with her and they got married—they got
two little girls.
A-a-nd she's carrying one now—she'll have a new baby in April.[1]

And these little girls, I named the first one.
Barry says "I want my grandmother to name the girl."
So I said "The First Lady,
the president's wife, the First Lady—
with a-a-a-ll the women in the whole United States,
and the reservation,
she picked me
to visit my home one day"—and I said,
"She's Lady Bird"—I said "I'm going to name this little girl Lady Bird."
Now her [Indian] name is Lady Bird.

Yes sir—that was something I'll never forget.
She come to my house.

There was ei-i-ight Greyhound buses full of people
stopped there in my yard.

> 1. This is Stephanie Amyotte. She and Barry now have seven children, Allannah (the oldest), Aprille, Miranda, Barry Jr., Tom, Ambrosia, and Effie. (BL)

I Made More Names

I named this boy.
They had a big feast there—these are more like Christian people.
They always go to church—they don't go to the dances.
They're Christian people.
So he says "You're an old woman now and you're a good woman."
Says "I want you to name my boy."

A-a-nd
I think about a name—says
"Yes" I said, "I'll name him
'He Went Too Far'—Awateelesh"—that say "Will Go Far."[1]
I said "When there's any church meeting,
they say,
'You're selected to go.'
Red Lodge or Cody or San Francisco.
Or Philadelphia—I went to church in Philadelphia."
I said "That's a lo-ong ways.
That place is a long ways but I go."[2]
Says,
"Lo-ong ways
to go"—so I name him that.

And then I name a little girl
Likes To Work.
Or "A Good Worker," something like that.
And I named—let's see, what other name?
Lucky.
"Is Always Lucky."

I name a girl—they had a big feast, lots of people there,
a-a-nd they had me—the mother got up and she says "We want her to name our daughter."
So I called her Very Lucky.
So I called her that.
She's a big girl now.
Growed up and she's married and has two kids.
She's good [she's a good woman].

And what's the other one?
You [Barbara]—the fourth.³
That's all I name.
Made four more names.⁴

1. I would translate this to Long Distance Traveler. (MP)
2. She has traveled to many places and is telling everyone the background for the name. (BL)
3. She named me Aassahkálaashtesh, Respects Her Clan Relatives. (BL)
4. She later named my granddaughter, Montana Sky Scalpcane, too, and also gave away her own name, Ties the Bundle Woman, to her great-grandniece. She offered three names to Sky, and we took them all. Later, when Sky is asked to name others, she can give names away without losing her favorite. Two of the names come from thoroughbred race horses her father once owned (see endnotes in "My Indian Name," chapter 1, and "Horses Run Over Caleb," chapter 7.) (MP)

CHAPTER TWENTY-ONE

I'm an Old-Timer

Lillian was already eighty-eight years old when she recorded the stories in this chapter, but she still wanted to make Apsáalooke arts, camp for gatherings such as Crow Fair, and collect and cook Indian foods. Sometimes her knees or back got in her way, but she participated as often as she could. (BL)

Sleeping in Our Teepee

I think Mary pawn—sold—our teepee.[1]
I haven't asked her yet.
I roll it up and tie it up good.
But since she move I think she
need some money and she took it and pawned it.

I haven't asked her yet,
but if she did, I have to buy me a new teepee.
If I want a teepee up for the fair.
Where we always set?
Where we always set our teepee there.
You [Barbara] over there and our big tent over here and then Adam.
And [my granddaughter] Fay Dean—they come from New York [last year],[2]
and she made the family go back to Billings so she can sleep in a teepee.
   (laughs)
She did.
She made her husband go—says "You go on to Billings,
and take the folks over,
while I camp here and sleep in the teepee"—says "I want to!" she says.
   (laughs)

   1. Mary pawns her teepee for proper storage and retrieves it in August. (MP)
   2. Fay Dean is Adam's daughter. She's married to an Italian from New York. They met in the US Army. (MP)

Teepee Poles

We Indians look forward for Crow Fair.
Like if it is June
and July, we say "We'd better get ready for the fair.
We'll have to go after teepee poles."
Sometimes we have a teepee pole
from last year,
but when the Crow Fair comes,
some people want new ones for the fair.
You can save your poles and have them all the time if you want to,
but it's just the idea of having new poles because there's plenty.

Up the Browning Indians, Piegan Indians,[1]
they have big mountain there—they go after teepee poles I guess.
Other tribes like Crees and Sioux and
all them, they don't have the timber,
like us Crows have.
So-o,
we go any time we want to.
We have plenty,
and we enjoy every year to go up on the mountain and
get our poles.
Take the bark off and dry 'em up.
And then they get ready for the fair.

The men get
big saw, chain saw.
They used to use just ax,
good ax and chop them down.
They'd say "Here goes one!"
And someone pulls them [the felled trees] out on the open.
And I know I get a little ax and
chop the little branches off.
And then they come straight [smooth] and they
pile them up alongside of the road.[2]
And pretty soon they bring in the pickup.

And they're heavy!
They're green and they're aw-w-ful heavy.
But that's fun.
We all look forward to going after teepee poles.

We used big knives [to take the bark off].
And that—I don't know the name of that.
O-oh we have some tools for this.
A handle there, a handle there [on each side],
big, sharp—just like big, sharp knife
on both side.
We go over to the pole
and skin—take all the bark off.
We do that up there in the mountains.[3]
Once in awhile we take them down—what we don't finish,
we take it down—I know we always lean it out to that
front big tree there [near the house].
We lean it on there—we work and work. (chuckles)

There're lots of people go up to the mountains to cut teepee poles.
I went couple times too and we camped there.
[One time] we had all my boys and George and them—we camp here,
and Regina camp here,
a-a-nd Lorena Mae camp here,
a-a-nd Delma Jean camp here a-a-nd—
who was it now camp over here?[4]
We all have one big fire.

And these others had camped there ahead of us.
And they were getting their dinner ready
and dishing out plates and they were sitting down to the meal.
And I know we stopped there and was unloading our stuff,
and one lady called me over and she says,
"Here—here's a plate full of food.
Sit down and eat before you unload your things."
So I sat down and they make some coffee for me.
And here my whole family was just having lots of fun unloading the stuff.

And we were going to pitch our tent this way and
my-y that mountain is pretty when you camp up there.

[Another time] when Mary work—while she was working in the hospital,
there was a colored man in there.
And they say this colored boy come along and says,
"Can I call you Mama?"
Talked to Mary
and [she] said "Yes you can.
I'll take you as a mother."
He says "I'll do <u>anything</u> for you."
Says "I'll even go to your house and clean.
Build fences or anything you want.
I want to help you out."

We all start cleaning the poles
and
shaving the little twigs off of the side.
And pull them out here—
say "Here's a spot you didn't find"—we start to peeling.
And Adam would cut the bottom part.
He said "Let's not saw it off."
And he takes an ax and make it this way and that way to make it stick in the ground.[5]

Last year Adam went down to Wyoming.
Down to Sheridan.
There's a whole bunch—like Lorena Ma-ae,
they're a bunch.
And who was it now?
Somebody else—Victor.
And Adam.
They all went up there at Kane.
Kane, Wyoming.[6]
They got our teepee poles from there.
Kind of scarce up at Pryor now
since everybody, all the Lodge Grass people,

Black Lodge people and
Saint X people, they all go to Pryor
to get poles, teepee poles.
They say not too many
now but they do go up there every year, get new ones.

I can't do it now.
We had a big tent—we took bedding along.
We'd take lots of food.
And my,
we had good times up there.
But I can't do it any more.

1. Piegan Blackfeet live in northwestern Montana. Browning is the main town on their reservation. (BL)
2. After the small branches are removed, teepee poles are straight and smooth, except for a few small knots. (MP)
3. Generally we'd skin poles immediately after chopping down. If you wait too long, the bark dries and is hard to shave. (MP)
4. Regina and Delma Jean are Cedric's sisters. (MP)
5. Some Crow cut the bottoms of teepee poles at a sharp angle. Others cut both sides so the ends form a somewhat sharp "V." Once on the ground, the poles sort of sink into the earth, so you cannot see the thick ends. Dan Plainfeather, personal communication to Mardell Plainfeather, 2009.
6. Kane, Wyoming, was a small town south of the Crow Reservation and about ten miles east of Lovell, but residents left when the Yellowtail Dam was completed and the reservoir flooded the region. Crow people who want to cut new teepee poles in the Big Horn Mountains sometimes get there via the highway through the old Kane area. (BL)

We Only Dug a Few Bitterroot

La-ast spring, last year,
around May,
me and Adam, we rode in a pickup—he has a pickup.
We rode in that pickup but we had two little boys with us too.
And then Mary and Nelson, they got a car too.
And, and who was the other third car now?
Anyway there was about four cars, four of us, took off where the bitterroot were.

We hardly find—just a few.
They used to be a-a-all over,
but we hardly couldn't find, hardly find enough to
make a dessert.

It was last year—I don't know but if it rains,
good weather, rain lots of moisture,
then a-a-all that plenty [might come back]—it was just you could
pretty near step on them.
<u>Lots</u> of it grow among the grass.
But last year we only dug a few.

It seems like
other women don't go out to dig that
root they call the bitterroot.
They don't
do it anymore—Lorena Mae and me and
a few others go out.

I want to go.
Maybe-e
at Decoration Day [Memorial Day] when we
start to
decorate the graves.
Go up there and put flowers on there and pretty soon we go down—have a
   picnic.
And when you get through we can go out on the hill and
pick a few
sackfuls of that bitterroot.
We like it.
People sure like it.
The younger people, the young
generation, they don't know what that is.
But I do—I like it.

Nellie's Hide

It's been a long time [since I tanned a hide].
I never have the hide.
Last fall Nellie had one out in the shed.
I said "I'll show you how to tan this.
Get some old grease and we'll grease it up and put it on top of that roof
and turn it around till it's through.
All that grease work down and we'll make that solution like my mother did,
and we'll make it and you'll have a buckskin."
[She said] "All right, I'll learn how to do it!"

She never did, so we didn't have the buckskin. (chuckles)
And that hide was laying on the porch,
at Nellie's house,
and I don't know what become of that hide.
No hair on it.
It's <u>goo-o-d</u>.
She [wanted to] learn how to do it—she didn't know.

Now my back would hurt,
but you have to just
use your strength.
Pull it, pull it, turn it around, pull it.
A-a-ll turn
white—gray.
You have to rub flour on it a-a-nd make it white.

I Always Want to Make Something New and Sell It

My mother is a har-rd worker.
She's not well off
like some of these people are.
She has no income.
She works hard.
She always want to make something and sell it.

I'm that way too. (laughs)
I always want to make something new and sell it.

Like the Cheyennes—one time
we made some quilt tops and
went over to Ataloa.¹
She says "Why don't you make some quilts? You always making quilts,"
and says "why don't you make some and take them over to Lame Deer,
a-a-nd they'll just buy them off the batch"—she says "They just sell so nice.
They want them too."
A-a-nd
these Cheyennes,
they get their monthly checks,
they always have plenty of money.
Says "They all want to buy these quilts."
If it's a quilt that's finished,
nice, neat work,
tie them and
good, soft comforter,
they sell about fifty or eighty—if it's a good one it's eighty dollars.
And if it's not a good one, thin one, it cost about
forty-y or fifty.²
That's what Ataloa told me.

So one time we went—I took two
like Agnes [Deernose] told me.³
I took it over and I know a man there—he's a preacher,
a-a-nd I just left it there with him.⁴
I said "You sell those quilts for me.
I can't stay—I can't go around
different houses to sell these quilts"—I said "I don't want to do that."
Said "Yeah I'll just leave these quilts with you and sell them."
And that man,
he's so quiet he doesn't go around. (chuckles)
Took him about a month before he could sell those comforters.
And I never did that after that.
I don't want to sell any more quilts. (chuckles)

[Now] Donna Mae said "Make three or four and we'll take them over
   there."[5]
She said "Just the top.
Not the comforter.
Just the top—we finish that, just the top,
and one sell for twenty dollars.
There are always lots of women there at the store.
People.
Just go to
one and say 'You want to buy a
quilt top?'
And they just go for that."

So I never done that but just once,
but I left mine with that man.
That man, he's so qui-iet.
He talk to you in small voice and he just grin a-a-nd
he's not like other men.
He's got a wife and two children.

1. Ataloa Harris is my father George Hogan's daughter and my mother's stepdaughter. She raised by Lizzie Yellowtail, my father's sister. She married a Cheyenne man and lives in Lame Deer. (MP)
2. A number of Plains tribes value quilts for gifting. The Cheyenne and Lakota especially favor quilts when honoring people publicly. (BL)
3. Ataloa told Agnes that there were garage sales in Lame Deer at the first of each month and a person could make money. After this, Mom was forever creating stuff to sell there. She took berry puddings, her blankets, and anything else she wanted to get rid of that might be of use to someone. (MP)
4. This was probably Joe Walks Along, who eventually became an ordained minister of the Mennonite Church. He's quiet and very nice. His wife Victoria was ill when I was about thirteen or fourteen, and the BIA Social Services asked Mom to care for their son Joe Jr. while she convalesced. Joe Jr. was with us for quite awhile. We girls sure enjoyed taking care of him. (MP)
5. Donna Mae Chavez, née Knows His Gun, is one of Lillian's step-granddaughters. Her mother was Frances Hogan Knows His Gun, George Hogan's daughter. Work was being done on Donna Mae's house when we were recording, so she and her family were living with Lillian. She married Pete Chavez, of Mexican descent. (MP, BL)

I Make Beading Designs

I make beading designs myself.
I copy a lot of things from magazines and,
a-a-nd see some beadwork when they're dancing.[1]
I like to do that, so I just think about it.
I like to draw [see fig. 18].

A-a-nd I put colors together.
I look at a flower and especially
when they dance a-a-nd I see an outfit,
I say "That's pretty,
and that color is pretty—bring in the color
with that would make nice-looking beadwork."
I just have the ideas—put my colors on.
I guess
I'm no expert on it but
I put the colors on good.[2]

Some people come and ask me to draw-w a design on a belt
or on a glove and I do that—I cut them up [cut out the garment pieces]
and put designs on there and give it to them.
They go and bead.[3]
I made
quite a bit designs.

People sometimes ask me to make a belt in
Indian design or with flowers.[4]
A-a-nd some say "Make roses.
Make carnations."
And that apple blossom flower,
it's easy to make.
I make a lot of that.
But the roses, they're kind of hard.

Now [my granddaughter] Merrie Lillian is pretty good,
making designs now—her husband helps her.
Her husband designs flowers real good.[5]

1. Crow beaders do not copy or repeat designs, so each outfit is unique, but they do watch for ideas. They study other beadwork, and in the case of flower designs, take images from magazines, tablecloths, curtains, dresses, and any other sources they encounter. Some women keep notebooks of new ideas. (BL)
2. My mother was an excellent artist. If she admired a flower on a cup or a live flower in a garden, she could sit down and draw it. She often embellished her drawings with unusual leaves and additional flower petals, and she came up with the most unusual-looking flowers. When people see her great-grandson Calvin Walks Over Ice's outfit, for example, they stop him to ask where the beaders got the design, but that was out of Mom's imagination [see fig. 19]. People also asked her to do drawings for them, but she usually saved her drawings for family. I asked her to keep a portfolio, so the family still has some of those drawings. (MP)
3. She would cut the garment of hide or canvas, depending on what the beader wanted, then draw the design on paper, baste the paper onto the hide or canvas pieces, and give them to the beader. (MP)
4. Most Crow women beaded geometric designs in the nineteenth century, but a few were already exploring floral images by the end of the century. Within two decades flower motifs were high fashion. In the mid-twentieth century, they added a new geometric style called "Indian design." Today they bead prolifically in all three fashions. For more details, see Loeb, "Crow Beadwork," 56–58. (BL)
5. Merrie Lillian is Nellie's daughter. Orrin Anderson is her former husband. (BL)

An Outfit for My Great-Grandson

Here Lillian describes a project she wanted to do. By age eighty-eight it was hard to do everything, so she never did bead this outfit. (BL)

Oh, I can see our new baby right now.
Chubby. (laughs)
He's awful light.
Robert—sure cute.
I told Lorena I said "I want a picture of him.
I says "He's
two months old or three months old" and I said "I want a picture of him."[1]

"All right Grandma, we'll get a picture"—maybe she'll forget it.
But really when she gets home,
we better get a picture now.
And maybe
in about ten months o-o-old, a year o-old, on and on.

Get lots of pictures of him.
I li-ike it.

It's been lo-o-ng time since I bead but now I kept thinking,
I'm going to make a little outfit for our new baby.
They're wa-a-a-y in Arkansas,
and this is a <u>ne-w-w</u> baby, one of my <u>great</u>-grandchild.
Great-grandchild, little boy, and I'm going to make a outfit for him,
and I'm going to dress him up—
next time, maybe-e Crow Fair.
If I finish it.

I know I have to buy me a good pair of glasses before I can start anything.
And beads.
I have to get a-a-ll kinds of beads.
I don't have any beads now.
Somebody stole my who-ole case.
I had a blu-ue fishing tackle box.
A big one I had full of beads.
We were going to make leggings.
And moccasins.
A-a-nd Mary had me pick the colors—we picked dar-rk red,
li-ight red,
dar-rk green, or-range color, white color,
different colors.
We put them in that case and they were downstairs.
Somebody stole them.
And there were ei-i-ight shawls.
In a bag, plastic bag, and we put it on the table a-a-nd
they took that too and my beads.[2]

> 1. Robert Scalpcane was born to Lorena Delrae, Mardell's daughter, on August 23, 1992. At the time, Mardell was working at the Fort Smith National Historic Site in Arkansas. (BL)
> 2. I never beaded him an outfit either. Too busy working, I guess. But I did finally purchase an outfit that I had laid away in Lammers store in Hardin. I made moccasins to match after the man at Lammers made a photocopy of the belt for me. I also made a tomahawk and a bustle and bought him a roach, but he is not interested in dancing, so the outfit is in my storage unit waiting for someone else to wear it. (MP)

I Was Going to Make a Dress for Camee

I have a bunch [of bone elk teeth] at home now.
I bought them from Mrs. Warren.
This is the first time I ever
was in there and found some
in a bag—
and she says there's a hundred in a bag,
in a plastic bag—and she sacked them all up.
A-a-ll lined out—I suppose Crows are buying that.
And Lammers has them.
And Buffalo Chip has them.
That's all the three stores have them now.
They're the only ones that's where you can buy the elk tooth.
And Mrs. Warren—she run a
good secondhand store now and she has those elk tooth.
And Bill Watt,
the merchant there at the Crow Agency.
He died just about three weeks ago—that Bill Watt, he died.
His boys take over now.
His wife and the boys all take over that store now.
They have elk tooth.
And they got be-eads of all kinds—like necklace beads
and the small beads.
They have a-a-ll <u>kinds</u> of beads—
Bill Watt's store,
in Crow [the Crow Mercantile].
And then Lammers too, have beads.
And then that other store,
that secondhand store.
Oh it's kind of new too, that store.
And she's aw-w-ful good to me,
that woman.
They're my neighbors and my lessee.
I like them people.
Warren, Darrell Warren's wife.
They're nice people.

And she has a store.
She has a-a-ll _kinds_ of beads.[1]
Oh,
that Indian Joe,
he has them too.
Indian Joe has them.
Bill Watt has them.
Lammers has them.
Mrs. Warren has them.[2]

They sack them up one hundred elk tooth in a sack.
I bought one [bag] from Mrs. Warren—I bought two.
I was going to make a dress for [my great-granddaughter] Camee,
so I bought two,
two bags—and they're still laying in my drawer.
And if finish her dress,
then I'll sew them teeth on.
Not every woman know how to sew these,
and I learned it from my mother.
I had to help her
finish some dresses.

1. Charlene Warren is an old high school friend of mine. She married one of my mother's lessees and owns a store called Custer's Last Stand, in Hardin, where she sells homemade items, mostly of wood, like shelves and things. She also carries beading and miscellaneous items. (MP)
2. Lammers Trading Post is in Hardin. Buffalo Chips Indian Art is in Billings. Bill Watt's store (the Crow Mercantile) is at Crow Agency. Bill Watt was of mixed blood and married a white woman. His son, Jimmy, now operates the store. Indian Joe is Joe Nichols, a white man who lived on the Crow Reservation for years and attends Crow events. He used to sell in Lodge Grass but moved to Red Lodge. (BL, MP)

I Still Have Some Deer Meat

If I had lots of meat I'd
slice them and dry them.
[Last time I dried meat] was couple months ago.

I still have some deer meat.
My grandson,
Nellie's son,
Nellie's boy,
Barry, Barry-y Bryan,
he goes hunting a lot.

He always goes hunting and
he's, he's a good worker.
He works.
Then sometimes you know how they spend money,
but he don't drink too much—he'll drink a little bit but
he don't spend money on booze, no.

I Like That Indian Food

One of my cousins—Amelia [Piiláako],
the one I said she's old?
They put her in a nursing home now.[1]
She says one day she said to a lady there she stayed with, she said,
"Let's go pick chokecherries."

And they did—they got up,
take some bags and then some pails.
She says "We took our pails, got ready"—and
said "What if we see a snake?"
And the other one says "Oh we'll kill it—we'll kill the snake.
We have to take a big heavy stick."

And they said they went in the brush, start to picking. (laughs)
And this lady, she start to reach up to draw one of the trees.
Pull the whole tree down so it'll bend
and get low so she can pick the cherries.
When she pull the limb down, there was a snake up there—crawl up in
   the tree.

And Amelia said
she ran—threw her pail away and she said "Let's go home!
We'll go without berries" she says—"there's a snake up there!"
They said Amelia said,
"Oh you said you gonna kill that snake if we see one."
Says "I'm afraid to" she says—"let's go home."
They went home without berries. (laughs)
Oh my.

I like chokecherries.
Mary sure can pick berries.
She help me to pound them up, dry them.
They sure like that dessert.
I guess I'm an old-timer.
I like all that Indian food.

I still have some dried berries.
I keep them in the little pail.
I used to go out there with other women.
I can't now with a bad knee and with a bad hip.
I can't go out and pick berries.

1. See "Piiláako Wanted to Go Hunting," chapter 17.

CHAPTER TWENTY-TWO

Education

My Parents Don't Know a Thing about Books

The old people
call the moon the grandmother.
And they call the sun the grandpa.
But this younger generation don't think about the sun
being a grandfather and the moon is the grandmother.
We don't believe in that.

But our parents,
they don't even speak English—they don't know
anything about
the white way—their parents had taught them how to talk.
And they taught them how to
honor their father and mother,
a-a-nd how to
talk to the moon and the sun because the sun is the grandfather,
a-a-nd the moon is the grandmother.
See the old people, it's very strange
how they
bring that up into their lives, [how they] think.
Awful strange but
we listen to them.

And just like my father and mother, they don't know a <u>thing</u> about
going to school or English and know nothing about books.
And they don't know about writing.
And if they have to sign their checks,
they have to use thumb pat.
So they don't know nothing [about school learning].

But us, we're different I think.
Wa-a-a-y [back] in that life it's just
way lot different but they put us
in the boarding school.
A-a-nd
said "Some of these days they have education,
and they'll be living on their own when the old,
old ways of living an Indian [are gone].
And they won't be living in a teepee and they'll be living in the houses and,
and they'll grow up to be men and women,
and in that generation it's going to be different."

We Couldn't Do without Education Nowadays

I said "I want my daughter [Mardell] to grow up,
have good education.
Might be wealthy or find her a good husband,
good children."[1]
I say "I make her give away
a quilt or money or tobacco to an uncle"—mostly a uncle,
on her father's side [a clan uncle].
So they prayed for her.

Now look at her—it's true that she's got good education.
If she neglected about education, not going to school,
she wouldn't be happy like that today.
She's got a good education.
Makes things go.
Live on her o-own
and make a living for her childre-en.

We couldn't go without education nowadays.
We live different than my generation.
We were allotted and we have income [from leasing land], although I never
   seen my money [as a child].
I never fuss about my money,

my leases—when we get our per capita money,
they just grab it and
I suppose my father use it to gamble
or do something—I never ask.
I don't know where my money goes.

Now I have pretty good money—I get about seven thousand,
more than seven thousand a year on my leases.
I take care of that.
[When] Father's gone, my mother's gone,
a-a-nd it's my husband and I, George and I,
he look into that—he make them
raise the price on the lease.[2]
That's how I get my more money—because he's wel-l-l educated.
He's a surveyor and he's had good education,
and he went through school like that and he knows.
And he work in the Office.
That's why I get good rent on my land.

1. Lillian called people "wealthy" if they covered basic needs, dressed well, had a car or pickup truck, lived in a reasonably comfortable home, and could afford horses and fine, traditional clothing. She did not necessarily mean they had large bank accounts. Like many Crow, she admired generosity. She thought people greedy and socially irresponsible if they accumulated excessive wealth. (BL)

    In modern life, a car and clothing are important. If you are well dressed, with a good coat, a hat, and perhaps new boots, these are also tangible signs of wealth. (MP)

2. The BIA served as federal "trustees" and developed regulatory market prices to "protect" Indians from being cheated, but even these were usually well below fair market prices. When Indian people lacked education, white ranchers leased their land for pittances. My grandma and grandpa signed "incompetent" leases. Only in the next generations, when most learned to read and write, did the BIA speak of "competent" leases and competent Indians. When Mom married Dad, he insisted on better rent for her lands, and she said her lease income nearly quadrupled. (MP)

Adam Learned by Experience

Adam went to the army [air force].
He went to Okinawa and lived there for about three years.
Came back and he never went back to school.
He said he wanted to but he never did.

I guess Adam never hard up.
He's a good worker.
Know [how to] build a highway.
A-a-nd build that highway from Hardin to Billings.
And then from Hardin to Livingston.
Now he's drawing pension [for hearing loss].
He draws five hundred dollars a month.
Pension.
And the-e-n he's got
social security money coming all the time.
A-a-nd
he's not hard up.
Although he has no education he,
he learned.
By experience.
He's a pretty good man.

Kids Fight Too Much

But I see now,
in this generation now,
kids fight.
They fight too much.
Like just last week,
my [great-]granddaughter Camee
went to school in Lodge Grass.
They start to fight her.
A couple girls want to fight her.
A-a-nd Mary didn't like it.[1]

Then Camee didn't either—she
didn't want to fight.
So they change school just last week.
So I see now too much fight in the school.

Maybe it's different from what we lived through.
They a-a-ll go to school in a bunch—there's children,
big school—there's <u>lots</u> of pupils.
So I guess that they quarrel and fight and all those.
So I see now it's different from what we
lived through.
Too much fight.
I don't know what my grandchildren, I don't know what
our little grandson,
the new baby now—
I wonder what's going to happen when they grow up.
Maybe they live different.

   1. Camee is Meredith's daughter and Mary's granddaughter. (BL)

Graduation Exercises

After Crow students graduate from college, proud families may honor them with a giveaway at a large Crow gathering such as Crow Fair or the New Year's dances, where they praise them for their accomplishment and give generous gifts to clan relatives to ask for their prayers. But this story is about graduation day itself, when many Crow families combine their own custom of feeding guests with the Western custom of giving gifts directly to the graduates. Lillian preferred homemade gifts for these more personal gatherings, but she often purchased presents because she could no longer sew or bead easily. (BL)

Now next Saturday,
there's Ataloa.
In Lame Deer.
They're going to put on a big feed over there,
and they want the family to come.

But we're going to have a big feed up
in Billings.
At MetraPark.
They're going to have a big feed there.
Graduation exercise there on the lawn.
And then one at the Rocky Mountain College.[1]

So we have to go and get presents for them. (chuckles)
O-o-oh my [a lot of presents this week].
Christmastime too you have to buy (laughs)—and Mother's Day and
    graduation.

And when I don't have the money I feel sa-ad.
When Nellie's daddy is living,
I used to make shirts
and make dresses,
blouses to give.
But I don't
sit down long enough to finish a shirt. (laughs)
They'd say I make the nicest buttonholes.
I don't use this buttonhole stitcher.
I didn't know it then—but after I
finish lot of shirts,
they tell me that I could get a
buttonhole stitcher.
And I made several buckskin outfits—like western shirt.
Pants.
Beads [beaded pants].

I can't bead anymore now.
My eyes.
Yeah like this one—it's hurting now.
This morning I kept rubbing—it start to hurting.
This is dim now.
I'm eighty-two.
I'm eighty-two years old [she was eighty-eight].
(chuckles) Yeh.

Ferole Mae—Mrs. Pease,
o-oh she's pretty.
She is <u>pretty</u>—her-r granddaughter's graduating now—they send me a card,
a-a-nd I like to be there Saturday.
I don't know what to give to her.
Tell me what to get for her.
A clothes?
Or a blouse?

And now before I left Lorena Mae's, "Mama, Mama, Mama" she says.
"Don't you forget next Saturday."
Says "Be right there—I'm afraid you're going to be laid off way up in Big
   Sky and you won't come."
And I said "No Lorena Mae—we can be back
Friday, Friday night"—I said "We'll be here for Saturday."
Saturday's the exercise.
Come and sing at the school,
out on the lawn.
We have to be there.

   1. Rocky Mountain College, a small liberal arts school in Billings, is Montana's oldest institute of higher education. Many Crow study there. Mardell graduated there in 1979. (BL)

CHAPTER TWENTY-THREE

Life as an Elder

I'm Getting Old

By this time, Lillian's family no longer depended on her, but readers should not misunderstand this story to imply that she was isolated. Crow rarely leave their elderly alone. Her children visited her almost daily, and family members almost always lived with her or at least stayed with her at night. If they couldn't, she stayed with one of them. Nor was she housebound. She still drove, so she visited friends and family and traveled to Hardin and Crow Reservation towns regularly. If she wanted to go further, other family members drove her. She was a woman with places to go and a houseful of people. (BL)

Well,
I grow to be an o-o-o-old woman now, o-old.
I'm eighty—
eighty-six—I'm eighty-six now? [eighty-eight]
Anyway I'm getting old and I'm glad the Lord's
helped me to live these [years].
Have all my children.

My-y children all growed up—growed up ni-ice.
They have their o-own family,
and I love them all.
Like Mardell, she lives wa-a-ay down in Arkansas,
but she calls me once in a while.[1]
Glad to hear her.
I went down there last fall.
To see family.

And I was really glad—I have my o-own car, my o-own home a-a-nd
I had my home built—I says "I'm going to be o-old,

and maybe some of my grandchildren will stay with me and take care
  of me."
A-a-nd
I draw pension and I said "I'll buy their grub and then go on living like that,
till the Lord takes me away some of these days."
No human being
live over a hundred years—if they're over a hundred,
they're helpless.
Like children.
I say leave it up to the Lord.
Just carry on like this—I raised these children up and I raised some of my
  own grandchildren,
and they're a-a-ll good to me.
But they don't live with me anymore,
although they come to see me—visit me and all that.

And I make my own living.
And I like it.
I don't fight my children.
Some women do, get mad.
Yeh.
I did with Adam one time—he was drinking too much and I got after him.
But he's all right now.

None of the girls drink.[2]
I have my daughter,
Lorena Mae, Lorena Mae Walks—she's smart, she's
got education, she make her o-own living.
I'm glad she does.
Now she's on her o-own [financially independent].
She gets pension.
I go visit her once in a while.[3]
A-a-nd Mary used to live with me.
Now she went back to her husband.
I don't cater to her any more.
And Nellie's about the only one—she always come and
take me to Billings or

take me to Sheridan or different ones because I have my o-own car,
I have my o-own money.
Sometimes I gave her a little cash.

1. When away, Mardell telephoned her once or twice a week. (BL)
2. Adam and I both drank, but we stopped because of our upbringing and the sorrow it caused our mother, plus clan feeds and lots of prayers. I know the exact day I quit, in May 1975. (MP)
3. Lodge Grass is about twenty-six miles from Dunmore. Lillian drove there once or twice a month, and Lorena Mae called or visited almost daily. (BL)

I Don't Like Writing Checks

This August,
that's when I get a big lease check.
And then it's in December.
In March,
I don't get so much but maybe eight hundred,
but I get about
fourteen hundred in this August.
And in December I get a check for seven thousand
and another check for five thousand—and then
some little checks like four hundred and
maybe a hundred and eight or
other small checks come in.

Sometimes my family come and borrow money from me.
Sometimes they come and say,
"Grandma give me some money—I need some money."
And I give—I give them money.
I don't say I have lots of money.
But even if I have
a hundred dollars, maybe seventy-five, maybe twenty-five
in my purse,
and fold awa-ay in my jar,
they come and says,
"We're out of gas a-a-nd we need some money—can you lend us some?"

Some pay back.
And some don't.
And I don't
say that they must pay it.

But I don't let them know where my money is.
Some know it when
I had my money deposit in Little Horn Bank [in Hardin].
A-a-nd Lorena Mae says "Now don't you
deposit your money there.
Take it out."
So she picked that place [in Billings].
[She] said "That's where my money is and I don't let nobody know.
So you do that too—put your money in that.
Them people will take care of it."
So that's why I didn't put my money in Hardin bank—I used to long time ago.

But I don't like writing checks.
If I have about fifteen hundred,
a big sum of money,
I fold them up and put them away (chuckles)—in my jar
somewhere.
A-a-nd if I go,
take a long trip,
I wrap it up,
all in bills.
Wrap it up and put it in the car.
And if I want any,
I take it out—say maybe a couple hundred, maybe hundred.
And
I like to be my o-own boss. (chuckles)

My Land

[My land is from] my mother.
I get some of my father's too.
I don't know about my brothers.
They have land—I should look into that.
I got a big brother that died when he was about twenty-eight years old.[1]
He died.
And I have a little brother that died at nine.
And that's the two brothers I lost.
And of course my sister Ida.
She's allotted.
She's got land.
A-a-nd
I get her land.

We have homestead allotted.
Homestead, we can't sell those.
But these grazing lands or if you inherit
a piece of land,
inherit land [from someone] that's related to you-u,
if you want to sell this land you can.
But you can't sell your own allotment.
The government won't let you sell it.
I guess that's good,
for your homestead.[2]

Now my homestead is right above Pryor and I can build a house there.
Adam's going to build a house—I thought Mardell was going to build a house there,
and they didn't—but Samuel, he build a house down there.
They got a good house there.
And I wish Mardell's family would build there.
Right close to the highway.
I think it's good.

I have
a lot of grazing land I lease to Scott.
Scott Company.
And some to Hamilton.[3]
That's a-a-ll in Pryor.
So I get
pretty good money now.
The welfare and the state knows—
they won't help me.
Like if I needed help,
like this fall the furnace broke down.
Clara, that's my niece, the chairman, said "We'll help you out!"
And I waited and waited for about four months and they never start nothing.
Couple times I went over—and says "Yes we'll look it up, we'll help you out."
They never did.
So one day I went to the man that's going to fix.
[He said] "You've got to pay me,
and I'll just start.
Have you went to the Office?"—and "I did and they won't help me."

Now I heard that
they didn't want to help me because I got too much income.
All those land they figured up I got too much income.
Some people don't and that's when they help these people.
Said I got too much income—they won't help me.
So I said "All right, I do,
I get quite a bit.
And I'm alone now."
I said "I got a car, I got a Buick,
and I paid for it."

1. She must mean Daniel who passed away when he was nineteen. (BL)
2. See "George Helped My Father Make a Will," chapter 16, for details on Lillian's land, the Dawes Act, and the Crow Act. (BL)
3. This was Herman Hamilton. She also leased to Chester Schwend of Joliet and several others. If you are talking about your lessee, you say "my white man." If you are talking to someone else about their lessee, you say "your white man." (MP)

I Broke My Hip

I fell and broke my hip.
I fell in one of the stores,
and I couldn't move then.
I scream—I said "I can't move!"
So there were
four men had to take me up, lift me up.
They moved me—it hurts!
Picked me up in the car and said "Now rush her to the hospital!"
And they did (claps hands)—they got me to the hospital and they
took me in and examine and x-ray.
They knew it was broken hip so they rush me to the hospital in Billings.
And I laid there one night,
in pain—but the next morning (claps hands) I went through surgery—after that,
never felt it.
Never gave me trouble.
I don't know where it broke. (laughs)
No I don't know. (laughs)

They kept me at St. Vincent's Hospital for four, four weeks.
But I got all right and they said I can go home [to the hospital in Crow].
And when I went home,
when the car backed up, drove in the entrance,
a-a-nd door opened, the nurses and the doctors all help me to the car.
A-a-nd said "Do you want some fruit juice or a sandwich or something?"
And I looked around and I said "Oh yeah,
I'll take your sandwich and some fruit juice."
And I already
was in the car and they going to take me to Crow hospital,
and they brought me some and
they laugh and said "bye-bye." (laughs)

They took me over to the hospital [in Crow],
and they kept me there another couple weeks and they let me out.

I walk just fine!
Never bothered me.

And it's through prayer.
Pra-a-y.
Pra-a-y.
Not afraid.
I don't say "Come on and help me up [in high-pitched pitiful voice]."
I don't do that.
Try to get up, help myself.
So therefore it's a-a-ll the Lord help me through.
Yeh.
I'm glad.

Caleb Died Last February

My brother died last February.
Poor thing—he never
walked again.
He's always
in the-e nursing home.
A-a-nd
he got re-eally sick.
He was living in the nursing home for about four—
four or five years.

One day I said "Let's go see Caleb."
We did a-a-nd
they put him in a wheelchair.
He rolled up to the corner
where nobody was watching.
He push himself to the corner,
and he sat there and he start to motion.
He talk a-a-nd talk and point in-n different ways.
And here we were standing way back here watching him.
He don't know we were there.

We're watching,
and I laughed and laughed and Nellie and Mary says "Don't laugh.
Don't laugh at him now—that might mean something."
So Mary came over and pushed the wheelchair,
a-a-nd he turn around, look—"O-o-oh, o-o-oh" he says,
"I didn't know you were here.
I'm talking to somebody up there, well-educated"—and
he started going funny.
We laughed.

But he never come out of the hospital.
Poor old fellow.
He's my only brother.
He had pneumonia and they got him to St. Vincent's Hospital.
Then he died there.
I didn't think he'd die when I went in there.
They tell me Caleb had pneumonia and laying in the hospital,
and Mary and I said we'd better go see him.
First time I was there he just
slee-e-p and then look at us and went back to sleep again.
I ask him how he was feeling—he says,
says "O-o-oh I guess I'm all right."
A-a-nd
he doesn't answer me too good but he laid there—just
doze off—I guess the medicine
they gave him made him sleep all the time.
But after that he,
he died.

Rebecca's Son Was Killed

Samuel's got a big family.
Let's see now—
Russell's the oldest.
Samuel's only got one son.
All the others are girls. (chuckles)

There's Russell,
Mary Doe [Renita Sue]—she's Mrs. Hill.
She su-u-re is a ni-ice-looking lady.
She talks so ni-ice and smi-iles so ple-easant.
She's su-u-re nice.

Millie—her husband and her, are staying
over to Lodge Grass with her mother-in-law,
because her mother-in-law is alone.
They went over there.[1]
Her house [is in Pryor].
Sammy gave it to her I guess.
It's her house but she lets Russell live there
so she can go back to Lodge Grass with her mother-in-law.
She's up to Lodge Grass now.
She only has,
I don't know—
two daughters I think
is all she has but
she adopted two [granddaughters].
She adopted a little girl.
Now she adopted another girl.
A baby.
So she's down there Lodge Grass now.

But let's see now—Mary Doe,
Millie,
Billie,
Rebecca,
Sara.[2]
Rebecca [Falls Down], she's in Lodge Grass too.
She's married and has a family.
Last fall,
been a year now,
last fall,
her son
was killed.
Right at the house.

The boys,
the cousins,
two cousins, two boys, come after him.
Said "You want to go with us? We're going hunting."
And this was in the evening,
and he said "Yes I'll go."
He went in and told his mother and father—says,
"I want to get my gun so I
go with the boys to hunt."

And the mother said "Be careful now."
And the father said "You'd better not go—it's too late now.
You'll be out a-a-ll night.
Maybe you won't kill nothing."
Says "You better not go."
But he said "They're out there waiting for me—I better go."
And he went out—took his gun and set it in the back seat.
Set the gun there and there were several guns there,
and one discharge
and shot him.
Through the heart.
Killed him instantly.

And they took him to the hospital,
and Rebecca didn't know he died.
Laid him there in one of the rooms there,
in the emergency room.
He laid there and I could see his hand.
She called right away—right after they brought the boy in,
Rebecca called—says "Grandma,"
said "come over right away."
And this was arou-n-nd twelve o'clock [midnight],
and she says,
"Come over right away because there's
the family—all of us are here,
and you should come right away"—and,
"My son"—she called his name—I forgot his name.

She said "He was shot.
And he's laying right here in the emergency room.
And we're all here waiting"—she didn't know he died,
but she was crying.

She went out of her head couple times while we were there.
And we all waited there for Samuel and Adeline,
to come to the hospital from Pryor.
Samuel, that's my son—Adeline is his wife.
And we were all waiting there.
A-a-nd the doctors and the nurses all around there but they took off and left us alone.
Got some more chairs for us to sit there.
Wait.
And we look in there once in a while—he just laid there on the
emergency but he—he died.
A-a-nd we waited for Samuel from Pryor.
They made it—they got ther-re must have been about—
one o'clock.
A-a-nd then after that,
Samuel look at him and he said "He's dead."
And that Rebecca just scre-eam—<u>scre-eam</u> and run out of her head.
We all had to get around her.

She come to,
but anyway,
she lost her boy.
She lives at Lodge Grass,
and she sure took it hard.
She's better now.
Yeh that was a bad accident.
But we were all there, Nellie and me and Mary.
All there.

That was recently—last year, I don't think it's a year yet.
But
she's such a nice woman.

And
I feel bad for her.
They're nice girls.

Rebecca has other children there.
She has
a ni-ice girl, nice daughter.
She's a teenager.
She's maybe about
fourteen or fifteen—she's re-eally good.
Good-looking too. (chuckles)
I don't know her name.
I've got too many grandchildren—I don't know their names,
I don't even know her name.
She's pleasant-looking,
and Rebecca, she has a ni-ice home.
The government build a house for them.
They gave them the house.
They maybe about fifty homes in that area.
Maybe forty—I don't count them.
And they live right close to the school,
and that makes it nice.

1. Millie was married to Jude Old Crow, since deceased. (MP)
2. She left some offspring out of the list. Samuel's daughters, from oldest to youngest, are Cerise, Mary (Renita Sue), Millie, Billie Desta, Rebecca, Teatta, and Sara. In addition to Russell, sons include Gregory, who died, and Jason Shane, born outside his marriage. Mary was named Renita Sue, but she was sickly, so her parents symbolically "threw her away." In reality, she remained with her parents but was ritually adopted and renamed by the good people to whom she was "given." Her Indian and Christian names were both changed, and Renita Sue became Mary. (MP)

I Stayed at Russell's

Russell's wife [Benita] went down to Havre.[1]
I don't know what she's taking up,
but she had to be transferred from Crow,
to Havre.

And at Easter time,
I went over to Russell's and stayed with the girls.
A girl a-a-nd two boys and Russell.
I stayed at the house and
we went to church at Easter time.
I went back after Easter—I went back home to Crow.
And she's back now.

I stayed at Pryor
while Benita's down in Havre
for some work—some kind of a
study o-or—I don't know what it is.
Too much for me and I don't know that but I stayed at Russell's
with one daughter—she took the other daughter with her,
and I stayed
with the daughter, Russell a-a-nd a little boy-y,
eight years o-old, and his son is about—
eleven years old.
And we spend Easter time together.

And after Easter,
about a week after that,
I stayed there because they don't have no car.
I had to stay, take them around, take them to Billings and
[to the] store.
It's so-o-o muddy there, the road is so muddy,
and it was stormy.
Sno-ow and ra-ain.
A-a-nd Russell had to take the kids
to school—they don't live
too far from the highway,
but he takes them to school in my car because they don't have no car.
So I went home
after that—it's been just about a week since I went home.

> 1. Havre is in north central Montana, forty-six miles west of Fort Belknap Agency where Benita grew up. (BL)

George's Grandchildren Are So Nice to Me

Lillian had many step-grandchildren who were fond of her, and they sometimes kept her company too, as in this brief story. (BL)

This time when I get home I'm going to be alone,
a-a-nd I think one of my grandchildren
fro-om George,
George's grandchildren,
a ni-ice girl—I think she's going to stay with me.
They're a-a-all,
oh they're so-o-o <u>ni-ice</u> to me!
They all call me "Grandma! Grandma!"
Yeh they hang onto me when I get out of the car and
<u>ev-v-very</u> one of them is nice to me.

The Senior Citizens Center at Crow Agency

They have a big house [with] a dining room,
a-a-nd
the senior people go there for dinner.
Ladies work there—about four.
Four ladies work there,
cook for the seniors.
A-a-nd we go over there and eat our dinner there and come back.

And right in that area
there's houses, rows of houses,
a-a-ll around—down top of the hill and then
drive on up to the school and then
there's another row of houses there—it's sure good.
The government built them.
And those that don't have no land or no houses,
they give it to them.[1]

So,
they ask me if I want to live in that
great big house.
They got senior,
old people there.
And when they first build it,
they asked me if I wanted a room.
"You have the preference of senior citizen."
And I said no.
I said "Don't give me one.
I have my own home—I don't want to leave my home."

> 1. Government houses are Housing Authority structures that Housing and Urban Development (HUD) built for tribal members. A cluster of homes is near the Senior Citizens Center, another up the hill, across Interstate 90 and the railroad tracks. Those who had land had their houses built on their own properties, but the tribe also sold 2.5 acres to anyone who lacked land and wanted to live in the country. After twenty-five years of small payments, the tracts and homes became theirs. (MP)

I Feel Proud

Seems like my family don't treat me as if I'm old.
They don't care—
even if I'm old they just don't say it or don't feel like it.
I'm old but I'm still there helping out.

But other people, friends,
my nie-e-ces and
some of my nephews,
some say,
"O-oh you done a lot—you raised your children.
You got a good home.
Even if you're an o-old, old woman,
you got a car of your own,
a-a-nd you feed yourself, you buy your own groceries,
and you still can drive." (laughs)

They laugh at you when you drive—say "Look at her!
Look at that old woman driving." (laughs)
But I don't drive to Billings though.
Just around Crow.
If I want to go to Pryor,
I just take off and go to Pryor—I drive.

[If they asked me to go into a nursing home] I'd say I would.
I would cause they sure take good care,
and I don't want
my children, my daughters, to
take care of me.
I'd still look on the bright side.
I don't take it bad.
Look forwards to a good time.

And I go to church a lot—they know.
There's a big feast going on,
or-r maybe box social or-r
some people putting on a feast, feed,
and lots of people there,
they ask me to get up and pray.[1]
Get up and pray for the people.
And afterwards some of them [say],
"We sure feel good when you pray."
Yes, so God gave me those.
To pray.
Yeh.
I pray for different ones.
I like it.
I enjoy.

Yeh—but the good thing about this is just driving around. (laughter)
I got a good eyesight.
Just this eye gets a little blurry now.
I feel all right [about being older]—I feel proud. (chuckles)[2]

1. When Lillian said everyone knew she attended church a lot, she was explaining why they chose her to offer a prayer. Prayers carry more credence if given by someone "especially attuned to and involved in religious life and recognized as such by others." See Frey, *The World of the Crow*, 52. (BL)
2. Later my mother moved to a small apartment in the Senior Center. At the end of her life, she was in the Awe Kuualawache Rest Home at Crow Agency, so we could visit her daily. The home is named for our famous leader, Chief Sits In the Middle of the Land. She passed away July 2, 2003. (MP)

Bibliography

Adams, David Wallace. *Education for Extinction*. Lawrence: University Press of Kansas, 1995.
Albright, Peggy. *Crow Indian Photographer: The Work of Richard Throssel*. Albuquerque: University of New Mexico Press, 1997.
Alcoff, Linda Martín. "The Problem of Speaking for Others." In *Who Can Speak*, edited by Judith Roof and Robyn Wiegman, 97–119. Urbana: University of Illinois Press, 1995.
Algier, Keith. *The Crow and the Eagle: A Tribal History from Lewis and Clark to Custer*. Caldwell IN: Caxton Printers, 1993.
Big Man, Max. "The Beaver Dance and Adoption Ceremony of the Crow Indians." In *Lifeways of Intermontane and Plains Montana Indians, in Honor of J. Verne Dusenberry*, edited by Leslie B. Davis, 43–56. Occasional Papers of Museum of the Rockies, no. 1. Bozeman MT: Museum of the Rockies, 1979.
Bradley, Charles Crane, Jr. "After the Buffalo Days: Documents of the Crow Indians from the 1880's to the 1920's." Master's thesis, Montana State University, 1970.
———. *The Handsome People: A History of the Crow Indians and the Whites*. Billings MT: Council for Indian Education, 1991.
Brien, Luella. "Chapter 5: Present-Day Life." In *Apsáalooke Writing Tribal Histories Project: The Apsáalooke (Crow Indians) of Montana: A Tribal Histories Teacher's Guide and Lesson Plans*, directed by Hubert B. Two Leggins, compiled and edited by Phenocia Bauerle, Cindy Bell, Luella Brien, Carrie McCleary and Timothy McCleary, 66–71. Crow Agency MT: Little Big Horn College, 2008.
———. "Fading Fluency." In *Apsáaloke Writing Tribal Histories Project*, Little Big Horn College, http://lib.lbhc.edu/history/5.11.php.
Curtis, Edward. *The North American Indian, vol. 4, The Apsaroke (Crow) and Hidatsa*. New York: Johnson Reprint Corporation, 1970. First published 1909.
Denig, Edwin. *Five Indian Tribes of the Upper Missouri*. Edited by John Ewers. Norman: University of Oklahoma Press, 1961.
Fitzgerald, Michael O. *Yellowtail: Crow Medicine Man and Sun Dance Chief*. Norman: University of Oklahoma Press, 1991.

Frey, Rodney. *Stories That Make the World: Oral Literature of the Indian Peoples of the Inland Northwest as Told by Lawrence Aripa, Tom Yellowtail, and Other Elders*. Norman: University of Oklahoma Press. 1995.

———. *The World of the Crow Indians: As Driftwood Lodges*. Norman: University of Oklahoma Press, 1987.

Hayden, F. V. "On the Ethnology and Philosophy of the Indian Tribes of the Missouri Valley." *American Philosophical Society Transactions* 12 (1863), 281–462.

Hoxie, Frederick E. *The Crow*. New York: Chelsea House Publishers, 1989.

———. *Parading through History: The Making of the Crow Nation in America, 1805–1935*. Cambridge: Cambridge University Press, 1995. Paperback edition, 1997. Citations are to the 1997 edition.

Larocque, Francois. *Journal of Larocque from the Assiniboine to the Yellowstone, 1805*. Publications of the Canadian Archives, vol. 3, edited by L. J. Burpee. Ottawa: Government Printing Bureau, 1910.

Linderman, Frank B. *American: The Life Story of a Great Indian, Plenty Coups, Chief of the Crows*. New York: John Day, 1930. Republished as *Plenty-Coups: Chief of the Crows*. Lincoln: University of Nebraska Press, 1962. Citations are to the 1962 edition.

———. *Red Mother*. New York: John Day, 1932. Republished as *Pretty-Shield: Medicine Woman of the Crows*. Lincoln: University of Nebraska Press, 1972. Citations are to the 1972 edition.

Loeb, Barbara. "Classic Intermontane Beadwork: Art of the Crow and Plateau Tribes." PhD dissertation, University of Washington, 1984.

———. "Crow Beadwork: The Resilience of Cultural Values." *Montana: The Magazine of Western History*, Autumn 1990, 48–59.

———. "Crow Fair." *Native Peoples*, Winter 1990, 16–24.

Lowie, Robert H. *The Crow Indians*. New York: Farrar and Rinehart, 1935. Reissued by New York: Holt, Rinehart and Winston, 1956. Citations are to the 1956 edition.

———. *Minor Ceremonies of the Crow Indians*. Anthropological Papers of the American Museum of Natural History, vol. 21, part 5. New York: American Museum Press, 1924.

———. *The Tobacco Society of the Crow Indians*. Anthropological Papers of the American Museum of Natural History, vol. 21, part 2. New York: American Museum of Natural History, 1919.

Marquis, Thomas B. *Memoirs of a White Crow Indian (Thomas H. Leforge)*. New York: Century, 1928.

McCleary, Timothy P. "Akbaatashee: The Oilers Pentecostalism among the Crow Indians." Master's thesis, University of Montana, 1993.

———. *The Stars We Know: Crow Indian Astronomy and Lifeways*. Long Grove IL: Waveland Press, 1997.

Medicine Crow, Joseph. *Counting Coup: Becoming a Crow Chief on the Reservation and Beyond.* Washington DC: National Geographic Society, 2006.

———. "The Effects of European Culture Contacts upon the Economic, Social, and Religious Life of the Crow Indians." Master's thesis, University of Southern California, 1939.

———. *From the Heart of Crow Country: The Crow Indians' Own Stories.* Lincoln: University of Nebraska Press, 2000.

Medicine Crow, Joe, and Daniel S. Press. *A Handbook of Crow Indian Laws and Treaties.* Crow Agency MT, 1966.

Nabokov, Peter. "Cultivating Themselves: The Inter-play of Crow Indian Religion and History." PhD dissertation, University of California, Berkeley, 1988.

———, ed. *Two Leggings: The Making of a Crow Warrior.* Lincoln: University of Nebraska Press, 1967.

———. "Vision Quests of Crow Women." *Indian Notes*, Summer 1974, 66–83.

Poten, Constance J. "Robert Yellowtail, the New Warrior." *Montana: The Magazine of Western History*, Summer 1989, 36–41.

Ramsey, Jarold. "From Mythic to Fictive in a Nez Perce Orpheus Myth." In *Traditional Literatures of the American Indian; Texts and Interpretaions*, edited by Karl Kroeber, 25–44. Lincoln: University of Nebraska Press, 1981.

Roscoe, Will. "That Is My Road: The Life and Times of a Crow Berdache." *Montana: The Magazine of Western History*, Winter 1990, 46–55.

Simms, S. C. "Cultivation of Medicine Tobacco By the Crows—a Preliminary Paper." *American Anthropologist*, New Series, vol. 6 (1904), 331–35. New York: Kraus Reprint Corporation, 1962. Citations are to the 1962 edition.

Snell, Alma Hogan. *Grandmother's Grandchild: My Crow Indian Life.* Edited by Becky Matthews. Lincoln: University of Nebraska Press, 2000.

Swanton, John R. *The Indian Tribes of North America.* Smithsonian Institution, Bureau of American Ethnology Bulletin 145. Washington DC: Government Printing Office, 1952.

Thomas, Davis, and Karin Ronnefeldt, ed. *People of the First Man: Life among the Plains Indians in Their Final Days of Glory: The Firsthand Account of Prince Maximilian's Expedition up the Missouri River, 1833–34.* New York: E. P. Dutton, 1976.

Tushka, Belva. A Dictionary of Everyday Crow. Crow Agency MT: Bilingual Materials Development Center, 1979.

Two Leggins, Hubert B., director. *Apsáalooke Writing Tribal Histories Project: The Apsáalooke (Crow Indians) of Montana: A Tribal Histories Teacher's Guide and Lesson Plans.* Compiled and edited by Phenocia Bauerle, Cindy Bell, Luella Brien, Carrie McCleary and Timothy McCleary. Crow Agency MT: Little Big Horn College, 2008. *Available online (with some changes), Apsáalooke Writing Tribal Histories Project, Little Big Horn College,* http://lib.lbhc.edu/history/.

U.S. Census Bureau. United States Census 2000, *http://www.census.gov/main/www/cen2000.html (accessed July 19, 2011)*.

Voget, Fred W. *The Shoshoni-Crow Sun Dance*. Norman: University of Oklahoma Press, 1984.

———. *They Call Me Agnes: A Crow Narrative Based on the Life of Agnes Yellowtail Deernose*. Norman: University of Oklahoma Press, 1995.

Williams, Walter L. *The Spirit and the Flesh: Sexual Diversity in American Indian Culture*. Boston: Beacon Press, 1986.

Wolf, Helen Pease. *Reaching Both Ways*. Laramie WY: Jelm Mountain Publications, 1989.

Yellowstone Western Heritage Center. *Parading through History: The Apsaalooke Nation*. American Indian Tribal Histories Project. Aberdeen SD: Coyote Publishing and Printing, 2006.

Yellowtail, Robert. *At Crow Fair*. Albuquerque: Wowapi Press, 1973.

———. "A Brief Review of the History of Big Horn County, The Crow Reservation and the Crow, 1884–1973." In *Lookin' Back, Big Horn County*, 315–18. Hardin MT: Big Horn County Historical Society, 1976.

Index

Aakkeetaash. *See* Bull Well Known (Aakkeetaash)
accidents, 302–4, 393, 397–98
adoption, xxi, 10–12, 143, 145n1, 289n2, 396; of Alex Plainfeather, 216n3; of captives, 14, 15; by grandparents, 14, 15, 113n2, 220, 230, 277n2; inheritance and, 289n3; of Iris Bullshow, 287, 289n2; of sick children, 9n7, 399n2; Tobacco Iipche and, xxxiii, 195–96; Tobacco Society and, 180–82, 189, 225–28
agents. *See* Indian agents
Alasíia Áhush. *See* Shows Plenty
alcohol, xix, xxxiv–xxxv, 333, 377; Bull Shows and, 140–41, 197, 198, 200–201; Caleb Bullshows and, 137, 140–41, 227–28; dances and, 115–16; Elizabeth Fitzgerald and, 274; Paul Singer and, xix, 236, 244–45
allotments, land. *See* land allotments
Amyotte, Stephanie, 360, 361n1
Anderson, Orrin, 372, 373n5
"Apsáalooke" (name), xiii
Apsáalooke biographies, xxi–xxii
Apsáalooke history, xv–xix
Apsáalooke language, xiv, xvi, xx, xxviii(n31), xxxvi, 31; boarding school and, 79; gender and, xxiii, xxix(n45), 68n1
Apsáalooke names, xi, xx, 5–10, 33, 361–62

Armstrong, Henry, 39, 42n5
army scouts, 39n2, 39n6
Arrow Creek, 42n6–7, 97n4. *See also* Pryor Creek
arrow throwing (game). *See* throwing arrows (game)
asbestos, 336–37
Asbury, C. W., 75, 80n5, 189n9
Asshee Aakeennáhkush. *See* Stays On Top of the Lodge
automobiles. *See* cars and trucks

babies. *See* infants
babysitting, 206
bags. *See* medicine bags; purses
Baker, Lee, 293, 304n3
baking, 94, 109, 129, 163, 210
Bank. *See* Bull Well Known (Aakkeetaash)
banks and banking, 390
barter, 241
Battle of Pryor Creek, 59n6
Battle of the Little Bighorn, 116n2
Battle of the Rosebud, 128n1, 128n3
battles, sham. *See* sham battles
beads and beadwork, xvii, xx, xxvii(n32), 148n1, 298n3, 384; for brides, 213; Crow Fair and, 106, 108, 110n4; dealers, 375–76; on dresses, 9, 98, 100nn3–4, 258, 260; by Lillian, 149–53, 270–72, 296–98; Little Horse and, 49, 149–53, 160; on medicine bags, 189, 190, 191; on medicine necklaces, xi,

beads and beadwork (*continued*) 68–71, 341, 342–43; Nez Perce and, xxvii(n15); Ohchiish and, 130; prayers and, 88–91; on saddles, 160, 161, 162n7; for Tobacco Society adoption gifts, 227n4
Bear Below, Joanne Horn, 259
Bear Cloud, Martha, xxxiii
Bear Cloud, Ted, xxxiii
bears, 66–68
Bear Tail, Mary Ann, 10–12
Beaver Dance. *See* Tobacco Society (Medicine Dance)
beets, 243
Before the White Man Came, 104–5, 149, 150
Bell, Benita Fay. *See* Plainfeather, Benita
Bell Rock, Annie, 81
belts, 270–72, 372
Benson, Theodore, 351, 353n1
Bentley, Chester, xxxii, 263, 306
berdaches, xiii, 124–31
berries and berrying, 18, 95, 117, 163–66, 268, 322–23, 371n3, 377–78
best friends, 117–24
betting. *See* gambling
Bible, 334, 336
Big Day, Annie, 217, 254, 296–97
Big Day, William, 217–18, 264–65, 268–69nn2–3
Big Eyes, 216n3
Big Hail, Julia, 81–82, 117–24
Big Lodge Clan, xiii, 14
Big Man, Cordelia, 249, 253n4
Big Man, Max, 248, 252
Big Ox, xxxv, 360n5
Biillíiche Heeléelash, 128
Billings Fair, 239, 327
Billings mt, 36–37, 239; Caleb Bull Shows and, 278; colleges, 385n1; commerce in, 49, 99, 204, 317, 318, 375, 376n2; medical care in, 57–58, 133, 136, 266, 277, 310, 393, 395; Paul Singer death in, 245–46
birth. *See* pregnancy and childbirth
bitterroot, 172–74, 253–57, 367–68
Blackfeet, xvi. *See also* Piegan Blackfeet
Black Hair, Mike. *See* Fitzpatrick, Mike
Black Hair, Sidney, 296n1
Black Hawk, Edith, 212n4, 249, 251, 358
Black Lodge District ("Dunmore"), 42n7, 234n1, 244, 304–5, 312, 323
blankets, 236–37, 371n3
boarding schools, xix, 33n8, 380; Arizona, 309; child labor in, 78; Crow Fair and, 108; Lillian and, xiv, 73–88, 175–77; Oregon, 211–12; Pennsylvania, xxxiii, 31, 33n8, 34, 91n6, 269n6; renaming and, 4n2, 33–34
bone saving and processing, 168–69
bone teeth. *See* elk teeth (carved bone)
bone tools, 154
"boss farmers," 5–6, 8n3, 205–8, 245, 246, 328; Lillian's naming and, xxxi, xxxii, xxxiii, 5–6
bow and arrow, 29, 31, 65. *See also* throwing arrows (game)
box elder trees, 161, 162n4
boy-girl relations. *See* girls: relations with boys
brain tanning. *See* tanning
bread making. *See* baking
brides, outfitting of, 213–14, 216, 217–18, 229, 231, 232n7, 247–48, 264

Brings Back Ten. *See* Passes, Amelia
Briskow, E. P., 127n8
buckskin, 296; decoration of, 101, 104n1; in medicine bag making, 189; in moccasin making, 158–59; outfits, 384; saddles and, 161; tanning of, 109, 130, 153–58, 297
buffalo, xv, xviii, xix, 70n4, 168
Buffalo Bill Historical Center, 152
Buffalo Chips Indian Art, 375, 376n2
Bull Don't Show, 23n5, 204n1
Bull Shows, 74, 253, 285–86; alcohol and, 140–41, 198, 201; bitterroot and, 256; death, 289–95; farming and, 111; film role of, 105; gambling and, xxxv, 197–98, 199–200, 381; horses and, 48–55, 138, 139, 199, 202–3; lack of schooling, 285, 379; land allotment and, 285; Lillian's first marriage and, 215; Lillian's fourth marriage and, 263; Lillian's illness and, 175–77, 179, 225–26; Lillian's new shoes and, 204; Lillian's renaming and, 4, 5–8; Lillian's second marriage and, 230, 231, 239; marriage, 47–48, 198, 201, 353; Mary Ann Bear Tail and, 10; medicine necklaces of, 341–42, 343; names of, 7–8; shinny game and, 222, 223; story of cow herding, 43–44; story of Crow leaving western lands, 39–42; story of herbal healing, 25–28; story of government school, 28–33; story of watermelon, 36–39; Tobacco Iipche and, 195; Tobacco Society and, 179, 180, 225–26, 227n2, 339; tool making of, 154; as widower, 283; will of, 287–89
Bullshows, Caleb (Charles), xix, 1, 3n5, 57, 59, 144; alcohol and, xxxiv, 137, 140–41, 227–28, 278, 280–81, 293–94; bia renaming of, 4n2; children, 142; death, 2, 394–95; dog and, 103; father's death and, 290, 293–95; horses and, 108, 111, 112, 138–39; inheritance, 287, 288; Lillian's first marriage and, 215; Medicine Porcupine and, 60; mother and, 278, 280–81; quits school, 210; Sun Dance and, xx, xxxiii, 265–66, 268–69nn2–3; Tobacco Iipche and, 195; Tobacco Society and, 227–28
Bullshows, Daniel, 1, 3n5, 49, 59, 391
Bullshows, Davene, 309–12
Bullshows, Effie, 3n5
Bullshows, Grace, 280–81, 291, 309
Bullshows, Harry, 287, 288
Bullshows, Harry Austin, 2, 3n5
Bullshows, Hulda, 3n5
Bullshows, Ida, 1, 2, 391
Bullshows, Iris, 280–81, 287, 288, 289nn2–4, 291
Bull Shows, Iva, xxxiv, 283n4
Bullshows, Johnny, 10n15, 323
Bullshows, Lillian: Apsáalooke names, xi, xxxi–xxxii, 9n10; beadwork and, 270–72, 372–74; best friends, 117–24; birth and infancy, 1–3; "boss farmer" and, xxxi, xxxii, xxxiii, 5–6, 205–8; correspondents, 212; dancing and, 204, 208–9, 357–60; death, 404n2; English name ("Effie"), 4, 294, 327; eye problems, 310, 313, 403; father's death and, 289–93, 294, 306; father's drinking and, 198, 201; first memories, 57–71; foster children, 321–22; gift-giving of, 384; green-bead medicine and, xi, 68–71; as healer, 346–49; hunting and, 323–24; illness of, 6, 7,

Bullshows, Lillian (*continued*) 175–80, 225, 266; income and finances, 325, 380–81, 389–90, 392; inheritance, 285, 286, 287, 288; injuries, 393–94; in-laws, 238, 240n3, 244; marriages, xxxii–xxxiii, xxxviii–xxxli, 131, 212–19, 229–40; marriage to George Hogan, 263–64, 269n6, 270, 272, 278, 281, 297, 298–306; mother's cancer and, 278–81, mother's death and, 281–82, 286, 306; Old Dwarf and, 141–46; pension, 303, 388; prefab house of, 325–27; quilt making and selling, 370–71; reading and, 212n2, 334; religion and, 63, 227, 234n1, 333–36, 355–56, 394, 403, 404n1; religious conflict of, xiv, xix, xxxiv, 269n6; school and, 73–88, 209–10, 211; stepchildren, 230; step-grandchildren, 401; travels, 295–96, 307–12, 361, 387, 390; wealth and, 381n1; will, 286

Bullshows, Percy, 3n5, 131–36
Bullshows, Rose, 2, 3n5
Bullshows, Samuel ("Mugger"), 289n4, 319, 320n3, 323
Bull Tail, 251
Bull Tail, Alice, 182n4
Bull That Shows. *See* Bull Shows
Bull Weasel, 239
Bull Well Known (Aakkeetaash), 13, 14, 58
Bureau of Indian Affairs (bia), xxxv, 331n3; agencies, 29, 32n4, 34, 314; George Hogan and, 303, 381; name changing and, 4n2. *See also* government schools
Burgess Memorial Baptist Church, xxxii
burial, 61, 62n3, 283, 283n5

camps and camping, 39, 41, 110n1, 110nn3–4, 357, 365–66, 367; Billings Fair and, 327, 331n1; cow herding and, 43; Cree, 95; Crow Fair and, 106–7, 110n6; dances and, 114–15; epidemics and, 25–28; filmmaking and, 105, 150; sheep shearing and, 119; Sun Dance and, 267, 269n7
cancer, 278–83
canning, 208n2, 242
captives, 13, 14, 14–15n4, 127–28
Carlisle Indian Industrial School, xxxiii, 31, 34, 91n6, 269n6
cars and trucks, 229, 242, 246, 254, 255, 295, 392; accidents, 302–4; Arizona trip and, 309–10; as gifts, 320–21; hunting and, 323. *See also* elderly drivers
carved elk teeth. *See* elk teeth (carved bone)
Cashen, Ella, xxxi, 5, 6–7, 9n9
Catholicism, 333, 334
cattle, 43–44, 98n7, 242, 245
cemeteries, 282, 283n5
ceremonies, tobacco-planting. *See* tobacco-planting ceremonies
Chavez, Donna Mae, 371
Chemawa Indian School, 211, 212
Cheyenne, xvi, 310, 312n4, 313, 370, 371nn1–2
chickens, 241
Chief, Walter, 113, 202–3
Chief Iron Bull. *See* Iron Bull
Chief Medicine Crow. *See* Medicine Crow
Chief No Intestines. *See* No Vitals (No Intestines)
Chief Plenty Coups. *See* Plenty Coups
Chief Pretty Eagle. *See* Pretty Eagle
Chien, Elizabeth. *See* Yellowtail, Lizzie Chien

Chien, Emma, 88–91
Child, 68–71
childbirth. *See* pregnancy and childbirth
child mortality, xix, 2, 25–26, 28, 133, 247n6, 282
childrearing: by Lillian, 276, 320n3, 321–22; shared, 32n5, 248, 250, 251, 371n1
children's forced haircuts. *See* forced haircuts
children's growth, 62–63
children's play. *See* games; girls' play
children's schooling. *See* schools and schooling
children's songs, 65–66
Childs, Susie, 231, 232n8, 264
chokecherries, 95, 147, 165–66, 169, 377–78
Christianity, xix, 361; boarding schools and, 77; Bull Shows and, 32, 289–90, 291; Crow marriage and, 216; George Hogan and, xxxii, xxxiii, 304n3; Lillian and, xiv, xix, xxxiv, 63, 227, 234n1, 269n6, 333–36, 403, 404n1; Little Horse and, 17; Old Dwarf and, 141, 144; Tobacco Society and, 187, 189n9. *See also* Catholicism; Church of God
Christian names. *See* English names
Christmas, 114, 170, 229, 307
Christmas gifts, 237, 320–21
Church of God, 234n1, 293, 304n3, 306n1, 326, 327n4, 334n2
clan system, xvii, 9n8, 15n6
clan relatives, 248, 354; gifts to, 140n3, 217–18, 233, 380, 383; names from, xxxii, 5, 9nn9–10; praising by, 120–21, 123; prayers and, 383, 389n2; teasing cousins, xxxii

Clark, William, xvii
Clarks Fork Yellowstone River, 19–23
close calls, 34–36
clothes. *See* dress
coal, 299–300
Cody WY, 152
colleges and universities, 295–96, 330, 380, 383–84, 385n1
Collier, John, xx, xxviii(n30)
Colville Indian Reservation, 314–15, 316n1
commerce. *See* selling
compulsory haircuts. *See* forced haircuts
cooking, 18, 129, 147, 162–63, 197, 210, 301; Crow Fair and, 109; garage sales and, 371n3; outdoors, 298, 301, 302n3; recipes, 172n1. *See also* baking; desserts
corporal punishment, 75–76, 80–85, 91n4
Costa, Arnold, 344
cottonwood trees, 88–91
Coulson MT, 38n2
counting coup, xvi, xix, 55n4, 120–23
courts, 85–88
Courts of Indian Offenses, xviii
cows. *See* cattle
Crazy Man, 68
Cree, 94–100, 253n5, 267, 268
Crooked Arm, Myranne, 162n8
"Crow" (label), xiii
Crow Act of 1920, 221n1, 285, 289n1
Crow Agency MT, 32n4, 42n7, 85–87, 272–73, 304; boarding school, 34, 88–91; businesses, 375, 376n1; George Hogan's death in, 305–6; seniors' residences, 401–2; sewing project in, 248–53

Crow Agency Social Services, 322n2, 371n4
Crow biographies. *See* Apsáalooke biographies
Crow Fair, xii, 14, 106–10, 113, 137, 138, 297–98, 383
Crow history. *See* Apsáalooke history
Crow Indian Reservation: districts, 42n7, 115, 360n4; size, xviii, xxviii(n23), 42n8. *See also* Black Lodge District ("Dunmore"); Garryowen District; Reno District
Crow language. *See* Apsáalooke language
Crow Mercantile, 375, 376n2
Crow names. *See* Apsáalooke names
Custer Battlefield, 302n1
Cuts the Bear's Ears, xxxv

dances and dancing, 20, 114–16, 204n2, 229, 244, 357–60; beadwork and, 372; nonnative, 204, 204n2, 208–9, 358–59; outfits, 372, 374n2; at powwows, 117n5; tobacco planting and, 183–85; at Tobacco Society adoption, 226. *See also* Sun Dance
Dawes, Alice, 247–48
Dawes, Ambrose, 247, 277n1
Dawes Act, xviii, 3n2, 221n1, 285
Daxpitchée Baaalapésh. *See* Kicking Bear
Day Child, Berneice. *See* Singer, Berneice Day Child
death: of Bull Shows, 289–93; of Caleb Bullshows, 2, 394–95; of Lillian, 404n2; of Lillian's great-grandson, 396–99; of Little Horse, 280–82; Old Dwarf and, 144–45; of pets, 104n4; of Plenty Coups, 248. *See also* burial; child mortality; funerary beliefs and customs

Decrane, Christine Rides Horse, 9n10
Decrane, Melanie, 9n10
Decrane, Roy, 124n2
Deernose, Agnes Yellowtail, 237, 251, 370
Deernose family, 251
Denig, Edwin Thompson, xvi, xxvii(n12), 100n2, 180n1
depression, 307
desserts, 171–72, 174, 256, 371n3, 378. *See also* ice cream
disease, xix. *See also* cancer; polio
divorce, 219, 239, 333
dogs, xvi, 101–4, 154, 156, 158n6, 168. *See also* puppies
dreams, 5, 22, 48–55, 175, 177–78
dress, xvii, xxvii(n19); Bull Shows and, 289–90; dog and, 101–4; hand games and, 117n4; Lillian and, xiii–xiv, 162n2, 296n3; Little Horse and, 162n2; poverty and, 200, 203; Tobacco Society adoption and, 227n4. *See also* brides, outfitting of; dances and dancing: outfits
dresses, xvii, xx, 130, 207, 279, 384. *See also* elk-tooth dresses
drinking. *See* alcohol
drinking water, hauling of. *See* water hauling
drivers, elderly. *See* elderly drivers
driving. *See* cars and trucks
drummers and drumming, 184, 188n1, 230, 232n2
Dunmore. *See* Black Lodge District ("Dunmore")

eating. *See* food
Edgar mt, 19, 198
education. *See* schools and schooling
elderly drivers, 402–3
elders, 40, 42n1, 68–71, 387–404

elk hunting, 97n3
elk teeth, 97n3, 99
elk teeth (carved bone), 94–100, 375, 376
elk-tooth dresses, xvii(n18), 95–100, 257–61, 376; bride outfitting and, 213, 214, 216, 217, 218, 231; display of, 109, 261–62; uncommon color of, 232n10
employees, government. *See* government employees
employment, 119, 197, 198, 245, 382. *See also* government sewing project
English language, xiv, xxiii, 3n3, 15, 207; boarding school and, 79; Bull Shows and, 43, 44, 285, 379; literacy, 381n2; Little Horse and, 2, 379
English names, xx, xxxv–xxxvi, 4, 33–34
epidemics, 25–28, 131, 133
Estep, E. W., 75, 125–26
ethnopoetics, xxiv–xxv, xxxvi

face painting, 23, 24n9, 120; of dog, 101
Fallen Bell District. *See* Reno District
Falls Down, Rebecca Plainfeather, 395–99
family violence, 198, 201, 227
farming, 8n3, 91n6, 111, 202, 205, 241–43, 246. *See also* "boss farmers"; irrigation
farm workers, Mexican. *See* Mexican farm workers
fasts and fasting, xvi, 18, 21–22, 24n10, 181, 264, 334–37
feasts, 115, 214, 283, 384
feathers, 193, 194
fighting, 382–83
filmmaking, 102–3, 149, 150

Finds Them and Kills Them. *See* Ohchiish
firearms. *See* guns
first words, 235–36
fishing, 134
Fitzpatrick, Elizabeth, 273, 274, 277nn1–2, 296n1
Fitzpatrick, Mike, 296n1
Fog In the Morning, 85–88
food, xix, 39, 40–41 58, 242; boarding school and, 77, 78, 80–81; costs, 198–99; at First Lady visit, 329; gifts of, 6, 129, 170; preservation of, 19, 23n4, 41, 163–71, 173–74, 208n2, 242, 376, 378; selling of, 200; sharing of, 68–69, 70n3; shortage of, 197; at Tobacco Iipche ceremony, 195. *See also* cooking; feasts; gardening; government food rations; meat; picnics; wild foods
forced haircuts, 28, 30–31, 32, 32–33nn6–7
Fort Assiniboine Military Reserve, 97n5
Fort Belknap Indian Reservation, 221n2, 400n1
Fort Custer, 35
Fort Laramie Treaty. *See* Treaty of Fort Laramie (1851); Treaty of Fort Laramie (1868)
Fort Parker, xviii, 28
Fort Shaw, 109
Fort Washakie wy, 265
foster care, 321–22, 388
Fourteen, 233, 234n1
Frey, Rodney, xxiii, 180n1, 284n1
friends, best, 117–24
Fromberg mt, 351
fry bread, 163, 329
funerary beliefs and customs, 61, 120, 282, 293

416 INDEX

gambling, xxi, xxxv, 111–12, 116, 197–200
games, 113n1, 197. *See also* hand games; shinny (game); throwing arrows (game)
gardening, 77–78, 242, 243; of tobacco, 182–89, 192
Garryowen District, 116n2
gender roles, xxxiii, 199n2. *See also* berdaches
gifts, xi, xx–xxi, 68–71, 129, 170, 181, 380; for healers, 85, 86, 345, 356; for name givers, 5; for new or potential in-laws, 12n5, 140n3, 217–18, 229, 231, 232n7, 247n4, 264; as payment for wrongs, 223; for wet nurse, 16n2. *See also* brides, outfitting of; Christmas gifts; giveaways; graduation gifts; offerings
girls: boarding school and, 73–83; friendship, 117–24; horses and, 93–94, 112–13; relations with boys, 94, 120, 123
girls' play, 93–94, 117–20, 150–51, 211
giveaways, 116, 217–18, 359, 383
gleaning, 211
gloves, 270–71, 372
Goes Ahead, Clem, 277n1
Goes Ahead, Helen, 91
Goes Ahead, Regina, 277n1, 365
government, delegates to. *See* political delegates
government employees, 295, 296, 303, 314. *See also* "boss farmers"; Indian agents; Vista workers
government food rations, xix, 40–41, 42n5
government housing. *See* houses: government-built
government land purchases, 331n4

government schools, 28–33, 34, 73–88
government sewing project, 248–53
graduation gifts, 383–85
Grand Canyon, 310–11
grandparental adoption. *See* adoption: by grandparents
Graves, Walter, 247n3
Gros Ventre, 15n5, 221n2
guns, 323, 397

hair, long. *See* long hair
haircuts, 23, 24n8, 33n6. *See also* forced haircuts
Hamilton, Herman, 392
hand games, 115, 116, 117n4
Hardin MT, 2, 3n4, 231, 232n6, 244, 272, 293, 314–15; commerce in, 374n2, 375, 376nn1–2, 390
Harris, Ataloa Hogan, 370, 371n1, 371n3, 383
Haskell Institute, 296n1
Haun, Dave, 293–95
Havre MT, 399, 400
Hayden, F. V., xvi
healers. *See* medicine men and women
healing, 2, 7, 175–80, 341–50, 354–56, 393–94; of dog, 103
heirlooms, 261–62, 281, 284n2, 341–43
herbal medicine, 2, 26–27, 118–19, 185, 343–50, 352
Her Medicine Is Sacred. *See* Medicine Porcupine
Hidatsa, xv, 196n2
hide tanning. *See* tanning
higher education. *See* colleges and universities
hired labor, 242–43
Hogan, Alma. *See* Snell, Alma Hogan
Hogan, Amy Agnes, 270, 283n5

Hogan, Ataloa. *See* Harris, Ataloa Hogan
Hogan, Camee, 382–83
Hogan, Ferole Mae. *See* Pease, Ferole Mae Hogan
Hogan, Frances. *See* Knows His Gun, Frances Hogan
Hogan, George W., xiv, xxxii, 371n1, 371n5; alcohol and, xxxiv–xxxv; Apsáalooke name, 33; boarding school and, 88–91; death, 305–6; education, 33n8, 269n6, 381; father-in-law's death and, 290, 291, 292–93; father-in-law's will and, 287; house in Crow Agency, 251, 253n7; marriage to Lillian, 263–64, 269n6, 270, 272, 278, 281, 297, 298–306; religion and, xxxiii, 269n6, 334n2, 338; Sun Dance and, 266, 338; travels, 296n1
Hogan, Mardell. *See* Plainfeather, Mardell Hogan
Hogan, Meredith, 330, 383n1
Hogan, Mary Elizabeth. *See* Wallace, Mary Hogan
Hogan, Pearl, 322n2
homemaking, 147–48, 208n3. *See also* cooking; sewing
homesteads and homesteading, xviii, 391
Horn, Joanne. *See* Bear Below, Joanne Horn
Horse. *See* Little Horse
"horse medicine," 319, 320n4, 341
horse racing, xxi, 106, 112–13, 137–39, 199, 218
horses, xvi, 11–12, 39n3; Bull Shows and, 48–55, 138, 139, 199, 202–3; Crow Fair and, 106, 107, 108, 110, 113, 297; C. W. Asbury and, 80n5; as gifts, 12, 16n2, 51, 54, 138, 140n3, 217–18; girls and, 93–94, 112–13, 119, 121–23; Henry Russell and, 35–36; Lillian and, 93–94, 108, 110–13, 119, 121–23, 209, 210–11, 238, 317–20; Lorena Mae Walks Over Ice and, 316; Old Dwarf dream and, 48–55; painting and decoration, 42n3, 110n4, 162n7; as payment, 98n7; Percy Bullshows and, 132–33, 136; raids and, 59n6
hospitality, 52–54, 68–69, 70n3
hospitals and hospital care, 59n3; Bull Shows and, 290; Caleb Bullshows and, 139; childbirth and, 234, 277; Lillian and, xxxii, xxxiv, 7, 302, 354; Nellie Singer and, 245, 246, 247n6; Ohchiish and, 130–31; Percy Bullshows and, 133, 136
houses, 70n4, 380; government-built, 399, 401, 402n1; heating, 298–302. *See also* log houses; prefab houses
Humphrey, Mary, 249
hunting, xviii, 39, 199n2, 323–24, 377; boys and, 29–30; Bull Shows on, 41; fatal accidents and, 397; women and, 19, 323–24. *See also* elk hunting

ice cream, 135
illness, 7, 25–28, 59n3, 245–46; adoption and, 9n7; child mortality and, 2, 25–26, 28, 133, 247n6; Lillian and, 6, 7, 175–80, 225, 266; natural remedies, 42n3; renaming and, 5, 7, 10n15; Sun Dance and, 266, 270n9. *See also* herbal medicine
incense, 193, 194n1, 350

Indian agents, 32n4, 39, 42n5, 106, 208n1, 248–49; berdaches and, 125–26, 127n8; boarding schools and, 73, 75; Courts of Indian Offenses and, xviii; Crow marriage and, 216; Tobacco Society and, 189n9
Indian doctors. *See* medicine men and women
Indian Reorganization Act, xxviii(n30), 264
infants: death, 2, 270, 282, 283n5; first words, 235–36; giving up of, 10–11; transportation, 180n3; wet nursing, 15. *See also* babysitting; lullabies
inheritance, 285–89
Iron Bull, 131n2
irrigation, 247n3
Isis, Gloria, 14

jails, 85–88, 89, 116
Jefferson, Lester, 358
jewelry: worn by berdaches, 129, 130; worn by dog, 101, 102. *See also* necklaces
jobs. *See* employment
Johnson, John ("Liver-Eating"), 216
Johnson, Lady Bird, 327–31, 360–61
jokes, xxii
Joliet mt, 28, 32n3, 47
jumping toward the moon, 62–63

Kane wy, 366, 367n6
Kicked In the Bellies, xvi, 42n7
Kicking Bear, 178, 179
Kills Good, 23n5
Knows His Gun, Donna Mae. *See* Chavez, Donna Mae
Knows His Gun, Frances Hogan, 371n5
Kurz, Rudolph Friederich, xxvii(n18)

La Forge, Alice Mae White Clay, 9n10
La Forge, Frank, 9n10
Lakota, 16, 59n6, 127–28, 320n4, 371n2. *See also* Sioux
Lame Deer mt, 310, 312n4, 313, 370, 371n1, 373n3, 383
Lammers Trading Post, 374n2, 375, 376n2
land allotments, xviii, 1, 3n2, 221n1, 285–86, 380, 391
Lander wy, 311
land leases, 199n1, 295n1, 380–81, 389, 392
land loss, 42n8
land sales, 331n4, 401
LaPointe, Sam, 205–8
Larocque, François, xvii
leases of land. *See* land leases
Leforge, Thomas, xxvii(n15), 9n10, 32n6, 188n2, 220
leggings, 271, 374
lessees. *See* renters
Lewis and Clark expedition, xvii
Lincoln, Albert, 33–34
Lion Shows, Oliver, 12, 138
Lisa, Manuel, xvii
literacy, English. *See* English language: literacy
Little Bighorn, Battle of. *See* Battle of the Little Bighorn
Little Horse, 13–24, 47–50, 147–74, 203, 369, 376; bitterroot and, 253–57; Catholicism of, 334; child bearing, 1–3, 353–54; Crow Fair and, 108, 109; fasts, 334–35; giving up of Lillian, 10–11; as healer, 343–46; husband's gambling and, 197–98, 200; illness and death, 278–83, 286; lack of schooling, 285, 379; Lillian's boarding school and, 73–74, 82–88; Lillian's children and, 234, 236, 239, 248, 250;

Lillian's first marriage and, 215; Lillian's new shoes and, 204; Lillian's second marriage and, 230, 231, 239; marriage, 47–48, 198, 201, 353; medicine necklaces of, 342, 343; story of singing bear, 66–68; Sun Dance and, 267–68; Tobacco Iipche and, 195
Little Light, Eddie, 24n9
Little Light, Roberta ("Blue"), 322
Lives On High Ground, 213
loans, 325, 389–90
Lodge Grass mt, 88, 89, 376n2, 382, 396
Lodge Pole mt, 220
Loeb, Barbara, 70, 362
log houses, 49, 57, 59, 199, 202, 235
long hair, 32–33n6, 130, 296n3
"Loves Man" ("Loves Men") (name), xi, xxxi–xxxii, 5, 6
Lowie, Robert H., 188n2
lullabies, 63–65

magazines, 211, 372
Male Bear, Gibson, 211–12
Many Irons. See Uuwutáhosh
marriage, 48, 123, 124nn2–3, 131n5, 247n4; gifts and, 12n5, 140n3, 217–18; Bull Shows and Little Horse, 47–48, 198, 201, 353; Cedric and Lorena Mae Walks Over Ice, 272–77, 314–16; Lillian and Alex Plainfeather, 213–19; Lillian and George Hogan, 263–64, 269n6, 270, 272, 278, 281, 297, 298–306; Lillian and Paul Singer, 241–48; Lillian and Robert Yellowtail, xxxii, 229–40, 359. See also brides, outfitting of
marriage licenses, 215, 219n2, 231

Masterson, Carl, 208
matrilineality, xvii, 9n8
Matthews, Becky, 110n2
McAllister, Ethel, 81
McCleary, Timothy P., 189n9
meat: preservation, 19, 23n4, 41, 166–71, 376–77; processing, 199n2
medicine, xxvi(n2), 85–88, 266; beads as, xi, 68–71, 341–43; dreams as, 48–55; Tobacco Society and, 181, 182nn3–4. See also herbal medicine; "horse medicine"
medicine bags, 188n2, 189–94, 283–85
Medicine Crow, xxi, 42n7, 44n1
Medicine Crow, Joseph, xv–xvi, xxi, xxviii(n40), 180n1, 233n12, 236n1; horses and, 113n3; on Sun Dance, 268n1
Medicine Dance. See Tobacco Society (Medicine Dance)
Medicine Horse, 358
medicine men and women, 85–88, 118–19, 175, 177–80, 225
medicine necklaces, xi, 68–71, 341, 342–43
Medicine Porcupine, 60, 61, 62nn2–3
menstruation, 192n2, 194
Mexican farm workers, 242–43
midwifery, 118–19, 350–54
Miles City mt, 317
military service, 382. See also army scouts
milk, 242
missionaries, 189n9, 216n2, 333
mission schools. See boarding schools
moccasins, 130, 204n2, 270–71, 281; Little Horse and, 49, 109, 153, 157, 158–59; Mardell Plainfeather and, 374n2
mock battles. See sham battles

420 INDEX

moon, 379. *See also* jumping toward the moon
Morton, Howard, 331n4
motor vehicles. *See* cars and trucks
Mountain Crow, xvi, 25, 41, 42n7
mourning, 18–24
movie-making. *See* filmmaking
Movius, Arthur J., 266
murder, 18, 20–21
Musselshell River, 41

names and naming, xi, xxxi–xxxii, 304n3, 357–62. *See also* Apsáalooke names; English names; renaming
necklaces, xi, 68–71, 341–43
Nespelem wa, 314–15
New Year's celebrations, 114, 116n1, 383
Nez Perce, xxvii(n15), xxiii
Nichols, Joe ("Indian Joe"), 376
Nomee, Clara, 16n3, 392
Northern Pacific Railway, 38n2
No Vitals (No Intestines), xv, xvii, 182n5
nursing homes, 394–95, 403, 404n2

offerings, 88–91
Ohchiish, xiii, 124–31
Old Black Bird, 13, 14, 23n5, 57, 58
Old Coyote, Barney, 105n1, 196n1
Old Coyote, May, 105, 231, 232n8, 264
Old Crow, Jude, 399n1
Old Dwarf, 29, 32n5, 48–55, 113n2, 141–46
Old Elk, Colleen, 322
Old Elk, Dan, 322n1
Old Elk, Evelyn, xxxiii, 182n4
Old Elk, George, xxxiii, 182n4
Old Man Coyote, 9n8
One Goose, Mary, 249

On the Other Side (On the Other Bank). *See* Bull Well Known (Aakkeetaash)
outfitting of brides. *See* brides, outfitting of
owl dance, 116, 117n5
Owns All, 233–34

painting, face. *See* face painting
painting, horse. *See* horses: painting and decoration
pants, 296–98, 384
Passes, Amelia, 322–25, 377–78
pawnshops, 262, 363
payments, per capita. *See* per capita payments
Pease, Bill, 331n3
Pease, Major Fellows David, xxvii–xxviii(n22), xxviii(n38)
Pease, Helen. *See* Wolf, Helen Pease
Pease, Ferole Mae Hogan, 305, 306, 328, 330, 385
pemmican, 166–71
Pentacostalism, 234n1, 269n6, 333
per capita payments, 197, 199n1, 331n4, 380–81
Pettey, Allannah, 360, 361n1
Pettey, Barry Bryan, 33, 360, 361n1, 377
Pettey, Merrie Lillian, 372, 373n5
Pettey, Nellie. *See* Sings In the Mountains, Nellie
Petzoldt, W. A., 131n4
peyote, 344, 349n1
pheasant, 41
Phinney, Archie, xxiii
Phoenix az, 295–96, 307–10
Picket, Nellie, 232, 232n9, 264
picnics, 298, 368
Piegan Blackfeet, 120–21, 364, 367n1
pigment, 101, 104n1, 190
Piiláako. *See* Passes, Amelia

pine needles, 193
pipes, 193, 194
Plainfeather, Adeline Rock Above, 296, 297, 398
Plainfeather, Alexander ("Alex"), xxxii, 12, 213–19
Plainfeather, Benita, 220, 399, 400
Plainfeather, Laramie ("Mosey"), 10n15
Plainfeather, Lee, 193n5
Plainfeather, Leo Dan ("Dan"), 219n3, 300
Plainfeather, Lorena, 10n15, 373, 374n1
Plainfeather, Mardell Hogan, 70, 270, 281, 289, 374nn1–2, 391; alcohol and, 389n2; Arizona and, 309, 312n1, 312, 313; Arkansas and, 387; "crier" right of, 360n5; education, 380, 385n1; first car, 321–22; First Lady visit and, 330, 331; herbal medicine and, 347; horses and, 319, 320n2, 320n5; Tobacco Society and, 338–39; woodcutting and, 300, 302n1
Plainfeather, Mary (Renita), 10n15, 399n2
Plainfeather, Millie, 396
Plainfeather, Rebecca. See Falls Down, Rebecca Plain Feather
Plainfeather, Russell, 220–21, 278n1, 395–96, 399–400
Plainfeather, Samuel, 130, 219, 220, 223, 278n1, 339n1, 391, 398; children and grandchildren, 395–99; as namesake, 289n4
Plateau tribes, xvi
Plenty Coups, xiii, xx, xxvii(n22), 42n7, 75, 80n4, 87; boarding schools and, 75, 84; Bull Shows's dog and, 103–4; Cree and, 96; death, 248; Ohchiish and, 125–26

Plenty Good, Rose, 219n3
Plenty Hoops, Winona, 183, 188, 190–91
police, 75, 83–84, 85–86, 88, 125
polio, 131–36
political delegates, 238, 239n1
poverty, 197–204, 252
powwows, 106, 117n5
Pratt, Richard, 33n8, 269n6
prayer, 187, 193, 270n9, 336, 380, 403, 404n1; healing and, 354, 355–56, 394
prefab houses, 325–27
pregnancy and childbirth, 1, 3, 118–19, 234–35, 277–78. See also midwifery
Pretty Eagle, 42n7
Pretty Shield, xviii–xix, 94n1, 128n1, 127n4
Pretty Weasel, Josephine, 273
Pryor mt, xix, xxxiv, 62n3, 113, 202, 239, 250–51, 278–81
Pryor Creek, 59n6. See also Arrow Creek
punishment, 79. See also corporal punishment
puppies, 101, 143
purses, 149–53, 270–71
Pushes Himself, 38, 39n6, 234n1

quilt making, 16–17, 369–71

railroad trains, 47
rattlesnakes, 102–3
rawhide, 159
reading, 212n2, 334
Real Bird, Edison, 331n4
Real Bird, Florence, xxxi
Red Lodge mt, 28, 216n5, 376n2
Red Star, 10–12, 82
Red Star, Selmer, 124n2
Red Star, Wallace, 11–12

Reed, Mary Kate, 249
religion, xiv, xix, xxxiv; George Hogan and, xxxiii, 269n6, 334n2, 338. *See also* Christianity
renaming, 5, 7–10, 399n2; by government, 4, 29, 30, 33–34
Reno, Marcus A., 116n2
Reno Creek, xix, 39, 40, 41, 42n3
Reno District, 42n7, 115, 116n2
rental of land. *See* land leases
renters, 294–95, 297, 308, 375, 376n1, 392n3
revenge, 22–23, 264, 268n1
Reynolds, Samuel Guilford, 106
Rides Horse, Christine. *See* Decrane, Christine Rides Horse
River Crow, xvi, xviii, 42n7
Rock Above, Adeline. *See* Plainfeather, Adeline Rock Above
Rock Above, Julia, 296–97
Rocky Boy's Indian Reservation, 94–95, 97, 97–98n5
Rocky Mountain College, 385n1
Russell, Henry, 1, 3n3, 28–36
Russell, William, 250

Sacred Pipe Society. *See* Tobacco Iipche (Sacred Pipe Society)
Sacred Weasel. *See* Whiteman, Ruth
saddle making, 160–62
Salem OR, 211, 212
salvaging and gleaning, 211
Scalpcane, Montana Sky, 140n2, 362n4
Scalpcane, Robert, 373–74
scarves, 279
schools and schooling, 209–10, 211, 382–83. *See also* boarding schools; colleges and universities; government schools
Schwend, Chester, 392n3
scouts. *See* army scouts

Scratches His Face, 232n9
self-mutilation, 24n8, 24n10
selling, 200, 239, 242, 246, 369–71; of heirlooms, 283, 284n2. *See also* land sales
Senior Citizens Center (Crow Agency), 401–2, 404n2
settlers, xviii, 19–21, 39
sewing, 18, 147–48, 205, 207, 257–61, 279, 384; by berdache, 130; of moccasins, 159. *See also* government sewing project
sham battles, 120–24
Shane, Jason, 278n12
sheep, 119
Sheridan WY, 239, 299, 366, 389
shinny (game), 221–23
Shoshone, 13, 14, 16, 264, 268, 311, 312n5
Shows Little, 23n5
Shows Plenty, 178–79
sickness. *See* disease; illness
Singer, Adam, 250, 315, 320, 321, 324, 382, 391; alcohol and, 388, 389n2; Arizona and, 309–12; father's death and, 246; grandfather's death and, 291; grandmother and, 248, 250, 251; horses and, 317, 318, 319; hunting and gathering, 323–24, 367; prefab house and, 325; teepee poles and, 366; woodcutting and, 300, 302n1
Singer, Ambrose. *See* Dawes, Ambrose
Singer, Berneice Day Child, 97, 98n6, 323
Singer, Fay Dean, 363
Singer, Laura, 196n1
Singer, Paul, xxxii, 131n5, 236, 241–48, 305n1
Sings Good family, 128n2, 344
Sings In the Mountains, Nellie, xii,

245, 246, 250, 251, 269n3, 296, 369, 388–89; in Arizona, 307–9, 312, 313; Caleb Bullshows and, 395; fasts and, 336; first car, 321; First Lady visit and, 328, 330, 331; grandfather's death and, 291, 292; grand-nephew's death and, 398; herbal medicine and, 347–49; horses and, 319; prefab house and, 325–26; woodcutting and, 302n1
Sioux, 59n6, 205–8, 210, 364. See also Lakota
snakes: fear of, 60, 134, 377–78. See also rattlesnakes
Snell, Alma Hogan, xxi, 91n6
soap, 79, 155
songs, 48, 50–51, 232n2; bears and, 67–68; bride outfitting and, 213, 214; hand games and, 116; Tobacco Iipche and, 195, 196; Tobacco Society and, 182n4, 183–87, 338–39. See also children's songs; lullabies
Southwest Indian School, 309
Spotted Horse, Clara, 235
Stanton, Harold, 303, 304n6
Stays On Top of the Lodge, 351–53
steamship supply, 36–38
stepchildren and step-grandchildren, 12, 230, 235, 401
Stewart, Frederick, 233, 234n1
Stewart, Sarah, 273, 277n2
Stone, Harold, 212n4
stone tools, 165, 167
storytelling and storytellers, xiv–xv, xxvi–xxvii(n7), xxxv
Stray Calf, Myrtle, 344–45
Strong Enemy, Myrtle, 214
sugar industry, 243, 246n2
sun, 379
Sun Dance, xvi, xix, xx, xxviii(n30), 264–70; George Hogan and, xxxiii, 338; Lillian renaming and, 5, 6

sweat lodges and sweat baths, xvi, 44, 44–45n2; children's, 93, 94

Takes the Gun, Mary, 24n8, 232n8, 277–78, 299
tanning, xxvi(n5), 18, 109, 130, 131n2, 153–58, 296–97, 369
"teasing cousins," 9n8
teepees, xvi, 24n6, 70n4, 116n3, 131n2, 363, 380; Crow Fair and, 106, 107, 363, 364; poles for, 364–67; Tobacco Society and, 182n4, 194
terminal care, 278–81, 290–91, 394–95
theft, 283–85, 374
throwing arrows (game), 111, 113n1, 115, 197
Thunder Iron, Albert. See Lincoln, Albert
Ties the Bundle Clan, xiii
Ties the Bundle Woman. See Bullshows, Lillian; Cashen, Ella
"Ties the Bundle Woman" (name), xxxi, 7, 9n10, 362n4
timber cutting. See wood cutting and gathering
tobacco, xv, xvii, xxxiv, 182–89, 192; seeds, 181–82nn2–3, 227n1
Tobacco, Bernard, 274, 277n2
tobacco bags. See medicine bags
Tobacco Dance. See Tobacco Society (Medicine Dance)
Tobacco Iipche (Sacred Pipe Society), xiv, xv, xvii, xx, xxxiii–xxxiv, 195–96
tobacco-planting ceremonies, 182–86, 190–91, 192
Tobacco Society (Medicine Dance), 116, 117n6, 146n4, 179, 180–87, 225–28, 338–39; Ohchiish and, 125, 129

tools, 301, 365. *See also* bone tools, stone tools
trading, 241
traditional medicine. *See* healing; herbal medicine; medicine men and women
trains, 47
transgender people. *See* berdaches; Ohchiish
translators and translation, xiii, xxii
trash gleaning, 211
travel, 295–96, 307–12, 361, 387, 390
Treaty of Fort Laramie (1851), xviii
Treaty of Fort Laramie (1868), xviii, 8n3
trees. *See* box elder trees; cottonwood trees
tribal police. *See* police
trucks. *See* cars and trucks
turnip, wild. *See* wild turnip
Turns Back, Blanche, 23–24n5, 134
Turns Plenty, Roger, 23n5
Two Leggings, xxi

Udall, Morris, 331n5
universities. *See* colleges and universities
Uuwutáhosh, 162n1

vengeance. *See* revenge
Vietnam War veterans, 24n9
violence. *See* family violence; fighting; murder
visions and vision quests, xxvii(n22), 24n10, 175; of Fog In the Morning, 87–88; naming and, 5; of Plenty Coups, 42n7
Vista workers, 322
Voget, Fred, xx–xxi, 55n4

Wagon, Suzette, 312n5

Walks Along, Joe, 371n4
Walks Over Ice, Calvin, 357, 359, 373n2
Walks Over Ice, Carson, 24n9, 271, 277–78, 295, 296n1, 296–98, 307
Walks Over Ice, Cassandra ("Sandy"), 295, 296n1, 307, 317
Walks Over Ice, Cedric, 272–77, 295–96, 312, 314, 315, 316, 367n4
Walks Over Ice, Lorena Mae, 272–78, 319, 321, 385, 388; in Arizona, 295–96, 297, 307–10, 312, 313, 314; birth and childhood, 234–36, 239; bitterroot and, 368; First Lady visit and, 329; in Nespelem wa, 314–15; Tobacco Society songs and, 338, 339
Walks Over Ice, Louis, 273, 274
Walks Over Ice, Louis ("Louie"), 307, 312n1
Wallace, Mary Hogan, 9n10, 70, 281, 289, 296, 388; Arizona and, 307–9, 312, 313; Barbara Loeb and, xii; beadwork and, 374; berrying and, 378; birth of, 270; bitterroot and, 367; Caleb Bullshows and, 395; First Lady visit and, 330, 331; grand-nephew's death and, 398; horses and, 317; Tobacco Society and, xxxiii, 338, 339; woodcutting and, 302n1
Wallace, Nelson, 9n10, 314, 367
war dance, 116
warfare, xvi, 127–28. *See also* sham battles
Warren, Charlene, 375–76
warriors, xvi, 24nn9–10, 59n6, 127. *See also* women warriors
Washington dc, 238
water hauling, 59–60, 302, 304n1
watermelon, 36–39, 242, 243, 347

Watt, Bill, 375–76
wet nurses, 15
wheat, 111, 202, 239, 241, 242, 246
Where They Left the Yellow Blanket, 25
White Clay, Vernon, 253n7
White Hip, Clara, 16, 58, 108–9, 201, 281
White Hip, Jerome, 346
Whitehip family, 343n3
White Man, Amy Yellowtail, 233n12
Whiteman, Maud, 249, 251, 253n5, 358
Whiteman, Ruth, 213, 251, 253n5
white settlers. See settlers
wild foods, 171–74, 253–57, 376–77. See also berries and berrying; fishing; hunting
Wildschut, William, xiii, 284–85
wild turnip, 171–72
Wind Blowing, 15
Wind River Indian Reservation, 269n4, 312n5, 331n3
Wolf, Helen Pease, xxi, xxvii–xxviii(n22)
Wolf Mountains, 42n3, 304n3
Woman Chief, 128n3

women warriors, 128n2
wood cutting and gathering, 19, 20, 37, 298–302, 364–67
workers. See government employees; Mexican farm workers
Wyman, Moses, xxi

Yarlott, Delma Jean, 273, 277n2, 365
Yellow Mule, 354–56
Yellowstone National Park, 261–62
Yellowstone River, xvi, 38n2, 42n7
Yellowtail, Agnes. See Deernose, Agnes Yellowtail
Yellowtail, Lizzie Chien, 232n8, 236–37, 264, 371n1
Yellowtail, Lorena Mae. See Walks Over Ice, Lorena Mae
Yellowtail, Robert, xiv, xx, xxvi(n6), xxviii(n28); Crow Act and, 289n1; daughter Lorena Mae and, 272–73; on Indian agents, 32n3; marriage to Lillian, xxxii, 229–40, 359; Max Big Man and, 248, 252
Yellowtail, Thomas, xvii, xxi, 131n4, 196n2
Yellowtail Dam, 331, 367n6

www.ingramcontent.com/pod-product-compliance
Lightning Source LLC
Chambersburg PA
CBHW021813300426
44114CB00009BA/152